RECENT EXPERIMENTS
IN PSYCHOLOGY

BY

LELAND W. CRAFTS
Professor of Psychology, Washington Square College
New York University

THEODORE C. SCHNEIRLA
Curator, Department of Animal Behavior
American Museum of Natural History

ELSA E. ROBINSON
Assistant Professor of Psychology, Washington Square College
New York University

RALPH W. GILBERT
Associate Professor of Psychology, Washington Square College
New York University

SECOND EDITION

McGRAW-HILL BOOK COMPANY, INC.

NEW YORK   TORONTO   LONDON

1950

RECENT EXPERIMENTS IN PSYCHOLOGY

McGRAW-HILL PUBLICATIONS IN PSYCHOLOGY
CLIFFORD T. MORGAN Consulting Editor

RECENT EXPERIMENTS IN
PSYCHOLOGY

McGraw-Hill Publications in Psychology

CLIFFORD T. MORGAN

CONSULTING EDITOR

Barker, Kounin, and Wright—CHILD BEHAVIOR AND DEVELOPMENT
Brown—PSYCHOLOGY AND THE SOCIAL ORDER
Brown—THE PSYCHODYNAMICS OF ABNORMAL BEHAVIOR
Cattell—PERSONALITY
Cole—GENERAL PSYCHOLOGY
Crafts, Schneirla, Robinson, and Gilbert—RECENT EXPERIMENTS IN PSYCHOLOGY
Davis—PSYCHOLOGY OF LEARNING
Dorcus and Jones—HANDBOOK OF EMPLOYEE SELECTION
Dunlap—RELIGION: ITS FUNCTIONS IN HUMAN LIFE
Ghiselli and Brown—PERSONNEL AND INDUSTRIAL PSYCHOLOGY
Gray—PSYCHOLOGY IN HUMAN AFFAIRS
Guilford—FUNDAMENTAL STATISTICS IN PSYCHOLOGY AND EDUCATION
Guilford—PSYCHOMETRIC METHODS
Hurlock—ADOLESCENT DEVELOPMENT
Hurlock—CHILD DEVELOPMENT
Johnson—ESSENTIALS OF PSYCHOLOGY
Krech and Crutchfield—THEORY AND PROBLEMS OF SOCIAL PSYCHOLOGY
Lewin—A DYNAMIC THEORY OF PERSONALITY
Lewin—PRINCIPLES OF TOPOLOGICAL PSYCHOLOGY
McNemar and Merrill (Eds.)—STUDIES IN PERSONALITY
Maier—FRUSTRATION
Maier and Schneirla—PRINCIPLES OF ANIMAL PSYCHOLOGY
Miller—EXPERIMENTS IN SOCIAL PROCESS
Moore—PSYCHOLOGY FOR BUSINESS AND INDUSTRY
Morgan and Stellar—PHYSIOLOGICAL PSYCHOLOGY
Page—ABNORMAL PSYCHOLOGY
Pillsbury—AN ELEMENTARY PSYCHOLOGY OF THE ABNORMAL
Richards—MODERN CLINICAL PSYCHOLOGY
Seashore—PSYCHOLOGY OF MUSIC
Seward—SEX AND THE SOCIAL ORDER
Stagner—PSYCHOLOGY OF PERSONALITY
Terman and Miles—SEX AND PERSONALITY
Wallin—PERSONALITY MALADJUSTMENTS AND MENTAL HYGIENE

John F. Dashiell was Consulting Editor of this series from its inception in 1931 until January 1, 1950.

PREFACE

The aim of the revised edition, like that of the first edition, is to make available to the college student and to the general reader investigations which are representative of the modern experimental treatment of important psychological topics. The title *Recent Experiments in Psychology* means that the book is designed to reflect contemporary trends in the science. However, not every experiment reported is recent in the sense that it has been performed within the last decade.

The investigations reviewed have been selected on the basis of their psychological importance and of their value and interest to the student. In general, each chapter includes an introductory section designed to orient the reader to the topic under consideration, a review of one or more pertinent experiments on the problem, and a concluding discussion in which the experimental results are interpreted from the viewpoint of their theoretical significance and of their application to problems of everyday interest. Only two chapters, XI and XIX, present material that is not chiefly or primarily experimental in nature.

All the experiments in this book are presented in a manner designed to make their aims, methods, results, and interpretation as clear as possible to the student who is not technically prepared to read the experimental literature in its original form. For this reason it has been necessary to make many changes in the terminology employed by the original author, to define terms possibly unfamiliar to the student, to amplify the descriptions of the methods used in the various experiments, to present the results in somewhat simplified form, and to include appropriate illustrative material. Hence, no chapter is in any sense a verbatim reproduction of the articles or books on which it is based. In order to bring the chapters to a convenient reading length, sections of the original experimental reports have been deleted or greatly condensed in certain cases. However, the reviewers have been careful to present with accuracy the factual material of every experiment. It is only in the theoretical interpretation and application of the data, especially in those chapter sections entitled "Introduction" and "Discussion," that the reviewers may at times have differed from the original author.

Of the chapters in the first edition, seven have been reproduced with only minor changes. Twelve other chapters have been retained but have been extensively revised, especially with regard to the inclusion of additional experimental material and, in several cases, the substitution of more recently reported experiments for those described in the first edition.

In addition, the revised edition contains seven entirely new chapters which deal with the following topics: belief in mysticism among college students, the perception of obstacles by the blind, conflict and experimental neurosis in cats, the value of organization for retention and transfer, the perception of the vertical in space, projection and the Thematic Apperception Test, and the opinion-poll technique.

The revised edition reflects various trends in psychological interest and research which have become conspicuous since the first edition was published. Among these are the extensive experimentation in the field of perception which originated in connection with the necessities of the Second World War; concepts of an organizational or Gestalt nature, which are related to the current interest in perceptual problems; the "dynamic approach," which is associated with the increasing emphasis now being placed upon clinical psychology; and the expansion of research in social psychology as exemplified especially by the opinion-poll technique. However, the present reviewers, though giving heed to these contemporary trends, have not committed themselves in their selection of chapter topics and experiments to any single systematic theory or type of interest.

For permission to use the articles reviewed in this book, the reviewers wish to express their indebtedness to the respective authors and to the following publishers and journals: *The American Journal of Psychology*, American Medical Association, American Psychological Association, *Archives of Psychology*, *The British Journal of Psychology*, Columbia University Press, Harper & Brothers, Paul B. Hoeber, Inc., Dr. Carl Murchison, W. W. Norton & Company, Rockefeller Institute for Medical Research, Springer-Verlag, Teachers College (Columbia University) Bureau of Publications, The University of Chicago Press,

University of Wisconsin, U.S. Government Printing Office, The William
Alanson White Psychiatric Foundation, The Williams & Wilkins
Company, and the Wistar Institute of Anatomy and Biology.   For
certain illustrative material the reviewers are also indebted to the
estate of Dr. A. A. Brill, Harvard University Press, Dr. C. V. Lyons,
Popular Science Monthly, and W. B. Saunders Company.

THE AUTHORS

NEW YORK, N.Y.
May, 1950

CONTENTS

CHAPTER IV

CHAPTER V

CHAPTER VI

CHAPTER VII

CHAPTER VIII

CHAPTER I

A STUDY OF ATTITUDES TOWARD MYSTICISM AMONG COLLEGE STUDENTS

INTRODUCTION

It is a well-known fact that popular interest in occult subjects such as "spiritualism" and "telepathy" is considerable at all times. It is also well known that such interests are likely to increase markedly when people feel fearful and insecure under social tension, as in wartime or during a period of major economic crisis. This tendency is not explained by ascribing it to "ignorance," a term which is often as meaningless and vague to the psychologist as "laziness." For beliefs in the occult may be held with equally uncritical credulity by people in all walks of life and by the educated as well as by the uneducated. The list of believers includes eminent physicists and physicians, and occasionally even college professors, as well as other types of ordinary and extraordinary citizens.

It is beyond the scope of this chapter to attempt to account for the persistence of such beliefs in an "enlightened modern world," or for the fact that they occasionally swell to the proportions of a major fad. We are concerned with the fact that "evidence" favoring the occult (*i.e.*, the mysterious, the unknowable) is often presented as though it were "scientific," although the conditions under which it was obtained are scarcely comparable to the controlled situations of a scientific investigation. We are also interested in the frequency with which "mystics" encourage their audiences to believe that occurrences which baffle their understanding and seem to defy any attempt at direct explanation are truly occult and "beyond the limits of scientific explanation." Writers such as Houdini,[1] Thurstone,[2] McComas,[3] and Dunninger,[4] who were

[1] Houdini, H. *A Magician among the Spirits*. New York, Harper, 1924.

[2] Thurstone, H. *400 Tricks You Can Do*. Garden City, Blue Ribbon Books, Inc., 1940.

[3] McComas, H. C. *Ghosts I Have Talked With*. Baltimore, Williams & Wilkins, 1935.

[4] Dunninger, J. *Inside the Medium's Cabinet*. New York, Kemp & Co., 1935.

1

themselves eminent performers of the "most perplexing mystical demonstrations" but who claimed no supernatural powers and, on the contrary, were interested in exposing fraud and chicanery in their field, have offered illuminating discussions of such problems. So, too, have many psychologists.[1] Honest masters of the occult craft have shown very clearly in their writings how fraudulent tricksters set out to baffle and amaze the public with their extravagant claims for supernatural powers and for the production of "inexplicable" mysteries. From such objective treatments of the matter, the reader has an opportunity to understand more adequately many practices of mediums and other occultists. For example, the reason why they insist upon performing in darkness or in very dim light when "materializing spirits" may not be due so much to the alleged preference of ghosts for faint light as to the need for providing conditions under which a skilled performer may carry out, unobserved, certain "critical" actions such as manipulating a microphone to shift "spirit" voices about the room, or presenting "spirit" faces by the adroit use of a long, collapsible rod.

However, the fact is that occult phenomena have a great fascination for many people. This attraction is based upon a variety of motives, often involving a desire to satisfy some intense need of the individual (*e.g.*, to communicate once more with a dead son or husband and to be assured of his happiness). Popular gullibility regarding the occult is fostered and increased by various groups and individuals in our culture. As McComas points out, psychic research societies contribute to the wide acceptance of occult beliefs by their frequent tendency—in all sincerity, as a rule—to publicize only those observations which they regard as "positive" evidence for occult phenomena, and which therefore tend to encourage a belief in spiritism. More important by far, however, are those individuals who find it financially profitable to exploit popular interest in the mysterious and the obscure. Lee Steiner in her well-known book, *Where Do People Take Their Troubles?*[2] describes and exposes a great variety of these ingenious and unscrupulous tricksters and shows how they are able to inveigle countless thousands

[1] For example, Jastrow, J. *Fact and Fable in Psychology.* Boston, Houghton Mifflin, 1900.

―――. *The Betrayal of Intelligence.* New York, Greenberg, 1938.

[2] Steiner, Lee R. *Where Do People Take Their Troubles?* Boston, Houghton Mifflin, 1945.

of ignorant or emotionally unstable persons into becoming their "clients" or "patients."

These mind readers, spirit invokers, and the like often make a practice of stimulating public interest and gullibility in their claims by giving public performances which vastly impress many of the people who attend them. In order to illustrate the kind of demonstration which may be presented to the witness or audience in such instances, and also to obtain some insight into the attitudes of university students toward occult interpretations of the occurrences, there follows a report of a public showing of "occult phenomena" in which the audience was composed of undergraduate students in psychology.

A CLASSROOM DEMONSTRATION OF "PSYCHICAL PHENOMENA"[1]

A few years ago an interesting test was carried out in a lecture class in psychology at a prominent American university. This test was planned and staged by two instructors who had been surprised at the number of students in their elementary courses who reported in all seriousness that they visited mediums, took their personal problems to the Ouija board for solution, or who at least expressed a sympathetic attitude toward belief in the occult although disavowing any active participation in such practices. Furthermore, the instructors suspected that among those students who expressed a serious interest in the occult there might be many who would require little further "evidence" to bring them into the category of "believers." When opinions were asked for in class, only a few students expressed outright skepticism about occult beliefs; moreover, the reasons they gave for their incredulity were often unclear and vague, however confidently they were expressed.

The instructors decided to present to their classes a special program which would open for discussion the general problem of occult beliefs and their basis, would demonstrate the power of group suggestion for the acceptance of presumably occult performances (as in theater or séance situations), and would also offer a lesson in the need for careful evaluation of the facts underlying so-called "psychical" phenomena before such phenomena are accepted as evidence for mystical beliefs.

[1] Adapted from Marcuse, F. L., and M. E. Bitterman. A Classroom Demonstration of "Psychical Phenomena." *Journal of Abnormal and Social Psychology*, 1944, vol. 39, pp. 238-243.

In other words, it was hoped that by using the methods of leading professional exposers of charlatanism (such as Thurstone, Houdini, Dunninger, and McComas), the students might be helped to take a more objective attitude toward such phenomena and to acquire a better insight into the difference between valid and seeming evidence. In effect, the aim was to develop a better understanding of the techniques of deception to the end of learning how to avoid being hoodwinked.

Accordingly, the following program was presented to an introductory lecture class of 171 undergraduate students in general psychology, at a point near the beginning of the course. Without any explanatory announcement of the real purpose, the students assembled for a regular class meeting were presented with the situation to be described.

THE LECTURE

First, the regular lecturer in psychology presented a purportedly serious discussion of psychical phenomena. Speaking slowly at a pace which permitted detailed note taking, he offered a predetermined set of pseudoscientific statements and suggestions, using 10 minutes in this way to "prepare the ground" for the main demonstration. In substance, the lecturer informed the class that he had been fortunate enough to work with Doctors A and B, who were pioneers in the field of psychical phenomena and who were the first really to put this type of work on a scientific basis. He decried the lack of understanding and appreciation of such work which is manifested by most modern writers in psychology and pointed out that any innovation in science must meet inevitably with opposition. The speaker than selected the problem of mental telepathy for special consideration. He defended the position that a good deal of the confusion now current about this topic in psychology was based upon a failure to realize the importance of individual differences in the capacity to "receive" telepathic emanations and upon the general neglect of evidence that telepathic capacities have a real physiological basis.

The latter point was then elaborated in terms of a discussion of (alleged) evidence from electroencephalography[1] and extended to a

---

[1] Electroencephalography is the study of the electrophysiology of the cerebral cortex, involving especially the analysis of the patterns of electrical activity in the brain which are commonly termed "brain waves" (see Chap. XII).

somewhat detailed consideration of the probable importance of individual differences in the thickness of various layers of the cerebral cortex for telepathic receptiveness. Here the presentation was made in measured tones, with liberal reference to complicated diagrams for illustration of the main points. Then, with every appearance of confidence, the lecturer offered a general hypothesis to account for telepathic capacities, along the lines of an analogy between telepathic occurrences and electrical circuits. He stated that "senders" of telepathic messages show more intense "brain waves," and that, as compared with nontelepathic individuals, both "senders" and "receivers" of such messages have thicker cortical layers and therefore offer a decreased resistance to the passage of these waves. This analysis was followed by the presentation on the blackboard of the physical formula relating resistance to the diameter of the electrical conductor. It was also stated that, as one might expect from the greater quantity of cortex which "telepathists" have been proved to possess, they are found to be superior in intelligence. Finally, it was pointed out that skeptics commonly tend to be irreligious and often are atheists or agnostics. This last remark was designed, obviously, to help create an atmosphere in which students who might be inclined to heckle could not do so except by associating themselves with a socially disapproved group.

The student audience was now in psychological readiness for the demonstrations themselves.

THE DEMONSTRATIONS

The lecturer ended his introductory remarks by announcing his intention to experiment with various psychical phenomena under "controlled laboratory conditions" and asked the students to judge for themselves the adequacy of the evidence to be presented. He stated as his only requirement that they remain quiet and ask no questions until the experiment was finished.

Tests of Telepathic Communication. To introduce the "demonstration" of telepathy, the lecturer modestly admitted that he himself possessed some ability as a "sender" and thereupon presented Mr. C as one of the two persons on the campus known to have ability as a "receiver."

After C had left the room, four students were selected at random and each was asked to write some number between 1 and 25 on the blackboard.   The four numbers obtained were then averaged on the board, after which the entire set of figures was thoroughly erased.   Meanwhile, not a word had been spoken by any participant.   This operation completed, a student selected at random from the class was asked to bring C, the "receiver," back into the lecture room.   The lecturer ("sender"), holding in one hand an object which he called a "psychic bulb," then stood face to face with C, the "receiver," in full view of the class and only 2 feet from the front row of students.   The two demonstrators then gazed intently at the "psychic bulb."   After several seconds C called out a number, which proved to be the correct one.

As a further test of the lecturer's telepathic ability, heavy envelopes and white cards were passed out at random to various members of the class with the request that these students write questions about the future on the cards, then carefully seal the cards in the envelopes without showing the contents to anyone.   The lecturer, now operating as a "receiver," announced his willingness to attempt to read and answer the questions sealed in the envelopes.   The envelopes were collected from the class by C, who passed them to the lecturer in full view of the class.   The lecturer then proceeded to pick up the sealed envelopes one by one and "discern" the contents of each without opening it. This he did by pressing each one of the heavy, sealed envelopes in its turn to his forehead and keeping it there until he had "read" and answered the question.   Then and only then did he open the particular envelope to confirm the "reading," and the writer of the question in hand was asked to state whether his question had been correctly revealed.   In this manner the questions were "read" in succession, all of them correctly as it proved, and "answers" were given to them.   Then members of the audience were free to examine the cards and envelopes, to satisfy themselves (as the lecturer explained) that there had been no trickery.

As an experiment in "long-distance telepathy," a committee of students designated by the class was asked to select some one playing card from a standard 52-card deck.   After having been told their choice, the lecturer stopped in quiet concentration for a few seconds, as if to transmit this knowledge to a distant "receiver," and then requested another class committee to phone "Miss Dwight" (described as a known "receiver" of ability) at a specified number and ask her to name the card.   The committee carried out these instructions to the letter and returned with the announcement that Miss Dwight had correctly identified the card, which had been the eight of diamonds.

While the class committee was telephoning Miss Dwight, the lecturer asked another member of the class to think of the last name of a friend, then to write a list of nine names in which the friend's name was "buried." When the list was handed back to the lecturer he looked intently at it, concentrated for a time, and then announced the friend's name, correctly.

An Attempt at Materializing Spirits. The lecturer then announced the last and most difficult test, an attempt to materialize (*i.e.*, to summon into visible form) one of the guiding spirits which commonly appear to aid mediums in their effort to communicate with the departed. The class was first asked to concentrate upon the lecturer, who was to attempt the materialization. The room was then darkened. After an interval of about one-half minute the lecturer inquired whether anyone could see anything. Several members of the class reported seeing "something ghostly." The lecturer than suggested that more "power" might help those who had not succeeded and asked the class to sing "The Battle Hymn of the Republic." During the singing, other students in the class exclaimed that they now saw a "ghostly face." A few seconds thereafter the room lights were turned on, and the demonstration was ended.

CLASS REACTIONS TO THE DEMONSTRATIONS

Immediately after the conclusion of the "experiments," the lecturer asked the class the following question: "On the basis of the evidence presented, how many of you are now convinced of the reality of psychic phenomena?" By a show of hands, 70 per cent of the class of 171 students answered this question in the affirmative. A special questionnaire on "before and after" attitudes[1] was then passed out, the results of which will be presented later in this chapter.

After all the students had indicated their attitudes on the general question and had answered the written questionnaire, the lecturer announced that the entire set of demonstrations was a hoax and that the so-called "experiments" were mere trickery. This statement was followed by "an embarrassed silence," after which there was a mounting tide of laughter. Requests for information about the ways in

---

[1] For a definition of "attitude" see footnote on p. 385.

which the various tricks had been performed were denied in order (as the lecturer explained) to promote good retention of the demonstrations and their significance.

To emphasize the frequent success of trickery in such matters, the lecturer than delivered a concise discussion of the general problem of psychical phenomena, the anecdotal nature of the evidence presented by most individual witnesses of such phenomena, the role of bias and "faith" in distorting observations, and some of the many types of deceptive techniques frequently employed by frauds and sharpsters. However, the students were left to their own resources to explain how the specific tricks used in their class demonstration had been worked.

The Postdemonstration Test of "Before and After" Attitudes

No tests of attitudes were made before the lecture and demonstrations were presented, in order to avoid arousing suspicions as to the purpose of the demonstrations or any doubts of their being "genuine experiments."[1]

After the demonstrations had been completed, and before the lecturer announced that the class had been subjected to a series of hoaxes, each member of the class, as has been said, was presented with a questionnaire designed to obtain further information concerning the effectiveness of the "experiments." In this questionnaire, each student was asked to indicate whether his attitude had been one of belief, uncertainty, or disbelief toward "psychical phenomena" before the lecture and experiments, and what it was immediately after the experiments (*i.e.*, before the lecturer exposed the hoax). The results for the 171 students are presented in Table I.

It will be noticed from Table I that the increase in the number of "believers" and the decrease in the "uncertain" group before and after the demonstrations were statistically significant, but that the number of "disbelievers" did not change to a significant extent. As noted above, considerably more than half of the students had raised their hands to indicate belief when asked for a verdict directly after the "experiments" had been finished. However, a show of hands is usually an unreliable indication of individual opinions, since it is obviously influenced by suggestion. It is probable that many of the students who raised their hands as registering "belief" responses later settled upon a

---

[1] The investigators believe that the procedure adopted actually had the effect of minimizing the obtained differences (*i.e.*, belief before and after the tests).

response of "uncertain" in the questionnaire. It is clear from the table, however, that the demonstrations had the effect of producing a significant increase in the direction of acknowledged belief in the reality of psychical phenomena.

TABLE I

Attitudes of the Students toward Psychical Phenomena before and after the Lecture and "Experiments"

$(N = 171)$

Attitude	Before lecture, per cent	After "experiments," per cent	Critical ratio[1]
Belief....................	15.8	42.7	5.7
Uncertainty..............	56.1	37.4	3.6
Disbelief................	28.1	19.9	1.8

[1] The *critical ratio* is a statistical measure of the significance of a difference between two sets of results (*e.g.*, per cent belief before and after the "experiments"). The formula for obtaining this value is $Diff./S.E._{diff.}$, which represents the difference between the groups (*i.e.*, between their arithmetical averages, or their percentages as in the present case) divided by the standard error of the difference. If a critical ratio of 3 or more is obtained between the groups, the probability that a similar difference would be obtained in a repetition of the experiment is indicated to be virtually 100 per cent, and the difference is considered significant.

The results given in Table II show the changes occurring within each of the three original attitude groups, that is, the shifts in attitude which occurred after the demonstrations among those initially expressing belief, those expressing uncertainty, and those expressing disbelief. It will be noticed, first of all, that—as the data in Table I also indicate— most of the changes in attitude were in the expected direction; that is,

TABLE II

Attitude Changes (after the Demonstrations) among Students Holding Given Attitudes before the Program

Attitude before lecture and demonstrations	Attitude after demonstrations							
	Belief		Uncertainty		Disbelief		Total change	
	Number	Per cent	Number	Per cent	Number	Per cent	Number	Per cent
Belief ($N = 27$).............	21	77.8	4	14.8	2	7.4	6	22.2
Uncertain ($N = 96$).........	44	45.8	39	40.7	13	13.5	57	59.3
Disbelief ($N = 48$).........	8	16.7	21	43.8	19	39.5	29	60.5
Total.................	73	....	64	....	34	....	92	....

40.7 per cent of those originally uncertain expressed belief after the demonstrations, and 60.5 per cent of those who said that they had been disbelievers shifted either to uncertainty (43.8 per cent) or to belief (16.7 per cent). However, some changes in the opposite direction occurred. Of those who said they had been believers before the demonstrations, 14.8 per cent changed to uncertainty and 7.4 per cent to actual disbelief; and of those who had been uncertain, 13.5 per cent finally expressed disbelief.

The experimenters interpret these changes toward a more skeptical attitude to mean that a few of the originally believing or uncertain subjects became less credulous because they were sufficiently acute to suspect the lecturer's purpose. In addition, 39.5 per cent of those who were originally disbelievers remained fixed in that opinion. It is probable that these students either guessed the aim of the demonstrations or were so convinced beforehand of the fraudulent character of telepathic and related phenomena that the "evidence" provided by the lecturer was insufficient to change their attitude.

DISCUSSION

The marked increase which occurred in the number of "believers," at the expense not only of the "uncertain" but also of the "disbelief" group, may be attributed to the convincing character of the lecture and demonstrations. University students as a group presumably rank fairly high in the general population in their ability to exercise a critical attitude toward new evidence; yet the results indicate that large numbers of students were "taken in" by these proceedings. This outcome indicates the great force of social suggestion and of prestige (here of the lecturer in psychology) in modifying attitudes—in this study, toward belief in the occult.

The fact that as a group the original believers were changed least of all is not surprising. For most of them, the classroom experience was satisfactorily perceived and understood in accordance with their existing uncritical attitudes, a familiar result in social psychology,[1] and few of them seem to have been made suspicious. In contrast, the initial disbelievers, as a group, shifted much more, changing in the direction of uncertainty and even of belief. In this investigation, attitudes of belief

---

[1] Murphy, G., L. B. Murphy, and T. M. Newcomb. *Experimental Social Psychology.* New York, Harper, 1937.

Sherif, M. *An Outline of Social Psychology.* New York, Harper, 1948.

in the reality of psychic phenomena appear to have been more stable and persistent than attitudes of disbelief.

It is quite probable that the attitudes of disbelief might have been less readily changed had they been based upon dependable knowledge and upon understanding of some of the ways in which such "tricks" are performed. The citizen who knows that "mind readers" often have excellent and extensive card-index systems of information about prominent members of the community, especially about confirmed "believers" and regular clients of mediums, crystal-gazers, fortunetellers, astrologists, and the like; or that such "psychic" gentlemen often employ astute "spotters" to listen in on lobby conversations before the show and during intermissions, is put on his guard when he attends a performance. He is then likely to think of other explanations than "telepathic waves" when his friend's name is announced from the stage and startling personal information about him is given. If he knows that mediums have many highly complicated and skillful techniques for the "materializing of spirits," which are not readily discerned by novices and outsiders and are generally guarded closely as valuable professional secrets, he will be less gullible during a séance with its atmosphere of darkness and soft music and its "spirit voices."

The tendency to conclude that something which cannot be explained on the basis of one's available knowledge is altogether "inexplicable" is understandably strong in people who lack an adequate education in the methods of science and is not always absent among the scientists themselves, particularly when they are concerned with problems outside their own special fields. Few people are sufficiently well acquainted with the facts and psychological principles of "occultism" to penetrate the deceptions of a practiced performance by masters of the craft. Readers of this chapter will appreciate the weight of the foregoing statement more fully if they, like the subjects of the experiment, will attempt to work out their own explanations of how each of the "tricks" was performed.[1]

One significant sequel to the demonstration should be mentioned. Within a few days after the investigation had ended, the two experimenters learned that a rumor was current on the university campus to the effect that they had carried out their lecture and demonstrations as a means of indicating their actual belief in the reality of "psychic" phenomena, a belief which the university authorities would not permit

[1] The solutions are given at the end of this chapter.

them to express openly. The fact that this story was false in all respects did not prevent its growth and energetic circulation, a familiar phenomenon to students of rumor psychology. An interesting question concerns which of the attitude groups represented among the subjects at the lecture and demonstration would be most likely to react to the postdemonstration "hoax-exposure" in this manner, and what their psychological motivation might have been.

The tricks employed in these demonstrations were very simple, and were selected from the elementary items in the extensive repertoires of specialists such as Thurstone and Dunninger. All of them depended greatly for their effectiveness upon the extent to which a receptive attitude on the part of the audience was developed by the lecture.

The version of the "psychic bulb" trick utilized here was made possible by the lecturer's ability to move his ears in a controlled fashion. The ear on the side away from the audience was used to signal the correct number to C, the receiver, who observed the movements in peripheral vision while fixating the psychic bulb. If no skilled ear movers are available, this demonstration may be carried out with any one of a variety of other minimal cues (*i.e.*, slight and usually unnoticed stimuli which, after more or less practice, become useful and perhaps of critical importance in perceptual judgments. Examples are verbal codes, musical signals from an on-stage pianist, and the like).

The envelope trick also can be carried out in many different ways. As used in these demonstrations, the trick requires a confederate in the audience who will ask a predetermined question, known to the receiver. In collecting the envelopes in this demonstration, C placed the one containing this known question at the *bottom* of the pack. In going through the envelopes, the lecturer started with an unknown one at the *top* of the pack. This envelope he pressed to his forehead, but while doing this he announced and answered the (known) question in the envelope at the bottom of the pack. Having done this, he opened the envelope which he had just taken from the top, apparently "for confirmation" but actually to learn what he would announce as the next question in the series. Then, after applying the next sealed envelope to his brow, he stated and replied to the question which actually had been read from the envelope opened just before. Proceeding in this way through the pack, in each case he was able to *read* the next question in actuality before seeming to read it "psychically."

In the telephone trick, the name of the person to be called was a code word which Miss D, the "receiver," with the code before her at the telephone, readily translated into the name of one of the 52 cards in a pack. Thus, the name "Miss Duforth" might have been the symbol for the four of diamonds, "Miss Cohn" the nine of clubs, and so on. Of course, it is possible to devise codes which may be used to transmit much more complicated information than this over the telephone.

The buried-name trick is based upon the observation of minimal cues and utilizes one of the most familiar principles in the psychology of attention. The individual who writes the list of names usually will write down the critical name without hesitation, but as a rule will hesitate, or show some other variation of behavior, before writing down each of the other names he is "thinking up." In the demonstration, the lecturer talked to the class while the names were being written down but observed the writer's behavior carefully without seeming to do so, and thus was quite sure of the *position* of the correct name in the series before he was handed the list for his process of "concentration."

The materializing of spirits was attempted last of all because of the fact that it involved a far greater strain on the credulity of the audience than did any of the other demonstrations. Dunninger and McComas, in particular, have described a number of ways by which a basis for the perception of "ghostly" figures may be produced. In the present experiment, an upright oval was painted with an anthracene solution on the projection screen at the front of the room before the class met for the demonstrations. This oval figure was quite invisible in ordinary light, but in the darkness it was caused to fluoresce by flashing ultraviolet light (invisible in ordinary daylight) upon it by means of a strong flashlight equipped with an ultraviolet filter. Readers familiar with personality tests such as the Rorschach ink-blot series will understand why, under such conditions, many members of an audience will imagine that they see a "ghostly" face or will interpret a patch of light or a vague outline as the visage of a person familiar to them. Even in audiences less credulous than those generally encountered at mediumistic séances, one may expect to find a few individuals who will report seeing or hearing "spirits" with very little external basis for the perception.

CHAPTER II

THE ORIGIN OF THE CAT'S RESPONSES TO RATS AND MICE

INTRODUCTION

The question as to what factors determine the behavior of cats toward rats and mice has constituted the problem of several psychological experiments. Since the "normal" (*i.e.*, the usual) reaction of cats to rats and mice is to kill and eat them, the major task of these studies has been to discover the causes of this rodent killing behavior. In popular language the question probably would be phrased, Is rat killing in cats "instinctive"? However, the word "instinct" possesses so many unscientific connotations that it has fallen into disrepute among most psychologists. For this reason a more satisfactory way to state the problem of these experiments is to say that their aim has been to ascertain the respective contributions of native and of acquired factors to the occurrence of rat killing in cats.

The meaning which will be attached to the terms "native response" and "acquired response" in this chapter requires a brief explanation. A response may be regarded as native insofar as it appears through the influence of maturation (*i.e.*, of genetic factors introduced through tissue growth) under the typical environmental conditions (both prenatal and postnatal) of the species. A response which is predominantly native in character is almost certain to appear in every member of a given species when its proper stimulus is presented, provided that the growth and development of the organism (1) have progressed under normal environmental conditions, both before and after birth (as we have said), and (2) have advanced far enough to make possible the reaction in question. Neither the appearance nor the nature of a truly native response is due primarily to modification through previous exposure to the stimulating situation (*i.e.*, to learning). On the other hand, an acquired response is generally understood to be a reaction which is determined primarily by the previous experience of the organism in some particular stimulus situation. If the organism has not had the experiences essential for the acquisition of such a response, the reaction does not appear at all. If different individual members of a species have had different experiences in connection with the particular stimulus situation, then their behavior in that situation will show corresponding differences. In other words, both the existence and the nature of an acquired response depend fundamentally upon learning.

When the psychologist attempts to determine whether a given kind of behavior is predominantly influenced by native or acquired factors, he resorts to controlled methods of investigation. It is obvious that such problems cannot be solved merely by speculating about them. But is is equally impossible to determine the origin of a given type of behavior simply by observing the frequency with which it occurs in a given species under uncontrolled conditions. For example, most people regard rat killing in cats as "instinctive" because all the cats of their acquaintance do kill rats.[1] Yet the universality of a response is no proof whatsoever that it is native. If it were true that all cats exhibited rat killing under the normal living conditions of the species, then it would appear that all cats must possess the bodily equipment (*i.e.*, receptor, nervous, and effector structures) essential to that act. But even then the possibility that learning played a role in producing this behavior would not be excluded, for notwithstanding the possession of the essential bodily equipment, each individual cat might still have to learn to use such equipment in acquiring the actual response of rat killing for itself. Only by controlling and varying the conditions in which an animal lives from birth and then repeatedly testing its responses to some chosen stimulus can one determine the true origin and development of its behavior to that stimulating situation.

Among the experiments which have dealt with the origin of the cat's responses to rats and mice, the investigation of Kuo is one of the most thorough and one of the most convincing. His work is significant, not only because it provides us with additional knowledge concerning the behavior of the cat, a favorite domestic animal, but also because it exemplifies sound scientific methods of handling the par-

[1] As a matter of fact, rat killing is not universal among cats, and many cat owners complain that their cats do not attack or kill rats and mice.

ticular problem which it raises and of analyzing a behavior pattern generally presumed to be "native." A review of Kuo's experiment follows.

KUO'S EXPERIMENT[1]

PURPOSE

The purpose of Kuo's experiment was to determine the origin of the cat's responses toward rodents (*i.e.*, toward rats and mice).

METHOD

Subjects. The subjects of the experiment were 59 kittens. Thirty of these, the "nonvegetarian" kittens, were fed throughout the experiment on beef, milk, and fish mixed with cooked rice. The other 29, the "vegetarian" kittens, were fed on milk and vegetables only and never tasted meat at any time. At the time that each of the tests described below was made, half of the vegetarian and half of the nonvegetarian kittens had eaten nothing for 12 hours, whereas the other half of each subgroup had just been fed.

General Plan of the Experiment. The general plan of the experiment was to rear different groups of kittens under living conditions which differed greatly with respect to the kind of experiences with rats and mice which the kittens underwent. To this end, three different living conditions were devised, the 59 kittens were divided into three groups approximately equal in size, and one group was assigned to live under each of these conditions. At certain prescribed times, the reaction of each kitten to rodents (*i.e.*, to rats and mice) was tested. In this way it was possible to discover to what extent certain defined experiences with rats and mice would influence a kitten's later responses to them. If, in the test situation, all three groups of kittens reacted to rodents in the same way, regardless of the differences in their previous experiences with them, then their response might be regarded as predominantly influenced by native factors. But if the different groups of kittens responded differently, and in accordance with the differences in their previous experiences, then their behavior toward rodents might be regarded as predominantly influenced by acquired factors. A description of the three conditions follows.

[1] Adapted from Kuo, Z. Y. The Genesis of the Cat's Response to the Rat. *Journal of Comparative Psychology*, 1930, vol. 11, pp. 1–30.

Condition 1. Twenty kittens were reared under condition 1. In this condition, the "isolated" one, each kitten lived entirely alone in a cage. The kitten was completely isolated and deprived of all contact with rats or mice except on those occasions when it was being tested for its response to them. Its cage was even kept covered at night so that, if a wild rat chanced to stray into the room, the kitten would not see it. It was also entirely isolated from any other kitten or cat, except that it lived with its mother up to the time of weaning, which occurred at the age of fourteen to eighteen days. But since no rodents were present in the environment during that early period, the kitten had no opportunity to observe the reactions of its mother to them. Of the 20 kittens in this group, 10 were vegetarian and 10 were nonvegetarian in their diet. Five of the vegetarian and five of the nonvegetarian kittens were always tested immediately after they had been fed. The other five of each subgroup were tested only after they had been without food for 12 hours.

Condition 2. Twenty-one kittens were reared under condition 2. Each of these kittens lived in a cage with its mother throughout the period of the experiment and saw her kill a rat or a mouse, just outside the cage, every four days. Three kinds of rodents were used for this purpose: large albino rats, medium-sized wild rats, and small dancing mice. Since each mother cat was always given the same kind of rat or mouse to kill, no kitten ever saw more than one species of rodent killed. Furthermore, since the mother was never permitted to eat the rodent she had killed, no kitten ever saw a rat or a mouse actually eaten. Each test was made immediately after the kitten had witnessed a killing. As in condition 1, the kittens were equally divided into vegetarians and nonvegetarians. Half of each subgroup were hungry when the test was made, and half were not hungry at that time.

Condition 3. Eighteen kittens were brought up under condition 3. Each of these kittens, from the age of six to eight days onward, lived in its cage with a single rodent of one of the three species named above. Until the kitten was weaned, it lived with the rodent during the day only; in the evening the rodent was removed and the kitten's mother was put into the cage for the night. After weaning, however, the kitten saw no other cats at any time. Furthermore, it was never permitted to see any rat or mouse other than the one with which it lived, excepting the rodents which were used for the tests. This group was subdivided as before with respect to diet and to degree of hunger at the time of the tests (see Fig. 1).

The Tests. The tests of the kitten's response to a rat or a mouse were identical for all three groups of kittens. Each test began with the introduction of a large albino rat into the kitten's cage. If this large rat was not killed within 30 min., it was removed and a medium-sized wild rat was substituted for it. If the wild rat was not killed within 30 min., it was also removed and a small dancing mouse was put into the cage. If the mouse was not killed within 30 min., the test was ended. The testing began when the kitten was six to eight days old. From that time on, each kitten was tested once every four days until it either had killed one rodent of each of the three species

Fig. 1.   A Cat and a Rat Which Have Lived Together Since Shortly after Birth, as in Condition 3. (*Courtesy of John Polo.*)

used, or had reached the age of four months. Hence a kitten, over a period of about 12 weeks, might be given more than 30 tests with each kind of rodent.

RESULTS

The Amount of Rat Killing in the Three Groups. The most important feature of the results is the number of kittens in each group that killed rats or mice. Table I shows for each condition the total number of kittens in each group, and the number which killed any species of rodent during the entire testing period.

These results show conclusively that whether a kitten killed rats and mice depended very largely on the nature of its individual experiences with them. Eighteen of the twenty-one kittens that saw their mothers kill a rat or a mouse very four days killed a rodent themselves sooner or later. Only 9 of the 20 kittens that were kept entirely isolated both from other cats and from rodents killed a rat or a mouse themselves. (Why nearly half of this group did kill rodents will be discussed later.) And among the 18 kittens which had actually lived with rodents, only 3 ever killed a rat or a mouse at all.

The Kind of Rodent Which the Kittens Killed. A record was also kept of the kind of rodent which each kitten killed. As will be seen, this phase of the results is of considerable importance. In condition 1 (the "isolated" condition), it was found that if a kitten killed a large albino rat, it also killed both the two smaller species, but that a kitten might kill a small rodent without ever attacking a larger one. Evidently, the *mere size* of the rodent often determined whether or not a

TABLE I

Showing, for Each Condition, the Number of Kittens That Killed Any Rodent

Condition	Number of kittens in the group	Number of kittens killing any rodent
1 (isolated).....................	20	9
2 (saw rodents killed).............	21	18
3 (lived with rodent)..............	18	3

kitten would kill it. In condition 2, every one of the 18 kittens that killed a rat or a mouse was certain to kill first of all one of the same species that it had seen its mother kill. However, after killing a rodent of this species, the kitten might then kill rodents of the other two species also. In condition 3, the three kittens which finally did kill a rat or a mouse never killed the kind with which they had lived, but always one of some other species. Hence, not only rat killing itself, but also the *kind of rodent* which a kitten kills, is dependent to a great extent upon experience. For the tests showed that a kitten always tended to kill the kind of rat that it had seen its mother kill, and that it never killed the kind that it had had for a cage mate.

Responses to Rodents Other Than Killing. Other aspects of the behavior displayed by the kittens toward rodents, aside from their killing or not killing them, are also of interest. This behavior Kuo classifies as *negative*, in which the kitten did not react to the rat or mouse at all; *oriented*, in which the kitten merely watched the rodent; *tolerant*, in which the kitten allowed the rodent to perch on its back, smell of its nose, etc.; *playful*, in which it played with the rodent just as it might have with another kitten; and *hostile*, in which it growled, arched its back, hissed, and the like. As might be expected, hostile responses during the tests were most common in Group 2. Negative, oriented, and playful reactions were common in Group 1. In Group 3, tolerant and playful reactions were most frequent in the test situation, though hostile responses to the strange rodent were sometimes observed.

As to the reactions of the kittens in Group 3 toward the rodents with which they lived, tolerant and playful behavior was very common. Six of the eighteen kittens showed "attachment" to the rat, in that they were restless and seemed to be searching for it when it was removed from the cage. Three kittens even showed "protective" responses toward the rodent, like those of a mother cat toward her young. Hostile reactions were never observed at all.

Effect of Age, Diet, and Hunger on Rat-killing Behavior. The average age of the kittens at the time of their first "kill' was about 83 days in Groups 1 and 3, and about 71 days in Group 2. On the average, 17 to 19 tests were given to the kittens before any actual rat killing occurred.

Whether the kitten's diet was vegetarian or nonvegetarian had no influence, in any of the groups, on its killing rats or mice. Just as many vegetarian as nonvegetarian kittens killed rodents. However, a nonvegetarian kitten was much more likely to eat a rodent it had killed.

Similarly, whether or not a kitten was hungry at the time of the test had no effect whatever on the likelihood of its killing a rodent.

Results of Exposing the Non-rat-killing Kittens of Groups 1 and 3 to Condition 2. It will be remembered that 11 of the 20 kittens of Group 1, and 15 of the 18 of Group 3, did not kill any rats or mice during the four months' testing, whereas 18 of the 21 kittens in Group 2 did kill a rodent during that period. Kuo decided to find out whether these 26 non-rat-killing kittens in Groups 1 and 3 could be induced to kill rodents by being subjected for a time to condition 2. Hence, he returned each of these kittens to its mother and had the kitten live with the latter and see her kill a rat or a mouse outside the cage every

four days. As before, the kitten was tested for its own reaction to
rodents immediately after each killing. The kittens were four months
old when they were placed under this condition, and they were kept
under it either until they had killed one member of all three species of
rodents, or until they were six months old. If they had not killed a
rodent by that time, the attempt to "train" them to do so was abandoned.

The results of this part of the experiment were that although 9 of
the 11 kittens from Group 1 killed a rat or mouse, only 1 of the 15 from
Group 3 ever killed one. Hence, seeing an adult cat kill a rodent
stimulated most of the kittens of Group 1, which had previously been
reared in complete isolation, to kill rodents themselves. But even
this experience was insufficient to cause rat killing by kittens that had
lived with rodents since their infancy. These results furnish additional evidence concerning the degree to which a kitten's own individual experience determines whether or not it will kill rats and mice.

Training Cats to "Fear" Rats. Kuo finally tried to find out whether
cats could be trained to "fear" rats. The subjects for this experiment
were 10 adult cats, all of them habitual rat killers. A large cage of
two compartments was constructed. Its outer sides were made of
wood, its top was covered with wire netting, and the two compartments were separated from each other by a glass partition. The cat
was put into one compartment, and a rat was then introduced into the
other. As soon as the cat saw the rat, it was given an electric shock
strong enough to make it jump and run wildly. The shock was continued until the cat ran out of the cage through a door which was
opened when the shock was given. Thirty minutes later, the cat was
put into another cage, the "test cage," which was identical with the
original cage except that it was somewhat larger and had its walls and
partition made of wire netting instead of wood or glass. A rat was
now introduced into the second compartment of this cage, and the
cat's responses to it were observed during a 15-min. period. No shock
was administered in the test cage. Three trials a day were given until
the cat had either acquired some definite and apparently permanent
response to the rat in the test cage, or until it had received a total of
50 trials.

The results were as follows: Three of the ten cats came to show
marked "fear" responses to the rat, both in the original cage and in

the test cage, after from 11 to 16 trials. Two cats showed fear reactions to the rat in the original cage after 9 to 17 trials, respectively, but at no time displayed any such response to a rat in the test cage. Five cats acquired the reaction of running out of the original cage before the rat was put into it. Those that learned this response usually showed it after as few as four trials. In all cases, fear responses were developed, either to a rat in either cage, to a rat in the original cage only, or to the original cage itself. Hence, even cats that are habitual rat killers can easily be trained to "fear" rats and to run away from them.[1]

DISCUSSION[2]

Kuo concludes his article with a discussion of his results, and an interpretation of them. "The behavior of the cat toward the rat," he says, "is much more complex and variable than most psychologists would have thought." The problem is how this behavior is to be explained.

The cat, Kuo points out, is "a small-sized tiger." Its bodily make-up is especially adapted for making swift movements and for capturing and devouring small animals. It is "a machine so manufactured that under ordinary circumstances it will kill and even eat animals smaller than itself, such as rats, birds, etc." But its bodily make-up also renders it what we term "playful" in its reactions toward small animals or small moving objects. Normally, either type of response may, and as a matter of fact does, occur. Is it necessary, Kuo asks, to add "that this machine has been endowed by heredity, through its nervous system, with the instinct to kill rats and other small animals, and also with another instinct to play with them"? Kuo believes that this assumption is entirely superfluous. The cat behaves as it does toward rats because of its size and its bodily make-up. The responses which horses, lions, apes and sparrows normally make to rats differ greatly from those usually made by cats. But this difference is not due to the absence in those other animals of a specific "instinct" which the cat alone possesses. It is rather that the bodily structure of

[1] When a human being habitually exhibits fear reactions to objects commonly considered to be attractive rather than dangerous, he is likely to be regarded as "neurotic," and his fear may be termed a "phobia."

[2] This discussion is based largely on Kuo's own interpretation and explanation of his findings.

horses, apes, etc., is sufficiently different from that of cats to cause the development of very different patterns of behavior.

But one must consider more than a animal's bodily make-up to explain any given instance of behavior, such as that of a particular kitten toward a particular rat. There is no basis for the frequent assumption that behavior patterns are inherited as such. Animals, like human beings, grow and change. Their behavior is constantly being modified by stimuli originating both outside and inside the organism. Although the nature of the responses which an animal can make depends on its bodily structure, the actual reactions of the animal at a given moment are also influenced by its "life history." Therefore, when we vary the latter we may, within limits, produce corresponding variations in the animal's behavior. Thus Kuo, by varying the "life history" of his kittens, caused some of them to kill rats, others to "love" rats and to play with them. In the opinion of most people, the "natural" response of cats to rats is to kill and eat them. However, in the general population of domestic cats, one finds good "mousers," fair mousers, and poor mousers. In reality, it is just as "natural" for the cat to play with a rat as to attack it, to behave affectionately toward it as to kill it; for either type of response can be developed without difficulty by the proper training. It is, therefore, evident that Kuo's experiment gives us a definite answer to the original question, To what extent is rat killing in cats a native or an acquired mode of behavior? His results show clearly that rat killing in cats, as a describable pattern of behavior, owes its existence primarily to the effects of individual experience.

A problem that still remains is to explain why almost all cats living in a state of nature do kill and eat rats, and why 9 of the 20 kittens which Kuo reared in the isolated condition finally became rat killers. The reason is that in the typical environment of the cat, any animal having the domestic cat's bodily structure will almost inevitably learn to kill rats sooner or later. Any normal kitten is reasonably certain to see rats (or mice) frequently. If the rat runs, the kitten is likely to pursue it, just as it will pursue any small moving object. Being structurally fitted for swift movements, the kitten will sometimes overtake the rat. Having claws and teeth, it may now claw and bite it, perhaps at first only "playfully," as it might a ball or a piece of string. Eventually, however, it may accidentally kill it. In the course of biting the rat, the kitten may draw blood, and the taste and smell of the blood may lead it actually to eat the rat. Many of the separate responses cited above, such as pursuing, clawing, and biting, may be predominantly native in origin. But it is certain that both the *conditioning* of these responses to the rat as a stimulus and their *integration* into the complex pattern of pursuit, killing, and devouring depend on learning. Since most environments provide such sequences of experience, most domestic cats form a *habit* of rat killing which becomes a part of their everyday repertoire of activities. But in the absence of such experiences, the cat's reactions to a rat, although they may be hostile, may equally be indifferent, or oriented, or tolerant, or playful. Such variability is characteristic of behavior which owes its pattern of organization essentially to learning.

CHAPTER III

MIGRATION AND THE "INSTINCT" PROBLEM

INTRODUCTION

To say that an animal performs an activity "instinctively" means that the performance of the activity, in all probability, mainly depends upon the activation of the animal's inherited equipment, *i.e.*, the sensory, nervous, and motor structures of the species, more or less independently of individual experience. Migration and pecking as they occur in various birds are examples of the "basic activities" which result. In such activities, the function of learning is by no means excluded, but it is of secondary importance in determining the *nature* of the act.

Contrary to the belief of the traditional "instinct psychologists," an acceptable and useful explanation of a given "instinct" can be attempted only when we have gained an adequate knowledge of the essential causes of the activity in question and of the manner in which the causal factors, in a given environment, produce this activity in a given animal. We learn nothing about such behavior from statements such as "the chick possesses a pecking instinct," an interpretation which amounts to saying nothing more than "the chick pecks because it pecks." Similarly, to speak of an instinctive *urge* for pecking, for migration, or for any other observed activity begs the question. The word "urge" has an appropriate psychological meaning and should not be misused. Unless a chick has pecked one or more times, to say that it possesses an "urge to peck" is a statement which seems actually incorrect. In any case, it leaves the problem unsolved, since the word "urge," like the word "instinct," is here merely a substitute for real knowledge of the causes of pecking.

Migration is one of the most typical "instinct" problems, and one which illustrates very satisfactorily the principal characteristics of such problems in higher animals. Furthermore, migration is a form of behavior which has long aroused much popular interest and which has been peculiarly subject to mystical and irrational explanations in the daily press and elsewhere. For these reasons, we select it for attention here, although it is by no means one of the best understood of such phenomena, and although the evidence on some of the other "instinctive" activities, such as pecking in the chick, is substantially more complete.

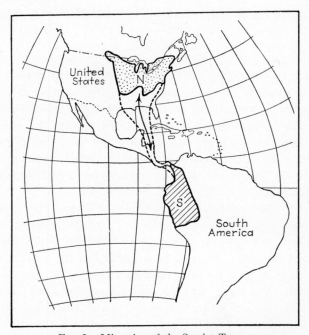

FIG. 2.   Migration of the Scarlet Tanager.

N, northern zone; *S*, southern zone.   The approximate limits of the tanager "flyway" are marked by dotted lines.   (*Redrawn from Dock, Harper's Magazine, October, 1937.*)

"Migration," as a problem in animal behavior, concerns the active movement of animals in numbers from one habitat to a different one often with a return journey. In higher animals, such as birds or fishes, the habitat of departure or arrival characteristically is the place in which breeding occurs. In the case of most migrant fishes and birds, the movement typically occurs periodically, with alternate phases involving "go" and "return" journeys. Our migrant birds of the North Temperate Zone move in the spring or early summer to a northern territory in which mating and breeding occur, then in the fall move southward to a more or less distant wintering habitat. A representative case is shown in Fig. 2.

Our treatment of the problem will be reduced to the consideration of two principal questions: First, what are the factors that cause animals of a given species to leave a particular locality in numbers at a predictable time of year? And second, what factors determine the route which the animals take in their passage and the place at which their journey ends? These questions will be considered in connection with the migration of certain birds and fishes.

I. MIGRATION IN BIRDS

Until comparatively recent years, the question as to the causes of bird migration received little more than speculative treatment. Hypothetical solutions of the problem included "the instinct to migrate," "decreasing temperature forces the birds from the northern territory," "decreasing food supply forces departure," and "the birds migrate in response to the gradual increase in daily illumination in spring, or to the gradual decrease in illumination in the fall." Granted that any one or more of these suggested factors (excepting the first one) may be important, the question arises as to which of them are basic in determining migration and which ones are of only secondary significance.

CAUSES OF BIRD MIGRATION

Rowan[1] suspected that the last-mentioned hypothesis, that of decreasing (or of increasing) daily illumination, pointed to the basic factor in the arousal of bird migration, and planned an experiment to test the question.

A Preliminary Test with Juncos. In Alberta, in early November one year, hundreds of juncos (snowbirds) were captured and were taken to Edmonton for experimental use. These birds normally spend the winter in the central part of the United States, hundreds of miles south of their summer home in Canada.

The birds in one group, the *control* group, were placed in an aviary in which they were exposed to a *regular decrease* in the daily amount of illumination as the autumn days progressively became shorter. In contrast, the birds in the *experimental group* were subject to a *regular*

[1] Rowan, W. *The Riddle of Migration*, Chap. IV. Baltimore, Williams & Wilkins, 1931.

increase in daily illumination. For them, electric lights were used to provide approximately 7½ minutes of additional illumination each day beyond the duration of the previous day's illumination. Thus, the normal group received the gradually decreasing daily illumination of the shortening autumn and early winter days, whereas the experimental birds were subjected to artificial springtime illumination conditions, with a progressive increase in the amount of radiation received daily. In all other respects (*e.g.*, feeding, and exposure to winter temperature in unheated coops) the two groups received the same treatment.

The specimens of the group of control juncos which were examined on January 7 had gonads (testes or ovaries) minimal in size and development, which is their normal condition during the winter months; whereas in specimens of the experimental group the gonads were found to have approached the normal springtime conditions, *i.e.*, they were growing. There were also important behavior differences which could be attributed only to the described increase in the sex tissues. The experimental birds sang actively (as in the springtime), whereas the control subjects were silent. More important than that, when 100 juncos of the control group were set free, they remained close to the laboratory. In contrast, all of the 92 experimental birds which were liberated flew away, and 38 of them were never seen again. Clearly, a relationship exists between a regular change in illumination, the physiology of the gonads, and the occurrence of migration.

A Repetition of the Experiment with Crows. Because of legal barriers against the trapping or shooting of snowbirds, it was not possible to gain information about the direction in which the experimental birds had departed. Hence crows, from which reports could be expected on the basis of legalized trapping or shooting, were used in a repetition of the experiment. (In the western part of North America this bird is a regular north-south migrant, *e.g.*, between Alberta and Kansas.) The experiment began at Edmonton, Alta., on September 28, with two separate groups of crows receiving treatment which corresponded to that of the experimental and the control subjects, respectively, in the junco experiment. At the time the experimental birds were liberated on November 9, their gonads were increasing in size, whereas the gonads of the control crows were definitely decreasing in size, as examinations showed.

As a result of good public cooperation in response to appeals issued in the press and by radio, reports were obtained concerning many of the released birds which were shot or trapped. Of 14 control birds, 6 remained in the general vicinity of the laboratory and 8 flew away. Of these 8, 2 were killed nearby and 4 were killed to the southeast of Edmonton, but *not one was killed in a northerly direction from Edmonton*. Among 54 experimental crows which were released at the Edmonton laboratory, 8 were killed to the north, 8 to the south, and 12 were killed locally. The remaining 26 were never captured. However, there were persistent reports of crows being observed in northern Alberta, an occurrence very unusual for that time of year. *Evidently, the great majority of the experimental birds must have flown northward*, since no such reports were received from southerly points. Moreover, it is notable that 50 per cent of the released controls and only 15 per cent of the experimentals were recovered to the south.

Conclusions from Rowan's Experiments. Rowan concluded from his results that the regular daily increase in illumination which occurs in the springtime produces physiological changes which cause the sex tissues of birds to grow, and that somehow this growth sets up an organic condition which results in the departure of the birds in a northerly direction. Since significant results were obtained in the low temperature of a Canadian winter, temperature would not seem to be normally an essential factor in *setting off* migration. Increasing illumination, leading to gonadal growth, would appear to be the primary cause in the investigated species. Conversely, a regular decrease in the amount of daily illumination causes the gonads to shrink, and during this change the birds are also caused to migrate. However, this condition *somehow* affects them differently, so that they move southward.

These results, together with others, clearly indicate that the arousal of bird migration depends upon endocrine changes which are controlled by the amount of light acting upon the bird.[1] The causal sequence

[1] What may be considered a "natural experiment" on this point has been reported by Bullough, who observed significant differences in the movements of two types of starlings in England, which, after study, he distinguished as different subspecies. The *B*-type of starling is essentially nonmigratory, a fact which Bullough attributes to the incomplete shrinking of their gonads in the summer after mating has occurred and to the beginning of a regrowth in the fall, when they exhibit further mating activities rather than migrating southward In the *C*-type starling, on the other hand, the gonads have shrunk to a mini-

therefore is: *A*, a regular environmental change (increase or decrease in daily illumination) produces *B*, a bodily change (an increase or a decrease, respectively, in gonadal secretion), which is responsible for *C*, a migratory movement in a northerly or in a southerly direction, respectively.   As Bissonnette[1] has found, the specific mechanism of *A* and of *B* must be worked out in further detail as a special physiological problem.   However, it may be said that the *causes* of modern bird migration are no longer obscure.

The Direction of Movement in Bird Migration

Although the available evidence furnishes a reasonable answer to the first of our questions concerning the fundamental causes of the migration of birds, it is difficult to investigate the second question, What governs the direction of their migration?   Rowan and other experimenters have not directly attacked this question (*C*, above) of how in one gonadal condition a bird is caused to migrate northward, whereas in another and very different condition it is caused to migrate southward.   The question is complicated by the probability that more than one factor is involved in any case, and that the direction-determining factors may not be the same in all species.[2]

One reasonable hypothesis to account for the direction of movement in bird migration is based upon the *temperature sensitivity* of the bird. The light-induced endocrine changes (*B*, above) are assumed to account for corresponding changes in skin circulation, which alter the general sensitivity of the skin to temperature.   Presumably in the spring a rise in gonadal activity increases the bird's sensitivity to temperature, so that it moves by stages away from the regions of relatively high temperature, until a regular northward movement is in progress.

---

mal size by early fall, when a regular southward migration occurs, and in the spring a fairly rapid regrowth of the gonads precedes a migration northward to their mating grounds. Subsequent investigation has shown that these two types of migratory and nonmigratory starlings, with their corresponding differences in sexual behavior, are also recognizable among the transplanted American relatives of the English starlings. (Bullough, W.   The Reproductive Cycles of the British and Continental Races of the Starling.   *Philosophical Transactions of the Royal Society of London*, Series B, 1942, vol. 580, pp. 165–246.   Bullough, W.   British and Continental Races of the Starling, *Sturnus vulgaris L.*, in Canada. *Nature*, 9945, vol. 155, pp. 756–758.)

[1] Bissonnette, T. H.   Sexual Photoperiodicity.   *Quarterly Review of Biology*, 1936, vol. 11, pp. 371–386.

[2] Lincoln, F. C.   *The Migration of American Birds*.   New York, Doubleday, 1939.

Conversely, in the fall gonadal changes of opposite nature may change temperature sensitivity in such a manner that the bird moves by degrees away from regions of low temperature, until a regular southward movement is in progress. Thus, in either case, nesting and feeding localities would be changed in response to local temperature conditions, and a more or less continuous migratory movement would be established in the northward or southward direction, respectively. It is possible that once the movement has been determined by temperature differences, for example, other and more specific factors (*e.g.,* visual) may enter to maintain the given direction of flight.

Another hypothesis is based upon the relationship between feeding activities and the length of the daylight period. We recall the fact that in the Northern Hemisphere in spring and summer the day is longer in the north, whereas in autumn and winter the day is longer in the south. It is pointed out that a change in gonadal secretion causes the bird to become more restless and to spend more of the available daylight time in finding food. It is conceivable that in its new condition of hunger-increased activity the bird would be more likely to move in the direction of longer daylight, toward the north in the spring and toward the south in the autumn. These factors, together with others of possible importance, should be tested experimentally.

Another problem concerning migration in birds is that of the factors which determine the "flyway" or general route of travel. It is reasonable to believe that the flyway (see Fig. 2) which is taken by migrant birds of a particular species may be governed by a number of factors, such as visual sensitivity, power of flight, nature of food, nature of sleeping place, and others.[1] These suggestions lack substantiation at present because it is very difficult to perform controlled experiments upon birds in the act of migrating. This type of problem may be more satisfactorily approached in a study of fish migration.

II. MIGRATION IN SALMON

The various migrant species of salmon have been extensively investigated by scientists. In the following sketch of the representative life cycle of this fish, it will be seen that salmon migration, like that of most migrant birds, has two phases, involving movements in opposite direc-

---

[1] Griffin, D. R. The Sensory Basis of Bird Navigation. *Quarterly Review of Biology,* 1944, vol. 19, pp. 15–31.

tions.   The salmon eggs are laid in the headwaters of inland streams where the adults previously spawned, and here the young undergo their early development.   Then, in their second year, the young salmon migrate by degrees downstream and finally they enter the ocean. They pass the next few years in salt water.   In their fourth or fifth year the salmon, now mature, make their way from the sea into a river and in this river they make their way upstream.   The two phases of salmon migration are treated below as separate problems.

CAUSES OF SALMON MIGRATION

The Downstream Migration of Young Salmon.   To explain the movement of young salmon downstream and into the sea, some writers suggest as the cause an "ancestral memory of the sea."   The kindest comment upon this hypothesis is that it is supported by no available evidence; but students of learning would go much further in demolishing it.   Certainly, explanations of a much more specific and satisfactory nature are available.

Roule,[1] a specialist in the problem of fish migration, offers evidence for his contention that the factor responsible for setting off and maintaining the downstream migration of young salmon is the rapid loss of skin pigmentation which occurs toward the end of the second year. This loss results from physiological changes incident to growth.

Previously, the dark chemical deposits in the skin acted as a filter to reduce the irritating effect of light upon the photoreceptive (light-sensitive) cells lying beneath the pigment layer throughout the skin of the body.   However, as the pigment disappears, these light-sensitive cells are more fully exposed to the action of light, so that at length light exerts a much more highly stimulative effect upon the fish and thus controls its behavior to a far greater extent than before.   Consequently, ordinary illumination becomes so irritating to the young salmon that during the daytime they are either driven into deeper pools or are rendered motionless and inert and so are carried downstream, tail first, by the current.   (Since light inhibits movement and greatly reduces regular activity during the daytime, feeding occurs mainly at night.)   Thus, by stages, the salmon reaches the sea, in the middle depths of which they spend the next three or four years of their life.

[1] Roule, L.   *Fishes: Their Journeys and Migrations* (trans.), Chaps. II–VI.   New York, Norton, 1933.

It is interesting to note that many species of trout (closely related to the salmon), which are not very subject to the reduction in skin pigmentation during growth, remain in fresh-water streams and do not migrate to the sea as do salmon. This fact clearly offers additional support to Roule's hypothesis.

The Upstream Migration of Adult Salmon. Although the basis of the upriver migration of salmon is far from clear, a considerable amount of useful evidence has been obtained. A theory that represents a reasonable interpretation of the evidence is as follows.

After two or more years of life in the sea, the salmon, now mature adults, undergo bodily changes which very probably initiate the migration that occurs at this stage. Although adult salmon may be found in the ocean far from shore, most of them probably are still within the extensive zone of the sea into which the river system from which they came originally pours its fresh waters. (It is important to remember that each large river empties its contents along a submarine valley, through which the waters may flow a long distance from shore.) Near the river mouth, therefore, the fresh-water content of the ocean will be high; but as the distance from shore increases, the water will become more and more "salt."

There are reasons for the statement that at the age of two years or older the adult salmon become more responsive than before to the chemical stimulation furnished by their environment. For one thing, when the salmon undergo the physiological changes of sexual maturity their tissues consume much more oxygen. Consequently, the less oxygenated waters farther out in the sea now inhibit respiration and hence tend to inhibit chance movements away from shore and favor movements toward shore. The fish are therefore caused to move (with some variability, of course) from waters of low oxygen content into the fresher waters of the river.[1]

The basis of the physiological change which apparently is in control of behavior at this stage is growth of the gonads. Sexual maturity,

[1] It is important that experiments in which a fish such as the salmon is tested as to its sensitivity in "gradient tanks" (in which it encounters a given chemical varying from a weak concentration at one end of the tank to a strong concentration at the other end) show that these subjects possess the delicate sensitivity to chemical differences which is essential to this type of behavior.—See Powers, E. B. Chemical Factors Affecting the Migratory Movements of the Pacific Salmon, a chapter (pp. 72–85) in *The Migration and Conservation of Salmon,* edited by F. R. Moulton. Lancaster, Pa., The Science Press, 1939.

therefore, brings into play internal factors which cause the adult salmon to migrate toward shore and into the river.   Oxygenation of the water, apparently, is the most important of the environmental factors which now influence behavior because of these internal changes,[1] but without much question there are other factors which also are of some importance.[2]   The reader will note the resemblance which this phase of salmon migration bears to the initiation of bird migration in the spring.

The Route Taken by Adult Salmon in Their Migration

Movement into the River Mouth.   Thus far we have considered factors which determine the *general direction* of salmon migration. We have seen that the downstream migration of young salmon may depend upon the action of light, which is rendered more effective because of a reduction in the amount of insulating skin pigment; and that the movement of adult salmon into the river mouth may depend upon a response to the oxygenation of water which is also based upon internal changes.   Another problem of great interest is presented by the specific route which adult salmon take in passing upward through a complex river system.

As the sexually mature salmon move into fresh water they begin to be more responsive to the current and move against it with increasing persistence.   This response may depend upon the fact that the fish, which for some time has been dominated by a tendency to move into waters rich in oxygen, soon develops a fixed reaction to the current alone as the result of a simple conditioned-response process.   That is, since movement into oxygen-charged water practically always brings head pressure from the current, the fish may presently respond more readily to the pressure itself as a "substitute" or conditioned stimulus.   Another possible cause for the strengthening of this reaction is the forcing effect of strong internal stimulation produced by the breakdown of digestive tissues with sexual maturation, and by chemical excitation

---

[1] Powers favors the view that a delicate sensitivity and responsiveness of the mature salmon to differences in CO_2-tension (*i.e.*, oxygen-depletion) of the waters provides a dominant factor in determining the passage of the fish from the sea to fresh water and upstream to the spawning grounds.   Powers, E. B.   Physico-chemical Behavior of Waters as Factors in the "Homing" of the Salmon.   *Ecology*, 1941, vol. 22, pp. 1–16.

[2] Greene, C.   The Physiology of the Spawning Migration.   *Physiological Reviews*, vol. 6, pp. 201–241.

from growing sex tissues. When there is strong pressure against the sensitive head region, the disruptive effect of the internal tensions is reduced, a phenomenon of "counterirritation" which would appear to provide a further basis for conditioning.

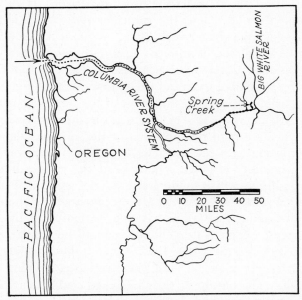

FIG. 3. The Upstream Migration Route Taken by Adult Chinook Salmon in an Experiment by Rich and Holmes.

The eggs were taken from the Big White Salmon River hatchery and were transferred to Spring Creek, where the young developed. 100,000 marked fish of this lot passed to the ocean in the fall run. Only 453 of these fish were recovered later as adults. Almost half of this number were captured at fisheries in the lower Columbia River, *i.e.*, when they were just beginning their upstream migration. However, 82 of the fish which escaped the nets reached Spring Creek itself and spawned there. Spring Creek is a small stream only about 100 yards in length, a relatively minute part of the Columbia River system. (*Adapted from Rich and Holmes, Bulletin, U.S. Bureau of Fisheries*, 1928, *vol.* 44.)

The reaction to the current (rheotaxis) soon greatly increases in strength. At first, while still in the mouth of the river, the salmon at intervals moves back toward the sea, against the pressure of inflowing tidal water when the tide is at flood. Presently, having passed farther up the river, it moves persistently against the steady outward current pressure from the river waters. This reaction becomes so strong that, as is well known, migrating salmon swim persistently against swift rapids and ascend waterfalls by leaping through them. Of course, casualties are numerous.

The Upstream Route through the River System. The facts which are known about the mature salmon and about the importance of its physiological changes for behavior provide the basis for a reasonable theory to explain the arousal of migration and the manner in which the general direction of migration (*i.e.*, upstream) is determined. There remains the question of the *particular route* which is taken by salmon in passing up a given river system. What is it that determines the turning of all salmon of a given "run" into one tributary stream rather than the other at a given branch, resulting in a route through the stream system which is zigzag and shows many turns (Fig. 3)? And what is responsible for the fact that most of the surviving salmon of a run finally reach an upland lake or small stream where spawning occurs?

Ward[1] made a study of this problem for the sockeye salmon of the Skagit River in southern Alaska. His method was to survey the consistency or variability of given conditions at the various branches of the river, conditions which might influence the movement of salmon into one or the other tributary at given branches by stimulating the fish in specific influential ways. If one or more conditions (*e.g.*, stronger current, clearer waters) were found to be regularly present at stream divisions on the side of the tributary taken by the migrants, obviously such facts might be those effective in determining behavior at the branch. The nature of their influence could then be investigated. On the other hand, environmental conditions which were found to be highly variable, or not always present, could not be of primary importance for the determination of the route.

Careful measurements at all stream branchings showed that *volume of water* could not be a factor, since the route taken by the salmon among the tributaries had no apparent or measurable relation to the amount of water which poured from the alternative branches at a given stream division. That is, the migrants turned into small, medium-sized, and large streams with approximately chance frequency. Similarly, records of the *velocity of flow* in the tributaries, the *depth* of the tributaries at the branching of the stream, and other conditions such as *relative clearness of the water* permitted the conclusion that none of these could be of importance for determining the route. For instance,

---

[1] Ward, H. Some of the Factors Controlling the Migration and Spawning of the Alaska Red Salmon. *Ecology*, 1921, vol. 2, pp. 235–254. Also see chapter by Ward in Moulton, ed., *op. cit.*

the tributary taken by all the salmon might be muddy, fairly clear, or crystal clear; or the waters of a given tributary might vary during the run, passing from one to another of these conditions without changing the manner in which the fish responded at the branch.

Finally, records of *water temperatures* were taken for the tributary streams at each junction. In this case the results were significant: The tributary into which the salmon moved in each case was the one with waters of lower temperature. Moving farther upstream, Ward finally arrived at the large lake which was the principal scene of spawning for the Skagit River migrants. As is typical, the salmon were found spawning only in certain places around the lake. By means of temperature readings, Ward ascertained that the places in which the salmon finally remained and spawned were always those of low temperature, below 37°F., whether their waters were clear or turgid, deep or shallow, fast or slow in flow. Certain apparently "good" places in the lake, in which salmon never spawned, always showed a temperature above 39°F. It seems clear from these results that the response of migrating salmon to temperature is a basic factor in determining both their route and their spawning place.

Because these tests of stream conditions were only exploratory and did not involve direct experiments upon the responses of the migrant salmon themselves, the results are to be considered suggestive rather than final. Ward inferred from experience that the chemical constitution of these mountain-stream waters is very much the same in different branches; so he did not carry out a chemical analysis of the waters in all cases. It is true that the streams into which the fish moved were not consistently acid or consistently alkaline; but it is nevertheless possible that features such as oxygen content, which are effective from the beginning of the movement, may also be of some importance in determining the upstream route and the spawning locality. At any rate, this study disclosed the nature of what apparently is the most essential factor in the behavior of these salmon and opened the way for further work.

DISCUSSION

We have noted that in the migration of both fish and birds an internal change brough about through growth serves to set off migration by changing the animal's sensitivity to the action of environmental stimuli. In experiments with birds, after the growth of the gonads is well started as a result of a regular daily increase in illumination, the subjects, when released, move from the vicinity, whereas control subjects with shrunken gonads remain in the vicinity when released. In the case of the salmon, it is suggested that the downstream journey is started by virtue of a decrease in skin pigmentation which occurs in the course of normal growth. This change accounts for a photokinetic effect (an influence of light upon movement), and, together with the transportive effect of the current, causes a downstream migration. As for the other phase of the salmon's migration cycle, sexual maturity brings with it internal changes which cause the fish to turn into water rich in oxygen and away from water containing little oxygen. The physiological changes of sexual maturation also are the source of great internal tension, which increases the vigor with which the adult salmon moves against water pressure. These suggestions offer a reasonable preliminary answer to our first question concerning the *causes* of migration.

Environmental stimuli play a *secondary* part in causing migration, since the origin of the movement depends upon the occurrence of internal bodily changes. (It is true that in birds environmental stimulation—change in the amount of light—is important for setting off the internal changes themselves.) Once the bodily changes have been effected, the answer to our second question, concerning the *direction and route* of migration, may be sought in a study of the animal's responses to the environmental stimuli which are then encountered. Adult salmon migrate toward shore and into the river because of their new response to waters rich in oxygen; birds may begin to move *away from* higher temperatures, or *toward* higher temperatures, according to seasonal changes in the sensitivity of their skin. It is also possible that the direction in which birds move is influenced by the length of the daylight interval itself, by a temperature gradient, or by other factors according to the species. In some such manner, although the exact nature of the process awaits experimental investigation, environmental stimuli influence the *direction* in which migration occurs. As for the *route* taken by the migrants, in birds it must depend upon a number of factors, and its explanation is far from being an easy problem. For the salmon the answer may come more readily; a good start is obtained when we know the manner in which the fish responds to temperature and other environmental differences between the tributary streams at places where the river branches.

It is clear that migration is basically an unlearned activity. It appears in young animals which have not previously performed the movement and under conditions which make it immaterial whether or not experienced animals are present. Neither the initiation of a migratory movement nor the general direction and main route of the migration is due to learning. In other respects, learning may acquire some importance, but in an essentially secondary way.

We have suggested, for the salmon, that movement against the force of the current may be intensified through the establishment of a conditioned response in which pressure is a conditioned (substitute) stimulus. When a bird migrates a second time, its response to the route may be somewhat different because of learning which occurred on the first trip; however, there is no reason to believe that the route may be materially changed in this manner. Also, on the second migration, when the bird enters the local territory occupied during the previous season, in all probability its response typically becomes one which may be called "homing," because it then flies with respect to learned stimulus cues (*e.g.*, a prominent hill) in the locality.

In vertebrate animals it is typical for *basic activities*, such as migration, to be supplemented or secondarily modified through learning. But that is a relatively minor fact in the case of activities such as migration. The reason that activities of this type are common to all animals of a given species and take a similar form in all individuals of the species is fundamentally because they depend upon the environmental activation of sensory, nervous, and motor equipment which characteristically appears as a result of growth, mainly or wholly in the absence of individual learning. As we said at the outset, this is the only sense in which the word "instinct" should be used, if it is to be used at all in psychology.

Although the problems of migration are far from being settled, our present evidence indicates the lines along which a more thorough explanation can be developed by further experimentation. Certainly, this evidence should dispel the notion that migration and similar phenomena are complete "riddles" to science, or that they can be "explained" only by invoking an "urge to propagate the species" or some other mysterious agency so occult that it lies beyond investigation.

CHAPTER IV

COOPERATION AND COMPETITION

Introduction

The aim of the present chapter is to consider the question whether cooperative or competitive situations are more effective as motives to work and effort on the part of human beings. A cooperative situation may be defined as one which stimulates an individual to *strive with* the other members of his group for a goal object which is to be shared equally among all of them. On the other hand, a competitive situation is one which stimulates the individual to *strive against* other individuals in his group for a goal object of which he hopes to be the sole, or a principal, possessor. Many situations which stimulate an individual to work cooperatively with others involve competition between his own group and some other similar organization. But in group competition the rewards of success accrue to the group as a whole. It is only in a competitive situation as we have defined it that a single individual strives to surpass other individuals in the acquisition of material goods, or of personal prestige and distinction.

At present the two principal sources of information relevant to this question of cooperation versus competition are the results of psychological experiments and the data obtained from anthropological studies of various human cultures.[1] Accordingly, this chapter will comprise a review of a psychological experiment in which the effectiveness of these two kinds of motive is compared, and brief descriptions of the cultures of two primitive tribes which differ markedly with respect to the relative importance of cooperative and competitive behavior in the life of their people.

---

[1] By "culture" is meant the social heritage of a people; that is, its language, customs, ideas, and values, its material goods and technical processes, and its social and economic organization.

I. AN EXPERIMENTAL STUDY OF COOPERATION AND COMPETITION[1]

The laboratory experiment which we have selected for review is the well-known study by Maller. The *general purpose* of this study was "to measure the effect of personal and social motivation," *i.e.*, of cooperative and competitive motives upon the work efficiency of American school children.

Subjects. The subjects of this investigation were 814[2] grammar-school children in grades V to VIII inclusive. These subjects ranged in age from eight to seventeen years. The group contained 417 boys and 397 girls. The children came from four different schools, which were representative of three different social and economic levels. One of these schools, hereafter designated as School W and attended by 277 of the children, was the only school in Walden, N.Y., a town of about 5,000 inhabitants, 65 miles distant from New York City. Most of the parents of these children were of the middle-class type characteristic of small communities, and 80 per cent of them were native born. A second school, designated as School L and attended by 314 of the children, was in New Haven, Conn., in a poor and crowded district of the city. The parents of these children were mostly unskilled laborers and two thirds of them were foreign born. The remaining two schools, hereafter designated together as School E because of their similarity in locality and in the social and economic status of their pupils, were attended by 223 of the children. These schools were also located in New Haven, but in a well-to-do neighborhood of that city. Most of the parents of these children belonged to the professional and business classes, and three-fourths of them were American born.

Experiment I[3]

Purpose. The purpose of Experiment I was to compare the work of the 814 school children under three different conditions of motivation: a relatively unmotivated (control) condition, a competitive condition, and a cooperative condition.

---

[1] Adapted from Maller, J. B. Cooperation and Competition, an Experimental Study of Motivation. *Teachers College Contributions to Education*, 1929, No. 384.

[2] The total number of subjects used by Maller was 1,538. However, only 814 subjects were used in the three experiments reviewed below.

[3] The numbering of the experiments differs from that of Maller.

Task of the Subjects. The task to be performed by the subjects was to complete as many simple problems in addition as possible within a given time. Each example consisted of the addition of two one-place numbers, such as 3 and 5, or 6 and 9. The examples were presented to the subjects on printed sheets, 100 problems to a page. The children performed these additions under the following three conditions.

The Control Condition. The purpose of employing the control, or unmotivated, condition was to discover how fast each child would work when he was not subject to the effect of any special type of motivating social stimulation. Hence, in this case the children were given only these instructions: "Do not write your name on this paper. This is only for practice. Write the word practice at the top, and when I say 'Go' begin adding and work until I tell you to stop."

The Competitive Condition. Under the competitive condition the children were given the following instructions: "You are now going to have a speed contest, to find out your speed of work in addition. This test will tell us who is the fastest worker, the second fastest, third fastest, and so on to the very slowest worker in this class. Prizes will be given to those who will do fast work. Every one of you has a good chance to win a prize. When I say 'Go' you will start to add and continue until I tell you to stop. The faster you work, the higher will be your score."

The Cooperative Condition. Under the cooperative condition the instructions were as follows: "This is to find out which class in the school is fastest, second fastest, third, fourth, and so on until the very slowest one. Class prizes will be given to those classes which will do fast work. This class has a good chance to win a prize. The classes that will not try hard will naturally be at the bottom of the list. . . . The score of your class will be the number of examples all of you do for your class." The children were told not to write their own names on the sheets, but to write the name of their class instead.

The Work Schedule. All of the work was done in one continuous session, divided into 13 periods of 2 min. each. Each of the periods involved 1 min. work on each of two separate sheets of addition examples. The subjects worked for one period under the control condition, and for six periods (a total of 12 min.) under each of the two motivating conditions. The period under the control condition always came first. After that, the subjects worked under the competitive condition for one period, then under the cooperative condition for one period, then for one period under the competitive condition again, then for another period under the cooperative condition, and so on in alternation until they had worked for six periods under each of the two motivating conditions. The score for each subject was the average number of examples done per minute (*i.e.*, per sheet), under the control and under each of the two experimental conditions.

Results. The results of Experiment I are given in Table I below.

TABLE I

The Average Number of Examples Done per Minute under the Control and under Each of the Two Experimental Conditions, by the Children of the Three Different Schools

School	Condition		
	Unmotivated	Cooperative	Competitive
W	41.0	44.9	45.9
L	44.8	45.6	50.1
E	37.3	40.4	43.0
Average, all schools	41.4	43.9	46.6

Table I shows (1) that the subjects were effectively motivated in both the competitive and the cooperative conditions, since in both of these cases the number of arithmetic examples performed significantly exceeded the number done under the relatively unmotivated (control) condition; and (2) that competition was a more effective motive than was cooperation of the work-for-your-class type. Moreover, these differences in the effectiveness of the three conditions appeared in the results for all three schools, in spite of the marked general differences in social and economic status and in cultural background which distinguished the children of the several schools. Furthermore, all of the differences between the three conditions are statistically reliable.[1] However, individual differences were found within each group; for example, one-third of the children actually worked faster under the cooperative than they did under the competitive condition.

The experimenter also computed the average number of examples done during each of the six periods under each of the two motivating conditions. These data show that the difference in the effect of the

[1] A note on the statistical reliability of differences is to be found on p. 9.

two conditions increased with practice.   The average score for the
first competitive period (*i.e.*, the number of examples done on the first
two sheets averaged together) was 45.4, and the score for the first
cooperative period was 44.8.   The initial difference between the scores
obtained under the two conditions was therefore only 0.6 examples.
But the score for the final (the sixth) competitive period was 46.8 and
that for the final cooperative period was 42.   Hence, although the
score under the competitive condition showed a gain of 1.4 examples
per sheet, the score under the cooperative condition showed a loss of
2.8 examples per sheet, and the difference between the two scores
increased to 4.8 examples.

Experiment II

Purpose and Method.   The *purpose* of Experiment II was the same
as that of Experiment I, namely, to compare the effectiveness of competitive and cooperative motives.   The *subjects* of the experiment were
the same 814 children who had served in the first experiment, and the
same task (the addition of pairs of one-place numbers) was assigned
to them.   The experiments differed, however, in the method by
which the effectiveness of the two motives was measured.   In Experiment I it was the experimenter's instructions that determined whether
each sheet should be done under the competitive or the cooperative
condition.   Regardless of the desires or preferences of the subject, the
score which a child made during certain periods (and so on certain
sheets) was credited to him individually, and the score which he obtained during other periods was credited to his class.   In Experiment
II, on the contrary, each child was required to choose whether he
would work for himself or for his class, and likewise had to make this
choice anew for every separate sheet of examples.

The *instructions* given to the subjects were as follows: "There are
seven more sheets.   You may work on as many of these as you wish
for yourself and on as many as you wish for your class.   You may even
do all the tests for yourself or all of them for your class.   Whatever
you do for yourself will add to your own score and whatever you do for
your class will add to the class score.   At the end of the test I will
collect all the papers at one time.   Look at the next sheet.   If you
write your name on it, it will count for yourself and for your own score.
If you write the name of your class on it, the additions will count for

your class. When I say 'Go' write either your name or the name of your class on the sheet and begin to add."[1]

In Experiment I the effectiveness of each type of motivation was measured in terms of the speed of the work performed under its influence. But in Experiment II the effectiveness of each motive was determined primarily by the number of sheets which each subject chose to take for himself or give to his class.

Results. The results of Experiment II are given in Table II below.

TABLE II

Giving, for Each School Separately, (1) the Average Number of Pages and (2) the Percentage of the Total Number of Pages, Which the Subjects Chose to Assign to Themselves or to Their Class, and (3) the Average Number of Examples Done on the Sheets Thus Assigned

School	Aver. number of pages assigned to		Per cent of pages assigned to		Aver. number of examples done on pages assigned to	
	Self	Class	Self	Class	Self	Class
W	4.77	2.23	68	32	45.5	40.1
L	4.66	2.14	69	31	57.2	47.0
E	5.70	1.30	81	19	32.8	28.9
Average, all schools	5.06	1.94	76	24	46.5	39.7

The results of Experiment II are both consistent and definite. In all three schools the children assigned many more sheets to themselves (*i.e.*, to be added to their own score) than they did to their class. The extent of this preference is indicated by the fact that the entire group of 814 subjects took 76 per cent of all the sheets for themselves, and gave only 24 per cent of them to the class. Likewise, on the average, the children worked 17 per cent faster on the sheets which they assigned to themselves. All of the seven sheets were given to the class by 5 per cent of the subjects, but 27 per cent did not allot even one sheet to their group. It is of interest to note that, as the table shows, the children of School E, whose average social and economic status was higher than that of the children of the other schools, were the least responsive to the cooperative situation.

[1] Each subject was given an odd number of sheets so that he could not solve the problem of working for himself or for his class by assigning an equal number of sheets to each.

These results are in complete agreement with those of Experiment I. *Both experiments testify that a competitive situation surpassed a cooperative one as a motivating stimulus for American school children.*

Individual Differences. As Maller's data show, on the average the competitive situation was more effective than was the cooperative situation, both as a stimulus to rapid work and as a determinant of the subjects' choices. However, the relative effectiveness of the two situations varied with different children, and there were many children who were more stimulated by the cooperative situation than they were by the competitive one.

In order to discover the factors responsible for these individual differences, Maller made an extensive study of his subjects (especially of those individuals who were most strikingly influenced by either kind of motive) from the viewpoint of such characteristics as sex, age, intelligence, physical condition, popularity, social and economic status, number of brothers and sisters, nationality and religion of parents, and the like. In general, however, this lengthy investigation produced only meager results.

The two sexes, for example, did not differ significantly in cooperativeness. Although in Experiment II the girls gave a somewhat larger proportion of their sheets to their class than the boys did, in Experiment I they tended to exceed the boys in their responsiveness to the competitive situation. Likewise, no age differences were found; there was no difference between the younger and the older children with respect to the effect of the two motives upon them. Intelligence showed a very slight positive relationship to cooperativeness in that (in Experiment I) the more cooperative children averaged a little higher in intelligence-test scores than did the less cooperative children. In tests of social intelligence the more cooperative children also tended to obtain slightly higher marks. On the average, the more cooperative children were slightly inferior in health and physique to the more competitive, had more personal friends, and came from families of somewhat superior cultural standing. Moreover, "only" children were inclined to be less cooperative than were children who had brothers and sisters. However, the nationality and the religion of the parents had no consistent influence upon the cooperativeness of their children.

Some of these results offer interesting suggestions as to the factors which may affect the competititiveness or cooperativeness of individual American school children, but they are inadequate to explain the marked individual differences which Maller found. Probably, an individual's own past experience in particular competitive and cooperative situations, together with the influence exerted upon him by the advice, suggestion, and example of other persons, are the factors which have most to do with determining his responsiveness to these two types of motivation.

Experiment III

Purpose. The results of Maller's first two experiments suggest that a competitive situation is a stronger motive than is a cooperative situation for most American school children. But it is essential to note, first, that these experiments involved only one kind of cooperative situation, namely, working with the other members of one's school class to secure higher scores for the class as a whole; and second, that this is a kind of cooperative situation which probably makes no strong appeal to most school children. It is quite conceivable that, even though the motivating effect of this particular type of cooperative situation was inferior to that of competition, some other kind of cooperative situation might prove to be a much more effective stimulus. Maller's third experiment was designed to investigate this possibility.

Method. The *subjects* of Experiment III were six groups of children from six different school classes, who had already served as subjects in the previous two experiments. (The exact number of subjects is not not stated by Maller.) Of these groups, four were from School L, one was from School E, and one was from School W. The *procedure* was identical with that employed in Experiment II. That is, each subject received seven sheets of addition examples and was obliged to choose in advance, for each sheet separately, whether he would assign the score made on that sheet to himself or to his group. But in Experiment III, five different kinds of cooperative conditions were employed, and different subjects were assigned to each condition. A description of these conditions follows.

1. *Teamwork.* The children elected two captains, who in turn chose two teams which competed with each other. Each child, therefore, worked with a group chosen by a fellow pupil.

2. *Partnership.* Each pupil was told to choose a partner. Contests between the various partnerships were then staged. The child was instructed to work for his partner, and to write his partner's name on his own paper. In this condition the subject cooperated with one other child only.

3. *Boys vs. Girls.* All the boys were placed in one group and all the girls in another. The two groups then competed with each other. The individual now cooperated with all the other pupils of his or her sex.

4. *Arbitrary Groups.* The experimenter himself divided the class into halves. The two groups thus formed competed with each other. Hence, each individual had to work with a group arbitrarily chosen by the examiner.

5. *The School Class.* This condition, which was introduced as a control, was a repetition of the work-for-your-class situation employed in the first two experiments. As before, each child cooperated with the other members of his class.

TABLE III

Giving, for Each Cooperative Condition in Experiment III, the Average Number of Pages, and the Percentage of the Total Number of Pages, Which the Subjects Chose to Assign to Themselves and to Their Group; Also the Number and the Percentage of Pages Which Those Same Subjects Had Assigned to Themselves and to Their Group in Experiment II

Cooperative condition	Experiment III sheets assigned to				Experiment II sheets assigned by same subjects to			
	Self		Group		Self		Group	
	Aver. no.	Per cent	Aver. no.	Per cent	Aver. no.	Per cent	Aver. no.	Per cent
Teamwork................	3.95	56	3.05	44	5.32	76	1.68	24
Partnerships.............	4.19	60	2.81	40	5.25	75	1.75	25
Boys *vs.* girls.............	2.12	30	4.88	70	4.08	58	2.92	42
Arbitrary groups..........	4.66	67	2.34	33	4.07	58	2.93	42
Class...................	6.48	93	0.52	7	5.33	76	1.67	24

Results. The results are given in Table III. For the purpose of comparison, the scores which the subjects had previously made in Experiment II are also given. Since the different groups in Experiment III were composed of different subjects, their scores in Experiment II were different. Maller does not report the speed of work under the various cooperative conditions.

The table shows that the incentive value of cooperation depends upon the kind of cooperative situation employed. Cooperation of the teamwork, partnership or sex-rivalry type was more stimulating to a child than was cooperation with his school class or with a group arbitrarily selected for him by the examiner. Cooperation with other children of the same sex with the aim of surpassing the children of the opposite sex proved to be a stronger motive than was competition itself. However, each of the other four cooperative situations was inferior to competition as a motivating stimulus.

Discussion. From a theoretical viewpoint, these data are of great importance. One might have been tempted to conclude from the results of Maller's first two experiments that, for American school children of the grades and ages tested, competition clearly surpassed cooperation in its motivating strength. Actually, this generalization would be justified only if cooperation with one's school class could be regarded as fairly representative of all of the cooperative situations available for use with school children. But cooperation with one's class was shown in Experiment III to be markedly *inferior* in effectiveness to as many as four other simple cooperative situations, and one of these four situations was found to be even more effective than was competition. It is therefore evident that neither the value of cooperation as a motive nor its status relative to that of competition can be accurately estimated by the use of one kind of cooperative situation alone.

Moreover, it should be noted that all the cooperative situations which Maller used involved competition between rival groups or pairs. It is true that the individual worked *with* the members of his own organization, but at the same time he worked *against* the members of another organization. There remains, however, the variety of cooperative situation which stimulates collective endeavor for a goal which is not contested for by another group (*e.g.*, the cooperative building of a playhouse by a number of children, all of whom will possess and use it equally). The motivating effect of a situation of this completely cooperative kind was not tested by Maller.

II. ANTHROPOLOGICAL STUDIES

In general, Maller's data suggest that for American school children the competitive motive is stronger than are most cooperative motives. Two other experiments which have been performed in this country, one with pre-school and high-school children[1] and the other with college students,[2] have yielded closely similar results. Consideration

[1] Sorokin, P. A., M. Tanquist, M. Parten, and C. C. Zimmerman. An Experimental Study of Efficiency of Work under Various Specified Conditions. *American Journal of Sociology*, 1930, vol. 35, pp. 765–782.

[2] Sims, V. M. The Relative Influence of Two Types of Motivation on Improvement. *Journal of Educational Psychology*, 1928, vol. 19, pp. 480–484.

of these findings suggests an inquiry as to the universality of this difference. Does competition surpass cooperation as a motivating stimulus for all peoples, regardless of the type of culture which they possess?

Fortunately, it is unnecessary to attempt a purely speculative answer to this question, since a considerable amount of information is available relative to the character and extent of competitive and cooperative activities in a number of primitive societies. In order to show as concretely as possible the nature and the significance of these studies, there follows a description of the competitive and cooperative behavior characteristic of two North American Indian peoples, the Kwakiutl and the Zuni.

A. The Kwakiutl Indians: A Competitive Society

The Kwakiutl Indians[1] present an excellent example of a people whose culture is characterized by an extreme emphasis upon competitive behavior and by a corresponding lack of cooperative activities. These Indians live on the coast of Vancouver Island, British Columbia. They subsist mainly on fish and other marine animals, though they also hunt game and pick wild berries and seeds. Food is plentiful, and they have an abundant supply of wood from which they construct their houses and fashion seagoing canoes, richly carved boxes, and totem poles. The Kwakiutl tribes once numbered from 10,000 to 20,000 members, but as early as 1904 successive epidemics had reduced their number to about 2,000. The following description applies to the conditions which existed among them at the time they were studied.

Inheritance as a Source of Prestige. The various tribes are subdivided into groups of related families called "numayms." Each tribe and each numaym is headed by a chief. Every tribe, every numaym within a tribe, and every family within a numaym is ranked according to a strict hierarchy of superiority and inferiority. Also, every individual Kwakiutl has a definite rank, which depends on whether the individual is a nobleman or a noblewoman (titles which are restricted to the first-born child of a family of rank) or a commoner,

[1] This account of the Kwakiutl is summarized from The Kwakiutl Indians of Vancouver Island, by Irving Goldman, which is Chap. VI in *Cooperation and Competition among Primitive Peoples*, edited by Margaret Mead. New York, McGraw-Hill, 1937.

and on whether he or she belongs to a superior or an inferior family, numaym, or tribe. There is also a slave class, which consists mainly of prisoners of war.

Accordingly, the social status of every individual is in great measure determined by the accident of birth. From the time of birth everyone is either a noble or a commoner, and is a member of a family, numaym, or tribe, of high or low social status. Noble children are taught to scorn and despise their inferiors, the first-born son of a chief, for example, being encouraged to throw stones at commoner children. However, the fierce rivalries of adulthood normally exist only between individuals (or numayms or tribes) of approximately equal rank. Noblemen compete with other nobles, but they do not usually enter into contests with commoners. The cultural practices of the Kwakiutl compel every individual to be constantly aware both of his own particular position in the social scale and of the crucial significance of differences in status.

The symbols of prestige due to birth are honorific names and titles, family histories and traditions, and ceremonial prerogatives, such as the right to perform a particular religious dance. These symbols are the property of specific numayms and families and are passed on to certain individuals in those groups as a part of their inheritance. A favored individual, e.g., a son of a nobleman, receives his first honorific name when he is one year old. If he is the first-born, he receives the most honored name of all at the disposal of his family. A few years afterward, he receives a second honorific name, and in later years he assumes still other such titles.[1] He also inherits dance privileges which entitle him to membership in certain of the important religious societies. His initiation into one of these societies occurs at the age of ten to twelve years. At a later age, he may claim admission, also by right of inheritance, into societies of still higher rank.

The great importance which the Kwakiutl attach to prestige derived from inheritance is reflected in the nature of many of their marital and religious customs. Usually, no Kwakiutl marries outside his rank; i.e., nobles do not marry commoners. The value which is set

---

[1] These honorific names are reputed to have been obtained originally by some ancestor from a supernatural being, after a series of heroic adventures. When an individual assumes a name, he regards himself as assuming all the greatness of the ancestor whom he is imagined to impersonate.

upon a particular woman is usually determined, not by her sexual attractiveness, but by the number and importance of the names and ceremonial privileges which constitute her dowry and which will be inherited by her sons. Every husband must pay for his bride, and the greater the names and privileges which she transmits, the higher her purchase price will be. Similarly, the prestige motive is dominant in the sphere of religion. The various religious ceremonials are essentially competitive displays and are valued primarily as opportunities for those who take part in them to exhibit their inherited prerogatives. These ceremonials reach their height in the initiations into the Cannibal society, in the course of which a slave actually may be killed and eaten. Although ordinarily the Kwakiutl abhors eating human flesh, the privilege of indulging in ritualistic cannibalism is one of his most valued hereditary rights.

The Use of Property in Maintaining and Increasing Prestige. The foregoing account might suggest that the accident of birth wholly determines an individual's social status throughout his entire life. However, this is not at all the case. In the first place, no individual can maintain the social position to which his inheritance entitles him unless he possesses material wealth and uses it in certain socially prescribed ways. Second, individuals who are of equal hereditary rank must compete with each other constantly by a similar prescribed use of property. To refuse to enter into such competitions would entail a loss of "face" for which no hereditary distinctions could compensate. In the same way, numayms and even whole tribes must frequently validate their claims to their rank by certain uses of material goods, and by internumaym and intertribal competitions.

From the viewpoint of material possessions, the Kwakiutl are a relatively wealthy people; that is, they have plenty of all the necessities of life, such as food, houses, canoes, blankets, and the like. However, there are great differences in the amount of property which different individuals possess, and the accumulation of wealth (especially in the form of blankets) is universally encouraged. Even so, property is not valued strictly for its own sake, nor are surpluses accumulated because of any additional material comforts which they might bestow. Like a name or a religious privilege, property is valued primarily because it is an essential instrument for maintaining and increasing individual prestige. Specifically, property is used for two distinct purposes: to validate hereditary claims to distinction, and to vanquish rivals. An individual may achieve these aims by purchasing certain copper plates on which huge values are arbitrarily set, by giving grandiose feasts, or by conspicuously destroying certain of his own possessions, *e.g.*, by burning quantities of valuable oils. But the most common method of accomplishing these ends is by giving a "potlatch," which is a ceremonious distribution of material goods, such as blankets and boxes.

The most curious characteristic of the potlatch is that the goods which an individual distributes must later be returned to him with an interest which may equal or exceed 100 per cent. Anyone who does not make such a return is regarded as profoundly disgraced. Thus, a boy twelve years old may begin to distribute blankets to his friends, who must repay him within a month at 200 per cent interest. Hence, if his numaym can furnish him with the necessary initial capital, it is not difficult for him to accumulate considerable wealth. Indeed, the only obstacle to his speedily becoming rich is the fact that he will have to return with interest any property which anyone else chooses to present to him.

There are numerous occasions when social tradition demands that the individual give a potlatch if he is to maintain his claims to distinction. Many of these occasions are connected with the institution of marriage. When a man marries, he must potlatch his bride's father, and the amount of goods which he distributes on that occasion serves as public testimonial both to his own rank and to that of his bride. When the first child is born, the father-in-law must return part of the goods which he has received and by the time that two or more children have been born, he is supposed to have repaid the original potlatch with 300 per cent interest. Since the father has now redeemed his daughter, the marriage stands annulled, and if the husband wishes to retain his wife with honor he must give another elaborate potlatch to his father-in-law. In this way, potlatching is prescribed not only to validate a marriage in the first place but also to legitimatize its continuance.

Other occasions upon which a potlatch is required are the celebrations which mark an individual's assumption of an honorific name or a dance privilege. When a father gives his child its first name (at the age of one year) and likewise its second name (some years later), he must give at least a small potlatch to the tribe. Thereafter, however, it is the boy himself who must conduct the potlatches. A young nobleman may accumulate sufficient property to give his first potlatch and thus validate his first *adult* name by the time he is twelve or fourteen years old. In similar fashion, he must undertake a new distribution of property every time he assumes any one of his other hereditary distinctions.

Most of the competitions between individuals (or between numayms or tribes) consist of a series of potlatches and feasts. Each individual potlatches or feasts his rival, who is then expected to repay him by a more lavish distribution of goods or by an even more elaborate banquet. In such contests, the one who spends the most is the victor. The wealthy Kwakiutl may also compete in the purchase of the copper plates mentioned above. The possessor of one of these plates may offer to sell it to his rival for, say, 1,000 blankets. The latter must meet this challenge and pay the price demanded, or else be greatly humiliated. Later, however, he can offer the plate to the original seller at a higher price, *e.g.*, 1,500 blankets and the latter must buy it back on these terms. In this way, a copper disk of very small intrinsic value can finally bring as much as 7,500 blankets. In such contests, the one who cannot pay the last price demanded is the loser. Thus wealth is used, like a weapon of war, to validate one's claims to superior rank and to defeat and crush one's rivals.

In these property battles, a Kwakiutl will go to almost incredible lengths in giving away property (always to be repaid with interest, however), in buying copper plates, in squandering vast quantites of food, and in publicly destroying valuable articles. As an accompaniment to this conspicuous display and waste of wealth, there occur verbal battles in which each contestant boasts of his own rank and power in truly egomaniacal fashion and heaps scorn and vilification upon his rival. Thus a chief's retainers may sing: "Our great famous chief is known even outside the world, O! he is the highest Chief of all. . . . [He is] the great one who cannot be surpassed by anybody, the one surmounting all chiefs." To which his rival rejoins: "What will my rival say again? That spider woman, what will he pretend to do next? . . . Will he not brag that he is going to give away canoes, that he is going to break coppers,[1] that he is going to give a great feast?

---

[1] The great value which may be attached to a copper plate renders the destruction of it an act which redounds greatly to the prestige of its owner.

... This I throw in your face, you ... whom I have maltreated; who does not dare to stand erect when I am eating; the chief whom every weak man, even, tries to vanquish" (page 192).

The winner of a property contest invariably acquires added prestige in the eyes of the people, and the loser is correspondingly shamed and abased, sometimes to such a degree that he commits suicide. Detailed descriptions of these potlatches and feasts may sound almost farcical to an American or a European, but to a Kwakiutl these occasions are among the most important events of life.

All the hereditary distinctions that we have mentioned may also be held by certain women (*e.g.*, by the first-born daughter of a nobleman), and such women may also potlatch and give feasts. Likewise, commoners are encouraged to compete with each other and to give potlatches and feasts as munificent as their comparative poverty permits.

In addition to the acquisition of prestige through birth and through the use of property, a Kwakiutl may also achieve personal distinction by murder, since the killer is allowed to assume the names and privileges which were formerly possessed by his victim. However, the murderer incurs the risk of being killed in his turn by his victim's relatives.

Incidentally, it is worthy of note that the Kwakiutl show the same aggressiveness toward their gods as they do toward their fellow men. They do not humble themselves before their deities. Some of their mythological heroes are reported to have demanded supernatural powers from a god, and even to have killed a god in order to seize his powers. Also, in times of misfortune the Kwakiutl do not meekly beseech their gods for aid, but rather try to compel their assistance by insults and obloquy.

Cooperative Activities. Despite the prevalence of intense and exacting competition, a certain amount of cooperative behavior exists among the Kwakiutl. A given numaym may own a fishing, hunting, or berry-picking territory which any member of the group is entitled to use freely. (However, trespass upon this territory by a member of another numaym may be punished by death.) The chief of each numaym is responsible for providing food for all his people, especially during the winter. For this reason, an individual fisherman turns over half of his catch to his chief and consequently retains only half of it for himself. Work, such as building a log house, which requires the labor of several men, is collectively organized. But since the laborers are hired and paid individually, their motivation is scarcely of the true cooperative variety.

The Kwakiutl show their greatest degree of cooperative endeavor in connection with the intense rivalries which are fostered between the various numayms and tribes. In these competitions, everyone cooperates with his group (*e.g.*, by donating blankets) in its attempt to vanquish the other, and although the chief of the winning group acquires the most prestige, all of his followers share in the glory also. It should be pointed out, however, that a cooperative group activity the goal of which is to surpass and humiliate another group bears a closer resemblance to competition than does a cooperative group activity which is pursued in order to achieve a common good without deprivation or injury to others. Cooperative behavior of the latter type appears to be practically nonexistent among the Kwakiutl.

Summary. For the most part, then, the Kwakiutl live an existence as fiercely competitive as any known among human beings. As Goodman writes (page 196): "Every aspect of Kwakiutl life is oriented to the basic drive for prestige, which is maintained and augmented by the possession of two types of property, the nonmaterial—*e.g.*, names, special privileges—and the material." Neither kind of property has much value without the other, since the possessor of nonmaterial distinctions must validate them by a display of wealth, and since the rich man cannot rise far unless he has claims to nobility as well. The inordinate value which the Kwakiutl place on self-glorification and on the public humiliation of a rival may seem almost "insane" (*e.g.*, paranoiac) to the average American. But a Kwakiutl Indian who displays such behavior is acting in entire accordance with the education which he has received and with the demands of the social organization to which he belongs. For him, self-glorification is the loftiest of human ambitions, and the ideal man is one who is born with names and privileges and who, in addition, validates them and crushes his rivals by certain prescribed manipulations of property.

B. THE ZUNI INDIANS: A COOPERATIVE SOCIETY

Just as the Kwakiutl Indians exemplify a people among whom competitive behavior is developed to an extraordinary degree, so the Zuni Indians[1] stand as an example of a group whose members are

---

[1] This account of the Zuni is summarized from The Zuni of New Mexico, by Irving Goldman, which is Chap. X in Mead's *Cooperation and Competition among Primitive Peoples.*

distinguished by their cooperativeness, and by an outstanding lack of aggressiveness and rivalry in their dealings with each other. The Zuni are a Pueblo tribe, living in New Mexico on one of the high arid plateaus characteristic of that region. They subsist almost entirely by means of sheep herding and agriculture, although they are also highly skilled in fashioning articles from silver, turquoise, and leather. The climate is so excessively dry that, as Goldman puts it (page 313), "The prayer for rain dominates most of Zuni religion." However, in recent years the introduction of modern irrigation has greatly eased their lot and has eliminated entirely the famines which were formerly prevalent. The Zuni can now be described as rich in material wealth. They possess great numbers of sheep, and raise large quantities of maize, wheat, beans, onions, chili, melons, squash, alfalfa, peaches, etc. Most of the Zuni live in the pueblo (*i.e.*, village) of Zuni, where some 1,900 people are gathered together in a group of compactly clustered and terraced adobe (sun-dried brick) houses. However, many of them live in outlying farming villages and go to the main pueblo only to participate in the various religious ceremonies.

In marked contrast to the Kwakiutl, the Zuni have no rigid class or caste distinctions. Every Zuni belongs to one of the 13 clans, but these clans are not ranked in any hierarchy of superiority and inferiority. Also, there is no division of the families within each clan into superior and inferior, nor is there any classification of individuals as nobles or commoners. Some families are wealthier than others, and there is inheritance not only of land, sheep, and other material possessions, but also of things of nonmaterial value, such as religious songs, prayers, and dances. No particular social emphasis, however, is attached either to wealth or to poverty. Furthermore, no formalized rivalry exists between individuals, families, or clans either for material goods or for any kind of prestige.

The Cooperative Attitude toward Property. The two most important kinds of material property among the Zuni are land and sheep. The productive land, *i.e.*, the orchards and tilled fields, is owned either by individuals or, more commonly, by families. The fields are worked cooperatively by all the men of a household, and all the produce is the common property of the family as a whole. Although such land is privately owned and can be given or bequeathed to anyone at the pleasure of its owner (whether individual or family), a fertile field which has lain unused can be appropriated by anyone who is willing

and able to cultivate it.   Land which has never been used is owned by
the people as a whole.   Anyone is free to stake out for himself as large
an area of this land as he can cultivate, and if he continues to use it
he becomes its owner.   The attitude of the Zuni with respect to property rights strikingly contrasts with the attitude which prevails in
our culture.   Both on ethical and on legal grounds, we distinguish
sharply between "possession" and "use."   In our culture, a man who
fails to use that which he owns does not thereby jeopardize his rights
of possession.   Similarly, the employment of another man's property
does not entitle the user to any proprietary rights to it.   But for the
Zuni, use and owership are strictly correlative, so that they can scarcely
conceive of the one without the other.   In Zuni reasoning, that which
a man owns he uses and the fact that he uses it shows that it is his.

Sheep are the major source of wealth among the Zuni, and the returns from the sale of sheep and wool are what make possible the
purchase of such luxuries as furniture, guns, and automobiles.   All
the sheep are owned by individuals (usually by men only) or by families.
Every sheep is marked with its owner's brand, and all the wool sheared
from it belongs solely to its owner, but sheep are always herded,
lambed, and sheared cooperatively by groups of male kindred.   Moreover, in spite of the great economic value of sheep, there is no competition for them, and a young man just starting his economic life is
helped by gifts from the older men to acquire a herd of his own.

Articles of personal property, such as strings of turquoises (which
may be worth as much as $700), silver necklaces (which are valued up
to $75), women's dresses, and moccasins (a woman's pair may bring as
high a price as $100) are individually owned.   However, such property
is loaned freely, and no one loses in prestige by appearing at a feast
adorned with jewelry and clothing which is recognized as belonging
to another.

The Zuni, then, do place some value upon material property, and
do recognize the right of individuals and of families to own, bequeath,
and inherit it.   But they place no *great* value upon such property.
Material wealth may be esteemed for the immediate comfort it can
bring, but the possession of it confers little of power and still less of
prestige.   Moreover, any excessive accumulation of property is discouraged, and hoarding is practically unknown.   Economic competition is frowned upon; greed, avarice, and stinginess are regarded as

shameful and repulsive traits. Even skilled craftsmen do not compete with each other, either for social recognition of their skill or for material reward. Sharp practice in economic transactions is tolerated only in dealings with the neighboring tribes of the Navaho.

If any individual (or family) happens to accumulate any unusual amount of material property, he is expected to redistribute it among other members of the group. Such behavior is not considered particularly virtuous, but only proper. Those who can afford to do so make lavish gifts on occasions such as marriages and religious initiations. They likewise pay generously for work which others do in their fields, and for prayers which others say for them or for the group. They also give large amounts of food, clothing, and other goods to their friends and poorer relatives. At the numerous religious festivals, the wealthier individuals and families give huge feasts and make liberal gifts to the "masked impersonators of the gods." In such ways, any large amount of surplus wealth which may come into the hands of one individual is soon dissipated.

In general, each Zuni is expected to give as much as he can, especially at the various religious festivals. Though the richer families give more than the poorer ones, they acquire no great prestige by so doing. Even if a rich family gives a really sumptuous feast, much more emphasis is placed upon the collective good done by the feast than upon the merits of its donor. Furthermore, it should be noted that all this giving is a "one-way" giving; that is, the donor expects no gifts in return. Among the Kwakiutl, however, giving is exactly opposite in character to that among the Zuni. In the case of the former, any gift must be returned with interest, so that gifts are often made with the sole aim of placing upon some other individual an obligation which he will be unable to discharge.

This lack of regard for property as a source of prestige or power is further illustrated by the marriage customs of the Zuni. Again in contrast with the Kwakiutl, Zuni marriages are usually based on sentiment only. The Zuni man or woman marries primarily "for love," and no property exchanges of any importance are required. The bride brings no dowry, nor does the husband make any payments (save that he presents his future wife with a dress, as proof of the seriousness of his intentions).

Cooperation in Religious Practices. Religious rituals and ceremonials are of such enormous importance among the Zuni as to be said to constitute their major interest. Ancestor worship is the basic cult. But there are several other principal cults, *e.g.*, the cult of the sun, the cult of the rain makers, the worship of the katcinas (mythological beings alleged to dwell at the bottom of a lake), and the medicine societies. Throughout the year there occur a great number of religious ceremonies, each of which has its own inviolable date. The amount of ritual which must be memorized verbatim is so great that the average Zuni man devotes more time to its mastery than he does to any other activity. This practice is due to the belief that the relationship between man and his gods should be a "sober and dignified" one, and that a desired blessing can be obtained only through "an orderly process of painstakingly accurate ritual." "One error and the rain may not come. Crops will wilt in the sun, Misfortune may strike the community" (page 337).

The essential cooperativeness of the Zuni is nowhere more clearly shown than in their religious beliefs and practices. To be sure, there is individual ownership of certain sacred songs, prayers, and ritual formulas, and since these are the properties most valued by the Zuni, the possession of them may give an individual considerable prestige and authority. Likewise, unusual proficiency in the rituals can confer upon an individual a degree of social distinction which no amount of wealth can bring. Nevertheless, all the religious ceremonies are performed collectively, "group must cooperate with group," and individuals with other individuals in the group. Furthermore, all the ceremonies are performed for the common good. There are no "individual visions," no personal relationships between one man and his gods. To become a priest is to acquire a position of some prestige and esteem; yet even a priest must not try to secure too much individual prominence.

Cooperativeness in Other Spheres. There are many other aspects of Zuni culture which similarly illustrate the remarkable cooperativeness of this people. The newly married man becomes a member of his mother-in-law's household, and lives there with his wife, his wife's parents, his wife's unmarried sisters and brothers, and her married sisters with their husbands and children. Although the house may contain from two to six rooms, most of its chambers are used for storing food, so that the entire group works, eats, and sleeps in one communal living room. All the economic activities of the household are cooperative. The men work together in the family's fields and turn over the produce to the women. The latter distribute the food, to everyone in accordance with his need.

The Zuni attitude toward contests of skill is also illuminating. Often, races are staged as a part of certain religious ceremonies. One of these is a 4-mile foot race, the purpose of which is to bring rain. Although scores of men compete in it, the name of the winner is never announced. In another race, the runners have to kick two sticks (representing the older and the younger gods of war) for a distance of 25 miles. Two sides are chosen, with three to six runners on each side. There is great public excitement and much heavy betting. Yet the winners acquire no great prestige from their victory, and if a man wins too frequently he will be excluded from future competitions.

It is also worthy of note that murder, assault, and theft are very rare among the Zuni. Even legal disputes are uncommon and are almost always settled quickly by some mutually agreeable compromise. Among the Kwakiutl, in contrast, every dispute of whatever sort must terminate either in victory or in defeat, since to compromise is regarded as a sign of weakness and of cowardice.

In the education of Zuni children, stress is constantly laid upon the value of the nonaggressive, sober, cooperative aspects of life. The child is taught to regard with aversion any aggressive or strongly individualistic behavior. Physical force and punishment are rarely used. Instead, parents endeavor from the first to make their children extremely sensitive to social criticism and to be ashamed of any behavior to which others in the group might object.

As various observers have noted, even among the Zuni there exist numerous personal grudges, antagonisms, and resentments, together with considerable gossip and scandalmongering. Nevertheless, there is a general and marked dislike of overt bickering and quarreling. Hence, if husband and wife disagree, they usually do not openly quarrel; instead, the husband quietly leaves his wife's household.

Summary. In general, the Zuni constitute an example of a people among whom cooperativeness is very highly developed. The personal characteristics which they value most are not individual initiative or ambition but a "yielding disposition and a generous heart" (page 344).

Their ideal man is one who cooperates readily in both the economic and the religious field. He is "the ceremonially minded individual ... willing to devote himself to the ritual routine of bringing supernatural blessings upon the group." He is a person of dignity and kindliness "who has never tried to lead and who has never called forth comment from his neighbors" (page 343).

DISCUSSION

It was pointed out at the beginning of this chapter that the results of the experiments of Maller and others suggest that among American children and young adults competition is a stronger motive than are most forms of cooperation. We then raised the question whether competition might be the stronger type of motivation among all human beings and in all cultures. The results of the anthropological studies indicate that this question must be answered in the negative. A comparison between the Kwakiutl and the Zuni alone is sufficient to demonstrate that human beings raised in different cultures may differ markedly in the extent to which they display cooperative and competitive behavior. Studies of eleven other peoples in North America, Africa, and the islands of the Pacific[1] have shown that other groups also vary greatly in this respect. Moreover, certain groups, such as the Eskimo, cannot be validly characterized as either cooperative or competitive, but are more accurately described as "individualistic," in that each family (or individual) tends to be a self-sufficing unit and to work by and for itself without any great interest either in rivaling other persons or in cooperating with them.

If, as these studies show, differences in culture can produce such profound and far-reaching differences in the extent to which a given people are habitually cooperative or competitive, at least two important conclusions follow:

First, there exist no valid reasons for assuming that either cooperative or competitive behavior is "instinctively" rooted in human nature, or that either is inherently a more powerful motive than the other.

Second, the results of the experiments of Maller and others can be explained in terms of the basically competitive nature of the culture in which American children are brought up, and of the emphasis which they are led to place upon personal ambition, rivalry, and individual

---

[1] These studies are also to be found in Mead, *op. cit.*

success.   As May and Doob[1] point out, such experiments demonstrate "the *relative* strength of certain incentives in *specific* cultural circumstances," but they do not prove "the *absolute* strength" of these different types of motivation "under *all* cultural circumstances" (page 39). In all probability, if Kwakiutl children were placed in an experimental situation similar to that employed by Maller, they would be even more responsive to the competitive stimulus than were the American children.   It is equally probable that the cooperative stimulus would be far more effective with Zuni children than it was with the average American school child.

In conclusion, it seems clear—from the evidence provided by studies of such people as the Kwakiutl and the Zuni—that the relative capacity of cooperative and competitive motives to influence the behavior of a given individual depends upon the nature of the cultural influences to which he has been subjected.   If a child of a typical American family were taken from his parents at birth and reared by Kwakiutl foster parents in the Kwakiutl culture, it is virtually certain that he would become a fiercely competitive individual.   Similarly, if such a child were taken from his parents and brought up by a Zuni family, he would eventually exhibit the cooperative traits which are characteristic of the Zuni culture.   The problem whether human life and human ideals are better served by a social order which fosters cooperative behavior, or by one which is devoted to the creed of competition and of individual rivalry, is an issue which is beyond the scope of this chapter.

[1] May, M. A., and L. A. Doob.   Competition and Cooperation.   Social Science Research Council, 1937, *Bulletin 25*.

CHAPTER V

FACTORS INFLUENCING THE RECALL OF COMPLETED AND OF INTERRUPTED ACTIVITIES

INTRODUCTION

Behavior usually occurs, not as disconnected reactions to unrelated stimuli, but in the form of more or less coherent groups of reactions. Such a series of actions as perceiving an empty feeling in the stomach, looking at one's watch, walking into the kitchen and asking whether dinner will be ready soon cannot be described adequately as responses A, B, C, and D, evoked by stimuli A_1, B_1, C_1, and D_1. Rather, this is a sequence of actions in which each member must be understood as deriving from the individual's hunger and his need or his desire for food. The responses appear to be the product both of a continuing state of hunger and of other elements in the situation, presumably unrelated to each other, such as the watch, the kitchen door, and the mother at the stove. It is to the *continuing* state that we must look for an understanding of the organized character of the series of actions. The psychological definition of the basis on which responses are thus organized into groups has long been a subject of discussion and investigation. A variety of terms, such as *drive, motive, set,* and *direction,* has been suggested to designate the principle which underlies and unifies such sequences of behavior on different levels of complexity.

In certain instances, the organized character of a series of responses can be attributed to a persisting physiological state called a "drive" or "tissue need." These disturbed states of the organism include dryness of the mucous membranes of the throat (underlying the thirst drive), distention in the bladder or colon (the excretory drives), tensions in the genital organs (the sexual drive), and spasmodic contractions of the stomach wall (the hunger drive). As long as these tissue needs persist, they continue to arouse responses; the series of responses comes to an end only when the disturbance subsides.

At the present stage of our knowledge, however, it is not possible to refer all cases of continuing organized activity to localizable physiological conditions. What tissue need, for example, furnishes the stimulation which causes one to read a novel, or to write home every week, or to complete one's preparation for an examination? Furthermore, even in cases in which physiological drives are clearly involved, why do we often continue the activity after the disturbance has subsided, as, for instance, when we go on with our dinner even though hunger contractions may have ceased some time ago?

Kurt Lewin,[1] with the aid of a group of his students, has attempted a theoretical and experimental investigation of such problems. He postulates that to begin an integrated activity of any kind creates a "completion tendency" which persists and determines the nature of the individual's behavior until that particular unit of activity is finished. It is in terms of this "completion tendency" that Lewin accounts for the behavior of the child who begs to be allowed to finish his game even though he appears to be thoroughly exhausted, or of the bridge players who unanimously insist on finishing the rubber even though it is long past midnight.

The integrating quality of a physiological drive resides in the fact that while it persists the individual's actions continue to be influenced by it. But the completion tendency postulated by Lewin goes beyond the state of the individual; it includes also influences stemming from the nature of the situation with which the individual is dealing, and the possible organizations of this situation for this individual. How long a person continues to work at a task depends, according to Lewin's hypothesis, not only on the needs of the person but also on the particular character of the task: the intricacy of the mathematical puzzle, the quantity of kindling necessary to start the log burning, the complexity of the personal problems presented by someone seeking advice.

Lewin's theory leads to the posing of a number of interesting questions. Suppose that a certain activity has been started but that a powerful obstacle to its completion is encountered. What happens to the completion tendency in this case? According to Lewin, the result is the creation of a "tension" which continues to exist after the overt activity has been interrupted. Is this tension manifested in any way, *e.g.*, in the individual's attempt to resume the activity as soon as possible, or in his persistent thinking about the uncompleted task? Does

[1] Lewin, K. *A Dynamic Theory of Personality.* New York, McGraw-Hill, 1935.

the tension finally die out, if there is no opportunity to resume the unfinished activity? Does the strength of the completion tendency depend on the nature of the task which aroused it? On the attitude with which the individual approaches it? The experiments now to be reported are typical of the researches by means of which Lewin and his students have tried to answer such questions.

I. THE RECALL OF COMPLETED AND OF INTERRUPTED TASKS[1]

PURPOSE

The aim of Zeigarnik's investigation was to discover whether any differences exist in the ability to recall activities which have been completed, as compared with activities which have been interrupted and left uncompleted.

METHOD

Procedure. The general procedure was to present a series of tasks, ranging in number from 18 to 22 for different groups of subjects. The tasks were presented one after another during a single sitting. The various tasks differed considerably both in nature and in difficulty. Among the tasks were the following: molding an animal from clay, filling a sheet of paper by drawing crosses over its entire surface, counting backward from 55 to 17, solving matchstick puzzles, naming 12 cities beginning with K, stringing beads, finishing the drawing of an incomplete pattern, combining the pieces of a jigsaw puzzle, consecutively numbering a large pile of papers, punching holes in a sheet of paper with a pin, finding a German philosopher, actor, and city all of whose names begin with a designated letter. Most of the tasks required from 3 to 5 min. for completion; only a few could be finished in less than 2 min.

The subject was permitted to finish one-half of the total number of tasks presented. He was interrupted in the performance of each of the remaining half of the tasks by the sudden introduction of a new task. A task which was thus interrupted remained permanently unfinished; *i.e.*, the subject was never permitted to resume it. The order of presentation of the tasks to be completed and of those to be broken off before their completion was wholly random. Hence the subject

---

[1] Adapted from Zeigarnik, B. Über das Behalten von erledigten und unerledigten Handlungen. *Psychologische Forschung*, 1927, vol. 9, pp. 1–85.

could never know in advance whether or not he would be allowed to complete the task which he was about to undertake. The subjects did not know why they were interrupted, nor did any of them ever suspect that the interruptions were one of the major conditions of the experiment.

Zeigarnik adopted the general procedure of interrupting each task "at the point of maximal contact between the subject and the task," *i.e.*, when the subject appeared to be most engrossed in it. Since this point was usually near the end, most of the tasks were not interrupted until they were close to completion. Occasionally, however, the tasks were cut off at earlier points, the interruptions occurring about midway in the performance of the task or shortly after the task had been started.

As a control against the possibility that certain of the tasks would be more interesting and, therefore, more memorable than other tasks, those which were completed by half of the subjects were interrupted for the other half, and vice versa.

All the materials and work products of each task, unfinished and finished alike, were placed in a drawer as soon as the task had been performed. The subject was told that this was done in order to "keep the table neat." The actual purpose of this procedure was to remove from the subject's immediate environment everything which might provide any special aid to him during the subsequent test of recall.

The Recall Test. The recall test was given as soon as work on the series of tasks ceased. The experimenter asked the subject to tell her what he had been doing during the experimental session. The subject responded by naming as many of the tasks as he could remember. The experimenter listed all the tasks which the subject recalled, and later classified them with respect to their completeness or incompleteness. In this way she was able to discover whether either of these two types of task was better remembered.

Subjects. The total number of subjects was 138. The experiment was carried out individually with 32 adult subjects (Group A) to whom 22 tasks were presented, and with a second group of 14 adult subjects (Group B) who were presented with 20 tasks differing from those on which the subjects of Group A had worked. Two "group" experiments were also performed: one with 47 college students (Group C); the other with 45 elementary-school children between the ages of thirteen and fourteen (Group D). Group C was given 16 tasks and Group D, 18. In these two "group" experiments, each task was presented in written form on a separate sheet of paper, and the subject performed each task by writing (or drawing) the answer on the appropriate sheet.

RESULTS

1. Table I gives the number of subjects in each group who remembered more interrupted tasks than completed ones, the number who remembered as many interrupted as completed tasks, and the number who remembered more completed tasks than interrupted ones. Mem-

TABLE I

Showing for Each of the Four Groups of Subjects: (1) the Number of Subjects Remembering More Interrupted Tasks Than Completed Ones; (2) the Number of Subjects Remembering Interrupted and Completed Tasks Equally Well; and (3) the Number of Subjects Remembering More Completed Tasks Than Interrupted Ones

Group	Number of subjects	Number of subjects remembering		
		(1) More interrupted tasks	(2) Both kinds equally	(3) More completed tasks
A (adults)............................	32	26	3	3
B (adults)............................	14	11	1	2
C (college students)...................	47	37	3	7
D (elementary-school students)........	45	36	4	5
Total............................	138	110	11	17

ory for interrupted tasks under the conditions of this experiment obviously was much more effective than memory for completed tasks. In each of the four groups, the number of subjects who remembered more interrupted tasks was about four times the combined number of subjects who remembered more completed ones and who remembered an equal number of both types of task. Of the 138 subjects, 110 remembered more interrupted tasks than completed ones.

2. The degree of the preference in recall for interrupted tasks may be expressed by (*a*) calculating the average number of interrupted tasks recalled by all the subjects (that is, average recalled-interrupted,

or Average RI), (*b*) calculating the average number of completed tasks recalled by all the subjects (that is, average recalled-completed, or Average RC), and (*c*) expressing the relationship between these two figures as a ratio Average RI/Average RC. For all four groups of Zeigarnik's subjects the value of this ratio was found to be very close to 1.6.[1]

3. The subjects characteristically showed both a strong resistance to interruption and a decided tendency to resume an interrupted task after they had finished a task which they were allowed to complete. In general, the children took the tasks far more seriously than did the adults and showed a more intense desire to resume uncompleted ones. For days following the experiment, certain children persistently asked to be allowed to finish the tasks which had been interrupted. They never asked to repeat a completed task, no matter how interesting the task may have been to them.

4. Analysis of the results showed that the effects of interruption on ability to recall varied considerably for different tasks. Thus it was found that four tasks (drawing a vase of flowers, bending a wire into the form of a bow, writing a favorite poem, and solving riddles) were remembered, on the average, more than three times as often when interrupted as when completed; several other tasks were remembered equally often whether they had been interrupted or completed; whereas a few tasks (*e.g.*, stringing beads, multiplying 5,457 by 6,337, printing the initials of one's name, filling a page with crosses) were remembered somewhat more frequently when they had been completed than when they had been interrupted.

5. A comparison of the frequency of recall of tasks interrupted early, toward the middle, and near the end of their performance showed that tasks which had been cut off when they were nearly completed were remembered far more frequently than were tasks interrupted shortly after they were begun. On the average, 90 per cent of tasks interrupted in the middle or near the end of their course were recalled,

[1] The procedure by which this index has been calculated differs from that originally used by Zeigarnik. She established the ratio of remembered-interrupted to remembered-completed tasks for each subject, and then obtained the average of these ratios. By this procedure her ratios ranged between 1.9 and 2.1 for the four groups of subjects. However, Marrow and other investigators have criticized her method as statistically unsound and have used the procedure that we have adopted here. (Marrow, A. J. Goal Tensions and Recall. *Journal of General Psychology*, 1938, vol. 19, pp. 3–35; 37–64.)

whereas, of the tasks left incomplete shortly after they were started, only 65 per cent were remembered.

The most significant result of Zeigarnik's experiments is the more frequent recall of uncompleted as compared with completed activities. This superiority was very marked and was shown with striking consistency by the subjects of all three age levels (adults, adolescents, and children). The conclusion that unfinished tasks were better remembered is supported by the additional finding that when the subjects listed the tasks which they remembered, unfinished items were named toward the beginning of their lists far more frequently than were finished ones. The marked superiority of the recall of uncompleted tasks is especially striking in the light of the fact that a longer time was generally spent on the completed than on the uncompleted tasks.

Memory for certain tasks was particularly favored by interruption. These tasks were those which required what Zeigarnik calls "final activity." In such tasks, the achievement of the goal demands the fitting together of all the part-activities into their proper relationships to each other and to the goal. Drawing a vase of flowers, a task remembered three times as often when it was interrupted as when it was completed, is an example of a task which requires "final activity." Each individual crayon stroke must be related to every other stroke in the picture if a satisfactory end is to be reached. Zeigarnik contrasts "final activity" with "continuous activity." A task involving "continuous activity" is one in which the part-activities have no organic relation either to each other or to the goal but merely follow one another in a series. Marking a page full of crosses and stringing beads are examples of such activities. Each bead strung and each cross marked are related to previous and to later beads and crosses only in the sense that they constitute members of a uniform series. The end of the activity does not depend on the relationship among the parts, but on extrinsic factors, such as the size of the page or the length of the string. Tasks of this kind, as a rule, were not more readily recalled as a result of interruption. Since the end of a "continuous activity" depends only on the arbitrary limit set by the experimenter who prescribes the size of page or the length of string, it is not surprising that interruption of such activity before the goal is reached should have had little effect on recall. It should be remarked, however, that these relationships were not without exceptions. One matchstick problem which, like almost all "puzzles," certainly would seem to require "final activity," was remembered no more often when interrupted than when completed.

Another significant finding was that the tasks which had been cut off toward the middle or end of their performance were more frequently recalled than tasks which had been interrupted shortly after their beginning.   Apparently, when one has made considerable progress in a defined task, the need or urge to complete the activity is stronger than it is when one has only started. This finding of Zeigarnik's may be illustrated by many everyday experiences. For example, if we are interrupted when we are just starting to read a mystery story, the experience is not nearly so disconcerting as it is if the block occurs when we are near the end. When we have almost completed a task, the proximity of the goal seems to exert an intensifying effect on the motive which both started and sustained the activity.

The principal finding of the investigation is clear: unfinished acts were remembered with far greater frequency than were completed acts.   Moreover, experiments which have been performed by other psychologists, abroad and in the United States, have corroborated Zeigarnik's results, often reporting closely similar Average RI/Average RC ratios.

Zeigarnik recognized the possibility of alternative explanations for her main finding.   For example, it might be argued that interruption of an activity would produce an emotional shock which of itself could increase the attention value of the task and account for the more frequent recall of it. To test this explanation, she performed a new experiment in which subjects were first interrupted and then later were permitted to finish the uncompleted tasks. If shock of interruption were the primary factor, these subjects should have recalled the tasks as readily as those who were interrupted and not permitted to finish.   But the results failed to bear out this hypothesis: tasks which were first interrupted and later completed were remembered no better than tasks completed in one operation.

A second possible explanation which Zeigarnik considered was that the interrupted tasks became noteworthy to the subjects because they expected to be asked to resume them later.   To test this hypothesis, Zeigarnik compared the recall performance of two new groups of subjects.   The members of one group were forewarned that all interruptions would be final; the members of the other were told in advance that each time they were interrupted in a task they would be allowed to resume and complete it later. The superior memorability of the interrupted tasks was found to be fully as marked for the former group as for the latter.

Thus Zeigarnik concluded that she had eliminated all possible explanations of her findings, except that in terms of Lewin's theory of tensions. According to this theory, the inception of any need or want in an individual is equivalent to the creation of a "tense system" or "tension" between the individual and the environment. Thus, when a task is presented, a tension is set up; this tension may be thought of as a "need" or "urge" to perform and complete the task. The tension is dissipated when the task is completed. But if the performance of the task is interrupted, the tension is prevented from discharging itself and the individual remains in a state of disequilibrium.

Applying this theory to her findings, Zeigarnik reasoned as follows. Each task which she presented set up a tension in the subject. This tension was released only when the task was actually finished. When the task was interrupted, the tension remained unrelieved and persisted as a particular condition of the subject in relation to his environment. Similarly, the experimenter's question, "What have you been doing this hour?" resulted in a tension which was relieved only by the actual recall. Therefore, at the moment of recall, the subject's behavior was the resultant of two "tense systems." One was directed toward the recall of all the tasks, the other toward the completion of the unfinished tasks. The uncompleted tasks were more readily remembered because their recall was favored by both tense systems.

The fact that uncompleted tasks are more memorable is interpreted, therefore, as the result of *tensions* which continue to exist and to influence behavior in spite of the interruption of the task *activities*. The further question then arises, How long will a given tension persist? Zeigarnik argues that during our waking life, at least, new tensions are continually being created as new needs arise and are continually being relieved, or interrupted and frustrated. The result is that the tension resulting from any given need is continually being exposed to opposition from the "pressures" exerted by other tensions resulting from different needs.

It cannot be expected that in this constant strife of tensions, any given tension can long endure, unless it be of unusual strength and resistance. Applying this conclusion to the present problem, one would predict that the uncompleted tasks would no longer be better remembered if the recall were deferred for a sufficient time after the original performance. This last prediction was borne out by the results of further experiments. Eleven subjects were not given the recall test until 24 hr. after the original experimental session. Preference in recall for the interrupted tasks continued, but it was so markedly reduced that the Average RI/Average RC ratio was only 1.08. Zeigarnik concludes that unreleased tensions persist but that they weaken with the lapse of time.

One of the tests of the scientific value of an experiment is the number and variety of new investigations which it inspires. The asking and answering of a significant question almost inevitably leads first to attempts to challenge or confirm the answer, and then to more detailed analyses, and the posing of other, related questions. Zeigarnik's results have been corroborated by numerous experimenters. They have also stimulated a considerable body of new research.

As we have seen, Zeigarnik concluded on the basis of her experimental results that individuals tend to remember uncompleted tasks better than they do completed ones, at least over brief periods of time. However, psychologists came to suspect that the appearance of this tendency depended on the adoption of a particular attitude by the individual toward the task on which he was engaged. If that attitude were of a different sort, they argued, the Zeigarnik result might not be obtained—in fact, it might be that completed tasks would be better remembered.

One of the first psychologists to examine this viewpoint in detail, and to test it experimentally, was Rosenzweig, whose investigation is described below.

II. THE EFFECT OF TASK- AND OF EGO-ORIENTATION ON THE RECALL OF COMPLETED AND OF INTERRUPTED TASKS

1. ROSENZWEIG'S STUDY[1]

INTRODUCTION

Rosenzweig used the Zeigarnik technique to test the influence on recall of what he calls "need-persistive" and "ego-defensive" reac-

[1] Adapted from Rosenzweig, S. An Experimental Study of "Repression" with Special Reference to Need-persistive and Ego-defensive Reactions to Frustration. *Journal of Experimental Psychology*, 1943, vol. 32, pp. 64–74.

tions to frustration, specifically, to frustration by interruption during the performance of a task.

According to Rosenzweig, whether an individual's memory is better for completed tasks or for tasks on which his work has been interrupted may depend upon the nature of the interpretation he places upon the interruption, and this interpretation, in turn, may depend upon whether his attitude toward the work he has been doing has been "task-oriented" or "ego-oriented."

An individual whose attitude is *task-oriented* works at a task primarily because he is engrossed in the task itself. He does not view the work as a situation in which his pride and self-esteem are deeply involved, in which success is vitally important and failure humiliating. Such a task-oriented attitude might be present in a chess enthusiast working alone in his study on the solution of a chess problem, or in a gardener laboring to finish planting a new lot of tulip bulbs.

On the other hand, an individual whose attitude is *ego-oriented* works at the task mainly because of egotistic motives. He regards the task as an activity in which success is necessary for the maintenance of self-esteem, and his interest in the work as such may be negligible. An attitude of this kind might be characteristic of a factory employee working under the eyes of a critical and watchful foreman, or of a person training himself in some competitive sport with the sole intent of excelling and worsting all possible rivals.

According to Rosenzweig, if an individual whose attitude is task-oriented is interrupted in his work he will react in *need-persistive* fashion. That is, like Zeigarnik's subjects, he will give indications of the existence of a need or tension to complete the task, *e.g.*, by recalling an interrupted task better than he would a completed activity. By contrast, a person whose attitude is ego-oriented, and who is interrupted in a task under circumstances such that he interprets the interruption as signifying failure, will tend to react in an *ego-defensive* manner. The interruption may not give rise to any urge to continue and complete the task. Instead, the injury to self-esteem which the interruption produces may even lead to the repression[1] of the memory of the task and hence to its forgetting.

---

[1] Repression may be defined as the exclusion from consciousness (*i.e.*, the inhibition from direct recall and effective recognition) of thoughts, feelings, and wishes which are repugnant or painful to the individual.

The above discussion has dealt with the extremes of the two attitudes. In most everyday experiences our attitudes toward tasks appear to be a mixture of task- and ego-orientation, and when we are interrupted in the performance of them, our reactions to such frustration are similarly compounded both of need-persistive and of ego-defensive responses.

PURPOSE

Of Rosenzweig's aims the one most pertinent to the present chapter was his effort to determine the effect of task-oriented and of ego-oriented attitudes upon the recall of completed and interrupted tasks.

METHOD

The subjects of the research, 60 college students, were tested individually with a series of jigsaw puzzles representing objects such as a bunch of grapes, a house, a boat, a flag, etc. For almost all the subjects the series consisted of 18 puzzles. Before the presentation of each puzzle, a miniature picture of it in completed form was shown the subject for about 15 seconds.

Rosenzweig arranged his experimental conditions with the intention of arousing an ego-oriented attitude and ego-defensive reactions in one group of subjects, and a task-oriented attitude and need-persistive reactions in the other. The instructions which were given the "informal" group (30 subjects) were designed to arouse a task-oriented attitude, and included such statements as the following:

... I'm going to ask you to help me by doing some jigsaw puzzles. ... this is not in any way a test of your ability or anything else about you. The point is simply this: I intend to use these puzzles in certain experiments later on. Before I do so, however, I wish to get some idea of how they work out in actual practice and so I am doing this preliminary work with you. ... don't hurry or feel in any way constrained while doing these puzzles. ... I'm not in the least interested in seeing how well or how quickly you can do puzzles ... do not be surprised if I interrupt you before you finish some of the puzzles as I doubtless shall do so if I find out what I want to know about a particular puzzle before you finish. ...

The introspective reports from this group showed that the instructions had been "successful." For example, one subject said that he had felt "Very calm; mildly interested. ... Not a very important matter. No hurry."

On the other hand, the "formal" group (also 30 subjects) had included in their instructions various statements calculated to produce an ego-oriented attitude, *e.g.*:

... I am going to give you some jigsaw puzzles to do as an intelligence test so that you may be compared with the other persons taking the test. ... different times are allotted the different puzzles according to their difficulty. If you do not solve any puzzle in the allotted time, I shall naturally be obliged to stop you. You ought therefore to work as rapidly as you can.... Your work will be interpreted as representing the full extent of your ability, so do your best. ...

All the instructions were given curtly, and a stop watch was held visibly before the subject.

Introspective reports obtained later from the subjects showed that the procedure was highly effective in arousing the desired attitude. For example, one subject spoke of his "feeling of desperation" resulting from the tension and sense of failure which the situation produced.

Each subject was allowed to finish only one-half of the puzzles presented to him. An attempt was made to equalize the time spent on uncompleted and completed tasks by interrupting the subject only after he had worked on a puzzle for a period equivalent to the time he had taken to complete a previously presented puzzle.

The test of recall was made within 1 minute after the completion of the series. The instructions were simply, "Will you now please write down in any order in which they come to mind the names of all the puzzles I asked you to do."

RESULTS

1. The "informal" group yielded results showing the same tendency as that reported by Zeigarnik. Nineteen of the subjects recalled a preponderance of unfinished tasks; 7 remembered more completed ones; 4 showed no tendency either way. However, the ratio Average RI/Average RC was only 1.14, a much smaller ratio than that noted by Zeigarnik (1.6) and by most other experimenters.[1]

---

[1] It should be remarked that Rosenzweig does not himself calculate this ratio, arguing that the proper comparison in this experiment is between individuals working under different conditions, not between pooled totals of remembered and forgotten tasks. He therefore suggests an alternative index to represent the dominance of finished tasks in the recall of each subject: $100\left(\dfrac{\text{finished} - \text{unfinished tasks recalled}}{\text{total tasks recalled}}\right)$. By this method, an index of -100.0 would indicate an exclusive recall of unfinished tasks; $+100.0$, an exclu-

2. The group working under "formal" conditions, on the other hand, yielded results opposite in tendency to Zeigarnik's. Of this group 17 members remembered finished tasks better than unfinished ones; 8 remembered unfinished ones better; 5 showed no preference. The ratio Average RI/Average RC was .97.[1] It is to be noted that the preponderance of memory for finished tasks was even smaller for the "formal" group than was the opposite tendency for the "informal" group.

3. Analysis of the results shows that the subjects of the "formal" group remembered almost as many interrupted tasks as did the "informal" group, but that they remembered a larger number of finished ones. The average number of all tasks recalled by the members of the "formal" group was 11.1. Of these tasks, 5.6 had been completed and 5.5 interrupted ones (*i.e.*, approximately 50 per cent of each type). The average number of all tasks recalled by the "informal" subjects was 10.5. Of these tasks 4.9, or 46 per cent, had been completed, and 5.6, or 54 per cent, had been interrupted.

2. THE STUDY BY LEWIS AND FRANKLIN[2]
METHOD

A similar experiment, one of several performed by Lewis, corroborates and extends Rosenzweig's findings. The 24 subjects (college students) were presented with 18 heterogeneous tasks, similar to those of Zeigarnik, *e.g.*, circling vowels in a paragraph, cutting and pasting an article from a newspaper into a scrapbook, winding thread on a spool, arranging jumbled words into a meaningful sentence. Lewis instructed the 12 members of her "task-completion" group as follows:

I am planning some experiments for next semester, and would much appreciate your help in finding out something about the materials I want to use. You are a kind of preliminary "guinea pig" who will tell me something about these materials. Just do the tasks I have prepared so that I can find out about them. You see, of course, that this isn't at all a test of *you*. It's a test of the tasks. You are in no sense on the spot.

---

sive recall of finished ones; and 0.0, no tendency in either direction. Actually, the mean of the indices for the members of Rosenzweig's informal group was −7.65, which shows a small but probably significant preponderance of unfinished tasks in recall.

[1] By the scoring method proposed by Rosenzweig, the mean of indices was +2.95.

[2] Adapted from Lewis, H. B., and M. Franklin. An Experimental Study of the Role of the Ego in Work. II. The Significance of Task-orientation in Work. *Journal of Experimental Psychology*, 1944, vol. 34, pp. 195–215.

The instructions given to a second group were much less insistent in assuring the subject that no test of him was intended. These instructions were:

> I have some tasks here which I should like to have you do. Please work any way you like. This is in preparation for some experiments I want to perform next semester. This is a kind of preliminary.

The authors of the study believe that the latter instructions had the effect of inducing in the 12 subjects of this group what they call an "ego-enhancement tension-system," since the subjects appeared to suspect that they were being tested in some way and frequently asked such questions as, "How did I do?" "Please tell me my results and tell me I'm not a complete moron." For each subject 9 tasks were interrupted and left unfinished; the other 9 were completed without interruption. In order to control any possible differences in ease of recalling the tasks deriving from differences in their interest-values, each task was administered as a completed task for half the subjects and as an interrupted task for the other half.

RESULTS

The results of this study are similar to those of Rosenzweig's experiment. Of the 12 subjects in the task-oriented group, 10 recalled more interrupted tasks, 2 an equal number of interrupted and completed ones, and none recalled more completed tasks. Of the 12 ego-oriented subjects, 11 recalled a preponderance of completed tasks, 1 an equal number of each, and none recalled a greater number of interrupted tasks. The value for the task-oriented group was 1.75, expressed in terms of the ratio Average RI/Average RC. Thus this group showed a preference in recall for unfinished tasks fully as great as that noted in the Zeigarnik experiments. The second, or ego-oriented group, showed a marked preference in recall for finished tasks, its ratio being 0.625. The average number of tasks recalled by the members of the task-oriented group was 9.83. Of these tasks, 3.58 had been completed and 6.25 interrupted ones. The average number of tasks recalled by the ego-oriented subjects was 9.75, of which 6.00 had been completed and 3.75 interrupted. The opposite tendencies of the two groups are almost exactly equal in degree: of the tasks recalled by the "task-completion" group, 64 per cent had been interrupted and 36 per cent completed; for the "ego-enhancement" group, 62 per cent of the recalled tasks had been completed and 38 per cent had been interrupted.[1]

DISCUSSION

Why did most of the subjects of both the Rosenzweig and the Lewis and Franklin studies who felt that they, and not the tasks, were being tested remember more finished than unfinished tasks? If the Zeigarnik effect is caused by the creation of task-oriented tensions, then the conditions under which the subjects who showed the reverse tendency worked must have either inhibited the development of task-oriented tensions or produced other and competing tensions of opposite effect. The latter alternative, Rosenzweig believes, constitutes the best explanation of his results.

According to his reasoning, task-oriented tensions were aroused in both groups when tasks were interrupted. Such tensions would account both for the greater recall of interrupted tasks by the informal group, and for the fact that the formal group also remembered a large number of such tasks. However, Rosenzweig thinks that the subjects of the latter group—who had been directed to consider their work a test of their intelligence—also tended to *repress* the disagreeable memory of the unfinished (to them, the failed) tasks. It is in this way that he explains why 17 members of this group remembered the finished tasks better, as compared with only 7 members of the informal group. Rosenzweig concludes that the reaction to interruption of a task under conditions of ego-orientation is a complex one and is the result of two coexisting mechanisms, a task-completion tension and an ego-defensive repression.

Actually, however, Rosenzweig's interpretation is not altogether convincing. It is true that most of the ego-oriented subjects remembered more of the completed than of the uncompleted tasks. But it is also true that the ego-oriented group recalled almost as many of the interrupted tasks as did the task-oriented group, the average scores being 5.5 and 5.6 tasks, respectively. More conclusive evidence for repression would have been afforded had the ego-oriented group re-

---

[1] In Rosenzweig's study, it is to be recalled, the preferential memory for finished tasks shown by his ego-oriented group was less marked than was the preferential memory of the task-oriented group for the interrupted tasks.

called a considerably smaller number of the interrupted (from their point of view, failed) tasks. In the experiment by Lewis and Franklin, the ego-oriented group actually did recall many fewer of the uncompleted tasks, their average score being 3.75, compared with 6.25 for the task-oriented group. Hence it might appear that the results of this study furnish more support than do Rosenzweig's own findings for his hypothesis that when interruption is interpreted as signifying failure, ego-oriented subjects tend to repress, *i.e.*, to forget, the interrupted tasks.

However, Lewis and Franklin do not accept this reasoning. They argue that since the number of uncompleted tasks recalled by the ego-oriented group, though small (average, 3.75), was not *less* than the number of completed tasks recalled by the task-oriented group (average, 3.58), the score of the ego-oriented group represents only the number of tasks that members of any group might recall in the absence of any *special* motive for doing so (such as tensions toward completion). In their opinion, convincing evidence for repression would require that the number of interrupted tasks recalled by the ego-oriented group be substantially less than the number of completed tasks recalled by the task-oriented group.

Furthermore, the two mechanisms of task-completion tension and repression do not suffice to explain another finding of the Rosenzweig experiment: the fact that subjects of the ego-oriented group remembered a greater number of completed tasks (average, 5.6) than did subjects of the task-oriented group (average, 4.9). This finding not only is corroborated by the results of Lewis and Franklin but appears even more emphatically in their work. Members of the ego-oriented group in their experiment recalled an average of 6.00 completed tasks; members of the task-oriented group, an average of only 3.58. Lewis and Franklin attribute this result to a tendency on the part of ego-oriented subjects to remember experiences that support or secure the ego, that is, to what the authors term the motive of "ego-enhancement." Beyond much doubt, this same tendency, though apparently in smaller degree, was present among the subjects of Rosenzweig's formal group.

Problems similar to those dealt with by Rosenzweig and by Lewis and Franklin have been investigated extensively by a number of other psychologists. One of the most recent of these studies is an experiment by Glixman.[1] In general, these new experiments confirm the major conclusion presented above: the attitude of the subject toward the work in which he is engaged will determine whether the Zeigarnik effect is obtained, or whether, on the contrary, completed tasks are better remembered than interrupted ones.

SUMMARY AND INTERPRETATION

The experiments reviewed in this chapter reveal the importance of motivation among the factors determining recall. Earlier experimenters had found that the probability of the recall of an experience was increased by such conditions as its frequent repetition, its vividness or intensity, its occurrence at the beginning or the end of a series of experiences, etc. The work stimulated by Lewin's teachings shows that the likelihood of recall is also influenced by the motives and attitudes which characterize the individual as he enters upon the experience, deals with it, and leaves it.

One major finding of these experiments is that, frequently, an experience is more likely to be recalled if it is associated with an unsatisfied or unresolved motive than if it is associated with a satisfied or resolved one. Thus unfinished business often returns to mind more readily than finished business does.

However, the experiments in question also have shown that the better recall of interrupted activities occurs only under certain conditions, namely, when the individual's attitude toward his activity is one of task-orientation. The subject must be engrossed in the *task*, in the sense that he is given over to the work he is doing and is relatively free of feelings of anxiety or inadequacy, of hope for advancement, or fear of humiliation in connection with it. When a worker finishes such an absorbing task, his dominant motive is satisfied too. Should he fail to complete the task, this motive is left hanging, as it were, unsatisfied. According to the followers of Lewin, the experience is therefore the more readily remembered.

In contrast, if the individual's attitude during his work is one of ego-orientation, his dominant motive is to give responses which serve to enhance or protect his self-esteem. Under such circumstances, the task itself is for him a matter of secondary importance. What counts

[1] Glixman, A. F. Recall of Completed and Incompleted Activities under Varying Degrees of Stress. *Journal of Experimental Psychology*, 1949, vol. 39, pp. 281–295.

is the *impression his performance is making* on others (and on himself also).   If he considers that the impression is a good one, *e.g.*, when he is allowed to complete a task and interprets this completion as signifying success, he is proud, or at least satisfied with himself.   And, according to the results obtained by Rosenzweig and by Lewis and Franklin, he is likely to remember especially well the situations which were associated with such a result.   On the other hand, if he thinks he has created a bad impression, *e.g.*, when he is interrupted in the performance of a task and interprets the interruption as signifying failure, his self-esteem is wounded, and, according to most current theories of repression, he is likely to find the experience harder to recall.   As we have pointed out, it is doubtful whether either the experiment of Rosenzweig or that of Lewis and Franklin yields conclusive evidence of repression.   However, other experiments, among them that of Glixman,[1] strongly suggest that a tendency to forget the interrupted tasks is present in many subjects.   At any rate it is clear that if the individual is ego-oriented, he usually will not recall the uncompleted tasks better than the completed ones.   Indeed, in such cases, what we have called the "Zeigarnik effect" is often reversed, so that the individual remembers more of the completed than of the uncompleted tasks.

Thus, with respect to the problem of the influence of motives and attitudes upon recall, all the experiments reviewed in this chapter show the importance, under certain circumstances, of a kind of *tension toward completion* which results in the better recall of interrupted activities.   Furthermore, two of the experiments, those of Rosenzweig and of Lewis and Franklin, point to an additional motivating factor which may influence recall, namely, *ego-enhancement*, which results in a tendency to remember especially well experiences which are associated with success.   These experiments also may be regarded as suggesting, but not demonstrating, the existence of a third factor, an *ego-defensive motive*, which leads to the forgetting of experiences which are associated with failure; recent studies, such as that of Glixman, lend further weight to this suggestion.   In normal, everyday living it appears probable that all three types of motive affect recall in most people, and that our memory for past events is continually being influenced by whether those events represent completed or uncompleted activities, and whether the recall of them will enhance or diminish our self-esteem.

[1] *Ibid.*

CHAPTER VI

THE PHYSIOLOGY OF EMOTIONAL BEHAVIOR

Introduction

One of the most basic and important aspects of the study of emotion is the investigation of the various and widespread bodily changes which occur in the organism during emotional disturbance. The relationship of such bodily changes to the inclusive behavior patterns denoted by the term "emotions" is undoubtedly very complex. Few psychologists would deny that the role played by organic changes in emotional behavior is an essential and probably a basic one. One important contribution to the problem is to clarify the nature and principal characteristics of the typical organic changes associated with emotional excitement.

Among the more frequently mentioned of these organic responses are changes which take place in the *circulatory system*—specifically, in blood pressure, in pulse rate, in the force of the heart beat, and in the distribution of blood within the body (as when the constriction of peripheral blood vessels may force blood from outlying regions and from the limbs to the interior of the body). Of importance also are *respiratory changes*, such as changes in the rate of breathing, in the respiratory rhythm, and in the inspiration-expiration ratio (the ratio of inhalation time to exhalation time). During emotional excitation there also occur changes in the *gastrointestinal tract*, such as an inhibition of digestive peristalsis in fear and an increase in the tonus of the stomach muscles, together with an increase in the acidity of the stomach, which is thought to occur in anxiety. Basically important also is a variety of possible *glandular reactions*, such as the heightened activity of the liver and of the adrenal glands (*i.e.*, the medulla or inner part of the glands) in fear and other types of emotional disturbance, and increased activity of the sweat glands known to be responsible for that reduction in the electrical resistance of the skin which has been variously named "psychogalvanic reflex," "galvanic skin reflex," and "electrodermal response." Notable too are *changes in the tension of the skeletal muscles* and *changes in blood chemistry*. In addition to these better known reactions of the various bodily mechanisms there occur other physiological responses which, although much less frequently discussed in most treatments of the subject, are no less authentic or significant. We refer particularly to changes in the number ("counts") of *red blood corpuscles*, *white blood corpuscles*, and *blood platelets*. There are also activities of the *spleen* which seem to be associated with the changes in blood-corpuscle count.

Space does not permit us to outline experimental studies of all the known or suspected organic components of emotional response. In the following pages representative investigations dealing with some of these components will be reviewed. The first group of studies is concerned with *changes in blood count*. Such occurrences illustrate the extensiveness within the body of some aspects of emotional response. The second major study to be presented is concerned with *changes in the muscular activities of the stomach and intestines*. This latter type of research will serve to illustrate certain of the instrumental techniques commonly employed in the investigation of the gastrointestinal components of emotional behavior. The third and last group of studies to be reported deals with the gastrointestinal changes which appear to be related to the development and aggravation of *peptic ulcers*. The ulcer studies are taken from the literature in the recently developed field of *psychosomatic medicine,* which deals especially with pathological organic conditions that presumably are caused or complicated by emotional tensions.

I. THE EFFECT OF EMOTIONAL STIMULATION ON THE SPLEEN AND ON THE CONSTITUTION OF THE BLOOD

INTRODUCTION

For several reasons, changes in the blood during emotional excitement deserve the attention of students of behavior. In the first place, the fact that changes take place in the fluid which circulates throughout the body indicates how inclusive is the nature of emotional response in the organism. Furthermore, it is possible that the study of certain of these blood changes may aid in clarifying the problems of "mood" and "temperament,"[1] since both of these processes are characterized

---

[1] The term "mood" generally refers to a transitory emotional condition, such as one of "depression," or elation. "Temperament" refers to the individual's more permanently characteristic emotional dispositions. Thus an individual who is easily disturbed emo-

by the persistence of a given level of emotional response. Also, as several students of behavior have emphasized, these changes are of interest from the standpoint of their significance for personal adjustment. It is not too difficult to appreciate the adaptive value of many of the better known visceral components of an emotion such as "anger." For example, the increased action of the liver produces an augmented supply of "fuel" (in the form of sugar) for the muscles; the acceleration in heart rate causes an augmented flow of blood, and, consequently, both a more rapid distribution of oxygen to active organs and a more rapid removal of waste and fatigue products from them. In all probability, the types of blood change which are to be considered in this section are no less adaptive. Oxygen is essential for organic response of any kind, and because the red blood corpuscles are the carriers of oxygen, an increase in the number of corpuscles in circulation contributes an increased supply of oxygen for the active tissues. White corpuscles capture and remove foreign particles and bacteria from the blood stream. Thus, when the organism is wounded, an increased number of white corpuscles in the blood materially aids the individual to combat infection and therefore constitutes an effective adaptation to an emergency situation.

Before we enter into a description of experiments having to do with changes in blood count, some essential facts about the components of the blood may be passed briefly in review.

Blood consists of rounded cells or corpuscles which float in a fluid called "plasma" (Fig. 4). There are two principal kinds of blood corpuscles: *red corpuscles*, or erythrocytes, containing the hemoglobin which carries oxygen to all the tissues of the body, and various kinds of *white blood corpuscles*, or leucocytes. The plasma also has suspended in it structures called "blood plates" or *platelets*. It is possible to determine the number of platelets and of corpuscles of either type in a given volume of blood. By the usual technique (the "blood count"), a blood sample is first diluted to a known degree, then is placed in a special glass chamber for examination under the microscope. The top plate of this glass chamber has crosslines ruled upon it, and the technician is able to count the corpuscles within each square space

---

tionally is said to differ in temperament from one who is for the most part calm and placid. He who is inclined to be happy and enthusiastic about life in general is said to be different in temperament from the person who is usually depressed and melancholic.

formed by the ruled lines. From these counts he can then estimate the number of corpuscles in a cubic millimeter of undiluted blood. Making a blood count is an important element in a thoroughgoing appraisal of an individual's health and has many special uses in the diagnosis of disease.

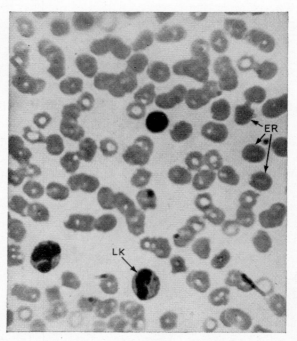

Fɪɢ. 4.   A Photomicrograph of a Preparation of Human Blood.   *Er*, Erythrocyte; *Lk*, Leukocyte.   (*Courtesy of Dr. Jacob Geiger, New York City.*)

There is evidence that the *spleen* is the organ in which some of the red blood corpuscles are destroyed when they are "worn out," and where perhaps others are rehabilitated. In addition, there is some evidence that during fetal development and in infancy new red corpuscles are also *formed* within the spleen. In older individuals most of the red corpuscles are thought to be manufactured in the bone marrow, but they are stored in the spleen, the latter organ serving as a reservoir for them, and probably for white corpuscles and platelets as well. The spleen is composed in part of smooth muscle tissue, and by the more or less rhythmic contractions of this musculature the circulation of blood through the organ is facilitated. An unusually vigorous contraction of the spleen has the effect of forcing an increased number of blood corpuscles from it into circulation in the blood stream.

EXPERIMENTAL RESULTS

Changes in the Spleen and in the Number of Red Corpuscles and Platelets. *Observations on Dogs.* Several investigators using dogs as subjects have reported that after vigorous bodily exercise and during emotional excitation a marked contraction of the spleen occurs, and also that following the contraction of the spleen there is an increase in the count of red blood corpuscles. This splenic contraction is not of the more usual mild rhythmic type mentioned above but involves a marked temporary shrinkage of the organ and an increase in the tonus of its muscular elements. It has also been reported that the injection of adrenin into the blood stream of dogs brings about a comparable contraction of the spleen and a consequent increase in blood count. However, when the nerves of the spleen are cut, or when the spleen is removed, neither exercise nor an emotional stimulus produces an increase in the corpuscle count; in fact, in some instances a decrease in the number of corpuscles results.

Field's Experiments upon Cats. Field,[1] working with cats, reported that following emotional excitation a sudden and striking increase in the number of blood platelets occurred in nearly all her subjects. Field first took control samples of blood under normal conditions. She next tied the cat to a board and after the animal had been excited for 3 min. by this restraint, she sampled its blood and then took further samples at intervals of 15, 30, and 60 min. following the period of excitement. In every one of 10 tests performed with 7 animals (some of the cats were tested more than once), an increase in the number of blood platelets occurred. The amount of this increase ranged from 26 to 90 per cent. When the increase was as large as 90 per cent, the number of platelets per cubic millimeter rose from 176,000 before excitation to 336,000 after excitation. Field repeated the tests with

---

[1] Field, M. E. The Effect of Emotion on the Blood Platelet Count. *American Journal of Physiology*, 1930, vol. 93, pp. 245–248.

several cats whose sympathetic nervous systems had been removed thereby eliminating the possibility of producing a contraction of the spleen by neural action. In these cases the change, on the average, was a *decrease* in platelet count of 4.3 per cent following emotional disturbance. With a group of cats whose spleens had been removed altogether there was an average decrease of 14.3 per cent under the same conditions.[1]

Observations upon Human Subjects. Even though the smooth muscle elements are less numerous in the human spleen than they are in the spleens of most lower animals, splenic contractions and increases in blood count following emotional stimulation have been observed in human subjects as well. In one experiment,[2] observations of the spleen were made with the aid of X-ray photographs taken immediately before and just after periods of vigorous exercise or periods of emotional excitement.

After vigorous exercise (*e.g.,* running a race), contractions of the spleen and an increase in red blood-corpuscle count were recorded in all cases. In one subject the increase in red corpuscle count was as high as 700,000 per cubic millimeter.

The following is an illustration of several special tests which were made. One subject was ready, in the laboratory, for an X ray of his spleen. The exposure intended for the "before exercise" record was first made, and immediately thereafter an explosion occurred which startled the individual considerably. An X-ray taken shortly after this emotional stimulation showed that the spleen had contracted, and later exposures made at various intervals indicated that the state of contraction persisted about 30 min. Some days later a count of red blood corpuscles was made, both before and after this subject had been emotionally disturbed in the same manner. The counts reported were as follows:

[1] Removal of the spleen would, of course, eliminate more corpuscles and platelets from circulation than would the mere removal of splenic innervation, since in the latter case the blood would still circulate through the denervated spleen. Either removal of the spleen or the removal of splenic innervation would account for a failure of an increase in blood count to occur following emotional excitation, but the explanation of the *decrease* in count which actually occurred is not clear.

[2] Benharnou, Jude, and Marchioni. La Splénocontraction à l'émotion chez l'homme normal. *Comptes rendu des séances de la Société de Biologie.* 1929, vol. 100, pp. 456–463.

	Number of Red Corpuscles per Cu. Mm.
Before "fear"	5,470,000
Immediately after "fear".................	5,860,000
7 min. after "fear"....................	6,980,000
14 min. after "fear"..................... .	5,630,000
21 min. after "fear"....................	5,450,000
28 min. after "fear".........................	5,510,000

As the table shows, the number of red corpuscles increased by as much as 1,510,000, or more than 25 per cent within 7 min. following the onset of the "fear" reaction. However, within 21 min. the red corpuscle count had approximately returned to its original value.

Changes in the Number of White Blood Corpuscles. *Experiments with Dogs.* Investigations by Mora, Amtman, and Hoffman[1] of changes in the number of white corpuscles (leucocytes) during emotional disturbance yielded results which are typical of experiments in this field. In one series of observations, dogs were used as subjects. The dog was first securely tied, then a cat or rat was placed in front of him but beyond his reach. Changes in pulse rate and in respiratory rate, together with behavior symptoms such as barking and growling, were used as criteria of emotional excitement. For control purposes leucocyte counts were made at intervals of a few minutes during a period prior to the emotional stimulation, when the dog was apparently calm. A count was also made immediately following the stimulation and at frequent intervals thereafter. In the 10 dogs used as subjects, increases in the leucocyte count of 10 to 150 per cent were observed after emotional excitement.

Observations upon Human Subjects. Mora, Amtman, and Hoffman also made a series of observations on human beings. Their subjects were 13 noninfected surgical patients at the Cook County Hospital in Chicago. The investigators assumed that the expectation of a surgical operation in the immediate future would cause most of these patients to become emotionally disturbed. Accordingly, control counts of leucocytes were made at frequent intervals during the third and second days before the operation, and a final count was made immedi-

[1] Mora, J. M., L. E. Amtman, and S. J. Hoffman. The Effect of Mental and Emotional States on the Leucocyte Count. *Journal of the American Medical Association*, 1926, vol. 86, pp. 945–946.

ately before the operation (when the patient was actually on the operating table). In the seven patients whose verbal reports and general behavior gave clear evidence of fear, an increase of from 12 to 100 per cent occurred in the leucocyte count as compared with counts made just before the operation. On the other hand, in the six patients who denied being afraid and who did not appear emotionally disturbed, no increase in the number of leucocytes occurred.

The following explanation is commonly accepted to account for the increase in leucocyte count following emotional stimulation. Normally, many leucocytes adhere to the walls of the blood vessels, and many also remain in the spleen. In emotional excitement innervation through the sympathetic nervous system brings about both a constriction of many blood vessels and a contracton of the spleen. These contractions cause an increase in blood pressure in these organs and an increase in the velocity of blood flow, the result of which is to release great numbers of blood corpuscles from the spleen and to detach others from the surfaces to which they have been adhering.

DISCUSSION

Reference has already been made to the adaptive significance of the increase in the number of blood corpuscles following emotional stimulation. Because *red blood corpuscles* are oxygen carriers, an increase in the number of these in circulation means that the oxygen supply to important effector groups is increased. Moreover, it is known that the higher centers of the brain are particularly susceptible to changes in the oxygen saturation of the blood. Hence it can be argued that the processes of thinking, reasoning, discrimination, judgment, and other complex operations may be carried out more effectively because an increased amount of oxygen is supplied. An increase in the number of *white blood corpuscles* may aid in making difficult and protracted adjustments by speeding up the removal of foreign matter from the blood stream. Furthermore, in cases of injury in the course of very strenuous or dangerous activities, infection is not so likely to occur if there is an abundance rather than a scarcity of white blood corpuscles. As regards the *blood* platelets, we are not in a position to judge whether an increase in their number constitutes an adaptive response, since the physiological functions of the platelets are not entirely understood at present.

We have limited our review of studies of blood changes to investigations dealing with changes in the number of corpuscles and platelets. Also important are changes in the chemical constitution of the blood. Much has been written about the adaptive significance of such changes as the release of adrenin into the blood stream, and the increase in the sugar content of the blood which occurs following emotional stimulation. In addition, new evidence shows that emotional excitement also involves an increase in the fat content of the blood. This reaction is clearly of adaptive value, since fat, as well as sugar, serves as fuel for the muscles and is moreover a type of fuel that can be absorbed readily and utilized quickly by them. Beyond much doubt future investigations will reveal still other changes in the blood which occur as parts of the total pattern of emotional response.

Due to the fact that changes in the constitution of the blood affect the general systemic condition of the individual, a more thoroughgoing investigation of these changes and of their organic effects should lead us to an improved understanding of the basis for those emotional conditions which we call "moods," emotional states more lasting than "flares" of emotion such as "startle" or "anger" which endure but a few seconds or minutes. Studies of individual differences in the constitution of the blood may also help to explain differences in "temperament," in levels of emotional excitability, and in strength of emotional response.

A further subject for research is the possibility of using blood changes as "indicators" of the existence of emotional disturbances. These changes are not perfectly correlated with changes in emotional state, since factors other than emotion (for example, physical exercise) operate to bring them about. Nevertheless it might be possible within limits to evaluate the current state of emotional excitement in a given organism by making counts of red and white blood corpuscles and by measuring the concentration in the blood of hydrogen ions (*i.e.,* acidity), sugar, fat, adrenin, and the like.

II. THE EFFECTS OF EMOTIONAL STIMULATION THE TONUS OF THE GASTROINTESTINAL MUSCLES[1]

Changes in the tone of the gastrointestinal musculature which occur as components of many emotional responses are of interest from several

[1] Adapted from Brunswick, D. The Effects of Emotional Stimuli on the Gastrointestinal Tone. *Journal of Comparative Psychology,* 1942, vol. 4, pp. 19–79, 225–287.

points of view.   In the first place, these changes may have considerable adjustive significance.   Cannon[1] observed that when a cat was excited by the barking of a dog, the peristaltic contractions of the animal's stomach and intestinal muscles were arrested and the smooth musculature of the digestive tract lost its tone, that is, it became flabby.   In an emergency situation it would appear advantageous to the organism to have its digestive processes retarded or stopped, so that the expenditure of energy might be maximally directed toward flight or combat. In the second place, it would be of interest to know if different types of gastrointestinal reaction are associated with different emotions, such as "fear," "rage," and "pity."   If this were found to be the case, differences in the "feelings" which characterize various emotions might be attributable in part to differences in concurrent gastrointestinal responses.   Furthermore, records of gastrointestinal changes, if they could be standardized, might come to be used as "indicators" of emotional disturbance, in the same way that blood-pressure changes and the galvanic skin response are now used for that purpose.

Brunswick's investigation of the effect of emotional stimulation upon the tonus of the musculature of the stomach and intestines was suggested by observations made by Cannon, referred to above.   The technique which Brunswick employed was derived from studies of hunger contractions in human subjects by the rubber-balloon method. In the investigations of hunger (by Cannon and Washburn,[2] by Carlson,[3] and by Wada[4]), the subject swallowed a rubber balloon which was then inflated within the stomach, and which was connected with the recording apparatus by a slender tube through the subject's mouth.   When hunger contractions occurred, the balloon was compressed correspondingly and a consequent increase in air pressure in the tube caused a stylus (*i.e.*, a writing lever) to rise on the surface of a smoked drum.   In this way a graphic record of stomach contractions was secured (see Fig. 5).   It occurred to Brunswick that the balloon technique might also be employed to investigate changes in

[1] Cannon, W. B.   *Bodily Changes in Pain, Hunger, Fear and Rage*, 2d ed.   New York, Appleton-Century-Crofts, 1929.

[2] Cannon, W. B., and A. L. Washburn.   An Explanation of Hunger.   *American Journal of Physiology*, 1911, vol. 29, pp. 441–454.

[3] Carlson, A. J.   The Relations between the Contractions of the Empty Stomach and the Sensation of Hunger.   *American Journal of Physiology*, 1912, vol. 31, pp. 175–192

[4] Wada, T.   Hunger in Relation to Activity.   *Archives of Psychology*, No. 57, 1922.

the tone of the stomach and intestinal muscles during emotional disturbance.

PURPOSE

The principal aim of the experiment was to determine whether any characteristic changes occur in gastrointestinal tone in association with different emotions which the subject reports under various stimulating conditions.

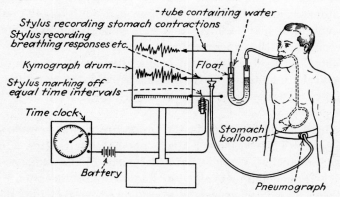

FIG. 5.   Schematic Representation of Apparatus Used for Recording Changes in the Tonus of Stomach Muscles.

METHOD

Apparatus and Technique.   As stated above, the rubber-balloon technique was employed.   In most cases Brunswick used two balloons, one placed in the subject's stomach and the other in his duodenum.[1] The balloons were connected through tubes with separate tambours, but their pressure changes were recorded on the same smoked drum. Because records of muscular activity in the stomach are also affected by changes in breathing, movements of the respiratory musculature (*i.e.*, muscles of the abdomen, thorax, and diaphragm) were recorded by means of pneumographs[2] attached to the chest and abdomen.

---

[1] The duodenum is that part of the small intestine into which food passes immediately upon leaving the stomach.

[2] A pneumograph consists of a rubber tube containing a coil spring, strapped around the thorax or abdomen, and connected by rubber tubing with a recording tambour.   Any change in the volume of the chest or abdomen brings about a change in air pressure within the pneumatic system, and the tambour rises or falls according to the direction of the change.

The subject was instructed to press a push button (or signal key), which he held in his right hand, as soon as he felt emotionally aroused. The pressing of the key activated an electrically operated stylus which traced a mark upon the kymograph drum. Because, in accordance with instructions, the subject held the key in the closed position until he no longer felt emotionally excited and then released it, his impressions as to the presence or absence of emotional disturbance were recorded on the drum together with the objectively obtained records of his stomach and respiratory changes. In addition, the subject's verbal reports of his "feelings" and any general comments he made were recorded by the experimenter in a notebook.

Subjects. Ten subjects served in the experiment. Seven of them were medical students, two were physicians, and one was a teacher of psychology. Twenty-eight tests were performed with these ten individuals.

Procedure. The first step in the procedure was the swallowing of the balloons. This was done about one-half hour after a normal breakfast or lunch. The adequate placement of the balloons in the stomach and duodenum was aided by fluoroscopic observation.[1] Once the balloons had been successfully swallowed, settled into position, and inflated, and after the recording apparatus had been properly adjusted, a series of stimuli designed to induce emotional excitement was presented and the subject's reactions were recorded. All of the stimuli were used serially with all 10 subjects, in the following order.

1. Without warning the light was turned off, plunging the room into total darkness. The light usually remained off for about 25 sec.

2. A pistol was fired just as the lights were turned off.

3. A pistol was fired and was then thrust in a threatening manner near the subject's head, where it was held for from 5 to 10 sec. Then the pistol was withdrawn with the explanation, "I just wanted to get your anticipatory reaction," but at the last word of this explanation it was fired again.

4. Cold water was unexpectedly dashed in the subject's face.

5. Containers emanating foul odors, such as those of decayed rat flesh, urine, and feces, were suddenly thrust beneath the subject's nose.

---

[1] The fluoroscope is a device which makes it possible to make direct X-ray observations instead of taking X-ray photographs.

6. A live rat was placed upon the subject's face.

7. The subject was threatened with an electric shock.

8. The electric shock was actually administered to the subject.

9. The experimenter announced to the subject, "I am going to try a subcutaneous injection of adrenalin," and followed the statement by actually injecting the substance. For purposes of control (*i.e.*, to determine whether any effects were caused specifically by adrenalin or by the mere operation of injection), saline solution (a 1 per cent sodium chloride solution) was sometimes injected after the subject had been prepared to expect adrenalin.

10. The experimenter read aloud personal letters belonging to the subject which the subject had been requested to bring to the laboratory.

11. Selected passages from Henri Barbusse's *Under Fire* were read to the subject. This is a book in which war horrors are vividly depicted.

RESULTS

Emotional Experiences Reported by the Subjects. It is not surprising to learn that the subjects reported intense emotional experiences in connection with many of these stimuli. Turning out the light without warning usually aroused "wondering," "expectancy," "tenseness," or "apprehension." When the pistol shot accompanied the turning out of the lights, subjects nearly always reported that they were "startled." Pistol threats followed by an unexpected shot also caused "surprise" or "startle" in most subjects. "Fear" or "anxiety" were reported following preparations for the injection of adrenalin. From the reports, many of the stimuli caused "fear," which varied in intensity in different subjects and also ranged from mild apprehension to actual terror according to the stimulus used. "Disgust," or at least "unpleasantness," was reported in response to many of the foul-odor stimuli. "Unpleasantness" was also elicited by electric shock, placing a rat on the subject's face, and reading selections from Barbusse's book. The termination of some of the disagreeable or startling situations usually produced "relief." "Wonderment" was frequently reported during the intervals between situations when the experimenter was getting ready to apply the next stimulus in the series. Curiously, the application of cold water seems to have been ineffective as an emotional stimulus. It is of interest that "anger" was never reported, perhaps because the subjects, mature individuals interested in scientific investigations, assumed a cooperative, "philosophical" attitude during the experiment, or perhaps because they were unwilling to confess to anger if and when it occurred.

Relationship between the Emotional Experiences Reported and the Gastrointestinal Changes.   Brunswick's primary aim was to determine whether there are characteristic changes in the stomach and intestines which are invariably or frequently associated with different emotional experiences as reported by the subjects.   An examination of the graphic records from this viewpoint revealed many inconsistencies. There were cases of marked individual differences in the direction of muscular changes when the same emotional disturbance was reported. Thus, for example, in "surprise" the gastrointestinal tonus increased in some subjects but decreased in others.   Furthermore, the types of change in muscular tone brought about in a given individual often varied at different times although the subject reported identical "feelings."   In one and the same individual "expectancy" was sometimes accompanied by an increased, at other times by a decreased, tonicity. Notwithstanding the inconsistencies, however, certain broad relationships between gastrointestinal changes and emotions of different types were observable.   These relationships may be summarized as follows.   In general there was a loss or a decrease of gastrointestinal tone when subjects reported "fear," "envy," "disappointment," "irritation," "pain," and "unpleasantness."   When "surprise" and "startle" were reported, there was usually an increase in the tonus of the stomach and duodenum.   In "amusement," "delight," "admiration," and "appreciation" no consistent changes of gastrointestinal tone occurred.

DISCUSSION

Although the results of this experiment do not permit us to conclude that there are several identifiable patterns of change in gastrointestinal tone, each associated with a given specific emotional state, they do provide experimental evidence that emotional excitation involves stomach and intestinal reactions in human subjects as in Cannon's cats. But Brunswick's data also indicate that, contrary to Cannon's reports, the same kind of change in gastrointestinal tone does not occur in all emotions of the so-called "emergency" type.   Although both "startle" and "fear" were characterized by Cannon as belonging to the *emergency* type of emotional response, in Brunswick's subjects these conditions were generally accompanied by different patterns of gastrointestinal reaction, since "fear" usually was associated with lowered and "startle" with heightened tonicity.

Brunswick's research was originally undertaken with the James-Lange theory of emotion in mind. According to this theory, the conscious aspect of emotional experience depends upon the stimulation of interoceptors and proprioceptors which results from the bodily reactions called out by an "emotional" stimulus. Brunswick's findings indicate that the nature of the subject's emotional experience, that is, whether he states that he is frightened or disgusted, angry or annoyed, cannot depend wholly upon the nature of his stomach and intestinal reactions, since a particular type of verbal report was not invariably associated with a particular pattern of gastrointestinal change. On the other hand, Brunswick's data cannot be interpreted as disproving the James-Lange theory. For, as we have noted, there are numerous other types of bodily change, both visceral and skeletal, which are elicited as parts of every emotional reaction and which may provide a differential basis for the more or less distinctive emotions we experience.

The basis of emotional differentiation cannot be very simple, and no type of differentiating factor (including visceral processes) should be dismissed from consideration until more thoroughgoing investigations have been made. Then too, even if many different emotions are accompanied by much the same visceral response pattern, as many writers contend, different emotions may still involve different skeletal muscular responses. In that event different verbal reports may well arise on the basis of differences in skeletal reactions.

It must also be considered that we name many of our emotions in accordance with the prevailing stimulus situation rather than with any special reference to a bodily experience. Suppose, for example, that two given situations arouse patterns of bodily change which are so similar that we cannot discriminate between them. In this case we cannot give two different verbal reports on the basis of the bodily reactions; but we tend, nevertheless, to assign different names to the experiences—the names which are traditionally associated with the different external situations themselves.

III. STUDIES OF THE RELATIONSHIP BETWEEN EMOTIONAL DISTURBANCE AND PEPTIC ULCER

Observations published by physiologists and medical men often indicate the finding of a definite relationship between emotional disturbance and *peptic ulcer*, *i.e.*, an ulcer of the stomach or duodenum.[1] It is often noted that patients with such ulcers suffer an increase of gastric distress, pain, nausea, or bleeding of the stomach following incidents which have caused anxiety, irritation, or resentment. Frequently the patients themselves notice an association of such gastric symptoms with emotional tensions. Although it is also true that an increase in the severity of the symptoms may fail to be accompanied by any state of anxiety or resentment of which the patient is aware, psychologists know that not uncommonly patients are "unconscious" of their emotional tensions, in that they are unable to describe them to any extent or even to note their occurrence. Furthermore, it is widely believed by physicians and psychologists that prolonged anxiety or resentment may *cause* as well as *aggravate* stomach or duodenal ulcers. Significantly, it has been observed that during an emotional upset in which anxiety or resentment predominates, there is a reaction of vasodilation (blood-vessel dilation) in the gastric mucosa, an increased secretion of hydrochloric acid in the stomach, and an increase in peristalsis.[2] It would appear that prolonged vasodilation together with the prolonged presence of excessive quantities of hydrochloric acid in the stomach could lead to tissue destruction, which might sooner or later assume the form of an ulcer.

In the following pages one of the outstanding studies on peptic

---

[1] In general, an ulcer is an open sore other than a wound. A peptic ulcer is an open sore occurring anywhere in the mucous-membrane lining of the stomach or duodenum. It would appear to be caused, in part at least, by the presence of an abnormal amount of hydrochloric acid—more than the amount required for the normal digestion of food. When free hydrochloric acid is present in the empty stomach, it may attack the gastric or duodenal mucosa (the mucous membrane lining the stomach or duodenum). Thus in popularized accounts of stomach ulcer the condition is often described as one in which the stomach "is literally digesting itself."

[2] At first glance it might seem that the increase in peristalsis is difficult to reconcile with Cannon's report of arrest of peristalsis in startled cats and Brunswick's reports of decreased tonus of the stomach muscles in fear. However, it would appear that fear and anxiety are two different states. Whereas a passing fear reaction involves decreased tonus and inhibition of peristalsis, anxiety, a more persistent condition, may involve increased tonus of the gastrointestinal tract and increased peristalsis.

ulcer will be reviewed, and another investigation will be described briefly.

EMOTIONS AND GASTRODUODENAL FUNCTION[1]

PURPOSE

The principal aims of this study were to determine what personality traits and types of emotion predominate in patients with peptic ulcer, what changes in gastroduodenal function are associated with these emotions, and whether such changes may be forerunners of tissue destruction in the stomach or duodenum.

A. PERSONALITY TRAITS AND EMOTIONAL REACTIONS OF PATIENTS WITH PEPTIC ULCER

The first part of this study is better characterized as a *clinical* rather than as an experimental investigation, since the principal data were obtained from personality and biographical studies of the patients. These studies were made by a trained psychologist who interviewed the subjects and learned as much as possible concerning their life histories and their outstanding personality traits.

Subjects. The subjects were 30 patients with definite peptic ulcers. In all of these cases unmistakable lesions actually had been seen, either at surgical operation or by X ray. Twenty-five of them had duodenal and five had stomach ulcers. Twenty-seven of the patients were men and three were women.[2] They ranged in age from nineteen to sixty-four years, but all except two were under forty-five. In addition three male patients with gastritis and duodenitis were included in the study,[3] as well as 13 people (used as controls) who were "normal" in the sense that they lacked any pathological conditions of the gastroduodenal tract or any complaints referable to it.

General Characteristics. The patients possessed a diversity of personality traits and reactions. Some were gregarious and "outgoing" in the sense of being socially expansive, while some were reserved and taciturn; some seemingly dealt lightly with responsibilities, while others were meticulous and overconscientious. However, one charac-

---

[1] Adapted from Mittleman, B. H., G. Wolff, and M. P. Scharf, Emotions and Gastro-duodenal Function. *Psychosomatic Medicine*, 1942, vol. 4, pp. 5–16.

[2] Peptic ulcer is more prevalent among males than among females.

[3] Gastritis and duodenitis are conditions involving an inflammation of the gastric or duodenal mucosa but without any specific ulcerous condition.

teristic, namely, an assertive independence, was shared by all the male ulcer patients. Seldom did any of these patients complain of anxiety, tenseness, or other emotional distress, or of personality problems or adjustive difficulties. Rather they complained of "physical" ailments, which were localized in the upper part of the abdomen and which included abdominal pains, nausea, and the like. Most of these men were "successful" people, presenting the appearance of sound adjustment. But in spite of their failure to complain about disturbing emotions, it was evident that they reacted frequently with anxiety, resentment, or hostility. They were characteristically unaware of the true nature of their attitudes, very possibly because any recognition of such matters would have been inharmonious with their conception of themselves as assertive, independent, and successful people. Yet uniformly, a summary of their clinical records revealed that behind a façade of independence and self-sufficiency was a background of severe and long-standing anxiety, frustration, and in some cases even of desperation. Although resentment was the most apparent emotional reaction, feelings of guilt and self-condemnation also were common. Indeed, in almost all the ulcer patients, remorse, guilt, and self-condemnation were found in association with the anxiety and resentment, and from clinical study were judged to be the basis of much conflict and personal stress.

The clinical investigation brought to light a variety of situations associated with the development of anxiety tensions in these male patients. In some cases the principal trouble was a failure of the patient to feel himself the object of unquestioning love, or failure to feel appreciated by family and friends, with a resulting sense of loneliness and desertion. Often the man had been made to feel inadequate by his wife's domineering attitude or had been unfairly treated by her, lied about, or denied sexual relations. Sometimes the wife had failed to provide such important symbols of security as the "well-kept home," "having the food ready," "taking proper care of one," and the like.

In contrast to the men, the three women did not show this assertive independence as a mask for insecurity. However, there was evidence that they too were suffering from chronic frustration and anxiety, since examination disclosed that their husbands were unable or unwilling to give them the emotional support which they wanted and to which they felt they were entitled.

Clinical Findings. In all of the 30 patients with ulcer it was possible to demonstrate a chronological relationship between the onset, recrudescence, and course of gastroduodenal symptoms and the occurrence of disruptive emotional reactions. The symptoms of ulcer did not appear until some time after the patients had become maladjusted and had developed emotional tensions. Thereafter, the severity of the symptoms varied strikingly in accordance with the degree of prevailing emotional stress. When gastroduodenal symptoms abated for a time, there were reliable indications that the patient's emotional stress was substantially reduced, and, when symptoms reappeared, it was usually evident that some event had occurred which intensified the emotional stress.

It should be noted that the history of complaints of discomfort or pain in the epigastric region and of other symptoms of an ulcerous condition was obtained independently of the biographical data. Had one person made both sets of observations, his descriptions and interpretations of behavior might have been influenced by his knowledge of the gastric symptoms.

We turn now to the experimental part of the study.

B. EXPERIMENTALLY INDUCED EMOTIONAL AND GASTRODUODENAL CHANGES

The evidence presented above suggests that situations which induce feelings of frustration, anxiety, and guilt in a persistent and lasting manner may be responsible for the development of gastroduodenal disorders and their symptoms or may increase the severity of such conditions where they already exist. Conversely, it is possible that long unbroken periods of experience with situations which engender security and contentment might restore normal functions and reduce or eliminate symptoms.

Having gained some knowledge of the predominant emotions of the patients investigated in the first part of the study, and of the factors responsible for their existence, the investigators attempted to induce in the laboratory emotional states similar to those resulting from the patients' real experiences in their everyday life, and to observe any changes in gastroduodenal functions that might occur.

Subjects. Twenty-six of the original subjects were used in the experiment. Nine of these had ulcer of the duodenum, one a gastric ulcer, and three, gastroduodenitis. The remaining 13 subjects were normal in that they were free from such symptoms. A total of 165 observations was made; 89 on the subjects with duodenal ulcer, 4 on the one with gastric ulcer, 12 on those with gastroduodenitis, and 60 on the normal subjects.

Method.   The subjects reported for the observations in the morning after a fast of at least 12 hr.   A rubber catheter[1] was introduced into the stomach through the nose.   By means of a syringe outside the body attached by rubber tubing to the catheter, samples of the gastric secretions were withdrawn at intervals of from 5 to 10 min. The activity of the stomach was recorded by the balloon method, previously described in our account of Brunswick's studies.   During the observations the subject was placed on his back on a comfortable table and was urged to relax.   A thermometer was placed against the fingers of the left hand so that changes in skin temperature could be recorded. Readings of finger temperature were taken every 1 to 5 min.

Each period of observation lasted from $1\frac{1}{2}$ to 2 hr.   At the termination of every period the volume of each specimen of gastric secretion was measured, the amount of mucous was noted, and the amount of bile, if any was present, was estimated by the color of the secretion. The quantity of free hydrochloric acid also was determined.[2]   In the results reported below, the numerical values given as measures of acidity refer to the number of cubic centimeters of a sodium hydroxide solution which was neutralized by the acid of the specimen.   The specimen was subjected to pepsin[3] determinations as well to as various other tests.

Observations on Emotional States.   In the preliminary control experiments, the subjects were simply urged to remain as relaxed as possible during the entire period of $1\frac{1}{2}$ to 2 hr.   Though they were not always

[1] A catheter is a tube used to drain or discharge fluid from the bladder, the stomach, or any hollow organ or vesicle.   Different types of catheter are used for different purposes.

[2] Substances may be said to be either acid, alkaline (or basic), or neutral.   An acid solution can be neutralized by the addition of an alkaline solution, and an alkaline substance can be neutralized by the addition of an acid.   In this study the amount of acid present in the specimen of gastric secretion was computed by ascertaining the number of cubic centimeters of a tenth normal solution of sodium hydroxide (NaOH) that was neutralized by the acid in the specimen.

[3] Pepsin is perhaps the most important of the several enzymes or chemical ferments produced by the gastric glands.   It attacks the proteins of the food we have eaten, splitting them into simpler substances.   Although it is a very important agent in normal digestion, its secretion in excessive amounts, along with excess hydrochloric acid, may play a part in the causation of ulcers.

able to feel secure and comfortable because of the novelty of the situation or anxiety about personal problems, explanation and reassurance usually succeeded in establishing a condition of relative ease. In most cases the stomach condition tended to be disturbed at first, as shown by excess acidity and by other signs, but eventually it usually became more nearly normal.

In subsequent experiments, after a period of relaxation and when the acidity and activity of the stomach had become as nearly normal as during the preliminary experiments, the patient was subjected to an interview. Two varieties of interview were conducted. The first type was designed to arouse in the subject the anxieties which habitually disturbed him, in order to ascertain the gastroduodenal changes that accompanied such states. These interviews concerned the patient's emotionally charged personal problems which had been revealed by the earlier personality and biographical study. The second type of interview was designed to bring about the opposite effect, that is, to eliminate stress, to reassure the patient, and to induce more nearly normal gastroduodenal processes.

When all the observations on the subject were completed, the records made during relaxation were compared with those obtained during induced or existent stress, and during the attempts to induce relaxation and relieve emotional tensions.

Results. *Acidity and Stomach Activity in "Normals" and Patients with Peptic Ulcer.* The quantity of free hydrochloric acid obtained in observations on patients in a relatively relaxed state varied considerably from individual to individual among both the normal patients and those with gastroduodenal symptoms. In half the normal subjects no free hydrochloric acid was found during any of the "relaxation" observations. Among the other half there was found sufficient acid to neutralize up to 92 cu. cm. of the standard hydroxide solution. (In these subjects values from 80 to 92 usually seemed to be associated with anxiety and resentment.) Patients with gastritis, duodenitis, or peptic ulcer had free hydrochloric acid in all the observations. For most of the subjects in this group relative relaxation was associated with levels of free hydrochloric acid well below 100 (values ranged between 20 and 80), but with induced or already existent anxiety, resentment, or guilt the values increased to over 100.

In addition to the increase in free hydrochloric acid during the effective states of resentment, anxiety, guilt, and frustration, there very often was a marked change in peristalsis as revealed by the stomach-balloon record—a change from periodic to continuous activity. However, increase in acidity was not always accompanied by an increase in peristaltic activity, and when physiological changes occurred they were sometimes more evident in the one function than in the other. These changes were similar in nature in both groups of subjects. The difference between the normal subjects, whose emotional reactions of insecurity and hostility were accompanied by increased acidity and peristaltic activity, and the pathological group was one of degree, in that the pathological subjects exhibited changes which were definitely more intense and more persistent than those shown by the normal subjects.

The results recorded for experiments involving the first type of interview contrast sharply with those for the experiments in which the second type of interview was employed. During and following an interview of the second type, designed to reassure the patient and to relieve emotional tension, there was noted in nearly all subjects either a decrease in hydrochloric acid secretion or a cessation of such secretion, as well as a decrease in stomach activity. The degree of these changes varied from individual to individual.

The results of the investigation outlined above, taken together with observations recorded in many other clinical and experimental studies, leave little doubt that the emotional reactions known as anxiety, hostility, and resentment include among their components hypersecretion of hydrochloric acid in the stomach, increased motility of the stomach muscles, and perhaps other physiological changes associated with gastritis and peptic ulcer. Probably the most striking direct observations[1] supporting these conclusions are those made on a patient whose condition necessitated the installation of a large gastric fistula.[2] Through this fistula it was possible, with the aid of suitable illumina-

---

[1] Wolf, S., and H. G. Wolff. Evidence on the Genesis of Peptic Ulcer in Man. *Journal of the American Medical Association*, 1942, vol. 120, pp. 670–675.

[2] A gastric fistula is a tube, surgically inserted, and leading from the interior of the patient's stomach to an opening in his side. Persons who have suffered serious damage to the esophagus, making it impossible for food to pass from the mouth to the stomach in the normal way, are often provided with such a fistula to make feeding possible. The patient may chew and masticate his food, remove it from his mouth, and place it in the stomach through the fistula.

tion, to view the gastric mucosa directly and to withdraw specimens of the gastric secretions. By such means it was ascertained that the emotions of fear and of sadness were accompanied by an inhibition of the secretion of hydrochloric acid and by pallor of the mucosa, indicating vasoconstriction and a diminution of the blood supply. However, when events occurred to bring about states of anxiety, of hostility, or of resentment, there was an increase in acid secretion, an increased activity of the stomach muscles, and a flushed or florid appearance of the mucosa, indicating a condition of vasodilation and a consequent increase in the amount of blood present near the surface of the mucous-membrane lining of the stomach. Often while such emotions were in progress, the subject would report heartburn[1] and abdominal pain.

In this patient, the prolonged exposure of a small eroded surface of the mucous membrane to acid gastric juice during the course of the study resulted in the formation of a chronic ulcer. Thus we may say that a gastric ulcer has actually been seen to arise as a result of physiological changes which are closely correlated with, or which may indeed be integral parts of, certain emotional states.

DISCUSSION

No attempt has been made in the present chapter to deal with all the various physiological changes which occur in connection with emotional reactions. The studies of blood changes were selected because, in addition to being adaptive, these changes illustrate the widespread nature, the pervasiveness, of emotional disturbances. A large share of the available space in the present chapter was assigned to the studies of gastrointestinal reactions largely because of their great importance from the standpoint of health and adjustment.

Investigations such as those of Brunswick show that changes in the tonus of gastrointestinal muscles take place as components of emotional patterns of activity. The studies of normal persons as well as of patients suffering from gastric and duodenal ulcer show that changes in the activity of gastric muscles, increases in the secretion of hydrochloric acid, and vasodilation in the gastric mucosa occur (at least in many subjects) during states of anxiety and resentment. These studies

---

[1] "Heartburn" means an acid or burning taste or sensation at the back of the throat and tongue.

also suggest how such changes may aggravate or induce the development of ulcers.

We must be careful not to draw sweeping conclusions from the observations reviewed above. The evidence at present available does not justify the statement that *all* ulcers of the stomach or duodenum are caused by emotional stress. Presumably there are other causes for ulcers, such as faulty diet or excessive use of alcohol. Furthermore, anxiety, resentment, and allied emotions do not disturb greatly the gastric functions of all persons, and it is probable that ulcers do not occur in all persons who have gastroduodenal upsets of the kind discussed in Part III of this chapter. There are individual differences in susceptibility to physiological changes of various sorts, differences in physiological predispositions toward the development of all kinds of pathological conditions. It appears that the ulcer, as a pathological condition, is no exception to this principle. However, the studies do indicate that ulcers may occur—and undoubtedly do occur very frequently—because of emotional disturbances, and, further, that when ulcers exist, emotional disturbances of the kind discussed actually hinder a cure of the condition and may even serve to aggravate the ailment.

It should be added that, although only studies of peptic ulcer have been described in the present chapter, investigators in the field of psychosomatic medicine are also concerned with many other pathological conditions which are related to emotional stress. For example, in some patients chronic emotional stress is associated with a condition of hypertension in the musculature of the blood vessels. This condition produces an increase of blood pressure which, it is believed, may damage various tissues and organs and may even cause pathological changes in the blood-vessel walls, directly or indirectly. In other patients, continued emotional disturbances appear to be involved in causing difficulties as varied as the onset of diabetes, attacks of asthma, recurrent headaches, skin disorders, aberrations of heart action, and pains resembling those of neuritis or of rheumatism. Phenomena such as these may cause some people to say, "This substantiates the time-honored dictum, 'mind over matter,'" or, "Here we have evidence that a sick mind produces a sick body." Vague dogmatic statements of this kind do not appear to serve any useful purpose in clarifying either the causation or the nature of the disorders. A psychologist who favors the hypothesis that in the last analysis "mental" processes are themselves bodily activities will regard psychosomatic ills essentially as cases in which one kind of bodily state or activity induces or aggravates another bodily state or activity, in which one physiological process induces or influences another, without the assumption of two distinct realms of function, body and mind, which somehow mysteriously interact. We may say that psychosomatic medicine has become a very important field of investigation and therapy, and that its findings are certain to become of increasing interest and significance in psychology and medicine alike.

CHAPTER VII

FACIAL EXPRESSION IN EMOTION

INTRODUCTION

It is a familiar fact that the facial muscles are involved in many emotional reactions. Traditionally, the resulting facial expressions have been referred to as "expressions" of emotion, as though to imply that the emotion itself were an inner process perhaps purely "mental" in nature. But to many psychologists today an emotion is quite as much "physical," *i.e.*, physiological, as it is "mental." Facial reactions, gestures, and other observable responses are to them not "expressions" of emotion; rather they are component parts of the emotional pattern itself. However, the problem to be dealt with in this chapter is neither the nature of emotion nor the role which these facial changes play in it. Rather, it is the specific question, Do definite and distinguishable facial patterns characterize the emotional reactions to which we give such names as "fear," "pity," "anger," "disgust," "relief," and so on?

It is a popular belief of long standing that each type of emotional disturbance involves a facial expression which is not only relatively invariable in a given individual, but also is more or less constant throughout the species; that there is, for example, a particular facial expression which is characteristic of fear in almost all individuals and another, and different, expression which is characteristic of anger. Our problem is now to determine whether there are grounds for such a view.

Many studies have been made of the ability of observers to recognize emotions "registered" by actors in posed photographs or sketches. Very often an observer can name with a considerable degree of accuracy the emotions which these posed pictures were intended to portray. At first glance, this result might seem to indicate that certain facial expressions are usually, if not invariably, associated with certain definite emotions. But it is also possible that these poses represent

108

only stereotyped patterns which are based upon conventional ideas as to how the various emotions are "expressed." If so, then these "registered" facial expressions are not necessarily the expressions which would be produced during actual emotion, and the success of the observers in interpreting them is no evidence that any fundamental association between certain expressions and certain emotions really exists. Evidently, we need experiments which employ reproductions of "real" facial expressions instead of posed ones. During the past three decades several studies have been made in which the use of posed pictures has been avoided. Although they were performed a number of years ago, perhaps the most important of these studies are still the two experiments of Landis which are reviewed below.

I. LANDIS'S STUDY OF FACIAL EXPRESSION IN EMOTION[1]

METHOD

Subjects. In the experiment 25 subjects were used, 12 men and 12 women, ranging in age from twenty-one to forty-one years, and 1 thirteen-year-old boy. All the men were connected with a department of psychology in various capacities. Of the women, 8 were assistants or graduate students in psychology, 1 was a stenographer, 1 a clinical psychologist, and 1 a schoolteacher. The boy was a hospital patient who was suffering from high blood pressure.

Apparatus. The results of much of the earlier experimental work on the problem of emotion indicated that the reactions called out in laboratory tests of emotional expression were to a great extent reactions to the laboratory, to the apparatus, or to the experimenter rather than to those stimuli specifically designed to arouse emotional responses. Therefore, Landis tried in this experiment to make the situation in which the subject was placed as little like a laboratory as possible.

Two adjoining rooms were used for the experiment. One room was used for the experimenter, the subject, and the parts of the apparatus which were attached to the subject. In the other room were the rest of the apparatus and an assistant to operate it. In order to reduce to a minimum the suggestion of a laboratory atmosphere the walls of the subject's room were decorated, draperies were placed at the windows,

---

[1] Adapted from Landis, C. Studies of Emotional Reactions: General Behavior and Facial Expression. *Journal of Comparative Psychology*, 1924, vol. 4, pp. 447–501.

and paintings were hung on the walls. The subject was seated comfortably at a table. Behind him was placed a large screen to serve as a photographic background, and at either side of him, a 1,000-watt lamp in a diffusing reflector. In the apparatus room there was a special camera, which was focused upon the subject through a small opening in the wall. Forty pictures could be taken without reloading the camera, and a mechanism was devised for changing the film rapidly so that, when necessary, exposures could be made in quick succession. Remote-control devices were provided, both for the shutter and for the film-changing ("move-up") mechanism, making it possible for the experimenter to operate the camera while he was in the room with the subject.[1] The two experimental rooms were connected by speaking tubes and a buzzer circuit, so that the experimenter in the room with the subject could keep the assistant in the apparatus room in step with the procedure. Three Eastman timers, exactly synchronized, were used. (The Eastman timer is a clock having a large seconds hand, easily seen at a distance.) One timer hung on the screen just back of the subject, so that it appeared in all the photographs; one was used by the experimenter in timing the procedure and in making notes on reactions; the third was used by the apparatus assistant.

Procedure. The procedure was to place the subject in each of the situations described below, and in the order indicated. No rest periods were interpolated between exposures to successive situations; as a result, the emotional effects might be expected to be cumulative. Pictures were taken of every perceptible change in facial expression. Following the conclusion of each emotional situation, the subject was asked to give a brief verbal report concerning the emotional experience that had been aroused, but while in a situation he was not encouraged to converse with the experimenter. However, any spontaneous verbal reports from the subject which seemed significant to the experimenter were noted. The analysis of the photographs was facilitated by outlining the subject's principal facial muscles with burnt cork before the experiment began.

---

[1] In addition, a sphygmomanometer was provided for measuring blood-pressure changes, and a Sumner pneumograph for determing inspiration-expiration ratios. The findings regarding the blood-pressure and respiratory changes associated with emotional changes in this study are not reported in the present chapter.

Situations. The series of situations was as follows:

1. *Popular Music.* Three jazz records were played on a phonograph.

2. *Technical music.* Two violin records were played. Both pieces are marked by their virtuosity and technique, but have very little melody.

3. *Reading the Bible.* The subject was given an open Bible and instructed to read St. Luke 6: 18–49. In these verses Christ enjoins his disciples to love their enemies, to take part in the doing of good works, etc.

4. *Truth and Falsehood.* Two pieces of paper marked *T* and *L* respectively were placed face down on the table. The subject was instructed as follows: "Choose either *T* or *L* and place the other aside. If you choose *L* (Lie), you will find points of circumstantial evidence attaching you to some crime. You are to invent a lie which will clear you of these charges on a cross examination which I will make. If you choose *T* (Truth), you will find an alibi provided for the crime. All you have to do is to familiarize yourself with the story and tell the truth on examination. Try to deceive me on the *L* and to tell the truth in an unexcited way on the *T*. We shall do this twice. The second time, choose to do the opposite thing from what you did the first time. I will leave the room for 5 min. while you make up your lie or familiarize yourself with the alibi."

5. *Ammonia.* The subject was given a tray with a row of six bottles and instructed to uncork and smell each in turn. All except the fifth bottle contained substances with mildly pleasant odors. The fifth was labeled "syrup of lemon" but contained strong *aqua ammonia*.

6. *Unexpected Explosion.* The experimenter stopped and suggested that the subject had smeared some of the markings on his face, so that it would be necessary to burn a little cork and to re-mark his face. He then stepped behind the screen and lighted a firecracker, which he dropped behind the subject's chair.

7. *Faux Pas.* The subject was told to write out a description of the meanest and most contemptible or most embarrassing thing he had ever done. He was told, "Try to describe some event which still disturbs you even to think about." The experimenter then read the description aloud.

8. *Jokes*.   Jokes were read by the experimenter in an attempt to arouse laughter.   (Since Landis found this to be the least successful of the 17 situations, it was used with the first two subjects only.)

9. *Pictures of Skin Diseases*.   Ten colored illustrations of various skin diseases were presented, with the instructions: "Look these over carefully, imagining yourself similarly afflicted."

10. *Distraction during Mental Multiplication*.   The subject was given a card with two numbers (*e.g.*, 79 × 67) printed on it.   He was told to fix the numbers firmly in mind and then to multiply them together mentally.   While he was doing this, distracting noises were produced by filing a piece of brass clamped in a vise attached to the subject's table.   The subject was kept at the task until he called out the right answer.

11. *Pornographic Pictures*.   A set of French pornographic photographs was handed to the subject with the instructions: "Look these over carefully."

12. *Art Studies*.   Posed photographs of nude female art models were presented with instructions as in situation 11 above.

13. *Sex Case Histories*.   Several of the most vivid of the case histories from Ellis's *Psychology of Sex*, as well as several other brief case histories, were given to the subject with the instructions: "Read over these case histories."   (We are not told whether or not the subject read them aloud.)

14. *Frogs and Electric Shock*.   A pail was placed beside the subject, and he was told, "Without looking into the pail, shove the cover to one side and put your hand inside to the bottom of the pail and feel around."   While the subject was doing this, he received a strong electric shock.   The pail contained several inches of water and three live frogs.

15. *Decapitation of a Rat*.   A flat tray and a butcher's knife were placed before the subject, and he was handed a live white rat.   He was then commanded to "cut the rat's head off."   In the five cases in which the subjects refused to do this, the experimenter himself performed the operation in their presence.

16. *Electric Shocks*.   The subject was given repeated electric shocks while he was trying to multiply mentally such numbers as 347 and 89, which were presented to him on a printed card.   The shocks continued until some marked sign of emotional disturbance was given, or until it was apparent that the subject was not going to give way to any

such response.   Only one subject completed the multiplication under these conditions.

17. *Relief.*   The experimenter stepped behind the screen and rattled the electrical connections as though preparing for another situation. He then stepped out and said, "Well, that finishes it."

The entire series required a little more than 3 hr.

Photography.   Before the start of the experiment, a full-face and a profile photograph were taken of each subject to be used as standards recorded under essentially non-emotional conditions.   The subject's face was then marked with burnt cork, in order to set off the functional muscle groups and thus to aid in the later analysis of the photographs. To provide a scale for measurement, the photographs were taken through a screen of ½-in. lattice.   In order clearly to delineate every noticeable change of facial expression, from 16 to 42 pictures were taken of each subject in each situation.   The total number of photographs available for later analysis was 844.

Analysis of Facial Expressions.   Facial movements were classified into 22 types (each of which is fully described in the original report), in terms of the specific facial muscles involved.   The photographs were carefully examined, and in every photograph the involvement of each muscle or muscle group was rated as 0 = absent, 1 = slight involvement, 2 = moderate involvement, and 3 = full or extreme involvement.   The data were finally tabulated in terms of the percentage of involvement of each particular type of movement for each subject, for each situation, and for each type of emotion verbally reported by the subjects.

Two different analyses of the photographs were made.   The first analysis was conducted with full knowledge of the verbal reports, situations, blood-pressure records, etc., associated with each photograph; the second was carried out in entire ignorance of these data. In most cases, the estimates of involvement of muscle groups in the two analyses differed by less than 2 per cent.

RESULTS

Emotional and Other Behavior Evoked by the Situations.   The effect of the series of experimental situations upon the emotional and other behavior of the subjects was as follows:

1. *Popular Music.*   2. *Technical Music.*   3. *Reading the Bible.* These first three situations were introduced only for the purpose of

allaying the subject's initial apprehension. This they did in practically all cases as was indicated by the fact that the physiological and facial records were not significantly different from the non-emotional controls.

4. *Truth and Falsehood*. This situation failed to evoke emotional reactions and thus was worthless except to the extent that it served to prolong the initial adaptive period. The situation was probably too artificial to evoke the emotions typically associated with deliberate deception.

5. *Ammonia*. The sudden breathing of ammonia gas had a very different effect on different subjects. Some were unaffected by it, while others coughed, gasped, made arm movements, and gave other indications of disturbance.

6. *Unexpected Explosion*. The unexpected explosion of the firecracker usually caused a "startle" response. The subject gave a sudden jump or other convulsive movement, and turned toward the experimenter as if for explanation. Finally, he usually smiled or laughed.

7. *Faux Pas*. Most subjects seemed quite at a loss when asked to describe the meanest or most embarrassing thing that they had ever done. Several blushed and fidgeted considerably when the description which they had written was read by the experimenter. Almost all of the subjects laughed during the reading.

8. *Jokes*. This situation was omitted with most subjects, since the jokes failed to produce the expected laughter. However, laughter was so frequently aroused in other situations that in order to study its characteristics no stimulus especially designed to produce it was necessary.

9. *Pictures of Skin Diseases*. The subjects gave close attention to the pictures, and most of them inquired as to the nature of the diseases portrayed. However, they gave few if any visible indications of emotion.

10. *Distraction during Mental Multiplication*. The filing of metal during mental multiplication was the most effective of all the stimuli in causing overt bodily activity. The subjects talked aloud, looked at the ceiling, wrote the numbers in the air or on the table top with their fingers, readjusted their position in the chair, and kicked or struck in the direction of the noise.

11. *Pornographic Pictures.* In this situation, the subjects usually looked over the pictures in a rather hurried and nervous manner. The lack of remarks and of movements and laughter was very noticeable and probably testified to embarrassment and inhibition of "natural" reactions on the part of the subjects.

12. *Art Studies.* The nude art pictures were considered with more care and in a more critical manner than were the pornographic pictures. Talking and laughing were common. In general, discomfort and embarrassment were less marked than in situation 11.

13. *Sex Case Histories.* The reading of the sex case histories was accompanied by movements of clearing the throat, biting the lips, moistening the lips, and other reactions which are usually regarded as indicative of embarrassment and constraint.

14. *Frogs and Electric Shock.* The subjects followed the instructions given in this situation in a very cautious manner. Tension, rigidity of posture, and slowness of movement were marked. The electric shock caused a convulsive jerk, with a throwing back of the head and a raising of both arms.

15. *Decapitation of a Rat.* This situation caused a great variety of reactions. All the subjects argued about the instructions given them and most of them doubted the experimenter's sincerity in demanding that they kill the rat. They usually showed a great deal of vacillation and made many false starts. When they actually undertook the act of decapitation, their final reactions were usually so hurried that the operation itself was rather awkward and prolonged.

16. *Electric Shocks.* Many of the subjects insisted that mental multiplication was impossible with the electric shocks. Some were profane, some became angry and tore the electrode from the arm, others begged the experimenter to stop. A few of the female subjects cried bitterly.

17. *Relief.* When the subject was told that the series was finished, a marked relaxation was apparent, although some of the more seriously upset subjects continued crying.

It is clear from the evidence afforded by the subject's behavior that most of the experimental situations produced strong and genuine emotions, and that they produced a variety of emotions.

Facial Reactions of Individuals. The photographs indicate that certain individuals used particular muscle groups very frequently, and rarely or never used others. For example, one subject often threw his head back, wrinkled his forehead, and opened his mouth, but never showed vertical wrinkles between the eyebrows. Another subject usually pursed his lips, but never threw his head back. One subject almost always closed his eyes, another opened them widely. The reason for such variations in expression is not clear. Questioning the subjects themselves shed no light upon the problem. Many subjects did not know what facial reactions they characteristically showed, whereas others, though aware of their reactions, were unable to explain them. However, it was found that in many individuals these differences in facial expression were due more to the failure of certain muscles to function at all than to the occurrence of very marked and intense reactions of the participating muscle groups. Probably, many personal "mannerisms" are similarly due more to the nonfunction of specific groups of muscles than to the overfunction of others.

The Relationship between Situation and Facial Expression. It is a common popular belief that in a given emotional situation most individuals will show a facial expression which is sufficiently specific and distinctive to reveal the nature of the emotion aroused. This view was sponsored by Darwin,[1] who wrote, "We have seen that frowning is the natural expression of some difficulty encountered or of something disagreeable experienced, either in thought or in action, and he whose mind is often and readily affected in this way will be apt to be ill-tempered or slightly angry or peevish, and will commonly show it by frowning."

No evidence in favor of this view was found in the foregoing experiment. No given expression was present in enough photographs taken under the same or very similar conditions to be considered as typical of any situation. Smiling occurred more frequently than any other response, but even this reaction was not associated with any particular situation.

The Relationship between Verbal Reports of Emotion and Facial Expressions. Pictures which had been taken when the subjects reported definite emotions, such as "disgust," "exasperation," "anger," "revolting," "surprise," and "sex excitement," were carefully analyzed. Contrary to commonly held views, there were no facial expressions

[1] Darwin, C. *The Expression of the Emotions in Man and Animals*, 2d ed., p. 238, London, 1890.

which showed any clear correlation with any verbally reported emotion. To be sure, in every picture taken during "exasperation" the subject's lips were open. But the prevalence of this reaction was due merely to the fact that all the "exasperation" pictures were taken in situations 10 and 16, in which the subjects were multiplying by the talking aloud method.

Posing and Facial Expression. Three of the subjects who had served in the experiment were asked to "register" or "act out" the facial expressions corresponding to certain emotions which they had verbally reported as having experienced during the situation series. With these instructions they gave expressions which could for the most part be readily recognized as the traditional expressions of "religious feeling," "disgust," "fear," and so on. That is, their expressions then took the form of the definite facial patterns which we have traditionally regarded as expressive of certain emotions or feelings. But these expressions were not the ones they showed in the experimental situations when these emotions were actually present. In reality, these posed expressions were probably only socially learned and socially approved expressions in the nature of language gestures and did not reproduce the patterns of facial expressions which actually occur in real emotional situations.

Sex Differences. For the most part, the facial changes of the male subjects were found to be more expressive and dynamic than were those of the females. Also, in situations 15 and 16 certain differences in the general behavior of the two sexes were noted. During the decapitation of the rat, and also during the electrical punishment, seven of the women cried and begged the experimenter to stop the experiment. In situation 16 the male subjects became profane; a number of them tore off the electrode which was attached to the arm and threw it in the direction of the experimenter; several *demanded* that the electrical stimulation be stopped. However, no evidence for sex differences in the variety of facial expressions was found in the photographs from either situation.

DISCUSSION

The major result of Landis's experiment is that no common or describable correspondence was discovered, either between any specific facial expression and any of the situations employed or between any facial expression and any one kind of emotion (such as fear, anger, disgust) which the subjects reported.   Whether the same results would be obtained with different subjects and with a wider range of stimuli is a question which cannot now be decisively answered.   However, neither common sense nor traditional beliefs are adequate to solve such a problem.   To most psychologists, Landis's results strongly suggest that the emotions which we introspectively differentiate are not distinguished by characteristic and different facial expressions.

II. AN EXPERIMENT ON THE JUDGMENT OF FACIAL EXPRESSION IN EMOTION[1]

As we have already pointed out, various experiments have been performed in which photographs of posed or simulated facial expressions have been shown to groups of observers who were instructed to decide what emotion was portrayed in each picture.   Under these conditions, it is found that ordinary observers can infer what emotion is depicted more often than chance would account for.   But this finding does not justify the conclusion that observers would be equally successful in judging photographs of "real" facial expressions produced under the stress of actual emotion.   Obviously, an experiment in which *real* and not posed expressions are judged is necessary to answer the question which this statement implies.   Landis, by proceeding to use certain of the photographs obtained in the experiment just described, was able to carry out a study of this further and different type.

PURPOSE

The specific aims of this experiment were as follows:

1. Given a collection of photographs taken during "real" emotional situations, to determine what interpretations judges will place on the "emotions" portrayed.

2. To determine whether a judge can describe correctly the situation which aroused the expression shown in a particular portrait.

3. To determine whether one can interpret more accurately the "emotion" when a portrait depicts a real response to an actual situation, or when it depicts an acted response to an imagined situation.

[1] Adapted from Landis, C. The Interpretation of Facial Expression in Emotion. *Journal of General Psychology*, 1929, vol. 2, pp. 59–72.

METHOD

Seventy-seven photographs were selected from the 844 taken in the previous experiment. These particular pictures were chosen because the investigator thought they were "very expressive." Of the 77 pictures, 56 were taken in actual emotional situations, while the other 21 were of subjects who were giving acted responses to an imaginary reinstatement of the situations they had previously experienced. Pictures of 11 men and 11 women were used. Each picture was trimmed so that only the head and shoulders were shown.

The pictures were projected on a screen by a projection lantern. The judges were 42 students of psychology at Connecticut Wesleyan University. Each judge was given a set of mimeographed blanks. At the head of each set of blanks were the following instructions: "You will be shown a series of photographs which seem to be expressive of various emotions or feelings. Consider each photograph carefully and then try to state what emotion or feeling you think the subject is experiencing. Enter this in the first column opposite the number of the picture. Then try to imagine or guess what sort of stimulation would give the particular expression photographed. Enter this in the second column. In the third column enter the percentage of certainty you feel concerning your two previous judgments."

RESULTS

The results of the experiment may be briefly summarized as follows:

1. The titles given to the photographs taken in emotional situations were mainly such terms as "joy," "sorrow," "maternal," and "surprise." In some cases, two somewhat contradictory terms were applied to the same picture by the same individual.

2. In most cases, when the observers were asked to characterize the situations which might give rise to the expressions shown in the photographs, they made use of only four general terms: "pleasant," "unpleasant," "religious," and "maternal." For eight of the photographs the mutually contradictory terms "pleasant" and "unpleasant" occurred in more than 20 per cent of the judgments. One picture was classified as appropriate for a pleasant situation in 46 per cent, and for an unpleasant one in 49 per cent of the judgments.

3. Only 31 per cent of the judgments of the emotions depicted in

the "real" pictures agreed with the introspective reports of the subjects photographed. Similarly, for the posed pictures, only 28 per cent of the judgments were found to agree with the emotions which the pictures were intended to portray. As to the ability of the judges to name situations which might have given rise to the emotions shown, 43 per cent of the judgments of the "real" pictures and 38 per cent of the judgments of the posed pictures were classified by the experimenter as "appropriate." Hence, there was no significant difference in the accuracy with which the judges interpreted photographs which depicted "real" expressions in actual emotional situations and photographs which depicted posed expressions in imagined situations.

Discussion

How can the results of these experiments be reconciled with those of investigators who have found that pictures representing various emotional reactions could be named correctly by observers more frequently than would have been possible had they been merely guessing? Landis believes that the explanation of the differences between his results and those of others lies in the fact that the posed pictures previously used were not true portraits of facial expression during emotion, but rather were pictures of the socialized and, to a large extent, conventionalized reactions which are used as supplementary language mechanisms. There is little or no evidence that such expressions occur in "real emotion" except by chance. To be sure, Landis's posed photographs were judged no more accurately than were his photographs taken in actual emotional situations, but this somewhat surprising result may be due merely to the fact that his subjects were "poor actors," *i.e.*, they were unpracticed in acting and unable to produce correctly the conventional facial expressions.

Are we, then, to conclude that no facial expressions of emotional origin can be interpreted correctly, and that the general belief to the contrary is wholly mistaken? The answer to this question seems to be an affirmative one. What happens in most cases of so-called "reading emotion from the face" is that we observe not only the facial expression of an individual but also many other perceptible aspects of his behavior (*e.g.*, verbal, gestural, and postural signs), and, especially important, we observe, as well, the situation which is stimulating him. We may think that we are judging the nature and degree of his emotional reactions on the basis of his facial expression alone. But in actual fact, it is very probable that the other factors mentioned above generally contribute far more to our interpretation. As Landis's experiment shows, when we are forced to judge emotions from the face only, we have little or no basis for success in differentiating one emotion from another.

CHAPTER VIII

THE DUPLICITY THEORY OF VISION

Introduction

The retina of the human eye contains two kinds of receptor cells, the rods and the cones. These two types of cells differ with respect to their structure, their function, and their distribution within the retina. Within the *fovea centralis*[1] there are many thousands of cones, but no rods. As one passes from the center toward the periphery of the retina, the proportion of rods to cones steadily increases until, at the extreme periphery, rods are thickly distributed and there are few, if any, cones.[2]

According to the "duplicity theory" of von Kries, the cones and rods of the retina have two important differences in function: First, the cones are the receptor cells which function at daytime levels of light intensity, whereas the rods are the receptors for "twilight vision," *i.e.*, for vision at the low intensities of illumination which characterize twilight and night conditions. Second, the cones are the cells which are so constituted that they enable us to perceive colors and to discriminate color differences, whereas the rods make possible only colorless, or achromatic, vision. The evidence supporting this duplicity theory may be summarized as follows.

1. Foveal Night Blindness. It has been shown that under deep twilight conditions of illumination the fovea is in effect a *scotoma*, *i.e.*, a blind area. Many years ago astronomers observed that they could not see very dim stars when they were looking directly at them but that these same stars became visible when they turned their eyes away to view some neighboring star. Since they were now fixating the neighboring star, the light from the dim star would fall outside

---

[1] The *fovea centralis* is the small, central "area of clearest vision" upon which is impressed the retinal image of small objects or figures which are directly "fixated" by the observer.

[2] The total number of rods exceeds that of the cones by many millions. Estimates of the number of rods vary from 60,000,000 to 130,000,000, whereas the estimated number of cones is only about 7,000,000.

the fovea, in a retinal region where rods are known to be abundant. After the rods have become "dark adapted" by being shielded from intense light for a time, they are much more sensitive to low intensities of light than are the cones. Although under daylight conditions it is the foveal cones which give us our clearest visual impressions, their thresholds of excitation are much higher than are those of the rods.

2. Differences in the Processes of Adaptation between the Cones and the Rods. The human retina is capable of two kinds of adaptation process, "light adaptation" and "dark adaptation." *Light adaptation* refers to the *decrease in sensitivity* of the retinal cells under continued stimulation by light, especially by light of relatively high intensity. This process goes on very slowly in the cones, but in the rods it is both rapid and extensive. The effect of light adaptation is illustrated by the familiar experience of being temporarily "blinded" when one goes from a brightly illuminated place into a relatively dark room. The explanation of this experience is that the intensity of stimulation suddenly has been reduced to a level below the threshold for the cones, and the rods, in their state of extreme light adaptation, are temporarily insensitive.

Dark adaptation means the *increase in sensitivity* of the retina which occurs when light is either excluded from the eye altogether or is reduced to a very low level of intensity. This type of adaptation is due primarily to changes in the rods. After the cones have been responding to moderately intense illumination, removal of the light does not bring about any great increase in their sensitivity. But rods which have been rendered almost wholly insensitive by the continued action of intense light then become dark adapted to such an extent that they acquire a sensitivity to light at least a thousand times greater than that of the cones. The sensitivity of the rods is increased greatly within a few minutes after light has been excluded from the eye, but complete dark adaptation requires 30 minutes or more in normal individuals. The effect of this kind of adaptation is shown by the invariably rapid recovery from the "blinding" which we experience when we enter a relatively dark place. Although at first we can see very little (as a result of the previous light adaptation of the rods), soon we are able to perceive objects at least in outline, though not in color.

3. Daylight "Blindness" in Animals Whose Retinas Contain Rods or Rodlike Cells Only. Various nocturnal animals, such as owls and bats, are known to have only rodlike cells in their retinas. Such animals are "blind" under daylight conditions because their retinas contain no cones, and the rods become light adapted to such an extent that they are practically nonfunctional. However, under conditions of very low illumination, these animals "see" extraordinarily well. In fact, they are reputed to "see" in the dark. As a matter of fact, no organism can "see" in absolute darkness. What actually happens is that through dark adaptation the rodlike cells of their retinas become sufficiently sensitive to make "seeing" possible when only a very small amount of light is present. Similarly, human individuals of the albino type, who also have retinas devoid of functional cones, see so poorly under daylight conditions that they can get about only with the aid of smoked glasses, which serve to reduce the intensity of illumination to such a low value that the rods may become dark adapted and therefore sensitive. Albinos are also blind at the fovea, and are wholly unable to perceive colors.

4. Achromatic Peripheral Vision in Daylight Illumination. Individuals possessing perfectly normal eyes are totally color blind in the extreme periphery of the retina. This fact has been demonstrated in the following manner. A small object of any color—red, green, yellow, blue, etc.—is placed back of a subject's head. While the subject continues to look fixedly straight ahead, the object is moved slowly around the side and toward the front of his head (by means of a special instrument, the *perimeter*) and the subject is instructed to report his first glimpse of it. Under these conditions, the subject first sees the object when it is far out to the right (or left) of his line of vision, and from that position it appears to him to be almost or entirely colorless. Apparently, the reason for its lack of color is that light reflected from the object at that point reaches only the extreme periphery of the retina where there are many rods, but few, if any, cones. These observations suggest that the excitation of the cones is required for color vision, and that the rods are receptors for achromatic vision only.

5. Achromatic Vision in Deep Twilight: The Photochromatic Interval. When the intensity of illumination is just at the absolute threshold of visibility, that is, when it is so low that objects can be just barely perceived, everything seen appears to be black or gray. If the intensity of the illumination is increased, the objects continue to appear gray until a certain critical intensity value is reached which is called the "chromatic threshold." From this point on, the objects are seen as colored. The range of intensity values extending from the absolute visibility threshold to the "chromatic" or color threshold is known as the *photochromatic interval.* These facts suggest that the retinal cells which function at low levels of illumination are insensitive to color, and that only those cells which function at higher levels of stimulus intensity are responsive to wave-length differences.

6. The Absence of an Achromatic Threshold at the Fovea. However, at the fovea, where there are no rods, there is no photochromatic interval. If light of a given wave length is of sufficient intensity to excite the cones of the fovea at all, the light is perceived at once as colored. This fact indicates that under all conditions of illumination (save when the intensity is below their thresholds of sensitivity) the cones are sensitive to the wave-length character of light.

7. The Purkinje Phenomenon. More than one hundred years ago, the Austrian physiologist, Purkinje, observed certain striking changes in the brightness relations among various colors when the intensity of illumination was reduced below the threshold for color vision. The objects of his earliest observations were the colored figures of the carpet and of the hangings of his study. Under daylight conditions the yellow figures were the brightest of all, but under deep twilight conditions, when all the colored figures appeared as different shades of gray, the brightest gray figures were not those which had appeared as yellow figures under bright-light conditions, but rather those which had been seen as green. Moreover, reds and blues no longer appeared equally bright as they had under daylight conditions; the gray figures which had been blue were much brighter than those which had been red. In fact, in deep twilight the red figures became definitely black.

Subsequently, several investigators obtained quantitative experimental data from which they constructed curves showing how luminosity (*i.e.,* apparent brightness) varies with the wave length of the light stimulus. Brightness curves were plotted both for twilight and for bright-light vision. These two curves were found to have the same form, but the curve for achromatic (*i.e.,* twilight) vision was shifted somewhat toward the violet end of the spectrum, so that its maximal brightness was at about 520 mμ[1] (green) instead of at 560 mμ (greenish yellow) which is the maximum of the daylight curve.

In terms of the duplicity theory, this change in the apparent brightness of lights of different wave lengths can be accounted for readily. A decrease in the intensity of illumination to a value below the threshold of excitation of the cones causes the rods to become the sole functional receptors, and the relative brightness of lights of different wave lengths differs for the two types of retinal cells.

All of the seven lines of evidence which we have described lend support to the von Kries duplicity theory of vision, according to which the rods and cones of the retina perform characteristically different functions in the process of seeing. As an example of a quantitative experiment which has furnished data substantiating that theory, we shall review the study of Hecht and Williams.

BRIGHTNESS CURVES FOR TWILIGHT AND DAYLIGHT VISION: THE FUNCTION OF VISUAL PURPLE[2]

The experiment of Hecht and Williams had a twofold purpose. One aim was to make an exact quantitative study of the Purkinje phenomenon described above. In order to do this the experimenters planned (1) to determine accurately the relative brightness of lights of different wave lengths (or frequencies) when viewed under conditions of dim-light vision, (2) to construct from these data a brightness curve for dim-light vision, and (3) to compare this curve with one similarly obtained for lights of different wave lengths under bright-light conditions.

The second aim concerned the visual purple, a substance found in the rod cells. When lights of very low intensity act upon the rods, they bring about chemical changes in the visual purple. Hecht and Williams attempted (1) to determine the relative degree of bleaching effect which lights of different wave lengths exert upon the visual purple, and (2) to compare the curve which represents these effects

---

[1] The mμ (millimicron) unit is the one-millionth part of the millimeter, and is employed to measure the length of light waves. The normal human eye responds to light stimulation over a wave-length range of from about 390 mμ (violet) to 760 mμ (red).

[2] Adapted from Hecht, S., and R. E. Williams. The Visibility of Monochromatic Radiation and the Absorption Spectrum of Visual Purple. *Journal of General Physiology*, 1922, vol. 5, pp. 1–33.

with the brightness curve for dim-light vision. If the brightness curve for dim-light vision were found to coincide with the bleaching curve for visual purple, it might be concluded that visual purple is the active retinal photochemical substance in achromatic vision.

METHOD

Subjects. The subjects were 48 graduate students and instructors at the University of Liverpool. Their average age was twenty-five years. Forty-three of them were men, five were women.

Apparatus. It was necessary, first of all, to obtain pure homogeneous monochromatic lights, *i.e.*, lights which were of a single wave length. To secure these homogeneous lights, white light from a 500-

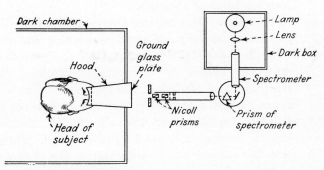

FIG. 6. Diagram Showing Ground Plan of the Apparatus of Hecht and Williams.

candle-power lamp was passed through a lens and then through a spectrometer. White light is composed of lights of all the various spectral wave lengths. Upon entering the glass prism of the spectrometer, the various wave-length components were refracted (bent) at different angles, and means were devised for selecting a beam of any desired wave length and diffusing it upon a ground-glass plate. It was also necessary to regulate with precision the intensity of the homogeneous lights. This was accomplished by having the beam pass through a pair of Nicol prisms. By a change in the angle between the prisms the intensity of the light could be changed at will.[1] A schematic representation of the entire apparatus is shown in Fig. 6.

[1] Measures of the relative intensities employed could easily be obtained, since the intensity of light transmitted by a pair of Nicol prisms is proportional to the square of the cosine of the angle between the prisms.

As was stated above, the monochromatic light was diffused upon a ground-glass plate. This plate formed the back wall of an observation box into which the subject looked through a hooded window.

Upon the inner surface of this plate (*i.e.*, the surface nearest the subject's eye) an oval figure was drawn in opaque radium paint (see Fig. 7). This figure constituted a constant visual stimulus, of an intensity which was above the absolute threshold of visibility but well below the threshold of color. The area covered by the oval figure was not completely painted. Instead, sections shown in black in Fig. 7 were left unpainted on the ground glass, which allowed light from the spectrometer to show through.

FIG. 7. Oval Figure Which the Subject Observed on the Ground-Glass Screen.

The white portion of the figure is radium paint; the dark part is where the light from the spectrometer shows through. When a perfect match for brightness is obtained, the dark portions of the figure disappear entirely, and the entire oval appears uniform in brightness.

Procedure. The subject was brought into the dark room and was fully informed concerning the object of the experiment, the apparatus, and the procedure. He was then seated in a curtained-off dark chamber, facing the oval window of the observation box described above. Light from the spectrometer was cut off, and at least one-half hour was allowed for the subject's eyes to become adapted to the darkness. During this time, the subject was able to watch and follow closely the gradual appearance of the radium-painted figure, which became progressively clearer as a result of the increasing sensitivity of his eyes. The figure usually became faintly visible after the first 10 or 15 min., and increased in brightness and clearness during the next 15 min., so that the subject soon became familiar with its shape. After about 30 min., the places at which the light from the spectrometer would later come through the ground-glass plate appeared as dark bars on a moderately bright background.

At the end of the adaptation period, the experimenter introduced a few practice trials in which light with a wave length of 412 mμ (violet, under bright light conditions) was projected upon the ground-glass plate from the spectrometer. The light at first was made very weak; then its intensity was increased by small steps until the subject reported that the dark bars mentioned above had disappeared. The disappearance of these bars meant that their brightness had come to match precisely the brightness of the radium figure. Every time such a match was made, the intensity value of the light required to produce the match was recorded. By the time the practice tests had ended, the subject had been in the dark chamber at least 45 min., a period which was sufficiently long to bring about complete dark adaptation. Then the same procedure was used to obtain brightness matches between the luminous figure and each of the following wave lengths: 412, 455, 486, 496, 507, 518, 529, 540, 550, 582, 613, and 666 mμ.[1] In order to test the reliability of the method, a final trial was made at the end of this series with wave length 412 mμ, the wave length used at the beginning of the experimental series. Another test of reliability consisted of having some of the subjects return to the laboratory for retests at later dates. Since all these retests gave similar results, the reliability of the method was confirmed.

RESULTS

For each subject a curve was plotted to show the particular intensity at which each given wave length exactly matched the brightness of the radium figure. As Fig. 8 shows, these curves were U-shaped. Hence, relatively great light intensities were required to match the standard radium stimulus when the wave lengths were from points near the two ends of the spectrum, and relatively little energy was required when wave lengths from the middle region of the spectrum were employed. The least intensity of all was required for light of wave length 511 mμ (which is green in daylight vision).[2]

---

[1] The hues which, in chromatic vision, correspond to these wave lengths are the following:

Wave length, mμ	Hue	Wave length, mμ	Hue
412	Violet	529	Green
455	Blue	540	Yellow-green
486	Blue	550	Yellow-green
496	Blue-green	582	Yellow
507	Green	613	Orange
518	Green	666	Red

[2] In plotting these curves, the *logarithms* of the intensity values were plotted against

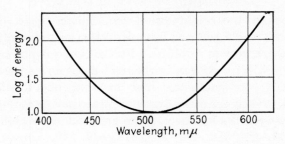

FIG. 8.   Curve Showing Relationship between Wave Length and the Light Intensity Required to Produce a Brightness Match with the Standard Radium Stimulus.   (*After Hecht and Williams.*)

TABLE I

Showing, for the Different Wave Lengths Used, (1) the Relative Intensities of Light Required to Match the Standard Radium Stimulus, and (2) the Relative Visibility Values of These Wave Lengths under Dim-light Conditions at a Constant Level of Energy, i.e., Intensity

Wave length, mμ	Color produced in bright-light vision	(1) Relative intensity	(2) Relative visibility
412	Violet	158.10	6.32
455	Blue	25.03	39.95
486	Blue	11.99	83.40
496	Blue-green	10.65	93.90
507	Green	10.06	99.35
518	Green	10.28	97.30
529	Green	10.98	91.10
540	Yellow-green	12.69	78.78
550	Yellow-green	17.99	55.60
582	Yellow	56.24	17.78
613	Orange	367.20	2.72
666	Red	5525.00	0.181

By a statistical procedure which need not be described here, the data for all the subjects were combined, and the average relative intensities required for the several different wave lengths were calculated.   These averages are given in column 3 of Table I.

the wave-length values, since a direct plot covering so large a range of values would have served to minimize the finer changes which occur at the lower intensities and to exaggerate the larger changes at the higher intensity levels.

The values given for the various wave lengths in column 3 represent the relative intensity of light which was required to produce a given, constant retinal effect (*i.e.*, to match the radium figure in brightness). The reciprocals of these values represent the relative stimulating effects of the different wave lengths with the energy factor held constant. These reciprocals, multiplied by 1,000, are entered in column 4 of Table I. A curve plotted for these reciprocal values resembles in form the "normal" or Gaussian probability curve.

Upon the same axes, Hecht also plotted a curve based upon data obtained by other investigators who used techniques similar to his own, but who worked with intensities of the standard stimulus which

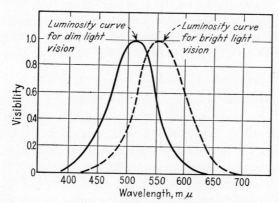

FIG. 9. Luminosity Curves for Dim-Light and Bright-light Vision. (*After Hecht and Williams.*)

were above the color threshold (*i.e.*, under bright-light conditions). It can be seen in Fig. 9 that the luminosity (or brightness) curve for bright-light (chromatic) vision has the same form as that for dim-light (achromatic) vision, but that the point of maximum brightness for the latter condition is shifted about 48 mμ toward the violet end (*i.e.*, the short-wave end) of the spectrum. Hence, these curves provide a quantitative representation of the change in brightness relations as the transition is made from daylight vision to twilight vision. The change as described from this study is precisely that which was more crudely described by Purkinje many years ago.

As we have said, the fact that a shift in the relative brightness of lights of different wave lengths occurs when the intensity of illumination is reduced below a certain level may be interpreted as constituting additional evidence in support of the duplicity theory. It is highly probable that the luminosity curve for dim-light vision is the curve of sensitivity of the rods, whereas the curve based upon data obtained under daylight conditions is the sensitivity curve of the cones. If this be true, then the same wave lengths differ in their relative stimulative effects upon the rods and the cones. At low, constant intensities light of wave length 511 mμ (green) has the maximum stimulating effect upon the rods, whereas at higher constant intensities it is light of 559 mμ (yellow) that has the maximum effect upon the cones (provided, that is, the intensity factor is held constant). The longest waves of the visible spectrum, those which range from 650 to 760 mμ and which appear as red under bright-light conditions, can excite the cones only if their intensity is relatively high; if their intensity is low, they have no appreciable effect upon either type of receptor cell.

Achromatic Vision and Visual Purple

Is visual purple the active photochemical substance in the rods of the retina? That is to say, is visual purple the substance which is chemically altered by light and which thereupon initiates the process of excitation in the retinal neurones associated with the rods? An attempt was made to answer this question by comparing the luminosity curve for achromatic vision with the curve representing differences in the action of lights of different wave lengths upon visual purple. Visual purple which has been extracted from the retina retains its purplish color only so long as it is shielded from light. When it is exposed to light, it loses its color, *i.e.*, it is bleached, but the velocity of this bleaching response differs for lights of different wave lengths, when the intensity of the lights is held constant.[1] Hecht and Williams determined as accurately as possible the times required for lights of the different wave lengths to produce the same bleaching effects. They found that bleaching times were far longer for violet and red, extreme red having scarcely any bleaching effect at all. They then converted their measurements into values which were comparable with the relative wave-length brightness values upon which their luminosity curves had been constructed. Comparison of

---

[1] Although bleached by light, visual purple regains its former hue when it is removed to a dark place.

the curve which represented the bleaching effects of different wave lengths with the luminosity curve for achromatic vision showed that the two curves were very nearly identical. The two curves did not coincide perfectly, but the amount of divergence was well within the limits of experimental error. The almost complete identity of the two curves lends further support to the view that the visual purple associated with the rods of the retina *is* an active photochemical substance.

If the visual purple is the photochemical substance associated with the rods, it might be inferred that the cones must contain a similar photochemical substance, since the luminosity curves for rod vision and for cone vision, although they do not coincide, are identical in form. In this connection, Hecht suggests two possibilities: (1) that the visual purple of the rods and the hypothetical photochemical substance of the cones may be two different, although closely related, substances; or (2) that the visual purple may exist in both the rods and the cones, but in media (or solvents) of different density. It has been shown that when a given substance which absorbs light is dissolved in different media its absorption curve shifts. Such a substance could well give luminosity curves 48 mμ apart, if it were dissolved in media which differed in density and refractive power.

DISCUSSION

Many of the facts and principles of retinal functioning which we have reviewed in this chapter acquired new significance during the Second World War, when they were applied in various useful ways both in the armed services and in civilian defense organizations.

One example of such application is that air-raid wardens who were trained to serve as observers under black-out or similar dark conditions were advised to try to identify an obscure object by "looking past" it instead of directly at it. Another example is the decision that red was the safest color of filter for an air-raid warden to place over the lens of his flashlight. It could be assumed that the eyes of an observer in an enemy plane would be dark adapted, and that his vision would be dependent upon the rod cells of his retinas. As we have seen, it has been established that the rods are least responsive to the long waves of the red band of the spectrum. Hence red would be the color of light least detectable by a plane flying at night overhead.

A further application of the fact that the rods do not respond to red light was the use of red goggles to facilitate the dark-adaptation process. An observer who is to stand watch in a black-out situation (*e.g.*, an aerial observer) must allow his retinas to become completely dark adapted, a process requiring 30 min. or more. By wearing red goggles, such an observer was able to spend a considerable part of the adaptation period in a normally illuminated room engaged in useful work instead of having to spend all of it in a dark room doing nothing. The reason for the efficacy of the red goggles is that red glass absorbs all the shorter wave-length components of white light and transmits to the eyes only the long red rays. Since the red rays do not excite the rods, the observer was able to enjoy modified cone vision while the rods became dark adapted.

Also of interest in this connection is the method employed to simulate night flying conditions in daylight during the training of airplane pilots. The windshield and windows of the cabin of the plane were coated with green acetate, and the pilot-trainee wore red goggles. The green acetate absorbed long and short waves, but allowed light of medium wave-length values in the green region of the spectrum to pass through it. Since most of this green light was absorbed by the red-goggle lenses, the world outside the cabin appeared dark to the pilot. However, he was able to see the lighted instruments inside the cabin, although they appeared reddish to him. The instructor, who wore no colored goggles, saw the instruments normally and had an adequate view outside the plane, although for him everything outside was tinted green.

Illustrations such as those above show that many of the experimentally determined facts concerning human vision and their interpretation in the light of the duplicity theory are far from being of academic interest only. Similarly, data concerning the visual purple can easily be shown to be relevant to everyday problems of human adjustment. An individual is often called upon to adjust visually under rapidly changing intensities of illumination. Suppose, for example, that a person is driving a motor car at night. If his eyes have been stimulated by bright headlights and the intensity of illumination suddenly falls to a low level, some dark adaptation of the rods must occur without too much delay if the driver is to avoid accident. Individuals differ greatly in the speed with which their retinas become dark adapted; in the so-called "night-blind" individual this process requires an abnormally long time. Obviously night blindness makes night driving hazardous. The possession of good daytime vision (*i.e.*, cone vision) is no guarantee that the individual will be able to adjust adequately under night conditions.

The speed at which dark adaptation occurs apparently depends upon the velocity with which the visual purple recovers after it has been acted upon and modified (and, incidentally, bleached) by light. It has been known for several years that visual purple is rich in vitamin A, the fat-soluble vitamin found in cod-liver oil, halibut-liver oil, and certain vegetables, notably carrots. Visual purple which is deficient in this vitamin shows an exceptionally long recovery time after exposure to light. Experimental results demonstrate that animals which have been deprived of vitamin A become "night blind," but that they recover their normal nocturnal vision after vitamin A has been restored to their diet. It has also been found that the administration of this vitamin in large amounts induces a more rapid dark adaptation in "night-blind" human subjects. Hence the adaptometer (an instrument employed to determine precisely the time required for dark adaptation) is used by some diagnosticians to detect and to estimate the magnitude of vitamin A deficiency in the diet. If adaptometer tests reveal an abnormally long adaptation time, it is concluded that the subject's diet has been deficient in vitamin A.

It is believed that a riboflavin (vitamin B_2) deficiency is also related to a slow dark-adaptation rate and to night blindness. Furthermore, there is evidence that the behavior of the visual purple is dependent upon the physiological condition of various organs of the body. For example, 96 per cent of a group of people suffering from kidney stones and 95 per cent of a group suffering from a liver disorder were found to be "night blind." There are also indications that many people adapt very slowly to darkness when they have severe colds, sinus infections, and the like. These disorders may be related to vitamin deficiencies or to disturbances in the metabolism of these vitamins.

In conclusion it is fitting that we call attention to the greatly increased interest among psychologists in problems relating to sensitivity. This interest developed during the war largely because of the urgent need for new devices to improve the accuracy of visual and auditory observation, and to test the sensory capacities of the men and women in the armed services. It also became important to identify the significant sensory cues controlling the activities of pilots and bombardiers and of observers of many types, since with increased knowledge of these sensory cues, more adequate training methods might be devised.

Among the many specific problems with which experimental psychologists became concerned during the war years were problems of visual organization, especially as related to the determination of the effectiveness of camouflage; problems of color perception and the extent to which the different varieties of color blindness might handicap men in specific branches of the service;[1] the investigation of the acuity of peripheral vision, and the development of possible methods for improving the accuracy of peripheral visual perception; studies of the visual cues made use of in landing a plane, with a view toward reducing the frequency of landing accidents; the determination of the optimal design of instrument dials and the optimal arrangement of instruments on the plane's instrument panel from the standpoint of quick and accurate visual perception; studies of the effect of oxygen deprivation at high altitudes upon dark adaptation, visual acuity, and the speed and coordination of eye movements. Worth noting is the fact that in the investigations on oxygen deprivation it was found that such deprivation brings about a lengthening of dark-adaptation time, a pronounced diminution in visual acuity, and a marked disorganization of the eye movements involved in reading instruments, examining maps, charts, and the like.

Related to these problems are numerous others involving complex perceptual processes, of which the perception of the vertical discussed in Chap. XXI is an example.

Consideration of such applications as have been mentioned above shows that the facts and theories of human sensitivity, despite their technical difficulty and their apparent abstruseness, are among the most important in psychology from the viewpoint of direct practical usefulness.

---

[1] It was discovered that persons afflicted with one variety of partial color blindness made valuable contributions as aerial observers, since they could detect certain modes of camouflage that were likely to go unnoticed by the normal observer.

CHAPTER IX

THE PERCEPTION OF OBSTACLES BY THE BLIND

Introduction

The remarkable and highly complex capacity of spatial orientation, that is, of finding one's way and maintaining a position with reference to surrounding objects, ordinarily is taken for granted by most people, including even students of psychology. The predominant and intricately organized role of visual sensitivity in spatial orientation is appreciated by few of the sighted individuals who depend upon it constantly in their everyday activities, although to scientific specialists the analysis of these visual abilities represents one of the most interesting and difficult problems in the field of space perception.[1,2]

When the normal-sighted individual must find his way and avoid obstacles in the dark, without a light and solely by nonvisual cues, his blundering inept movements stand in sharp contrast to the efficiency and precision of his orientation in the light and emphasize the extent to which his everyday activities depend upon visual stimuli from the surrounding environment. This contrast makes us wonder at the dexterity with which most blind individuals habitually make their way about in total darkness.

This capacity which the blind demonstrate strongly suggests the existence of environmental cues (*i.e.*, potentially useful stimuli) other than visual ones which can adequately guide one's spatial orientation when vision is not available. It is evident that these cues, whatever they may be, are not effectively employed by most sighted individuals, who are very unskilled at avoiding objects in pitch dark or when blindfolded. On the other hand, they must be utilized by blind individuals who commonly detect and avoid obstacles readily without the aid of vision.

Such comparisons have led to much speculation about the nature of the spatial orientation of the blind, the ways in which their accom-

---

[1] Carr, Harvey. *An Introduction to Space Perception.* New York, Longmans, 1935.
[2] Werner, H. Dynamics in Binocular Depth Perception. *Psychological Monographs*, 1937, No. 218.

plishments in orientation differ from those of sighted individuals, and whether such abilities can be acquired through long practice, as they seem to be by people who have lacked sight from birth or from the early years of life.

There have been many attempts to find a solution for these problems. For example, as long ago as 1747 the French scholar Diderot reported the "amazing ability" of a blind acquaintance both to perceive obstacles in his path and to judge their distance from him. Diderot advanced the idea that the action of air on the subject's face as he moved about somehow permitted him to localize and avoid obstacles, in other words, that the blind literally use their cheeks and foreheads as "feelers." This was an early specific form of what became a favorite general theory of many writers and investigators, namely a *sensory* type of explanation. According to this view, the blind avoid obstacles through the heightened responses of known sense organs, *e.g.*, through the action of air pressure and air currents (*i.e.*, as reflected from objects in the environment) on the cutaneous nerve endings of exposed skin, through auditory sensitivity proper, or through pressure or similar nonauditory effects on the tympanic membranes and other structures of the ears. This sensory hypothesis has been extended to include a *perceptual* process, through which blind individuals not only receive sensory cues to which sighted persons are usually not responsive, but also "interpret" and use them in special organized ways. There also has been advanced an *occult* (*i.e.*, mystical) hypothesis, according to which the blind person is assumed to possess a "sixth sense" different in nature from any sense yet known, to rely on such purely conjectural agents as magnetism and vibrations of "ether" or even on some assumed action of the "unconscious."

Prior to the experiments to be reported in the present chapter, the literature on this subject presented a rather confused picture which afforded no basis for determining which of the above possibilities (or which combination of them) might be correct. Some of the earlier investigators had concentrated upon one possible explanation and some upon another, with corresponding differences in their methods, but no thoroughgoing experiments had been conducted involving the adequate control of all possibilities in the same set of tests. One experimenter, Villey[1], supplemented his tests of blind soldiers with

[1] Villey, P. *The World of the Blind* (*A Psychological Study*). London, Duckworth, 1930.

a series of questions designed to discover how they thought they avoided obstacles. One-fourth of the men interviewed thought they used hearing, one-fourth thought they used contact in some way, and the remainder attributed their avoidance of obstacles to a combination of these. It is clear that a problem such as this can be solved only by adequately designed experiments.

The experiments to be reported in the present chapter were directed toward answering questions such as those discussed above. They are described here in considerable detail, not only because they represent an attack upon a problem which has long interested students of human behavior, but also because they provide an impressive example of how the investigation of such a problem may be undertaken by means of an appropriately planned series of controlled experiments.

THE CORNELL EXPERIMENTS ON OBSTACLE-LOCATION BY BLIND AND SIGHTED SUBJECTS

GENERAL PLAN

Three principal investigations were carried out. The first of these consisted of seven experiments designed to explore the nature of obstacle avoidance under different conditions by sightless individuals. The plan was to make a thoroughgoing study of the performance of blind subjects in avoiding a test obstacle, and to compare their ability with that of blindfolded sighted subjects. The object was to ascertain what factors are involved in the avoidance of obstacles by blind individuals, and whether sighted individuals can acquire such abilities, at least to some extent, through practice. In the second and third investigations, several deaf-and-blind subjects were used in further controlled experiments directed at a more precise isolation of the factors governing obstacle-avoidance by blind persons.

First Investigation: Obstacle Location in Blind and in Blindfolded Seeing Subjects[1]

In the experiments of the first investigation, all the subjects were blindfolded throughout. The first tests were conducted under conditions normal to the blind. These initial tests were exploratory, and their object was to compare the degree of skill of the blind and

---

[1] Adapted from Supa, M., M. Cotzin, and K. M. Dallenbach. "Facial Vision"; the Perception of Obstacles by the Blind. *American Journal of Psychology,* 1944, vol. 57, pp. 133–183.

normal subjects[1] (*i.e.*, to ascertain their standard performances) under a few simple variations of the experimental conditions.

SUBJECTS AND SITUATION

Four subjects served throughout all seven experiments of the first investigation. Two of them had normal vision and two had been blind from early life. The blind subjects were Mr. E.S., an undergraduate student twenty years of age who had lost his vision when five years old, and Mr. M.S. (one of the authors), twenty-two years of age and a graduate student in psychology, who had lost his effective vision at about twenty months of age, except for a slight sensitivity to light in the left eye. The normal subjects were Miss P.C. and Mr. J.D., both graduate students in psychology. Both blind subjects exhibited in their daily behavior a notable ability to perceive obstacles from a distance. This ability was attributed by M.S. to audition, in contrast to E.S., who thought that sounds were a hindrance and that reactions to air currents acting on his face accounted for his successful space perception. At the beginning of the experiments neither of the normal subjects could detect distant obstacles when blindfolded, and walked directly into objects in their path.

All seven experiments in the first investigation were performed in the large hall of the graduate psychology laboratory at Cornell University (except for Experiment IV in which a soundproof room was also used). This hall is 18 ft. wide, 61 ft. long, and 20 ft. high, with a beamed, center-ridged ceiling and skylights. There are seven doors on each side of the hall, together with two doors and a descending stairway with open stair well at one end, and one door near a side of the opposite end. During the experiments, all the doors were closed, small apparatus and movable furniture were placed out of the way at the unused (stairway) end of the hall, and only glass-door apparatus cases and larger pieces of apparatus were left standing along each side wall.

GENERAL METHOD AND PROCEDURE

The eyes of blind and normal subjects alike were covered with cotton pads, and a flexible leather blindfold was fitted snugly over

---

[1] The fully visioned subjects in this investigation will be referred to as the "normal" subjects, as distinguished from the blind subjects, although both sighted and blind subjects wore blindfolds in all the experiments.

the forehead, around the temples, and over the cheeks. Thus all the subjects were "blind" and had their exposed facial areas reduced by like amounts. In all experiments the subjects were tested separately.

In the first six experiments, each "trial" was conducted in the following manner. The subject was started at a predetermined distance from the obstacle with instructions to walk toward it, to stop and raise his right arm when he first perceived the obstacle (the *distance perception*), and then at a verbal signal from the experimenter to approach as near as possible to the obstacle without touching it, indicating when this point (the *close perception*) was reached by raising his left arm. In each trial, these two distances were recorded by the experimenter to the nearest 6-in. interval by means of a tape measure stretched taut on the floor in the subject's path. A further measure of performance was obtained by recording the number of actual collisions with the obstacle made by each subject.

In Experiments I and VII the obstacle was the end wall of the hall opposite the stairway, a stone wall which reflected air and sound waves very efficiently by virtue of its hard-plastered surface covered with semigloss paint. In Experiments II to VI, inclusive, the obstacle was a piece of masonite board[1] ½ in. thick, 4 ft. wide and 4 ft. 10 in. high, mounted on a portable stand so that its lower edge was 2 ft. from the floor and its upper edge was at a height (6 ft. 10 in. above the floor) well above the elevation of the subject's ears.

Experiments I to V, inclusive, were carried out under each of two conditions: in *condition A* the subject wore shoes and walked on the hardwood floor toward the obstacle, guided by two narrow carpet runners which kept him in a lane 2 ft. wide between them. In *condition B* the subject walked toward the obstacle in his stocking feet and was guided by having to keep on a soft carpet runner 30 in. wide and 40 ft. long.[2] The progress of the subject under conditions A and B is represented in Fig. 10. These two conditions were counter-

---

[1] Masonite (a composition board) proved to be the most satisfactory of all the surfaces tried. The subjects readily detected plywood boards, whether unfinished or finished with shellac, varnish, paint, or wax, through their odors at a distance. Masonite, however, furnished no cues of the olfactory type.

[2] The carpet guide was not used in Experiment IA. Instead, the subject was guided when necessary by means of appropriate hand taps by the experimenter on his shoulder, as explained below.

balanced in the five experiments by having condition A precede B in Experiments I, III, and V, and follow B in Experiments II and IV. Under each condition the trials were continued until a subject had achieved 25 "successes," that is, had approached the obstacle closely twenty-five times without colliding with it.   Further information

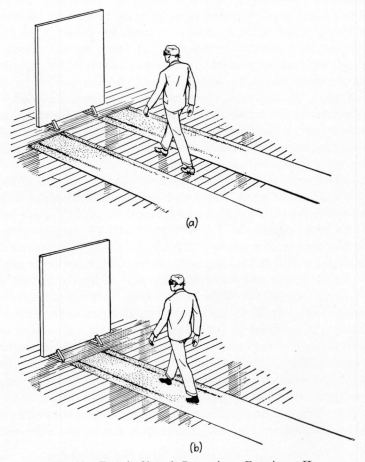

(a)

(b)

Fig. 10.   Tests in Obstacle Perception.   Experiment II.

    10*a*. The subject approaching the obstacle (a masonite screen) under condition A in Experiment II, walking with shoes on the hardwood floor and guided toward the obstacle by the lane between two carpet runners.

    10*b*. The subject approaching the obstacle under condition B in Experiment II, walking in stocking feet on a carpet runner which serves to guide him toward the obstacle.

about method and procedure is given in connection with the description of each individual experiment.

PRELIMINARY EXPERIMENTS (I–III)

Experiment I, Condition A.   The initial exploratory tests were made as favorable as possible for the perception of obstacles without the use of vision.   The subject wore shoes, walked on the hardwood floor toward the reflective end wall, and was permitted to make as much noise in walking (*e.g.*, by shuffling his feet) as he wished.   The subject was first led around the hall for 3 minutes to disorient him, then was started toward the wall from distances of 6, 12, 18, 24, or 36 ft., in a prearranged haphazard order on successive trials.   In Experiment I, condition A differed from the corresponding condition in the other experiments in that the two carpets and the lane between them were not used.   Instead, the subject was kept going straight toward the obstacle by appropriate taps on the right or left shoulder delivered by the experimenter whenever the subject deviated from a direct line.

Results. The blind subjects were successful on every one of 25 consecutive trials, and therefore were given no further tests under condition IA.   They stepped out unhesitantly, required no guidance to approach the wall directly, and did not walk into the end wall a single time.   M.S., who stepped heavily and clicked his heels on the floor as he walked, reported that he "listened" for reflected sounds. E.S., who performed best of all four subjects, walked quietly, and reported using cutaneous cues (*e.g.*, air currents?), which he localized in his forehead.

The sighted subjects, in contrast to the blind subjects, required many more than 25 trials in order to achieve 25 successes.   P.C. needed 40 trials, and J.D., 44.   Their advance was hesitant, their step shuffling and noisy.   Without any guidance, they would have walked repeatedly into the side walls of the hall.   At first they collided constantly with the end wall; however, after a few trials—eight for P.C. and nine for J.D.—they began to have some success.   In a second practice series under condition IA, P.C. collided with the end wall only six times as against fifteen in the first series, and J.D. only once as against nineteen times in the first series.

A comparison of the results for the four subjects, in Table I, shows

TABLE I

The Average Distance and the Mean Variation (in Feet) of Distance Perceptions and Close Perceptions of the Experimental Obstacle by Blind and Normal Subjects under Conditions A and B, Experiments I to VII, also the Number of Collisions with the Obstacle in Each Series

(D-P, Distance Perception; C-P, Close Perception; Coll., Collisions; MV, Mean Variation[1])

Experiment and series		Subjects							
		E.S. (blind)		M.S. (blind)		P.C. (normal)		J.D. (normal)	
		Score	MV	Score	MV	Score	MV	Score	MV
I. Wall as obstacle:									
A. Shoes on hard floor	D-P	18.04	±6.69	6.36	± .64	2.12	± .80	0.98	± .80
	C-P	.52	± .04	.54	± .07	.56	± .10	.56	± .11
	Coll.	0		0		15		19	
B. No shoes, on carpet	D-P	17.88	±7.17	3.46	±1.36	4.70	±3.38	1.18	± .46
	C-P	.62	± .19	.72	± .28	1.08	± .51	.88	± .48
	Coll.	2		4		4		6	
Repetition, Series I-A	D-P			6.08	± .92	2.58	±1.20	.93	± .36
	C-P			.56	± .09	.68	± .26	.77	± .17
	Coll.	0		0		6		1	
II. Screen as obstacle:									
A. Shoes on hard floor	D-P	15.60	±5.54	3.70	±1.50	3.22	±1.29	2.98	±2.30
	C-P	.58	± .13	.74	± .27	.62	± .20	.94	± .70
	Coll.	0		1		3		7	
B. No shoes, on carpet	D-P	13.62	±7.72	4.88	±3.25	4.54	±2.74	1.50	± .68
	C-P	1.10	± .80	2.86	±3.19	1.20	± .71	.66	± .24
	Coll.	4		4		3		15	
III. Screen:									
A. Same as II-A	D-P	17.08	±6.96	3.98	±1.18	3.34	±2.13	3.20	±1.70
	C-P	.50	± .00	.58	± .14	.84	± .34	.66	± .27
	Coll.	0		3		1		1	
B. Same as II-B (no shoes, on thick carpet)	D-P	8.16	±5.58	2.38	±1.03	1.08	± .36	1.72	±1.33
	C-P	.50	± .00	.54	± .07	.50	± .00	.52	± .04
	Coll.	1		3		1		1	
IV. Screen:									
A. Same as III-A except for felt head cover, etc.	D-P	8.56	±1.94	7.44	±2.01	1.44	± .81	3.64	±1.67
	C-P	.62	± .18	.56	± .11	.70	± .30	1.06	± .85
	Coll.	0		1		5		2	
B. Same as III-B except for felt head cover, etc.	D-P	4.88	±2.37	3.50	±1.08	1.64	±1.21	2.06	± .54
	C-P	.62	± .22	.64	± .20	.66	± .22	.78	± .29
	Coll.	3		7		2		2	
V. Screen:									
A. Same as III-A except for ear plugs and cover	D-P	0		0		0		0	
	C-P	0		0		0		0	
	Coll.	100[2]		100[2]		100[2]		100[2]	
VI. Screen—Masking tone									
A. Same as III-A except for masking tone	D-P	0		0		0		0	
	C-P	0		0		0		0	
	Coll.	100[2]		100[2]		100[2]		100[2]	
VII. Subject hears over phone									
A. series only	D-P	10.20	±1.12	6.04	±1.80	6.60	±2.77	2.92	±1.09
	C-P	2.74	± .34	.94	± .46	1.60	± .24	.82	± .35
	Coll.	1		2		3		4	

[1] The mean variation is computed by obtaining the deviation of every individual score from the average (or other measure of central tendency), then finding the average of these deviations.

[2] Collision on every trial (no successful perceptions of obstacle).

that the blind subjects were clearly superior to the normal subjects in their *distance perception* of the wall. Although the average distance of the *close perception* of the two groups was not different in the 25 successful trials, it must be remembered that the blind subjects had no collisions with the wall, whereas the normal subjects had 15 and 19 collisions, respectively, and so required many more trials to attain their 25 successes.

A comparison of the mean variations of sighted and blind subjects shows that on the whole the latter were less variable. One significant difference was that whereas both the normal subjects were thoroughly disoriented by being led circuitously around the hall before each trial, and needed guidance in approaching the obstacle, the blind subjects did not need guidance and could determine their approximate starting positions by reference to their perception of irregularities in the floor and of objects such as apparatus cases at the sides of the hall.

Experiment I, Condition B. In this series, the subject walked in stocking feet upon the long carpet runner toward the obstacle wall. The carpet both deadened the sound of the subject's footsteps and guided him toward the wall, a means used instead of shoulder taps to direct him to the obstacle in a straight line. Otherwise, the procedure was the same as in IA.

Results. As Table I shows, the efficiency of the blind subjects was less than it had been under condition IA. Their average distance-perception scores were lower (*i.e.*, they needed to walk closer to the wall for their initial perception of it), and their close-perception scores were higher (*i.e.*, they could not approach the wall so closely without collision). Both blind subjects had a few collisions with the wall, and their variability was greater than under condition IA. It was observed that M.S. now walked with his head turned to one side as if to aid hearing. It seems likely that his losses, as well as those of E.S., are to be attributed to the reduction of auditory cues, although E.S. said he was pleased by the absence of "distracting noise."

Like the blind subjects, the two normal subjects were less efficient in close perception and exhibited a marked increase in variability. Presumably their limited gains in the distance-perception scores were attributable to the practice in condition IA, and their losses in the close-perception scores to a decrease in auditory stimulation. Both subjects appeared to "miss" the auditory cues that had been present in IA.   P.C. shuffled her feet "to make some noise," and J.D. found the trips harder because "there were no sounds . . . upon which to base my judgments."

Experiment II.   After the normal subjects had learned to some extent how to perceive obstacles in the absence of visual stimuli and the blind subjects had become accustomed to experimental controls under conditions approximately normal for them, the masonite screen was used instead of the wall as the obstacle.   With the screen in different positions on successive trials the blind subjects were deprived of the advantage of their "absolute orientation" in the hall.[1]   To prevent the subject from confusing the screen with the wall, he was started at a fixed point near the wall and the screen was placed near the center of the hall at one of the predetermined distances of 6 to 36 ft.   These distances were used in variable order on successive trials.   Under condition A, as in all the experiments except I, the subject walked with shoes on the wooden floor in a lane between two carpet runners, and under condition B he walked in stocking feet upon the single carpet runner.   Before every trial, the subject waited outside the hall while the obstacle-screen and the lane were arranged; then he was led to the starting point, without knowledge of the position of the obstacle in the room.   Started by a tap on the back, the subject walked toward the obstacle without guidance except from the "lane" (condition A) or the single runner (condition B), indicating his distance perception and close perception of the obstacle as before by making the appropriate hand signals.

Results.   All of the subjects were usually able to perceive the obstacle at a distance and to approach close to it without collision, despite its smaller size and its variable position in the hall.   However, a comparison of the results of Experiments I and II shows that the new conditions usually did have an adverse effect, especially on the blind subjects.   In the normal subjects, this effect seems to have been largely neutralized by continuing improvement due to practice. E.S. again gave the best performance of the four subjects.[2]   M.S.,

---

[1] Circumstances indicated that this capacity for placing themselves accurately or judging their general position anywhere in a room was attributable to long experience in spatial orientation before the experiments began.

[2] In view of the fact that he was able to perceive the obstacle at the starting position of the three shorter distances (*i.e.*, 6, 12, and 18 ft.) the results for E.S. in the table should be corrected by taking only the data for starts at 24 and 30 ft. from the obstacle.   Thus

11*a*.

11*b*.

Fig. 11.   Tests in Obstacle Perception.   Experiment III.

11*a*. The subject, approaching the obstacle in Experiment III, condition A, signals his distance percep⁻ tion of the screen by raising his right arm.

11*b*. The subject, approaching the obstacle in Experiment III, condition B, signals his close perception of the screen by raising his left arm.

who seemed to lose proportionally more of his skill under the new conditions than did E.S., now did only slightly better than the normal subject P.C. in distance perception, and actually fell slightly below

corrected, the averages for his distance perception of the obstacle become 23.20 ± 3.41 ft. in series IIA and 21.42 ± 4.84 ft. in series IIB.   This correction is not necessary for the other subjects, since they did not perceive the obstacle at any distance until after they had started toward it.

P.C.'s score for the close perception on series IIA and below that for both normal subjects in IIB.

Experiment III.   The two conditions, A and B, were again employed, but under condition IIIB the carpet runner was twice as thick as the one used previously.   Also, in this experiment, the subject was started on each trial from a different one of five positions (0–12 ft. from the end of the room), instead of starting from a fixed position as in Experiment II.   As before, the screen was set at one of five distances from the subject's starting position, except that at random intervals a check trial was introduced in which no screen was used. The result was that the positions of both subject and obstacle were changed on each trial.   The circumstances of conditions A and B in this experiment are shown in Fig. 11.

Results.   As the results summarized in Table I indicate, all of the subjects were still able to perceive the obstacle at a distance and to approach close to it with very infrequent collisions.   The blind subjects, particularly E.S., were superior in almost all respects to the normal subjects in both series of the experiment.[1]

The subjects were evidently disturbed in their distance perception of the obstacle by the thick carpet runner, since the distance-perception scores of all except J.D. were poorer than in Experiment IIB.   However, for all four subjects the close-perception scores were better, their mean variations were smaller, and they had fewer collisions than in IIB.   It is possible, however, that with the thicker carpet the subjects were forced to make more sound themselves and to listen somewhat more attentively than in Experiment IIB, for all of them now shuffled and scraped their feet continuously in approaching the obstacle.

Discussion of Results, Experiments I–III.   It is not surprising that the blind subjects from the beginning possessed to a high degree the ability to perceive objects at a distance and to avoid collisions with them, considering that they brought to the experiment the advantage of long experience.   A comparison of the results of the different tests reveals that the skill of the blind subjects dropped sharply under both conditions A and B when they passed from Experiment I, in

[1] When the scores of E.S. are corrected as before for immediate perception of the obstacle at the starting point, his distance-perception averages improve to 23.6 ± 3.2 ft. in IIIA and 9.13 ± 4.08 ft. in IIIB.

which conditions were similar to their everyday problems in orientation, to the more artificial and controlled situations of Experiment II. However, that they could still benefit from practice is suggested by the fact that even under the more restrictive conditions of Experiment IIIB their close-perception scores were better and their collisions fewer than under the B condition in Experiments I and II.

Although the normal subjects at first did not possess to any appreciable extent the ability to perceive distant objects without the use of vision, they rapidly acquired it under the favorable conditions of Experiment I, condition A. For them, in contrast to the blind subjects, the effect of the more restrictive conditions of Experiments II and III was relatively slight, compared with the difficulty of the complex and new situation which had confronted them in Experiment I. Consequently, in Experiments II and III the normal subjects did better, in comparison with the blind, than in the other experiments.

Thus far the nature of the cues responsible for the subjects' successes has not been examined. The fact that in the check tests of Experiment III without any obstacle the subjects always kept going, until stopped by the experimenter, and failed to report the presence of any obstacle indicates that in the other tests their judgments depended upon real sensory effects of some kind. The finding that in most cases (and especially in Experiment III) the subjects did better under condition A than under B indicates that in some way the effective cues were deadened by the carpet, which suggests that sound cues may have been involved. Inspection of the data shows that the drop in efficiency from the A to the B condition occurred chiefly in the distance-perception scores, which may mean that these judgments were made on a somewhat different sensory basis than were the close perceptions. This possibility is also suggested by the fact that for P.C. the rank-order coefficient of correlation between the distance-perception and the close-perception scores is $-.97$, indicating that for her, experimental conditions which favored a good distance perception operated against a good close-perception score. However, for the other subjects the corresponding coefficient values were: E.S., $-.14$; M.S., $-.10$; and J.D., $-.21$—all values so close to zero that a virtually chance relationship is indicated between the distance-perception and close-perception processes.

We are put on our guard against an acceptance of the subject's opinion as a source of evidence by results such as those of the best subject, E.S., who despite his initial belief that his obstacle perception depended entirely upon cutaneous pressures localized on his forehead found himself in Experiment IIIB shuffling along on the double carpet, in his own words, "listening for the obstacle."

The preliminary experiments thus served a number of purposes. Besides accustoming the blind subjects to the experimental situation and disclosing the ability of the normal subjects to improve through practice, they furnished norms for all the subjects (*i.e.*, standards of their ordinary performance) with which the results of further special experiments could be compared.   Furthermore, these experiments were exploratory in the sense that their outcome guided the planning of procedures and controls to be used in the later investigations.

THE MAIN EXPERIMENTS (IV–VII)

Experiment IV.   The first of the main experiments was designed to test one principal variant of the "pressure theory," namely, that the avoidance of obstacles by the blind depends upon cutaneous pressure effects aroused by reflected air currents or air waves.   If the perception of obstacles has such a basis, the subject should be unable to perceive and to avoid obstacles when all ordinarily exposed areas of the skin are covered, even though auditory sensitivity remains unimpaired.   Experiment IV was designed to test this hypothesis.

Apparatus and Procedure.   The procedure of Experiment III was repeated, except that no area of the subject's skin was left uncovered. His head and face were covered with a heavy felt veil which hung loosely down over his chest, shoulders, and back and was prevented from touching his skin at any point by a headboard of insulite from which it was draped; his head was also covered by a felt hat.   The subject's arms were covered by rolled-down sleeves, thrust into the cuffs of wool-lined leather gauntlets which covered his hands.   Although in various preliminary tests this arrangement eliminated the tactual effect of air currents set up by an electric fan blowing toward the subject from a distance of 10 ft. and by the fanning movements of the experimenter's hand directly in front of the subject's face, the subject was able to hear through the veil with only a slight reduction in intensity.   Trials under conditions A and B, except for the differences noted, were performed as in Experiment III (see Fig. 12).

Results. Contrary to what would be expected from the cutaneous-pressure hypothesis, the results as summarized in Table I show that all four subjects were almost always able to perceive the obstacle both at a distance and close by. Although a limited impairment is indicated by the fact that the subjects were not quite so successful as in Experiment III, their performances were sufficiently good to demonstrate that a cutaneous type of stimulation (as by "air waves") is not a *necessary* condition for obstacle avoidance.[1] Furthermore, stimulation by air currents (*e.g.*, through the reflection of one's breath from an obstacle) cannot be a necessary condition for the close per-

FIG. 12.   Tests in Obstacle Perception.   Experiment IV.

The subject approaching the obstacle in Experiment IV, condition A.   Wearing the felt veil and head covering topped by a felt hat, with arm covering and gloves, he approaches the obstacle with every appearance of confidence and perceives it every trial.

ception of obstacles, in view of the fact that collisions were avoided at distances which, on the whole, differed but slightly from those of Experiment III.

In general, the results of Experiment IV corroborate those previously obtained, especially as concerns the superiority of the blind subjects.   As suggested above, comparison of the results with those for Experiment III suggests a partial impairment in sensitivity in some instances.   Thus, although E.S. was again superior to the others, his performance fell below his standard in Experiment III, as indicated by the act that his distance perceptions were shortened by 50 per cent and his close perceptions lengthened about 25 per cent

[1] A *necessary* condition is a requisite and basic condition in the absence of which the phenomenon (here, obstacle avoidance) cannot occur.

on the average, while the number of his collisions increased in series B. In contrast, the performance of M.S. was better than in Experiment III in all respects save collisions.

Discussion.   Although the results of this experiment indicate that the cutaneous effect of reflected air waves was not a *necessary* condition for perceiving obstacles by the subjects, further tests (see Experiment V) are required to find whether they are a *sufficient* condition.[1]   On the other hand, the results indicate that echoes of sound waves actually are a *sufficient* condition for the responses to obstacles. E.S. finally admitted his dependence on sound, through discovering that "making a little noise," as by scraping his stockings on the carpet under condition B, was necessary for getting "an impression of the screen."   M.S. reiterated his reliance on sound, and the behavior of both the normal subjects (*e.g.*, continuous scraping of feet) suggested a similar dependence.   Certain deficiencies in the scores, particularly in the general performance of E.S. and in the close perceptions of all subjects, might be attributed either to the loss of cutaneous cues or to a reduction in the effective reception of auditory stimuli through wearing the veil.   (To determine this special point, further experiments were undertaken.)   In this experiment, as before, a lack of consistency in the distance and close perceptions of the subjects suggests that the two appraisals of the obstacle depend upon sensory bases which are different at least in part.

Experiment V.   This experiment was directed toward answering three questions raised in Experiment IV: (1) Are reflected sound waves (either sensed tactually or heard) *necessary* conditions for the perception of obstacles?   (2) Are object-reflected air or sound waves which tactually affect exposed skin surfaces *sufficient* conditions for the perception of obstacles?   (3) Are the object-reflected currents of the subject's breath, effective tactually or through hearing, *sufficient* conditions for the close perception of obstacles?   In view of the fact that experimental conditions which would make possible the answer to the first of these questions would also be adequate for answering the

---

[1] A *sufficient* condition is one which is capable of producing the phenomenon under suitable conditions but is not "necessary" since the phenomenon presumably can occur in its absence.   Thus the odor of a wooden obstacle or the warmth of a radiator may be sufficient conditions for perceiving those objects without sight, but they are not necessary for such a perception.

other two, Experiment V was directed at question 1. It was decided that the complete elimination of audition should answer this question without incurring the technical difficulties of controlling possible cutaneous effects of sound waves. Because plugging the ears would also block nonauditory effects (*i.e.*, tactual stimulation) on the external meatus and the tympanic membrane, the outcome of this experiment could not be completely decisive for the auditory theory, although it would be crucial for the facial-pressure variant of the cutaneous-pressure theory.

Fig. 13. Tests in Obstacle Perception. Experiment V.
One of the subjects approaching the obstacle screen with ears covered in Experiment V, condition A. With his hearing reduced greatly in sensitivity, he walked toward the screen hesitantly and ran into it on every one of 50 trials, as did all of the subjects.

Apparatus and Procedure. For all tests in this experiment, the subject's ears were completely stopped with special plugs of the type used in mine-safety precautions, topped by beeswax and cotton-wool stoppers in the meatus and concha, a beeswax-cotton shield closely fitting the pinna, and over this two layers of cotton batting held in place by a pair of ear muffs lined with cotton wool. The entire device was held in place by the elastic bands of the regular blindfold. The subjects thus equipped could not hear the sound of their footsteps or an ordinary conversation. Except for the blindfold, the subject's face was uncovered and open to all types of cutaneous stimulation from air currents, reflected breath, and the like. The situation under condition A in this experiment is represented in Fig. 13.

Results. None of the subjects were able to perceive the obstacle under the conditions of this experiment. They all collided with the screen in every one of 100 successive trials, and were as completely lost in the A series as in the B series (see Table I). With contact of the feet on the carpet runner apparently serving as the only source of cues, all the subjects reported that they were "unable to hear," in spite of their walking with head thrust forward as if straining to do so. E.S. now walked with his hands held up "apprehensively" in front of him, and M.S. reported, "I cannot get any cues at all."

The results of this experiment may be taken as demonstrating that air and sound waves reflected to the skin of hands or face were not *sufficient* conditions for the perception of obstacles by these subjects.[1] The conclusion seems justified that "Aural stimulation, felt or heard, is a *necessary* condition for the perception of obstacles by our Ss. Under the conditions of this experiment we cannot determine whether pressure-stimulation from the external ear (meatus and tympanum) or audition is the necessary condition. Though willing to hazard the opinion that our Ss' failure to perceive the obstacle was due to the loss of audition . . . we have neither the right nor the desire to be dogmatic nor do we wish to transcend our results. A decision concerning this point can be reached only through further experimentation."[2]

A previous tentative conclusion that the distance and close perceptions derive from at least partially different sensory bases is not negated by the results of Experiment V, as might be thought at first consideration. The inability of the subjects to perceive the obstacle either at close range or at a distance indicates only that ear stimulation is a *necessary* condition for both, but does not mean that the distance and close judgments have precisely the same sensory basis. For example, the judgments might rest on auditory cues of different types, or one might depend on audition and the other on nonauditory

---

[1] One of the subjects, P.C., in some additional tests, was able to perceive the object when very close to it through the reflection of air from forcible breathing through the mouth. However, none of the subjects (including P.C.) could perceive the obstacle, even when very close to it when they breathed normally through the nose.

[2] "Experiments with deaf Ss having inner ear defects, who could serve without stopping their ears—thus leaving the meatuses and tympanums open to pressure stimulation—would be crucial." Such experiments were carried out in the second investigation, to be described.

pressure effects on meatus and tympanum. Such possibilities remained to be explored.

Experiment VI. In this experiment the investigators set out to test a possible objection to their conclusion from Experiment V, that reflected air and sound waves are not sufficient conditions for the perception of obstacles by the subjects. The question might be raised whether the failure of the deafened subjects to detect the screen was due to some deleterious effect of the loss of hearing on cutaneous perception. Although this might be considered a somewhat remote possibility, further experiments seemed desirable to investigate it. Experiment VI was therefore aimed at testing whether pressure stimulation of exposed skin might be a *sufficient* condition for obstacle perception when hearing is functionally intact although auditory stimuli are useless as cues.

Apparatus and Procedure. To eliminate usable auditory stimuli, a "sound screen" was used, a constant, continuous sounding tone of 1,000 cycles per second at moderate intensity, produced by an electrically driven tuning fork. This stimulus was delivered to both ears of the subject by earphones throughout each test, with the result that auditory cues from the obstacle were rendered useless although hearing was not functionally impaired. Any hypothetical interference with possible cutaneous facial cues through a complete blocking of audition thereby was ruled out. A failure to localize obstacles under these conditions could be due only to the elimination of necessary auditory cues.

Results. Without auditory cues, the subjects could not perceive the obstacle at any distance, but collided with the screen on every trial as in Experiment V. Because failure was complete under condition A, the even more difficult test of condition B was not run. The subjects behaved as in the preceding experiment, walking slowly and noisily, the blind subjects with hands held up before them, all subjects as if listening closely.

The experimenters conclude that the complete failure of obstacle-perception in Experiment V was not due to any secondary impairment of cutaneous perception through loss of hearing, but to the absence of indispensable auditory cues. In Experiment V such cues were eliminated through the deafening effect of the ear coverings; in Experiment VI through the masking effect of the sound screen. The previous conclusion thereby is strengthened, that auditory stimulation is a *necessary* condition and that air currents or sound waves which affect the skin are not *sufficient* conditions for obstacle perception.

Experiment VII. *Apparatus and Procedure.* In Experiment IV, a special felt covering of face, head, and hands eliminated the possibility that cutaneous-pressure stimuli (through air waves) might be responsible for obstacle avoidance. In Experiment VII the sound variant of the pressure theory was tested by eliminating sound waves that might stimulate exposed areas of skin and serve as cues, while permitting sound waves from the footfalls to reach the subject's ears. The critical experimental condition was obtained by placing the subject in a soundproof room and having him judge the experimenter's approach to an obstacle by means of the electrically transmitted sounds of the experimenter's walking. In his approach to the obstacle (the end wall of the hall) the experimenter held at shoulder height a microphone pickup through which the sounds of his leather shoes on the hardwood floor were transmitted by wire through a power amplifier to the high-fidelity headphones worn by the subject. In the successive trials under condition A, the experimenter walked toward the end wall from starting points ranging from 6 to 30 ft., as the subject himself had done in Experiment I.

The communication system was so arranged that the subject and experimenter could talk back and forth between trials, the experimenter could give "Ready!" signals, and the subject could make his reports directly to the experimenter. The experimenter walked at a moderately slow rate until the subject requested him to go even more slowly, as he did at points of critical judgment. After the subject had said, "There!" to indicate his distance perception of the wall, the experimenter stopped and recorded the distance. He then continued without a signal (to eliminate unwanted cues) until he had bumped the microphone against the end wall or until the subject had signaled a "close perception" of the wall by saying, "Stop!"—whereupon a second measurement was made. The situation of subject and experimenter in this experiment is shown in Fig. 14.

Results. As the summary of results in the table shows, the subjects made their distance and close perceptions about as effectively as in the control experiment (Experiment III) and did not "collide with the wall" very much more frequently than in that experiment. It is probable that the number of collisions would have been even smaller had the subjects been able to control the rate of the experimenter's

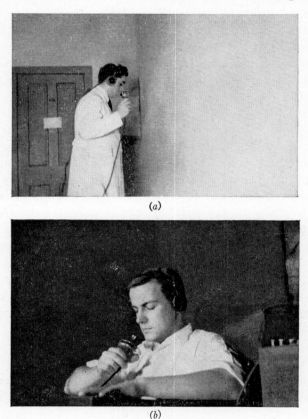

(a)

(b)

Fig. 14.   Tests in Obstacle Perception.   Experiment VII.

14a. The experimenter in Experiment VII approaching the obstacle wall with pickup microphone in his right hand at shoulder height.

14b. The subject, seated in a soundproof room, listens through high-fidelity earphones to the experimenter's footsteps, and speaks his "distance perception" and "close perception" over the phone system to the experimenter.

advance as precisely as they could control their own progress in Experiment III.   All subjects stated that the sounds of the experimenter's footsteps approaching the wall were different from the sound of their own steps as in Experiment IIIA.

In comparison with the results of Experiment III, the performance of E.S. was considerably poorer, whereas that of the other three subjects was only slightly different. The greatest loss for E.S. was in his close perception of the obstacle, which was 2.74 ± 0.34 ft. as against 0.50 ± 0.000 ft. in Experiment IIIA. On the other hand, the smaller sizes of his M. V.'s in Experiment VII (10.9 per cent as against 40.7 per cent in Experiment IIIA) suggests that the cues which served as the basis of his distance perceptions in Experiment VII were more constant in their effect, although weaker than in Experiment IIIA.

Discussion. The fact that the subjects were able to perceive the wall when auditory cues alone were available constitutes evidence that (1) sound-wave stimuli are a *sufficient* condition for obstacle perception in this situation, (2) cutaneous stimulation of exposed areas of skin is not a *necessary* condition for such perception, (3) both variants of the pressure theory are untenable, so far as they apply to exposed areas of skin, and (4) currents of air reflected to the subject from his breathing are not *necessary* conditions for the close perception of the obstacle.

Although these results confirm the conclusion of Experiment V that both the distance and close perceptions depend essentially upon auditory cues, they are not decisive with regard to the tentative conclusion from Experiments I to IV that these two judgments rest upon different sensory bases. The experimenters suggest that stimulation of the ears may involve pressure effects as well as audition, and that these effects might have different functions in the distance and the close perceptions. It is true that the subjects said that the principal basis of their judgments was audition, and that none of them at any time mentioned pressure; however, in such matters it is justifiable to regard the subject's comments as suggestive only and not as a necessarily valid item of evidence concerning what the cues actually were.

It is worth mentioning in this connection that in Experiment VII absence of the very high sound frequencies (*i.e.*, those above 12,000 cycles per second, which were not transmitted by the apparatus) was noticed and reported by the subjects. This fact suggests that the poorer performance of the subjects in Experiment VII (as compared with Experiment III) may have been due to the possibility that such high sound frequencies play a role of some importance in the perception of obstacles. As will be seen later, the results of the third investigation justified this interpretation.

GENERAL DISCUSSION OF THE FIRST INVESTIGATION

The results of this first series of experiments indicate that experienced blind individuals avoid obstacles in their path and thus guide their progress by responding to a pattern of reflected sound which may possibly be supplemented by ear-pressure effects. The complexity of the process is revealed by the fact that although the general nature of the cues was clear, the two blind subjects apparently utilized such cues in different ways. Thus M.S. ordinarily clicked his heels as he walked and asserted that he used auditory cues, whereas E.S. typically did not seem to need extra sound, and at first insisted that facial cutaneous cues were the basis of his judgments. However, the experiments yielded results which demonstrated that such cutaneous cues were not adequate guides for any of the subjects, and that all four subjects including E.S. needed auditory stimuli in order to avoid obstacles.

The initial ineptness of the sighted subjects in avoiding obstacles when blindfolded indicates that they, like most people, had never really begun the special process of perceptual learning which experienced blind individuals evidently master. If the sighted subjects had been individuals such as experienced woodsmen or night watchmen, who often have occasion to practice making their way about in the dark, different results might well have been expected. It would be interesting to know whether steamship pilots who frequently need to direct the immediate course of their vessels without visual cues, as in the fogs of Puget Sound, use the reflected sound patterns of their frequently used whistles much as blind persons depend upon sounds reflected from their footsteps.

SECOND INVESTIGATION: TESTS WITH BLIND-DEAF SUBJECTS[1]

PURPOSE AND GENERAL PLAN

Although the results of the first investigation demonstrated that the subjects were using sensory cues, and that these very probably were auditory stimuli, the latter point was not established beyond all question since the role of cutaneous cues affecting exposed surfaces of the outer ear was not altogether controlled in any of the experiments. The experiments of the second investigation, however, provided the basis for a crucial test of this question.

[1] Adapted from Worchel, P., and K. M. Dallenbach. "Facial Vision": Perception of Obstacles by the Deaf-blind. *American Journal of Psychology*, 1947, vol. 60, pp. 502–553.

For this test the experimenters decided to use subjects who were both blind and deaf but whose outer ears were intact and had normal cutaneous sensitivity. If blind persons without hearing should possess a good obstacle-avoidance capacity, this fact would indicate that the ear-cutaneous factor is a sufficient condition for the ability, and further investigations to establish the role of hearing would be essential.

Subjects. Ten blind-deaf persons were found (eight men and two women, ranging in age from thirty-four to fifty-five years) who possessed the qualifications judged essential for this investigation: although deaf, all had intact outer ear parts, and all were fairly active individuals who got about with some confidence, although clumsily. Thus they were likely to have learned to utilize all available sensory capacities to the full in their orientation. Their vision and hearing were examined by specialists. Most of them were found to be completely deaf and blind, and the others were judged sufficiently close to zero sensitivity in these sensory fields to serve as subjects. None had outer ear defects that might have affected cutaneous sensitivity in that region.

TESTS AND RESULTS

Tested under condition IA, the one most favorable to obstacle avoidance, these subjects made very poor scores in detecting the end wall, in complete contrast to the excellent scores made under this condition by the two blind-hearing subjects in the first investigation. Eight subjects collided with the wall in more than 33 per cent of the trials; four collided with it in more than 50 per cent. All subjects frequently collided with the wall before having made even a distance-perception report. With further trials, a few of them showed a limited improvement, but in all cases their scores were far inferior to those of the hearing-blind subjects in the first investigation.

Circumstances suggested that the limited success of some of these subjects was due to the use of special cues for judging distance, *e.g.*, to the use of floor irregularities to estimate the position of the starting point by means of foot contact. To test this hypothesis, the screen was used as the obstacle, and was placed in different positions on successive trials as in Experiment III. All of the subjects were poorer than before in every respect. When 25 "catch" trials *without the screen* were introduced at random, all except one of these subjects (F.B.) reported the obstacle as frequently as when it had been present.

These results indicate that in the absence of hearing there is no possibility of an obstacle perception at all comparable to that of hearing-blind subjects.

The only two deaf-blind subjects who had any success in obstacle avoidance, F.B. and M.St., had a slight degree of hearing, and both wore hearing aids. In further tests with M.St. involving random placements of the screen in the hall, it was ascertained that her first limited success was really due to the habit of walking about 10 ft. before reporting a distance perception, and 10 ft. more before reporting a close perception, *i.e.*, with her it was a matter of guessing. The results showed that she was not really helped by the hearing aid, except that it set her at ease and increased her confidence in moving about.

The really puzzling case was F.B., who had had some success throughout the tests up to the final one, described below. He objected to the pressures of the special light-tight blindfolds worn by the other subjects and would not permit his eyes to be taped or otherwise closely covered, complaining that unless his blindfold was loose there were distracting tensions and pressures which impaired his "facial-pressure sense." When tests were made in complete darkness he progressed very haltingly and collided with the wall on every trial, then objected to continuing, on the ground that darkness affected his nerves. At length a test was found to which not even F.B. objected. Trials were made in which F.B. approached the screen from varying distances and places wearing a special close-fitting cardboard blindfold which was open to light from above, but which was shielded otherwise so that no light would reach the eyes (even by reflection) from the obstacle. Wearing this device, F.B. had no more success in perceiving the obstacle at any distance than had any of the other blind-deaf subjects. He at last admitted that what he had always thought was "facial vision" must really be a very limited sensitivity to light.

THIRD INVESTIGATION: NATURE OF THE AUDITORY CUES IN OBSTACLE-AVOIDANCE BY THE BLIND[1]

Problem. After the second investigation had furnished conclusive evidence that auditory cues are responsible for the skillful avoidance of obstacles by blind individuals, a further study was conducted to

[1] Adapted from Cotzin, M. The Role of Pitch and Loudness in the Perception of Obstacles by the Blind. *American Journal of Psychology*, 1950, in press.

determine what characteristic of auditory stimuli may be critical for this ability.

Subjects.   Two blind and two sighted subjects served in these experiments.   One of the sighted subjects was P.C., who had participated in the first investigation.

Situation and general procedure.   The arrangement of the experimental situation resembled that in Experiment VII of the first investigation.   The subject, seated in a completely dark and soundproof room, was asked to judge the spatial relation to the obstacle of an experimentally produced noise reflected from the masonite obstacle screen in the distant experimental hall, and transmitted to him electrically.   His judgment was expressed specifically by his accuracy in moving the sound-source as close as possible to the obstacle, without collisions.

In different experiments, both noises and pure tones were used as critical stimuli.   The noise, a complex pattern of several frequencies all of equal loudness, was produced by means of a push-pull amplifier and amplified by the loud-speaker.   The pure tones were produced by means of an RCS beat-frequency oscillator, the frequency range of which was 30 to 15,000 cycles per second.   The sound used as stimulus was transmitted to the subject's earphones through a circuit leading from a microphone mounted below the loud-speaker at "ear height."   Both loud-speaker and microphone were attached to a carriage which moved smoothly and noiselessly along a wire track through the center of the experimental hall from one end to the other. The rate of movement of this carriage toward the obstacle was controlled by the subject through the use of a foot pedal.

Thus the subject made his close perceptions of the obstacle by "remote control," endeavoring to avoid "collisions" much as in Experiment VII, in which he controlled the experimenter's progress verbally. In the various trials of successive experiments with the noise and with several pure tones, four starting distances of 6, 12, 18, and 24 ft. between sound and obstacle were used in a haphazard order.   With the noise as stimulus, the judgments under these conditions were almost as good as in Experiments I and II of the first investigation, in which the subject himself moved toward the obstacle.   On this basis it was concluded that the apparatus and procedure were suitable for critical tests.   Preliminary series of trials were carried out, as in the first investigation, in which the inexperienced sighted subjects acquired the ability to perceive the obstacle with some accuracy under the conditions described above, and the blind subjects were demonstrated to have a high degree of skill in such obstacle-location.

Results. In the principal experiments of this investigation it was first desirable to determine whether the subject's judgments were dependent upon changes in intensity (*i.e.*, loudness) of the noise as the source approached the obstacle or receded from it. For this purpose, the threshold intensity (*i.e.*, the least intensity of sound necessary for hearing the noise) was determined at distances of 1 to 6 ft. from the obstacle. It was found that the intensity thresholds were the same for all these distances. This result indicated that perception of the obstacle under these conditions could not depend upon *intensity* differences of sounds reflected from it, for if intensity differences were critical, the intensity thresholds would have differed according to the distance of the sound-source from the screen.

To determine whether the obstacle-localization depended upon *frequency*, *i.e.*, pitch differences in the sound as the source was moved toward or away from the obstacle, pure-tone stimuli of particular frequencies were substituted for the noise.[1] On each trial, one particular tone of controlled pitch was used as the critical stimulus. By appropriate means, the different tones used for any subject on the successive trials of a series were held at constant loudness. The following frequencies were used: 128, 256, 500, 1,000, 2,000, 4,000, 8,000, and 10,000 cycles per second. Higher frequencies were not tested, since the apparatus—oscillator, loud-speaker, transmission, etc.—could not produce and transmit sounds higher than 12,000 cycles per second with fidelity.

The outcome was clear: all of the subjects, blind and seeing alike, were able to detect the obstacle at close range (typically at a distance of 1 ft. or less) when the tone of 10,000 cycles was used, but made poor and variable scores with the lower tones. With the 10,000 cycle tone as stimulus, both of the two blind subjects stopped the carriage very close to the obstacle in 40 out of 40 trials, and the two sighted subjects were successful in 39 and 37 trials, respectively, out of 40. With

---

[1] Oscillographic records of these tones, taken by a connection from the subject's earphones, showed that they were all "pure," *i.e.*, produced by sound waves of a single frequency.

tones of 8,000 cycles and lower, collisions predominated in most of the series, and in most of the relatively few successful trials the distances of close perceptions were considerably greater than with the 10,000 cycle tone.

The experimenter concluded that the most skillful avoidance of obstacles by the blind occurs when there is a reflection from them of very high tonal frequencies. Although an explanation of the superiority of the high-frequency auditory cue must await further investigations, it is considered likely that differences in the reflection and absorption of high and low frequencies by obstacles such as the masonite screen may be responsible for the results obtained.

General Discussion and Conclusions

These three investigations demonstrate very clearly that a solution to problems of this kind can be obtained only by means of precisely controlled experimental methods. The experimenters concluded that "auditory stimulation is both a *necessary* and a *sufficient* condition for the perception of obstacles by the blind," and that the cutaneous surfaces of the external ears are not sufficient for the perception of obstacles. The fact that active blind-deaf subjects, who lacked hearing but possessed intact outer ears with normal cutaneous sensitivity, could not avoid obstacles with any degree of adequacy but behaved much as had the blind-hearing subjects in Experiments V and VI when hearing was eliminated, demonstrates that the cutaneous factor is not a sufficient condition for obstacle perception. These results therefore point clearly to sound as the critical and necessary stimulus for the skilled avoidance of obstacles by the blind.

The results of the first investigation show that the blind efficiently make their way about through having developed a heightened perceptual responsiveness to sensory cues which are relatively ineffective in the orientation of most sighted individuals. That such performances actually represent complex learned acts of skill is indicated clearly by the manner in which both of the sighted subjects improved during the experiments in the first investigation. At first completely without competence in avoiding obstacles when blindfolded, both of them improved rapidly and soon acquired a considerable degree of skill in obstacle-avoidance without the use of vision. This skill was exhibited not only in perceiving the experimental obstacles from a distance but also in avoiding collisions when close by, although neither of the sighted subjects ever became as proficient as the blind subjects. It is quite probable that the superiority of the blind subjects over blindfolded sighted subjects would have been much greater if further tests had been made under the complex conditions of orientation in everyday situations, as for example in crossing streets and avoiding moving objects out of doors.

One rather impressive feature of the results was the manner in which they flatly contradicted the strong convictions of subjects, such as the blind E.S. and the deaf-blind F.B. in the first and second investigations, respectively, that their capacities depended upon some sort of "sixth sense" such as the term "facial vision" would suggest. Actually, the skilled object-avoidance of E.S. turned out to depend upon auditory cues, and the inferior performance of F.B. upon limited visual cues. A frequent practice in attempting to explain the many extraordinary phenomena of orientation in space is to postulate a "sixth sense" or a special "unknown direction sense" without having adequately investigated the functions of known senses. The elimination of "facial vision" as a new "sense," to account for the orientation of blind individuals, when that esoteric concept was tested in the investigations reported in this chapter, should suggest a measure of caution to those who prefer to answer difficult questions about human behavior by leaping at once to an occult type of explanation.

It should be mentioned in this connection that the term "sense" has been used in vague and misleading ways in discussions of orientation. "Unknown sense," as the expression is sometimes used in regard to orientation, should be interpreted to mean only the inadequately investigated sensory basis of an impressive known ability. Consideration of skilled obstacle avoidance in the spatial orientation of the blind supports this conclusion. The phenomenon is a striking and even spectacular one, and its basis has been obscure and subject to much speculation in the literature. However, when the problem was attacked by controlled experimental methods, it was shown that the sensory cues on which this orientation depends are furnished by a known type of sensitivity, namely audition, and that the hypothesis of a "sixth sense" is entirely unwarranted.

In addition to studies of spatial orientation in man, there have been numerous investigations of this ability in lower animals. As an example of the latter, an investigation of obstacle-avoidance in bats is reported below.

THE SENSORY BASIS OF OBSTACLE AVOIDANCE BY BATS

INTRODUCTION

The skill with which blind people avoid obstacles has its parallel in the amazing ability of many species of bats to fly at night through forest foliage or to negotiate the tortuous turnings of dark caves where it would seem that nonvisual cues of some kind must be depended upon. Although the problem has been the object of investigation since 1794 and numerous types of explanations have been offered, it is only in recent years and particularly in the experiments of Griffin and Galambos[1] that the question has received a convincing answer. Considered in relation to the foregoing experiments with human subjects, a brief summary of the principal results on bat orientation should serve to demonstrate even more convincingly that no mysterious kind of sensitivity need be postulated to explain these performances.

In bat orientation, as in the problem concerning the human blind, both auditory and cutaneous cues (*e.g.*, air currents on wing membranes or snout) have been hypothecated. One investigator found that bats strike obstacles when their ears are plugged, but not when other changes are made, such as blindfolding them or covering their wings. However, he had observed that a flying bat seldom makes any sound audible to man and was led by his observations to postulate that the basis of orientation was pressure effects upon cutaneous receptors in the ear. Eighteen years after the English physiologist Hartridge had suggested that bats in flight may emit extremely high-pitched sounds which, reflected from objects in their path, could serve as orienting and object-avoidance cues, Pierce and Griffin in 1938 demonstrated that bats actually make such notes during flight, as clicks or pulses of sound which appear in successive short bursts. With adequate recording devices, tones of frequencies from 30,000 to 70,000 cycles per second were picked up from flying bats. These very high frequencies are called "ultrasonic," since they lie considerably above the upper human threshold, which is as high as 20,000 cycles per second for

---

[1] Griffin, D. R., and R. Galambos. The Sensory Basis of Obstacle Avoidance by Flying Bats. *Journal of Experimental Zoology*, 1941, vol. 86, pp. 481–506.

many individuals but much lower for others.[1]   It remained to demonstrate that ultrasonic tones actually serve as orienting cues for the bats that make them.

THE EXPERIMENT OF GRIFFIN AND GALAMBOS[2]

Method.   Bats were made to fly through a barrier of parallel wires strung vertically from floor to ceiling so that the space between adjacent wires was 12 in. (a distance about 3 in. greater than the maximal flight wingspread of the bat species to be tested).   As the subject flew back and forth through the barrier, a count was kept of the misses and hits of wires (the latter being indicated by a clearly audible sound when wing brushed wire).   Thus a low percentage of hits meant high skill in object-avoidance.

A minimum of 50 trials was run with each of 144 normal bats, and with several subjects tested with eyes, ears, or mouth covered (*i.e.*, "blind," "deaf," and "gagged" subjects) before they were later tested in a normal condition.

Results.   Although the bats were somewhat groggy at the time because of an incomplete recovery from hibernation, the average for 144 *normal subjects* was 35 per cent hits (*i.e.*, contacts with wires). Twenty-eight of these subjects scored fewer than 25 per cent hits, and only seventeen of them had more than 50 per cent hits.   All of the normal subjects were considerably better in their scores than the 65 per cent level of hits which had been calculated mathematically in advance of the experiments as a *chance score*.   On these calculations, a score of 65 per cent would be made by bats flying through the interwire spaces used in these experiments without any means whatever of detecting the wires.   Moreover, slow-motion cinema records showed that in approaching the wires a bat would often modify its flight appropriately, as by folding its wings somewhat or by banking with vertically spread wings, thereby avoiding a collision.

Blinded subjects (eyes covered with a dark blue collodion preparation, noninjurious and removable after the test) were as efficient as normal seeing subjects in avoiding the wires.   When 28 bats of the same spe-

---

[1] Because the term "supersonic" is used increasingly to refer to speeds beyond the speed of sound, for the sake of clarity it is desirable to refer to "sound frequencies" above the audible human threshold as "ultrasonic" frequencies.

[2] Adapted from Griffin and Galambos, *op. cit.*

cies were tested under this condition, they scored 24 per cent hits; when tested as normal subjects, they scored 30 per cent hits. The difference was attributed to chance, and some nonvisual means of avoiding wires was indicated. In fact, most of the bats avoided wires more efficiently with eyes covered than when normal.

When 26 bats were *deafened* temporarily by stoppage of the meatus in each ear, their flight became abnormal, and obstacle-avoidance was drastically impaired. A group of 12 subjects averaged 34 per cent hits as normal fliers, but made 65 per cent hits when deafened. Another group of 17 subjects averaged 29 per cent hits when temporarily blinded, but their average was 67 per cent hits when both blinded and deafened. It will be noticed that these results for deafened bats were no better than the calculated chance score mentioned above. Clearly, the absence of hearing virtually destroyed the capacity for accurate orientation in flight. Deafened bats took to flight very slowly, then flew erratically, and when flying in an open room almost always came into head-on collisions with the walls. [The reader will be reminded of the similarity between this result and the finding with deafened (and blinded) human subjects.] It is clear from these results that the efficient avoidance of obstacles by bats depends in some manner upon auditory cues.

Hartridge had suggested that the effective sensory basis of orientation might be the ultrasonic utterances of the bats themselves when in flight. Such "cries" later were recorded from bats, in extremely short bursts lasting only about 0.002 sec., with 5 to 10 bursts per second from bats at rest, 20 to 30 per second from bats in flight, and 50 to 60 per second from bats approaching obstacles.[1] To stop such possible cues at the source (*i.e.*, to prevent the sound waves from issuing, being reflected from objects, and heard) the snout of each subject in a group of six bats was firmly closed with a loop of thread and a collodion seal, with nostrils open but lips tightly shut. This treatment raised the number of hits from 38 per cent to the chance score of 65 per cent on the average. "Gagged bats flew in the same clumsy hesitant and bewildered manner as deaf bats." From such subjects no ultrasonic utterances were detectable instrumentally; however,

[1] Griffin, D., and R. Galambos. Obstacle Avoidance by Flying Bats: the Cries of Bats. *Journal of Experimental Zoology*, 1942, vol. 89, pp. 475–490.
Also see Griffin, D. R. Supersonic Cries of Bats. *Nature*, 1946, vol. 158, pp. 46–48.

when a small opening was scratched in the collodion as a mouth hole ultrasonic tones were picked up by appropriate recording apparatus and the bats thus treated became able to dodge wires quite efficiently.

Discussion.   From the above results the authors conclude that

All this evidence points conclusively towards Hartridge's auditory theory in a slightly modified form which may be stated as follows: Flying bats detect obstacles in their path by (1) emitting supersonic (*i.e.*, ultrasonic) notes, (2) hearing these sound waves when reflected back to them by the obstacles, and (3) detecting the position of the obstacle by localizing the source of this reflected sound.   This localization is presumably accomplished binaurally by some auditory mechanism, similar in principal to that used by other mammals for sounds of ordinary frequencies.

The term "echolocation" has been advanced by Griffin to denote the use of reflected sounds in nonvisual orientation.   Although the sounds which are useful to bats in echolocation are considerably above the effective human range, it is clear that the abilities, as demonstrated in the foregoing experiments, have an auditory basis in both human subjects and bats.   As we know from the third investigation with human subjects, the skilled avoidance of obstacles by the human blind depends upon sounds in the upper ranges of human sensitivity.

Despite the similarity of sensory-and-response mechanisms, it appears safe to say that man's capacities for the acquisition of a wide variety of cues and for utilizing them in varied ways in space perception characteristically exceed those of lower animals—not because of a superior sensory acuity, but because of his resources for learning new cues and perceptual relationships.   The human blind use many obvious auditory cues such as the clicking of heels, tapping of canes, and listening for variations in traffic noises, and also various "minimal cues" that although important are difficult to identify.   There is little question that experienced individuals typically shift adroitly in the basis of their orientation, according to which auditory cues are most available and most useful under given conditions.   The further investigation of such matters represents a part of the general study of perceiving in which much work remains to be done.

CHAPTER X

THE FUNCTION OF THE BRAIN IN RELATION TO INTELLIGENCE

INTRODUCTION

It has been said that the problem of learning is the most important single problem in psychology. In a certain sense, Aristotle prophetically recognized this fact when he formulated his "laws of learning." For many centuries thereafter, the problem remained in the hands of philosophers and received no more than speculative attention until Ebbinghaus began his original and epochal experiments, shortly after 1880. Since that time, an important experimental literature has been developed from the investigation of conditions which are essential for efficient learning and retention. Later, the rapid development of animal psychology and child psychology as experimental subjects greatly broadened the study, particularly with respect to the theoretical understanding of learning.

That learning in a higher animal depends upon the setting up of changes in nervous tissue, and in particular upon changes in the brain, was widely assumed long before the experimental investigation of learning was undertaken. As a result, beginning even before 1840, an extensive knowledge of the structural and physiological characteristics of the human brain has been developed in neuroanatomy and related sciences. Although it was actually a general realization of the importance of the brain for behavior which led to these investigations, knowledge derived from them has not proved of much direct assistance in throwing light upon the manner in which the nervous system functions in learning and in retention. There have been no direct experimental studies of the neural changes which are brought about when learning takes place, although studies of reflex action and of the nerve impulse have excited great interest in the question. At present, psychologists have virtually abandoned "synaptic resistance," "drainage," and related hypotheses of a vague nature concerning the neural changes underlying learning, and new "leads" into the problem are developing from physiological studies on the brain as well as lower nervous centers. However, it cannot be said that any clear solution of the problem is discernible at the present time.

One helpful sign is the amount of knowledge which has been obtained as to the general function of the brain in behavior. Shortly before 1840, *extirpative experiments* (*i.e.*, experiments involving tissue destruction as the basic method) had been performed by Flourens and other physiologists on dogs and various other lower animals. Since that time there has been a series of investigations upon the sensitivity and the "mental capacities" of individuals with nervous injuries resulting either from experimental extirpation (as in lower animals) or from accident or disease (as in man). However, such investigations have yielded little useful evidence for the understanding of neural function in learning. Among the reasons for this deficiency have been the use of faulty operative techniques, inaccuracy in reporting both the amount and the location of brain tissue destroyed in a given operation, and the absence of adequate studies of the subject's abilities both before and after the operation. When experimentation is handicapped by such deficiencies, it is impossible to determine with precision the effect of brain-tissue injuries upon behavioral capacities.

However, an important contribution of these early experiments was to show the presence in the mammalian brain of certain cortical *projection areas*. The normal function of certain of these areas has been inferred from the fact that injury to them results in deficiencies in specific fields of sensitivity (*e.g.*, visual, auditory) or in motor deficiencies (*e.g.*, paralysis). Although the extreme doctrine of the phrenologists, that the brain is divided into many areas which control corresponding psychological "faculties" (*e.g.*, memory, morality, ambition, etc.), lost its scientific standing long before 1900, the existence of the projection areas has influenced many students to think of brain functions primarily as "localized." However, the doctrine of a cortical *association function* also arose as a consequence of the early brain investigations. That is, it seemed likely that different areas of the brain might work together in the same learning processes by virtue of their tissue interconnections. In their writings, most psychologists commonly treat this function rather vaguely, at least as regards the manner in which the brain performs it. To clarify such questions the need for a more direct attack upon the problem of brain function is very evident.

SYSTEMATIC EXPERIMENTAL STUDY OF BRAIN FUNCTION IN LEARNING

Shortly after 1900, a few psychologists began to experiment upon the problem of brain function. They were led into the work mainly by a growing interest in the nature and basis of the learning process. Chief among the early experimenters was Franz,[1] who in 1916 first interested Lashley in the question. Since then, Lashley has followed an organized program of research upon the problem and has succeeded in attracting a large number of research students to its investigation.

Lashley has investigated two problems in particular: First, the manner in which brain functions permit the learning and retention of particular habits; and second, which characteristics of the brain determine "intelligence," *i.e.*, the relative capacity of an animal for modifying its present behavior or for acquiring new behavior. He has consistently used the animal's learning ability as an indicator of its intelligence, studying in particular the effect upon learning ability of experimentally altering the brain tissue possessed by the animal. The present chapter constitutes a review of some of Lashley's principal findings.[2]

First of all, we should consider the principal variables which must be kept under control by any scientist investigating how the brain functions in the learning process, if he is to be successful in his experimentation.

1. It is important to know the *sensory control and the movements which are essential* to the particular habit to be learned. As for sensory control, this varies according to the nature of the problem which the animal must learn and also according to the setting in which this problem is presented. Under certain conditions, the mas-

---

[1] For a general summary of the problem see Marquis, Donald G. The Neurology of Learning, in Moss, F. A., ed., *et al. Comparative Psychology*, Chap. 7 pp. 153–177. New York, Prentice-Hall, rev. ed., 1942.

[2] Adapted from Lashley, K. S., *Brain Mechanisms and Intelligence*. Chicago, University of Chicago Press, 1929, and from more recent papers. For a summary and discussion of Lashley's work see Maier, N. R. F., and T. C. Schneirla, *Principles of Animal Psychology*, Chap. XIV. New York, McGraw-Hill, 1935.

tery of a habit may involve only one field of sensitivity (*e.g.*, vision alone), in which case we may speak of the habit as a "specific" one. In this sense, Lashley used the light-dark discrimination habit as a specific habit. Obviously, a blind animal would not be able to learn this habit, just as a deaf animal would be unable to learn a habit which specifically depended upon auditory control. On the other hand, when the mastery of a habit requires the availability of stimuli in two or more fields of sensitivity, we may speak of a "general" habit. For example, the learning and the performance of an elevated-maze habit have been found to require visual, olfactory, auditory, and perhaps other types of sensitivity as well.   Maze habits, characteristically, are of the general type.   In the same sense, a habit may be specific or general with respect to action: *specific* if one particular movement or series of movements alone will serve, and *general* if no one movement or movement series is indispensable for its performance.   In this chapter we shall be concerned mainly with the importance of brain function for *sensory control* in learning, attempting to determine whether there is a difference in brain function according to whether the animal learns a specific or a general sensory habit.

2. *The relative difficulty of the problem* which is used to test the animal's intelligence must be known and controlled, or the results will have little significance for the study of brain function.   In the studies to be reported, Lashley used the light-dark discrimination as a *simple* "specific habit," and the brightness discrimination as a *complex* (*i.e.*, more difficult) "specific habit."   In testing the formation of "general habits," he used three maze patterns of increasing difficulty.   *Difficulty of problem* was thus graded for both the specific and the general habits.

3. Another way in which to discover the importance of cerebral function for learning is to change in controlled ways *the amount of cortical tissue* possessed by the subject. Lashley studied this factor by operatively reducing for different groups of rats the percentage of intact cortex. Since he tentatively had adopted performance in learning given habits as a measure of "intelligence" by comparing the learning records of normal animals with that of various groups of cortically operated animals, Lashley hoped to find whether the intelligence of an animal would be reduced in accordance with the amount of cortex which remained.

APPARATUS

1. Specific (Visual) Habits. For the tests of simple and of complex specific habits a light-discrimination box was used (Fig. 15*a*). The rat was released into an enclosure, at the farther end of which he came directly toward the edge of a partition which separated two compartments. In the light-dark problem, which tested a *simple specific habit*, either compartment was lighted for a given trial while the other compartment was darkened. In the brightness-discrimination, which tested a *complex specific habit*, a light of different intensity was pre-

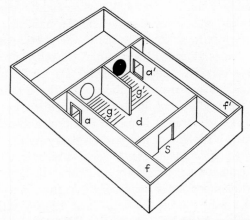

Fig. 15*a*. Apparatus Used for the Testing of Visual Discrimination Habits.

The rat starts from *S*, at *d* responds to the stimuli, and receives a shock at *g* (or at *g'*) if he turns to the "incorrect" stimulus. If the response is "correct," the animal is free to pass through door *a* (or *a'*), reaching *f* (or *f'*) where he receives food. (*Redrawn from Lashley.*)

sented through a round window at the end of each compartment. Side doors permitted the animal to escape from the apparatus after passing through either of the two compartments. The floor of both compartments was wired so that a shock could be given the animal when an incorrect response was made. (In later studies the "jumping apparatus," shown in Fig. 15*b*, has been used and has proved much more satisfactory than the discrimination box for the purposes of this experiment.)

2. General (Maze) Habits. In testing the learning of general habits, alley mazes of three degrees of complexity were used (Fig.

16). Maze I, the simplest of these problems, had a short true pathway with but one blind alley between starting point and food-box; Maze II, which was more complex, had a somewhat different true pathway with three blind alleys; and Maze III, which was the most complex of these mazes, had eight blind alleys, some of which turned off to right and some to left from the true pathway.

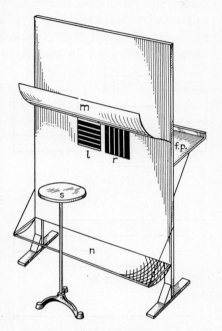

PROCEDURE

Procedures Common to All Tests. *Original Learning Tests.* In the five problems which were used (*i.e.*, the simple and complex visual problems, and the three maze problems of different complexity), hunger was the drive employed and food was the reward for each successful trial. First, each of the problems was given as a learning test, both to normal rats and to rats operatively deprived of part of their cerebral cortex. The training of the operated animals was started two weeks after they had been subjected to the brain operation. The normal and the operated animals were compared as to their efficiency in learning, on the basis of the total number of errors they committed in learning a particular problem, and also in terms of their trial-to-trial error scores.

FIG. 15*b*. "Jumping Apparatus" Used by Lashley to Test Visual Discrimination Habits.

The rat jumps from the stand *S* against card *l* or *r*. The "correct" card is loosely held in place so that it falls readily when the rat jumps against it, letting him pass through the opening to the food place (*f.p.*). The "incorrect" card is fastened securely so that the rat falls from it into the net (*n*). (*Rdrawn from Lashley.*)

Retention Tests. Each of the five problems was also presented as a retention test (*i.e.*, a test of memory) to normal animals as well as to animals which had been subjected to a cortical operation *after* they had learned the problem when in the normal condition. The purpose of this test was to discover how many trials were required and how many errors were committed by animals of the two groups in re-learning each problem.[1]

The Cortical Operation. The animals were operated upon under ether anesthesia. A hole was drilled in the exposed skull, and pre-determined portions of cortex were destroyed in each of the two hemispheres with an electrocautery. In the operation, from 1 to 50 per cent of the total amount of cerebral cortex was destroyed. All operations were bilateral (*i.e.*, in each case, both cerebral hemispheres were involved). In was arranged to have one or more groups of animals in which each of the principal areas of the cortex had been destroyed.

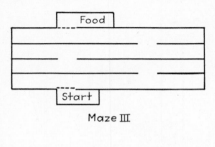

Maze III

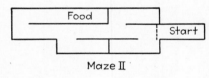

Maze II

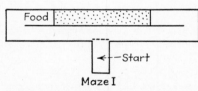

Maze I

FIG. 16. Maze Patterns of Graded Difficulty Used by Lashley in Testing General Habits. (*Redrawn from Lashley.*)

Two weeks after the operation, training was begun, provided that the animal had fully recovered. After the learning and retention tests had been completed, the animal was killed and a histological study (*i.e.*, a detailed examination of the cells and fibers) was made of its brain, in order to ascertain the exact amount of cortical or other nervous tissue which had been destroyed by the operation. The amount of tissue which had been effectively destroyed was measured by means of a special technique, and when corrected for surface curvature this amount was expressed as a *percentage of the total area of cortex.*

Procedures in Particular Tests. *Specific Habits.* In the light-dark discrimination problem, which was used to test the learning of a *simple specific habit*, each subject was given food after he had passed through the lighted compartment into a side alley and was shocked

[1] If the number of trials necessary to relearn a habit is smaller than the number originally required to learn this habit, the difference is interpreted as evidence of memory for the habit.

electrically when he passed into the darkened compartment. The lighted compartment was sometimes on the right side, sometimes on the left, in irregular order, so that the rat would be unable to solve the problem merely by learning a simple "position habit" involving constant entrance into the same compartment. For other rats, food was given after the rat passed through the darkened compartment, and shock was given in the lighted compartment. The trials were continued until the rat succeeded in responding to the "correct" stimulus at least 80 per cent of the time.

The same procedure was adopted in the intensity-discrimination problem to test the learning of a *more difficult specific habit*. In this

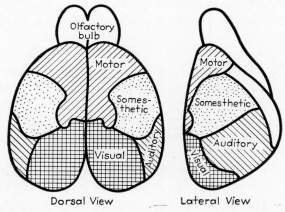

Dorsal View ——— Lateral View

FIG. 17. Schematic Views of the Rat's Brain to Show the Approximate Boundaries of the Projection Areas. (*Adapted from Lashley.*)

case, both compartments were lighted, with one light brighter than the other. Certain rats were rewarded after each response to the dimmer light, and shocked after each response to the brighter light. For other rats the reverse procedure was used.

The operated animals used in these specific-habit tests were deprived of given amounts of cortex within the "visual area" near the posterior pole of the cerebral hemisphere (see Fig. 17). As controls, certain other subjects used on these tests were deprived of cortex in various regions outside the visual area.[1]

[1] In other control groups, the destruction was effected in the subcortical neural center (*i.e.*, the lateral geniculate body of the thalamus) through which visual impulses from the retinas of the eyes reach the cerebral cortex.

General Habits. In the maze tests the normal and operated rats were made hungry and were given food at the end of each run through the apparatus. The criterion of learning, *i.e.*, the test of mastery of the problem, was 10 successive errorless trials. However, in the case of slow learners it was necessary to limit the number of trials given to any one animal. This limit was 60 trials for Maze I, 100 trials for Maze II, and 150 trials for Maze III. Both error and time records were taken for all maze trials.

The operated animals used in the general-habit tests were deprived of different amounts of cortex, ranging between 1 and 50 per cent of the original total. The operation was performed upon different parts of the brain in different individuals, so that each given locality on the surface of the brain had been removed in some of the operative cases.

RESULTS AND INTERPRETATIONS

Specific Habits (Simple). In their *original learning* of the simple specific habit (the light-dark discrimination), all operated rats considered as a single group required 80 trials on the average, whereas normal animals required an average of 107 trials to learn this habit. The operation on visual-area cortex certainly did not reduce the ability of rats to learn the specific habit used in this test.

The superior performance of the operated animals *cannot be attributed to a real superiority in their ability to learn*, but rather must be attributed to the fact that operated rats typically are much less easily distracted by incidental stimuli (*e.g.*, noises coming from outside the apparatus) than are normal rats. In other words, normal rats may be handicapped in simple problems by excessive response to such extraneous stimuli.

In tests on the *retention* of this simple habit, rats which had learned the problem with intact brains were deprived of varying amounts of cortex in the visual area before they were retested. These rats lost the habit as a consequence of the local operation. In contrast, the learned discrimination persisted in animals in which *cortex anywhere outside the visual area* was destroyed following the original learning. It is clear that although the *learning* of this simple "specific" habit was not impaired by any cortical injury, its *retention* was interfered with if the visual area of the brain was injured following original learning.

Further tests, however, have shown that the retention of this habit is not greatly interfered with unless visual cortex which receives impulses from the visual thalamus (a subcortical structure) is entirely destroyed.[1] The visual cortex may, therefore, be regarded has having a localized function (*i.e.*, a *projection* function), in that it serves as the "cortical inlet" of the visual system. Hence, the area is essential for the retention of a habit which specifically requires visual control. However, it should not be hastily concluded that cortical tissue within the visual area possesses *only* the projection function.

Specific Habits (Complex). From the test of the brightness-discrimination habit, which is a more complex specific habit, somewhat different results were obtained.[2] The *original learning* of this habit was retarded by the destruction of cortex in the visual area, although the same operations did not retard the learning of the light-dark habit. (In control experiments, lesions *outside* the visual area did not impair the learning of the brightness discrimination.) For this habit, the greater the amount of cortex destroyed in the visual area, the more retarded was the learning. The correlation coefficient, which indicated the closeness of the relationship between *retardation* in the brightness habit and *amount of destroyed tissue*, was $+.58$. From this it may be inferred that when a specific habit is complex (*i.e.*, fairly difficult), the *amount* of intact cortex is also a factor which affects the speed of its acquisition.

Similar results were obtained for the *retention* of the brightness-discrimination habit, in that the greater the amount of the visual-area cortex which had been removed following the original learning, the greater the reduction in the animal's ability to perform the already learned habit. Injuries localized elsewhere in the cortex had no effect upon the retention of this habit.

So far as these specific (visual) habits are concerned, cortical tissue in the visual area is thus found to have, as at least one of its functions, a specific importance for the learning and retention of habits which

[1] Lashley, K. S. The Mechanism of Vision. XII. *Comparative Psychology Monographs*, 1935, vol. 11, pp. 43–79.

[2] Lashley, K. S. The Mechanism of Vision. II. *Journal of Genetic Psychology*, 1930, vol. 37, pp. 461–480.

are dependent upon visual control.[1] Correspondingly, Wiley[2] has shown that the auditory area of the rat's brain (see Fig. 17) is essential for the retention of simple habits which depend specifically upon auditory control, and that no other area of the cortex has this particular function.

In this connection it should be mentioned that the motor areas of the cerebral cortex possess a projection function which we may term the "motor-outlet" type. When cortical tissue in this frontal area of the brain (see Fig. 17) is destroyed, partial paralysis will occur. There may also be incoordination in general activities, such as locomotion (as Maier[3] found), and the animal may be impaired in the retention of habits which specifically depend upon motor control (*e.g.*, a problem-box habit).

The possibility that the projection function may not be the only function of so-called "projection" cortex is supported by results from experiments such as that of Kirk[4] in which it was discovered that for rats, when a specific habit becomes very difficult (as when an F is to be discriminated visually from an Ⅎ), lesions anywhere in the cortex retard both learning and retention. A comparable result for problem-box learning was obtained by Lashley,[5] who tested rats with varying degrees and locations of cortical destruction in their ability to learn a series of five problem boxes. In each of these boxes the operation of a particular different type of latch fastener would permit the subject to escape from confinement and obtain food. The cortically operated animals made poorer records than did normal animals on three of the five problems. The degree of their inferiority in these problems was not significantly related to the *location* of cortical injury, but was found to be correlated with the *extent* of cortical lesion.

---

[1] This statement is, of course subject to the reservation that the original learning of very simple visual habits, such as the light-dark habit, does not appear to be affected by visual-area injuries, although their retention is affected by such injuries.

[2] Wiley, L. E. The Function of the Brain in Audition. *Journal of Comparative Psychology*, 1932, vol. 54, pp. 143–172.

[3] Maier, N. R. F. The Cortical Area Concerned with Coordinated Walking in the Rat. *Journal of Comparative Neurology*, 1935, vol. 61, pp. 395–405.

[4] Kirk, S. A. Extra-striate Functions in the Discrimination of Complex Visual Patterns. *Journal of Comparative Psychology*, 1936, vol. 21, pp. 145–158.

[5] Lashley, K. S. Studies of Cerebral Function in Learning. XI. The Behavior of the Rat in Latch Box Situations. *Comparative Psychology Monographs*, 1935, vol. 11, pp. 5–42.

The relationship between an inferior performance in the problem situation and the amount of cortex lost was indicated by correlation coefficients ranging between $+.48$ and $+.72$. The significance of this fact will become evident in the subsequent treatment of results for "general" habits.

General Habits (Simple and Complex). In *learning* maze habits operated rats were always significantly retarded as compared with normal rats. For instance, in learning Maze III, normal rats required an average of 19 trials, whereas operated rats required an average of 91 trials, and the error totals of all operated rats were significantly

TABLE I

The Relation between the Percentage of Cortex Destroyed and the Number of Errors during Learning

Per cent of cortex destroyed	Average total number of errors committed in learning (4–11 rats per group)		
	Maze I	Maze II	Maze III
0 (normals)	⎰7.3	₁⎰16.2	47.4
1–10	₁⎱6.6	⎱15.4	72.0
11–20	⎱7.2	40.0	266.0
21–30	31.8	43.5	396.0
31–40	29.3	63.2	485.0
41–50	34.7	52.8	580.0
50+	40.0	66.6	1446.0

[1] The operated animals obtain an artificial advantage in these error averages in that Mazes I and II were not learned in certain cases within the training limits, which were set too low.

greater than were the error totals of normal rats. For the three mazes, a comparison of the results for the various groups of normal and of operated rats may be made from Table I.

It is evident from these results that the retardation in original learning was greater, the larger the amount of the cortex which was injured. That *the amount of cortex lost is the condition which determines retardation in complex learning* was shown by a correlation coefficient of $+.75$ between amount of destroyed cortex and the degree of retardation in maze learning. On the other hand, in the learning and retention of general habits, the locus of destroyed cortex appears to be of indifferent importance.

The last point, that the ability to learn and to retain general habits depends upon the amount of intact cortical tissue, is particularly emphasized by a comparison of the results for the three mazes. It will be recalled that Maze I was designed to be a relatively simple problem, Maze II to be intermediate, and Maze III to be the most difficult. From an examination of Table I it becomes apparent that the operated rats in any given group had less difficulty in learning Maze I than in learning Maze II and clearly had their greatest difficulty in learning Maze III. For instance, rats which had lost 50 per cent or more of their cortex learned Maze I with an average total of 40 errors but committed 1,446 errors on the average in learning Maze III. In further studies by other investigators, general problems of great difficulty (or very difficult specific habits) have been presented to rats with extensive cortical destructions, and the subjects have been totally unable to make any progress in learning the required habits. This reminds us of the fact that human idiots and imbeciles are limited to the acquisition of very simple habits, and that such individuals are completely unable to cope with problems which are easily solved by other individuals.

The above results were substantially duplicated in *retention* tests on maze habits which had been learned prior to cortical operation. The extent to which the operations interfered with retention was greater, the greater the amount of the cortex which was destroyed after original learning had occurred. Here also, the location of the injury was of no detectable importance; the extent of the injury was the essential factor. These results thus support the previous findings in showing that the correlation function (*i.e.*, the general associative function) is nonlocalized with respect to brain areas.

Investigation of the Specific-pathway or "Storage-center" Hypothesis of Nervous Changes in Learning. It is a popular theory of learning that what is acquired is "stored" in certain parts of the brain, even in particular brain cells. This assumption is sometimes found in psychological treatments of learning, in the form of assertions that the process of mastering a habit occurs by effecting changes in specific pathways in the brain, and that after learning has occurred, given neurones have the particular function of carrying the impulses which appropriately arouse the learned movements.

Two features of Lashley's experiments are sufficient to weaken materially, if not to destroy, this view. First, it will be recalled that a given injury (*e.g.*, destruction of 30 per cent of cortex) had the same effect upon a general habit, regardless of where the cortex was destroyed.   The neural changes effected by the maze habit were definitely not "stored" in particular parts of the brain, but apparently involved living tissue throughout the brain.   Second, in experiments with animals which had learned Maze III, Lashley disconnected the various areas of the brain in different cases by means of long or short cuts through the brain tissue.   Thus, in one experiment or in another, all of the possible tracts of association fibers which might conduct impulses among the different brain areas were severed, but only negligible amounts of cortex were destroyed.   After their recovery, these animals were tested, but they did not show any retardation in the habit.   Since this result is good evidence that the neural changes essential to a given habit are not restricted to arousal through any particular fiber pathways, Lashley concludes that correlation cannot be "... expressed in terms of connections between specific neurones."

DISCUSSION

The results of Lashley's experiments on *specific habits* agree with the findings of other investigators in showing that the brain possesses a "projection" function which is localized in given areas.   Thus, the retention of the light-dark discrimination habit was impaired by injuries anywhere within the visual area, but injuries to cortex outside of the visual area had no effect upon retention of this habit. In a recent study, Lashley has shown that this simple specific visual habit is lost entirely when the visual cortex which has fiber connections with the visual thalamus is entirely destroyed.   From the results, it is reasonable to conclude that the projection functions of certain cortical areas (the visual, the auditory, the somesthetic) consist in the fact that through certain layers of neurones in these "sensory-inlet" areas, impulses from the corresponding sensory systems (*i.e.*, the related sense organs and subcortical nervous centers) gain access to the cortex.   The case appears to be similar for the "motor-projection area," as the center through which cortical impulses are discharged to lower centers of the nervous system.

The *retention* of the light-dark discrimination habit was not impaired by cortical destructions outside the visual area, apparently because in the case of a simple habit of this specific type the correlation function is required only to a minor extent. As has been said, this fact contrasts with the finding of Lashley and others that rats which have learned very difficult specific habits (*e.g.*, pattern-vision habits) are impaired in their retention of the habit, whether the cortical injury lies within or outside the visual area. Furthermore, the discovered habit impairment is greater, the larger the extent of the cortical injury. Such results show that for efficient performance a habit which is sufficiently difficult involves all uninjured brain areas, regardless of whether the habit is specific or general in its sensory control. This suggests the existence of a second cortical function which has essential importance for intelligence.

In the case of a *general habit*, such as the maze habit, the greater the amount of cortex removed, the less efficient are rats in their learning and in their retention of the habit. Furthermore, since for different animals the injury of equal amounts of cortex in different parts of the brain produces equal retardations in the learning or retention of the maze habit, the cortex as a whole (or all intact cortical tissue) is essential for most efficient learning, and no particular area is more important than is any other area. *Intelligence, defined as the capacity for modifiable behavior, may therefore be regarded as a function of the entire cortex.* This, substantially, is the meaning of Lashley's *theory of mass action*.

A brief reference to the anatomical relations of the brain areas will give further point to these remarks. Each of the sensory-projection areas (*e.g.*, the visual area) is connected by fiber tracts with a correspondingly different part of the thalamus, and through these cortical areas the respective sensory systems discharge impulses into the cortex. Thus, the projection area in question (*e.g.*, the visual area) has a specific importance for a habit which requires one *specific* type of sensory control, as visual control is required for the light-dark habit. Extensive destruction of cortex within the particular projection area will thus impair or prevent the performance of the corresponding specific habit. On the other hand, destructions outside the given projection area have no noticeable effect if the habit is very simple. In contrast, when a habit is complex and difficult, regardless of whether it is specific or general in its sensory control, the destruction of *any* part of the rat's cortex impairs its performance.[1] *The projection function is localized, whereas the correlation function is nonlocalized. The entire cortex, including the projection areas (which thus have two functions), participates in the correlation function.* This, apparently, rests upon the fact that all parts of the cortex are interconnected in every conceivable way by tracts of "association" fibers, the cell bodies of which comprise the bulk of the cortex itself. The different cortical areas are termed "equipotential" with respect to the correlation function, since in this function they participate similarly and with approximate, if not complete, equality in their importance.

Lashley believes that his conclusions as to the relation of cortical tissue to intelligence (*i.e.*, general capacity for learning) in rats may be applied to all animals which possess cortical tissue. "*Data on dementia in man,*" he says, "*are suggestive of conditions similar to those found after cerebral injury in the rat.*" That is to say, by actually destroying considerable amounts of cortical tissue in rats, Lashley produced rats which, in their greatly reduced intelligence, were equivalent to human individuals who become reduced in intelligence because of nervous degenerations occurring at some time after birth. Perhaps the comparison may be extended to include *amentia* (*i.e.*, feeblemindedness) as well. The principal difference is that in the case of human amentia, the defective intelligence is attributable to a nervous equipment which is inadequate for learning, not because of tissue destruction or deterioration but apparently because of fundamental shortcomings in the original development of the individual.

Although various objections have been raised to applying the massaction theory of intelligence to man, the effectiveness of such objections is materially reduced by the fact that they are not based upon thoroughgoing investigations comparable to those made upon the rat. For instance, one criticism is based upon the finding of clinical

---

[1] An effective demonstration of correlation function in the tissue of the visual projection area of the brain has been accomplished by Tsang, who blinded a group of rats in their infancy, then tested the animals as adults in the maze. In these animals, destruction of the cortical visual area at a time well before the maze tests resulted in a marked decrease in maze-learning ability. This decrease was much the same as was obtained from normal sighted rats after equivalent brain operations but was considerably greater than that shown by blinded rats with intact brains. (Tsang, Y. The Functions of the Visual Areas of the Cerebral Cortex of the Rat in the Learning and Retention of the Maze. *Comparative Psychology Monographs*, 1934, vol. 10, pp. 1 56; *ibid.*, 1936, vol. 12, pp. 1–41.)

neurologists that the degeneration of tissue within certain local areas of the cortex in man generally is accompanied by correspondingly different disturbances in language function (*i.e.*, *aphasia*). Those who object to applying the mass-action theory report themselves unable to understand how, according to that theory, a certain brain area could become more important than others for the control of a generalized language function in the individual. However, because of the relatively uncontrolled conditions under which the human evidence is gathered, it is quite possible that the results of injuries in projection areas (which we know are marked by particular kinds of defects, specifically sensory or motor in nature) have been stressed at the expense of the unrecognized or less apparent general retardations produced also as a result of these and other cortical injuries. It is unfortunately true that the evidence which is presented in the literature on aphasia is confused and, therefore, contributes little at present to the solution of the problem of brain function.

On the other hand, it should be mentioned that many contemporary investigators of aphasia have indicated their skepticism concerning the validity of any strict "cortical-localization" view of aphasic disorders. Thus in a leading source book on the subject, Weisenburg and McBride[1] have offered a classification of the principal types of aphasia which reduces the list essentially to *receptive, expressive*, and *mixed* aphasic patterns. Such a view involves no essential contradiction of the discussion of cortical function offered in the present chapter, since "receptive" types of aphasia may be interpreted as cases in which specific sensory-projection factors *predominate*, "expressive" types as cases in which motor-projection factors *predominate*, and "mixed" types as cases in which qualitatively different cortical functions are involved, not identifiably sensory or motor and frequently with a heavy emphasis upon what we have called "correlational" (*i.e.*, organizational) function.[2]

[1] Weisenburg, T., and K. E. McBride. *Aphasia*. New York, Commonwealth Fund, 1935.

[2] Lashley recently has reported experiments in which attempts were made to produce in monkeys a specifically "receptive" type of difficulty which is somewhat comparable to the traditional "visual agnosia" (*i.e.*, failure of perceptual recognition of objects) by destroying the portions of the pre-striate (visual) cortex most likely to have visual-associative functions. Specifically, the destroyed areas of cortex were those which corresponded most closely in their anatomical relations to the areas which have been thought responsible

The fact that under proper training procedures aphasic patients can regain their language and symbolic functions or can improve greatly in these functions shows that the psychological effects of damage to the various alleged "language areas" in the human brain need not be permanent. These results encourage caution against any dogmatic adherence to an oversimplified view of "strictly localized" cortical functions and suggest that the "equipotentiality principle" of brain function may apply even in connection with the cortical control of language functions in man.[1, 2]

Perhaps the generalized (*i.e.*, the correlation) function of the human brain will remain obscure until adequate tests of the patient's learning and thinking capacity are made *before* a brain injury occurs, are repeated *after* the brain injury reaches its height, and the study is completed with a thorough investigation of the condition of the brain after death. Until we have made as careful and thorough a study of man or some other higher primate as Lashley and his collaborators have made of the rat, dogmatic conclusions are unwarranted. It is better to leave the question open for the present, so far as man is concerned. However, we should not forget the probability that a line of evidence which has thrown light upon the nature of cortical function in one mammal may do the same for the others, which also possess cerebral cortex.

---

for "visual agnosia" in man. However, in a variety of postoperative tests the subjects were not found inferior to normal subjects in their recognition of objects, of form and movement, of distance, and of color. The experimenter found only that the cortically operated monkeys showed "some deterioration of higher level functions which are doubtfully visual, and this not consistent for all animals." (Lashley, K. S.   The Mechanism of Vision.   XVIII.   Effects of Destroying the Visual "Associative Areas" of the Monkey. *Genetic Psychology Monographs, 1948, vol. 37, pp. 107–166.*

[1] Granich, L.   *Aphasia: A Guide to Retraining.*   New York, Gruen and Stratton, 1947.

[2] Halstead, W. C.   *Brain and Intelligence.*   Chicago, University of Chicago Press, 1947.

CHAPTER XI

ORGANIC NERVOUS DISEASES IN RELATION TO BEHAVIOR

INTRODUCTION

Physiologists and psychologists have long known that it is the nervous system which makes integrated behavior possible, and that a sound nervous system is a prerequisite for the proper functioning of the entire human being. Thus, a healthy nervous system is essential to the normal operation of *the vegetative processes*, such as digestion, respiration, circulation, and excretion; *the sensory-motor processes* (sensation and movement); and *the so-called "higher" or "mental" processes*, such as thinking, intelligent action, adjustment to the social environment, and the like. For this reason disturbances in the functioning of the nervous system may cause serious abnormalities in behavior.

Injury or disease of the vegetative (*i.e.*, the autonomic) nervous system may be revealed in various kinds of malfunctioning, mainly of the viscera, which manifest themselves in numerous disorders of the glandular, vascular, respiratory, genitourinary, and gastrointestinal systems. Sensory-motor disturbances derive from disorders of the cranial and peripheral nerves, the spinal cord, the brain stem (*i.e.*, medulla, pons, midbrain, basal ganglia), the cerebellum, and the cerebrum. Such disorders are revealed in sensory disturbances and in disturbances in the integrated and balanced action of the various motor organs of the body. Personality disorders and disturbances in memory, sequential thinking, social adjustments, and the like are associated primarily with the malfunctioning of higher brain centers, in particular, of the cerebral cortex, whether this malfunctioning be due to disease, injury, or some other cause.

The initial problem of the neurologist is to determine the locus and nature of the disturbance in the nervous system. This *diagnosis* is based upon the concrete behavior abnormalities (*i.e.*, the *symptoms*) which he observes in the individual patient. After the diagnosis has been made, the neurologist is generally in a position to cope with the problem of treatment and cure.

It has frequently been said of neurology that no other branch of medicine lends itself so well to the correlation of symptoms with the diseased structures underlying them.   Nevertheless, the neurologist must exercise the greatest thoroughness and care.   First, he must adequately observe and record important aspects of the patient's behavior, such as the nature and distribution of reported pain; the existence of anesthetic areas; abnormalities of the reflexes; disturbances of gait, posture, and speech; and disorders of emotional and intellectual responses.   In the second place, he must obtain a complete "case history."   This consists of a family history and an account of the patient's previous life, of the mode of onset of the symptoms, and of the course and development of the illness.   A correct diagnosis requires a proper evaluation both of the patient's history and of his symptoms.   For the adequate performance of this task the neurologist should be trained both in the medical sciences and in psychology.

In what follows, a brief account will be given of the pathology and symptoms of a few important disorders of the nervous system.[1] Behavior disorders for which no organic basis is known will not be treated in this chapter.

ACUTE ANTERIOR POLIOMYELITIS (INFANTILE SPINAL PARALYSIS)

Pathology.   Infantile spinal paralysis is an intense inflammation which is almost wholly limited to the *ventral* (*i.e.*, the anterior) *horns of the spinal cord*, the region of the gray matter of the cord which contains the cell bodies of peripheral motor neurones.   The pathology of the disease can be followed by referring to Fig. 18.   The inflammatory process typically attacks the ventral-horn cells at certain levels of the spinal cord and destroys these cells more or less completely.   In certain cases, both the left and right ventral horns of a given level are affected; in other cases, the disease is confined to only one side of the cord.   When both sides are involved, the disease process is usually asymmetrical; that is, it affects one side more seriously than it does the other.   The inflammation causes the afflicted

---

[1] Of the several textbooks of clinical neurology which have been consulted, the one most utilized in the descriptions of the nervous diseases discussed below is Wechsler, I. S. *Textbook of Clinical Neurology*, 6th ed.   Philadelphia, Saunders, 1947.

motor cells to swell, and if the inflammation is severe, these cells presently disintegrate and disappear. The *degeneration of the cell bodies is followed by that of the associated processes* (axones and dendrites), since no nerve fiber can continue to live after its cell body has been destroyed. Subsequently these neurones are replaced by connective-tissue cells. In the course of time there is an *atrophy* (*i.e.*, a shrinkage) *of the ventral* (motor) *roots* of the spinal nerves on the levels of the cord which are affected. This atrophy results from the disappearance of the axones, the cell bodies of which, before they were

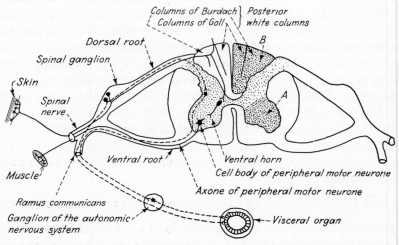

Fig. 18.   Diagram of a Cross Section through the Spinal Cord, Showing the Neural Elements Most Commonly Affected in *A*, Acute Anterior Poliomyelitis (Infantile Spinal Paralysis), and in *B*, Tabes Dorsalis.

destroyed, lay in the ventral horns of the gray matter. The *spinal nerves* also *atrophy* extensively because of the degeneration of the axones which formed their motor component. Similarly, there are changes in the muscle cells on which the motor neurones terminated when these neurones were intact. The *muscle cells* of each muscle which these neurones supplied *dwindle in size and weaken* as a result of disuse (since they cannot be aroused to a state of contraction by neural action), and also because these cells develop trophic (*i.e.*, nutritional) disturbances. Therefore, *each affected muscle as a whole undergoes a process of degeneration.* Occasionally the inflammation spreads up the cord and involves the motor nuclei of certain of the cranial nerves, in which case there may be paralyses of the ocular, facial, and tongue muscles, with difficulties in swallowing. The meninges[1] also may be somewhat affected. If the inflammation destroys the respiratory and cardiac centers in the brain (specifically, in the medulla oblongata), the patient dies.

Infantile spinal paralysis occurs mainly in epidemics, although "sporadic" cases also happen. It is primarily an affliction of childhood. It is most common between two and four years, and is practically unknown in infants younger than six months. But adults are sometimes stricken, and when they are, the form of the disease is usually more severe than it is with children, the mortality rate is higher, and the degree of recovery of function considerably less. After one attack, there is usually immunity, but cases of reinfection sometimes occur.

It has been ascertained that the cause of the disease is a filterable virus which so far has proved highly resistant to destruction. The virus enters the body by way either of the nasal passages or of the gastrointestinal tract and may be transmitted through the saliva or the nasal secretions, through the stools, or possibly through an intermediate host (*e.g.*, flies). It is claimed that a recent tonsillectomy may predispose to the disease, especially in the form of high spinal and cranial nerve involvement.

Symptoms. After an incubation period of 2 to 10 days, the disease proper is usually preceded by a *short prodromal* (*i.e.*, preliminary) *period*.[2] The main symptoms of acute anterior poliomyelitis may be discussed under five headings.

1. The initial muscular weakness rapidly increases and within a

---

[1] See description of the meninges and Diagram *B* of Fig. 21 on p. 199.

[2] The *prodromal period*, when it occurs, lasts from a few hours to a few days. Its characteristics vary considerably so that it often passes unobserved or is mistaken for a mild general infection. The patient may show any of several symptoms (such as a slight degree of fever, poor appetite, vomiting, diarrhea, redness of the throat, coughing, headache, restlessness, or drowsiness), or he may complain of vague pains in the limbs or at the back of the neck.

Following the prodromal period, one to several days may elapse with the patient apparently well. This, however, is followed by a *meningeal period*, signaling the onset of the spinal disease. At this time the mild inflammation of the membranes covering the spinal cord (see Fig. 21, Diagram *B*) may cause some rigidity of the neck and generally an exaggerated sensitivity.

few hours or a few days the maximum of *paralysis* for the given case is reached.   Since neural impulses cannot reach the muscles of which the pathways of innervation have been destroyed, the paralysis is of a *flaccid* (soft and limp) type.   The muscles are "lumpish" and lacking in tonus.   The paralysis usually invades a large group of muscles, generally of the extremities.   Thus, a limb or a part of a limb may be paralyzed, or one arm and one leg, both legs, both arms, or even all four limbs.   The precise region of the paralysis is always determined by the location of the diseased nervous tissue.   If, for example, the paralysis is limited to a leg, one can infer that the destructive process was confined to the lumbar[1] section of the cord and to only one side of the cord, the side of the paralyzed leg.   The muscles of the back may be affected and, more rarely, the neck muscles.   Occasionally the abdominal muscles are paralyzed.   As has been pointed out, when the disease process extends to high spinal levels and to certain cranial nerve nuclei, there may be paralyses of the diaphragm, and of the eyes, face, and tongue.   The patient dies if the centers of the cranial nerves controlling breathing and heart action are destroyed. After the maximum degree of paralysis has been reached (usually only 24 to 48 hr. after the onset of the disease proper), the inflammatory process begins to abate and the disturbed functions begin to improve.   The degree of improvement possible depends of course upon the number of neurones in the affected parts of the nervous system which were not irreparably damaged by the disease process.

2. The *reflexes* (*e.g.*, knee-jerk and ankle-jerk) which are exhibited by healthy limbs *disappear in the paralyzed members*.   This loss is due to the fact that the motor component of the reflex arc has degenerated and is therefore nonfunctional.

3. All through the acute stage of the illness, *pains* are frequently reported, especially when the affected parts of the patient's body are passively moved by an attendant.   The patient also commonly shows a general *hypersensitivity*.

4. In a short time, the *paralyzed muscles* begin to *shrink in size* because of trophic disturbances and lack of exercise.   This muscular

---

[1] The *lumbar section of the spinal cord* is the region which gives rise to the spinal nerves 21 to 25 inclusive.   (In all there are 31 pairs of spinal nerves which are numbered consecutively from those nearest the head to those farthest from it.   For further information about the spinal nerves, see footnotes 1 and 2, p. 202.)

atrophy is progressive, as may be seen clearly by comparing the healthy with the paralyzed limb of a crippled adult who was stricken in childhood with anterior poliomyelitis.

5. Subsequent to the disease, but associated with the paralysis, there frequently occur a *stunting of the bone growth* in the affected parts, *changes in the joints and circulation*, and *deformities*. The characteristic gait of many who have been afflicted with infantile spinal paralysis derives from inequality in the length of the legs due to atrophy of the bones in the paralyzed one. The deformities arise also from the overaction of healthy muscles which are unopposed by their paralyzed antagonists.

Prognosis[1] and Treatment. About 5 to 10 per cent of the cases, especially those with laryngeal, pharyngeal, cardiac, and respiratory symptoms, die during the active phase of the disease. Mild cases recover fairly rapidly, the acute symptoms ordinarily subsiding after a week or two. As has been said, the maximum damage is shown in the paralyses present after the acute stage has passed. Then begins the gradual process of recovery, which may continue up to two years or longer, depending both on the severity of the original inflammation and on the intelligence and skill with which the case is managed. The final recovery may be partial or, as in the majority of cases, complete, *i.e.*, without residual paralysis.

Various medical treatments are applied both to alleviate the symptoms and to combat the disease process during its active phase. Protracted rest in bed is considered very important. In the attempt to reduce the paralysis, warm applications, gentle massage, and passive movements are started almost immediately after the very acute period has subsided, although the patient must be restrained from walking or using his limbs too soon or too energetically. Warm baths are also given.

It is frequently true that, although most of the cells have been destroyed in the ventral horns at a given level of the cord, a certain number of cells remains intact. It follows that, although the degeneration of the greater part of the motor cells has caused the paralysis of a muscle or a group of muscles, some individual muscle fibers or even some small muscles in the affected group can be made to contract through the agency of such motor neurones as may have escaped

[1] A "prognosis" is a prediction of the probable course and outcome of a disease.

permanent injury.   By means of appropriate tests, the physician is able to detect the presence of those incomplete activities of which the afflicted muscles may still be capable.   On the basis of such an analysis, when the patient is adjudged ready for it, he may be "reeducated" in the performance of certain movements by practicing them separately and persistently under medical guidance.   Such practice can be undertaken under recreational conditions (*e.g.*, swimming in a warm water pool, bicycling), or in an occupational or creative work situation (as in working the treadle of a sewing machine, weaving, etc.).   In this way, also, the atrophy of muscles (chiefly as a result of disuse) may be markedly reduced.   But enormously valuable as such reeducational methods are, they of course cannot restore functions which depend on the integrity of tissues that have been permanently destroyed. Therefore, although the functions of a severely afflicted limb may be largely recovered through reeducational techniques, the limb may never regain its full capacities.

In the effort to minimize or avoid deformities, light braces and supports are sometimes used.   Orthopedic operations in the treatment of deformities are now far less frequently performed than they formerly were.   Since recovery of function, especially under a program of guided exercise, may continue for as long as 2 years after the acute attack, such an operation, even if desirable, should not be performed before the end of that period.

SYRINGOMYELIA

Pathology.   Syringomyelia is a chronic, slowly progressive disease which involves principally the spinal cord, but frequently also all of the central nervous system anterior to the spinal cord, except the cerebrum and the cerebellum.   The pathologic process (see Fig. 19) consists in the *development of a cavity* (syrinx) *or cavities which form around the central canal of the cord.*   The result is a *destruction of those neural elements which lie close to the central canal in the gray matter of the cord.*   Hence, *the earliest seat of destruction is the pain and temperature fibers which cross to the opposite side of the cord via the anterior commissure* (adjoining the central canal) to form the long ascending lateral spinothalamic tracts.   The destruction of the pain and temperature pathways is limited to the vicinity of the cavity. Then, as the destruction advances, the cavity becomes larger and encroaches upon the *ventral motor horns of the gray matter of the cord*. The pathologic process usually first attacks the cord at its upper levels, in the cervical enlargement.[1]

Subsequently, the destruction may take many forms. But the resulting abnormalities in behavior are always closely correlated with the location, extent, and form of the cavity or cavities. A given syrinx may extend up and down the cord through a great many segments. It may reach the medulla and include the nuclei of certain cranial nerves. It may progress dorsally and cut through the posterior white columns, thus interrupting the route for afferent impulses from

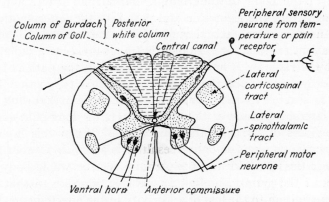

FIG. 19. Diagram Showing the Location of the Tracts of the Spinal Cord Most Commonly Involved in Syringomyelia.

kinesthetic and tactual receptors which are situated below the region of destruction. It may extend laterally and destroy the lateral corticospinal pathways, so that descending impulses from the motor area of the cortex can no longer reach the motor cells of the spinal cord. But the essential feature of the disease is a combination of (1) destruction of the pain and temperature fibers in the anterior commissures of certain segments of the cord, and (2) destruction of the ventral horns of approximately the same segments.

The cause of syringomyelia is not known, but it is thought to arise

[1] The cervical enlargement is a relatively thickened portion of the spinal cord. It extends from the point of emergence of the fourth cervical nerve to that of the second thoracic nerve, inclusive. (The positional relationships of the several divisions of the spinal nerves are described in footnotes 1 and 2, p. 202.)

from a congenital neural defect which is revealed by abnormality in the development of the central canal of the spinal cord. The disease usually afflicts adults and may drag on for 30 years or longer.

Symptoms. Since the pain and temperature fibers of a limited segment are almost always the first to be affected, the earliest symptom is generally a *loss of pain and temperature sensations in the skin areas corresponding to the diseased level of the cord.* These affected areas of the skin are usually restricted at first to the fingers, hands, and arms. They commonly occur on both sides of the body, *i.e.*, on both arms, since the anterior commissures contain fibers which cross from the left side of the body to the right spinothalamic tract, and fibers which cross from the right side and pass into the left spinothalamic tract. In most cases, tactual sensitivity is unimpaired. The blindfolded patient can tell, for example, that he is touching a radiator but not that the radiator is hot. In the beginning, the patient is characteristically unaware of the decrease in sensitivity, so that he frequently is scalded, burned, bruised, or cut without knowing it. A marked lateral extension of the syrinx affects the long pain and temperature fibers of the spinothalamic tracts. When this lateral extension occurs on one side only, the result is a *Brown-Séquard sensory disturbance* (loss of pain and temperature for the whole body below the level of the syrinx), limited to the side opposite to that of the syrinx, in addition to the loss of sensitivity in the affected segments on both sides of the body.

Associated with the neural disorders, there are *trophic and circulatory disturbances* in the affected parts. The latter disorders are responsible for the bluish or reddish appearance of the skin and probably underlie the patient's complaints of numb, tingling, and cold sensations in the involved areas.

The chief motor symptoms result from the slow process of destruction of the ventral horns. These symptoms are, first, *erratic twitchings and tremors* of muscles or parts of muscles (usually in the fingers and hands), and then *paralysis and atrophy* (the gradual process of muscular wasting as a result of lack of exercise). In time, the atrophy may extend to the arms and shoulders. The affliction of the ventral horns in syringomyelia produces the whole complex of symptoms which are typical of acute anterior poliomyelitis. If the lateral corticospinal tracts are involved, the muscles of the body below the corticospinal lesion become paralyzed. This paralysis is not a soft and flaccid one, accompanied by atrophy (as is the case in all afflictions of the ventral horns), but a *spastic* (*i.e.*, stiff and rigid) *paralysis* in which there is no atrophy. The neurological ground for the difference in the character of the paralyses resulting from damage to the ventral horns (*lower*

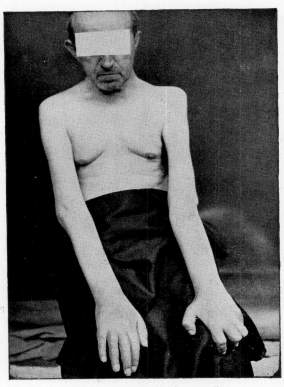

FIG. 20. A Case of Syringomyelia.

The patient shows the muscular atrophy which results from afflictions of the ventral horns of the spinal gray matter. (*Courtesy of Dr. L. V. Lyons, New York.*)

motor-neurone paralysis) and from corticospinal tract lesions (*upper motor-neurone paralysis*) is not entirely understood.

Prognosis and Treatment. As far as cure is concerned, the prognosis for syringomyelia is unfavorable. In certain cases, the symptoms remain unchanged for a long period of time, so that the course of the disease seems to be arrested. But, characteristically, the disease progresses slowly, the symptoms increase in severity, and the patient becomes more disabled as the paralysis grows. If the cranial nerve nuclei which are found in the medulla oblongata are afflicted, there result such disturbances as tremors of the tongue and facial muscles, atrophy of the tongue, paralysis of the muscles which control eye movements, difficulty in swallowing, regurgitation, and paralysis of one or both vocal cords. If the cavities involve areas of the nervous system which control the functions of the intestines and bladder, or if the cardiac or respiratory centers in the medulla oblongata become seriously involved, death soon ensues. Syringomyelia may last 20 or 30 years or even longer, with the patient finally succumbing to some complicating disease (*e.g.*, pneumonia, tuberculosis) which he is especially liable to contract because of his general condition of debility.

As regards treatment, there is no known remedy which will arrest the development of the disease, although good results have sometimes been reported from the application of X rays to the spine at the level of the syrinx. Spinal surgery has occasionally beeen performed for the purpose of facilitating such X-ray treatment and also in order to evacuate the syrinx. The symptoms are treated as they arise. The trophic disturbances and the paralysis are treated as in infantile spinal paralysis, but for the sensory losses no remedial measures are known.

MENINGITIS

Pathology. Meningitis is an *inflammation of the meninges* (*i.e.,* membranes or coverings) *of the brain or cord, or both.* Figure 21 presents diagrams of these membranes in relation to the brain and to the spinal cord. Three membranes cover the brain and spinal cord over their whole extent; these are the *pia mater* (closest to the brain or cord), the *arachnoid*, and the *dura mater* (the outermost of the three). The pia and arachnoid lie very close together, but they are separated by a space (the subarachnoid space) in which the cerebrospinal fluid circulates. This space is continuous with the four ventricles (*i.e.*, cavities) of the brain, which are situated deep in the brain tissue. Thus, just as the meninges form one continuous structure, the subarachnoid space and the brain ventricles constitute a single communicating system within which the cerebrospinal fluid is contained. It follows that an acute bacterial inflammation which starts anywhere along the membranes is apt to spread throughout their entire extent.   Any one of a variety of agents may be responsible for the inflammation, but the signs and symptoms of a meningitis are much the same, irrespective of the causative factor.   The symptoms depend chiefly on the locus and extent of the nervous tissue affected, and less clearly on the specific type of invading organism (whether

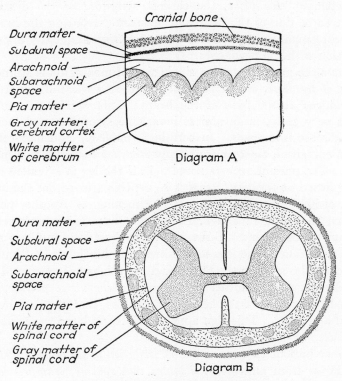

FIG. 21.   Diagrams of the Meninges.

Diagram A.   Frontal section through the skull, meninges, and brain.
Diagram B.   Cross section of the spinal cord and meninges.

meningococcus, tubercle bacillus, or some other agent).   When the meninges are invaded by organisms and their toxins, there is an inflammatory reaction in which many of the bacterial products are poured into the subarachnoid space, with a resulting increase in the volume of the cerebrospinal fluid.   Almost always, one can find an early increase in the amount and pressure of the cerebrospinal fluid and can detect the presence of microorganisms within it.   The best means of determining both the occurrence and the type of meningeal infection is by an examination of the cerebrospinal fluid, which is obtained by a puncture of the spine.   This puncture is usually made in the lumbar[1] region.

Symptoms.   *Headache,* the earliest symptom of the disease, is thought to be due to the increased pressure exerted on the brain by the cerebrospinal fluid.   *Dizziness* and *vomiting* frequently appear in association with the headaches.

Perhaps the most important single sign of meningitis is stiffness or *rigidity of the neck,* which probably is due to the inflammation of the meninges at the base of the brain.   This rigidity of the neck appears very early, is an almost invariable symptom, and increases as the disease progresses.   In certain forms (*e.g.,* epidemic cerebrospinal meningitis), *the neck is* actually *stretched backward* to a marked degree.   The patient reports acute pain if the leg is extended at the knee or flexed at the hip (*Kernig's sign*); this arises from the inflammation of lumbar and sacral roots and meninges.   Another peculiar symptom is *Brudzinski's sign:* the patient lies on his back and the physician bends the neck forward on the chest; the result is an involuntary flexion of the legs at the knee and hip joints, so that both legs become flexed upon the thighs and the thighs become flexed upon the abdomen.   Still another symptom is a *convulsive posture,* characterized by arching of the body backward so that the patient rests on head and heels.   This sign appears relatively late in the course of the disease.

In every patient there are *signs of irritation of the motor apparatus.* These range from *muscular twitchings and spasms, cramps, tremors,* and the like, to *generalized convulsions.*   In addition to these marks of irritation of the motor system, there are *paralytic phenomena* which occur later than the foregoing signs.   These paralyses result from the involvement of the motor cortex; they are spastic (*i.e.,* stiff and rigid) in type and may be very extensive or may affect only limited groups of muscles.

As the disease begins to involve the cranial nerves at the base of the brain, new disturbances appear.   A *paralysis of the eye muscles* (both internal and extrinsic) is revealed, first by *irregularity in the*

[1] See footnote 2, p. 202.

size of the pupils, later by sluggish pupillary reaction, and finally by complete *loss of pupillary reflexes*. *Cross eyes, squint,* and *double vision* are also common.

Fever is another very early and very constant symptom; it is low in certain forms of meningitis and high in others. A *slow pulse* is often the result of irritation of the vagus center (inhibitory to heart action) in the medulla.

A *hypersensitiveness to visual, thermal, tactual, and auditory stimuli* is common; it is undoubtedly due to irritation of the sensory cortex and of the nuclei of the optic and acoustic nerves.

Rashes and *skin eruptions* are frequently present.

So-called *mental symptoms* are almost invariable in meningitis. Early in the disease, these consist of restlessness, irritability, apathy, and drowsiness. The more serious symptoms which occur later are delirium, insomnia, stupor, and coma.

Associated with these signs and symptoms are many others which occur more or less commonly in meningitis. But for a general diagnosis of the disease, the especially significant early signs are headache, neck rigidity, vomiting or a convulsion, fever, and the Kernig sign. Such a picture calls for an immediate puncture of the spine for an examination of the cerebrospinal fluid, in order to determine the specific cause of the meningitis so that proper treatment can be initiated.

Prognosis and Treatment. Any one of a number of agents may be responsible for an acute meningitis (*e.g.*, the meningococcus, the pneumococcus, streptococcus, tubercle bacillus, syphilis spirochete). Both the prognosis and the course of treatment of each case depend upon the nature of the specific causative factor.

In the past the treatment of acute meningitis, for the most part, was unsatisfactory and often futile. The mortality was very high, complications were frequent, and in those who recovered permanent defects (*e.g.*, gait disturbances, noises in the ears, deafness, cross eyes, mental deficiency) were fairly common. At present, although tuberculous meningitis still does not respond to treatment, almost all other types do, and therefore are considered much less grave conditions than they formerly were. Epidemic cerebrospinal meningitis, caused by the meningococcus, now is successfully treated by the prompt and vigorous use of the sulfonamides (sulfathiazole and sulfadiazine, usually the latter). Other types, especially pneumococcus meningitis, yield more easily to penicillin therapy.

TABES DORSALIS (LOCOMOTOR ATAXIA)

Pathology. Tabes is a chronic progressive syphilitic disease of the nervous system. An understanding of the pathology may be facilitated by consulting Fig. 18. The disease affects the *spinal ganglia* and the *dorsal roots which lie between the ganglia and the cord.* It frequently spreads to the *rami communicantes* (which connect the spinal cord and the autonomic nervous system). The disease ascends from these tissues and causes a selective *degeneration in the posterior white columns of the cord* (the columns of Goll and Burdach). Only very rarely are other parts of the spinal cord involved. The degenerative process often extends to certain lower brain centers, where the curious selectivity of the disease is again shown by the fact that it almost always attacks the *nuclei of the optic nerve and of the nerves which supply the ocular muscles,* and only infrequently the nuclei of other cranial nerves.

Although the only cause of tabes is syphilis, only a small percentage of syphilitics ever shows tabetic symptoms. It is not known why some syphilitics develop tabes while the majority does not. Tabes usually occurs late in the course of syphilis, from 8 to 15 years after the initial infection.

Symptoms. The symptoms of tabes are clearly correlated with the disturbed condition of the specific structures involved. These symptoms may be divided into four general groups.

1. *Pain* is almost always a prominent symptom, because of the sensory disturbances which result from the infection of the spinal ganglia and dorsal roots. The site of the pain depends directly on the particular ganglia and roots involved. If the disease is at the lower cervical and thoracic[1] levels, the patient reports pains in the arms. If the lumbar and sacral roots[2] are affected, the pain is localized in the legs. The pains are sometimes acute but transitory

---

[1] The *cervical* section of the spinal cord is the section which lies closest to the head. It gives rise to spinal nerves 1 to 8 inclusive. The *thoracic* section lies between the cervical and the lumbar sections; it gives rise to spinal nerves 9 to 20 inclusive.

[2] The *lumbar* section of the spinal cord which lies immediately below the thoracic section gives rise to spinal nerves 21 to 25 inclusive. The *sacral* roots are the roots of the spinal nerves 26 to 30 inclusive. The sacral nerves, together with the 31st (the *coccygeal* nerve), emerge from the lowest part of the spinal cord.

and are described as "shooting" pains; at other times, they are both intense and lasting. "Girdle" pains which encircle the body at one or another level are common. The location of the girdle always corresponds to the distribution at the skin surface of the spinal nerves the dorsal ganglia of which are diseased. When, as frequently happens, the disease spreads to the rami communicantes, acute visceral pains, known as "crises," occur. These are abrupt in their onset, and after lasting from a few hours to a few weeks, disappear suddenly, only to recur again and again. Depending upon the level at which the rami communicantes are involved, the crisis may be localized in the rectum, bladder, or sexual organs (if the lowest roots are affected), in the larynx, pharynx, salivary glands, or tear glands (if the disease process extends to certain of the cranial nerves), but most frequently, the site of the crisis is the stomach, and the patient suffers not only from pain, but also from retching, vomiting, inability to retain food, and consequent emaciation.

2. *Ocular disturbances* result from the involvement of the motor cranial nerves (which control eye movements and the pupillary reflex to light) and of the optic nerve (which mediates vision). Thus, a lesion in the fibers underlying the pupillary light reflex produces the *Argyll Robertson sign*, in which the *pupils* do not react to changes in light, but do respond in convergence[1] and in accommodation.[2] In addition, the pupils are frequently contracted, irregular in outline, and unequal in size. Involvement of the nerves which control the movements of the eyeball itself results in the *paralysis of some or all of the six extraocular muscles*, so that the eyes can be moved only in certain directions or not at all. These paralyses usually are unequal in the two eyes. The patient often reports *diplopia* (seeing single objects double). The ocular paralyses may also cause a form of *strabismus* ("cross eyes") and *ptosis* (drooping eyelid). When the disease attacks the optic nerve, as it usually does, there ensues a gradual *impairment of vision* (the loss being first for colors, later for brightness), a decrease in the size of the visual field, and ultimately, blindness in most cases.

3. A *disturbance of the sense of position, movement, and vibration*

---

[1] *Convergence* is the process by which the eyeballs are automatically turned in toward the nose in adjusting for the seeing of near objects.

[2] *Accommodation* refers to automatic adjustments in the shape of the lens for the seeing of objects at different distances.

results from the destruction of the posterior columns (the columns of Goll and Burdach). This symptom, which is invariably found in tabetics, is due to the fact that the posterior columns contain the ascending tracts which convey impulses from receptors in muscles, tendons, and joints to higher centers in the brain. If the patient's eyes are closed, and a limb is raised or lowered or moved sideways by the physician, the patient will not be able to report the direction of the movement. If a tuning fork is held to the surface of the skin, he will be unable to detect its vibration. A disturbance of reflexes is shown by a *reduction or loss of knee-jerks and ankle-jerks*, reactions which depend for their occurrence on the presence of intact pathways through the dorsal roots and the posterior columns of the cord.

4. Because of the fact that the patient is partially or completely insensitive to changes in position and movement, *ataxia* develops. Ataxia is a loss of the power to coordinate voluntary movements. It may arise from any one of several causes, but in tabes it is due to the failure of impulses from muscles, tendons, and joints to reach the brain centers for coordination. The ataxia is almost always first manifested only in the lower extremities, the upper limbs being affected later. There is marked insecurity in walking, and a flinging about or flopping of the legs and feet. The feet are advanced irregularly and stiffly. The toe is turned upward and when the foot descends, it does so with a thump upon the heel. Moreover, the foot is raised abnormally high at the end of each step. The tabetic patient is less ataxic when his eyes are open, which is the reason why he closely watches his feet and the ground on which he walks. The tabetic sways markedly when he is simply standing still with his eyes closed (*Romberg's sign*). In fact, all motor acts of the voluntary type are jerky, uncoordinated, and lacking in precision. The ataxic gait which results from tabes is shown in the photographs of Fig. 22.

Symptoms of *trophic disorders* are often present. These arise from disturbances of the sympathetic division of the autonomic nervous system, by way of the syphilitic invasion of the rami communicantes. Of the trophic disorders in tabes, the most frequently encountered are afflictions of the joints (often resulting in deformities), as well as "spontaneous" fractures and perforating ulcers (especially of the soles of the feet).

"Mental symptoms, aside from the general mental change in a person who is afflicted with a chronic, progressive, and ultimately incapacitating and hopeless disease, do not occur in tabes . . . ,"[1]

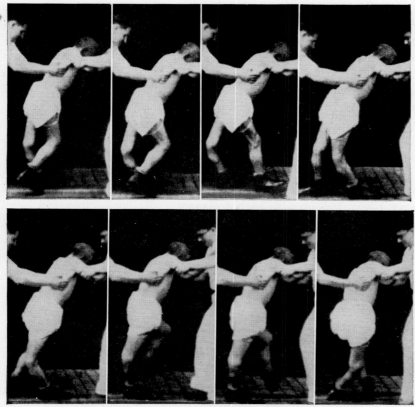

FIG. 22. Locomotion in Tabes Dorsalis.

The patient shows the tabetic gait, with severe ataxia and marked muscular weakness. (*Reproduced from photographs in the possession of Ernst Herz, M.D., by courtesy of Dr. Herz and of the King's Crown Press, publishers of Ernst Herz, M.D.; and Tracy J. Putnam, M.D.*, Motor Disorders in Nervous Diseases, *1946.*)

but constitute a prominent feature of paresis, also a syphilitic disease of the nervous system, which is described below.

Prognosis and Treatment.   Tabes is a gradually progressive disease. With the passage of years, the patient typically becomes increasingly incapacitated by the ataxia and by the pains, especially if these in-

[1] Wechsler, *op. cit.*, p. 460.

volve "crises." He often has recourse to the use of one or two canes, in time is limited to "locomotion" by wheelchair, and ultimately becomes bedridden.

There is no known cure for tabes. In the attempt to prevent the development of tabetic symptoms in syphilitic patients, it is customary to continue the antisyphilitic treatment until the blood Wassermann test for syphilis becomes negative and until examination of the spinal fluid shows no evidence of invasion of the nervous system by the *Treponema pallidum*, the syphilis spirochete. The likelihood of arresting the progress of the disease by the use of the usual antisyphilitic drugs (*bismuth*, *mercury*, or the *arsenicals*) is greater early in its course than when the disease has done extensive and irreparable damage. However, cases in which there is atrophy of the optic nerve often respond poorly to these drugs; in fact, in many cases acceleration of the atrophy and a more rapid advent of total blindness have been attributed to such treatment. Recently, *fever treatment*[1] has been used in tabes as it has in general paresis, but the success with the former condition has not been striking.

In the treatment of the tabetic pains, the usual analgesic drugs are used. Since these only control the symptom and do not cure the underlying cause, they must be administered often. But for the gastric crises, there are no known drugs or treatments which yield even appreciable temporary relief.

Nor can the ataxic process be reversed. Once the neurones have been destroyed, they cannot be regenerated and therefore there is no structural basis for a restoration of function. It is true that there are cases of even bedridden tabetics who have learned to walk again as a result of special retraining methods. The beneficial effects achieved by such methods depend not only on the physician's skill, but in large measure on the patient's learning to conquer fear and shame, to use more efficiently whatever intact nerve fibers have remained, and in the performance of his movements to rely more than do normal individuals upon stimuli which are not kinesthetic in nature (*e.g.*, visual stimuli).

GENERAL PARESIS

Pathology. General paresis is a disease of the nervous system which characteristically progresses gradually; if not treated it is

---

[1] See pp. 212–213.

usually fatal, although its course is often marked by periods of arrest of the symptoms or even of improvement. The cause is the same as that of tabes dorsalis, that is, the invasion of the nervous system by the syphilitic spirochete (*Treponema pallidum*). However, in tabes the infection is confined in the main to the spinal cord; whereas the brain, primarily the cerebrum, is the focus of the disease in paresis.[1] The disease usually appears between the ages of thirty and fifty, but is far from unknown at earlier and later ages.

The essential features of the disease consist (1) of *inflammation of the meninges, especially those of the brain* (see Fig. 21), and (2) of a *diffuse inflammation and degeneration, mainly of the brain, but to some extent of the cord and sometimes of certain of the cranial nerves.* Paresis involves the actual destruction of nervous tissue by the syphilitic organism and the poisoning of nervous tissue by the by-products of the infection. The most characteristic feature is an atrophy of the convolutions of the brain, especially in the frontal and parietal lobes, because of the damage to the cortex and to the nerve fibers. In some areas of the cortex the gray matter becomes extremely poor in cells. On the surface of the cortex there is a marked increase in the number of supporting (nonnervous) cells, forming a dense fiber meshwork.

The meninges of the brain—the dura mater, the pia mater, and the arachnoid—are always affected, all three of them showing thickening. The dura becomes adherent to the cranial bones (*i.e.*, the skull), and the pia and the arachnoid to the cerebral surface (*i.e.*, to the cortex).

Degenerative changes are also found in lower brain areas, such as the cerebellum and the nuclei of certain cranial nerves. The cranial nerve nuclei which are most frequently attacked by the syphilitic process are the cells of origin of the fibers which mediate vision and hearing and which control movements of the eye muscles.

The spinal cord is frequently involved by the infection of the posterior white columns (the columns of Goll and Burdach) and of the lateral corticospinal tract (see Fig. 19).

A common effect is *hydrocephalus*, a condition in which the quantity of cerebrospinal fluid is excessive, either because of a too rapid accumulation of the fluid or its failure to circulate at the normal rate.

When the paretic neural pathology includes degenerative changes

[1] As was pointed out in the discussion of *tabes dorsalis*, it is not known why only about 5 per cent of syphilitics develop syphilis of the nervous tissue.

which also occur in tabes dorsalis, *i.e.*, involvement of the posterior white columns and of the optic nerves, the disease is known as "taboparesis."

Other pathological signs exist, but they are not found as regularly as are those that have been described.

Symptoms. As a result of the diversified and widespread character of the pathologic processes in the nervous system, the symptoms are numerous and varied.

Certain of the symptoms are important primarily as clinical signs of brain damage. Among these are *ocular disturbances*, involving pupillary disorders and paralyses of the extraocular muscles, very similar to those seen in tabes dorsalis and deriving from the affliction of the same cranial nerves as in tabes. However, the optic nerve is less frequently involved in paresis and therefore optic atrophy and blindness are less common than in tabes. *Convulsive or paralytic attacks*, though not invariable, are very common, especially late in the course of the disease. The convulsion may occur in any part of the body, but usually it is generalized. It may last from a few minutes to a half hour, may be mild or severe, may occur as a single episode or be repeated again and again at short intervals. Sometimes the attack takes the form of a paralysis, either partial or complete, which usually disappears within a few hours or days; late in the disease, however, these paralytic attacks are followed by permanent impairment of movement.[1] *Abnormality in speech and writing* is very characteristic of paresis. Speech tends to become tremulous, slurred, marked by elisions and stammering. Writing, too, usually has a tremulous quality and shows omission, doubling, and transposition of letters. Certain features characteristic of tabetic handwriting are shown in Fig. 23. Thus, as a result of the irreparable damage to the neural structures underlying the language functions, the symbolic skills of the paretic patient are gravely impaired and his processes of communication and of organized thought disrupted. If the spinal cord (including the posterior columns), as well as the brain, is extensively involved, the symptoms include the disappearance of the ankle and knee reflexes, the Romberg sign and ataxia, bladder disturbances, and other symptoms of tabes.

---

[1] These gross muscular disorders have been ascribed to circulatory disturbances in the brain or to episodic invasion of the brain by increased "showers" of spirochetes.

From the viewpoint of psychological adjustment, general paresis is revealed as a *psychosis*, involving progressive mental deterioration (*dementia*). This deterioration is shown in the progressive impairment of intelligence, memory, moral judgment, and emotional control. These symptoms, as they develop, reflect the progressive involvement of various regions of the brain. Frequently the course of the disease is marked by *remissions* (transient diminutions or abatements of the

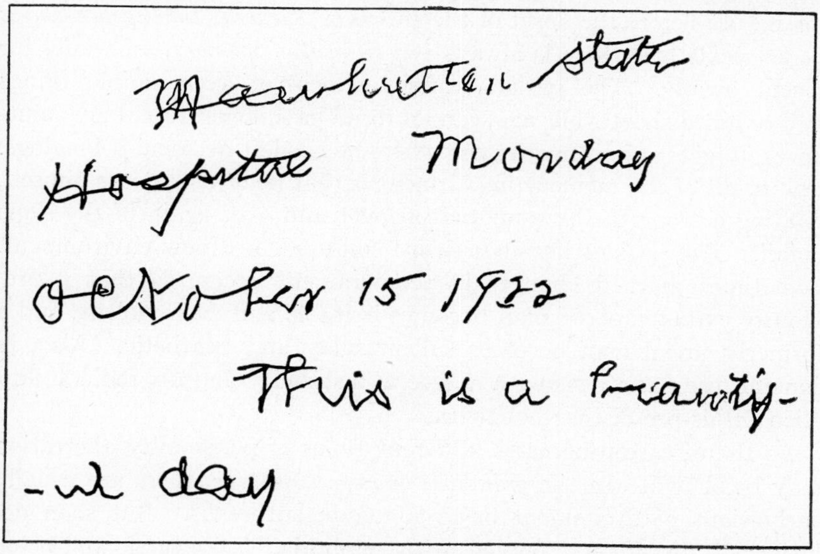

FIG. 23. Paretic Script.

Disturbance of coordination is especially plain in the **M** and in the word "beautiful," the former, showing this disturbance by the interruptions in the lines, and by the numerous but vain efforts to continue the strokes.

symptoms), which are thought to be due to a temporary subsiding of the pathologic processes that results from a physiological defensive reaction to the syphilitic invasion.[1]

The diagnosis of general paresis is based less on the nature of the individual symptoms, which often occur in other organic psychoses, than on their manner of onset, coupled with the typical signs of motor disturbance and the characteristic blood and spinal fluid changes.

As a rule, the first overt signs of the disease are *personality changes* or changes in general behavior. The individual may show lack of

[1] Wechsler, *op. cit.*, p. 445.

power of concentration, easy fatigability, and irritability. Sometimes he becomes overanxious and depressed and suffers from insomnia. Soon, however, symptoms of greater gravity appear. The person begins to avoid responsibility, becomes indifferent to all his affairs (business, personal, and social), and careless in his dress and manners. He may even commit moral delinquencies, such as theft, sexual excesses, or drunkenness, which would have been entirely foreign to his nature before the onset of the disease. *General intelligence shows degeneration* and there is always *impairment of memory*, especially for recent events. The patient cannot remember even simple things told to him a short while ago, cannot recall having met recent acquaintances, forgets appointments and where he has left personal belongings. One result of the memory impairment is that he often repeats himself, relating a story to the same person over and over again in the same detail. The patient becomes easily confused in a new environment. Sometimes marked changes in temperament occur, so that a previously even-tempered man becomes irritable and even violent, and a formerly jovial man becomes sullen, sulky and apathetic. Also, in general, the paretic shows a degree of instability and unpredictability alien to his pre-disease behavior.,

As the disease progresses, different types of personality aberration may be shown. In the *grandiose or expansive type*, there are usually early signs of excitement or even manic outbreaks. But soon delusions of grandeur, coupled with euphoria (feelings of well-being which are usually unfounded and exaggerated), dominate the scene. The patient "never felt so well in his life"; he has the physical power of Hercules; he has millions of dollars, is an emperor, or has 10,000 children. At the same time the "expansive" paretic is often very irritable and is incoherent in the expression of his fantastic ideas. The *depressed type* from the first tends to be overanxious and despondent. He often expresses feelings of inadequacy and self-accusatory ideas (*e.g.*, believing himself guilty of unpardonable sins for which he will be mercilessly punished). In time the depression deepens and the patient is obsessed with hypochondriacal delusions (*e.g.*, his heart has been filled with water; his brain has been removed; there is an obstruction which prevents him from ever moving his bowels). Profoundly melancholic, the patient may attempt suicide. The *demented type* is characterized by gradual mental deterioration, apathy, loss of memory (especially for recent events), neglect of personal hygiene, and personality defects. The patient often has mild grandiose ideas and other simple delusions. Finally, a *simple and slowly progressive type* of general paresis has been described, which is for years characterized by only a few mild behavioral disorders and physical symptoms of a pathological nature. The diagnosis of these cases is based primarily on the findings of tests of the blood and spinal fluid.

Without question, many of the behavioral symptoms of paresis (*e.g.*, loss of memory, disturbance in language) arise as a direct result of brain damage due to the inroads of the spirochete. However, it is very likely that some of the symptoms, especially those reflecting emotional and general personality disturbances, may be explicable, in part at least, by the patient's reaction to the effects of the organic damage, *i.e.*, to his illness. It may be the confusion and insecurity engendered by the patient's decreasing general competence that cause his depressions; the delusions of grandeur may result from an unconscious attempt by the patient to conceal from himself the knowledge that his personality is disintegrating. If it is true that the behavioral symptoms in paresis are partly a result of the patient's psychological reaction to the ravages of the disease, it is not surprising that individual paretics should show wide differences in the nature of their personality disorganization. As Wechsler says, "The psychotic manifestations can sometimes be correlated with the previous personality and character make-up of the individual. . . ."[1] Thus an excitable person may develop the expansive type of personality deviation, a phlegmatic individual the depressed type, etc. The same view is expressed by another neurologist who holds that the behavior pathology which a paretic develops is determined "by his premorbid personality structure and its underlying emotional trends and conflicts."[2]

Prognosis and Treatment. In untreated cases the prognosis of general paresis is very grave. Although the rate at which the disease process develops may vary from slow and insidious to very rapid, and although in some cases remissions and even apparent "spontaneous" recoveries enduring from two to six months may occur, ultimately all the symptoms become aggravated, mental and physical deterioration

[1] Wechsler, *op. cit.*, p. 447.
[2] Grinker, R. *Neurology*, 3rd ed. Springfield, Ill., Charles C Thomas, 1943 p. 905.

increases, speech becomes progressively more difficult and more incomprehensible, until finally the patient is bedridden, a completely demented, helpless, vegetative organism. Untreated, the disease is fatal, usually within two or three years, in almost 100 per cent of the cases.

Chances for recovery in treated cases vary with the nature of the treatment and with the time at which the treatment is instituted. Before discussing methods of therapy, however, it should be pointed out that it is more correct to speak, in most cases, of the arrest of paresis rather than of recovery or cure, since, as we have said, nervous tissue that has been destroyed cannot be restored.

Various methods have been used in the treatment of paresis, all of which have as their aim the elimination of the infectious process which underlies the physical and psychotic symptoms. However, the method in most common use today involves *fever therapy*, often combined with penicillin,[1] followed by antisyphilitic treatment with arsenic compounds and bismuth. The accepted mode of fever therapy in paresis at the present time is by the inoculation of the patient with the malaria organism, so that he develops malaria with its alternating high fevers and chills. This treatment is based on the knowledge that the human constitution can recover from internal temperatures (*i.e.*, of 104° to 106°F.) which are fatal to the *Treponema pallidum*. After the patient has had 10 to 15 chills, antimalarial treatment with quinine is begun.[2] Following recovery from the malaria, a standard antisyphilitic treatment is given, usually involving tryparsamide (an arsenic compound) alternating with bismuth. The administration

---

[1] During the fever therapy penicillin is often administered at 3-hr. intervals for a period of 4 weeks. Authorities state that experience has not as yet been sufficient to permit a full evaluation of the effectiveness of penicillin in the treatment of paresis.

[2] There are, of course, certain dangers in the use of this form of fever therapy, because of the hazards of malaria itself. The treatment is most effective when given to young and healthy patients in the early stages of paresis. For aged patients and for those in advanced stages who have undergone serious physical deterioration, the treatment may actually hasten death.

In certain cases "artificial" fever is induced, not by malaria, but by such means as wrapping the patient in an electrically heated blanket, placing him in a short-wave radio field, or surrounding him with hot humid air. These methods have the obvious advantage that the physician can control the degree of fever and its duration with precision. A number of authorities, however, agree that generally the malarial method gives better results; perhaps certain biochemical changes resulting from the malarial infection are valuable in neutralizing toxic products of the syphilitic infection.

of these drugs in accordance with the established regimen is necessary after the fever therapy, since in many cases improvement in symptoms following the malarial infection is not accompanied by a change from positive to negative results in the blood and spinal fluid tests for syphilis. This combined fever and pharmaceutical treatment has resulted in arrest of the disease in about 50 per cent of the cases, with "remissions amounting to permanent cures ... in about 30 per cent of cases. ..."[1]

Psychotherapeutic methods have also been used to aid in the readjustment of medically treated paretic patients.

DISCUSSION

Of the whole array of diseases of the nervous system, only a very few have been singled out for description here. These few have, of necessity, been presented briefly and incompletely. But even this short account should suffice to show how greatly human behavior depends upon sound structural and functional conditions in the nervous system and, further, how specifically localized disorders in the nervous system produce specific abnormalities of behavior. The ataxic gait which is a symptom of tabes dorsalis can be directly ascribed to injury of the fibers which ascend to the brain in the posterior white columns. The limp paralysis of infantile spinal paralysis results from the deterioration of the ventral-horn cells of the gray matter of the cord. In syringomyelia the loss of pain and temperature sensitivity in restricted areas of the skin is caused by the destruction of the anterior commissures which lie near the central canal of the spinal cord. A progressive deterioration of personality and of thinking functions parallels the progressive destruction of cerebral cortex in paresis. The foregoing pages furnish many other examples of the correlation between specifically localized disturbances in the nervous system and specific types of behavior disorder.

However, certain cautions are necessary with respect to our interpretation of these neurological findings. It must be pointed out that the close relationship between specific neural pathology and specific behavior abnormality may not be found when the disease or injury is principally confined to the cerebrum, or when the behavior abnormalities are disturbances of such "higher processes" as learning, memory, and thinking. Each particular spinal center has a function

[1] Wechsler, *op. cit.*, p. 452.

which is specific and relatively invariable. It follows that if this particular center is injured, a specific impairment of behavior will result. But for the most part no such specific functions can be definitely assigned to the various areas of the cerebrum. Hence, damage to one particular group of neurones in a particular region of the cerebrum may not result in one and the same variety of behavior disturbance in all individuals. In other words, there is no exact correspondence between symptoms, on the one hand, and the extent and location of certain types of cerebral injury, on the other. Furthermore, injury or disease of the cerebrum usually has a general rather than a narrowly specific effect on behavior and commonly produces profound disturbances of the most complex psychological processes, as well as of simple sensory and motor functions. An example of the evidence on which these conclusions are based is to be found in the description of general paresis in this chapter.

Another point which the reader should bear in mind is that there are no known neurological bases for many of the most common "mental" disorders. This statement does not mean that such disorders occur in the absence of any disturbance of neural functions. What is meant is, rather, that many "mental" disorders apparently do not arise as a result of any actual damage to the nervous system from tumors, hemorrhages, concussions, wounds, bacterial infections, or any similar cause. The loss of kinesthetic sensitivity in locomotor ataxia is clearly traceable to damage done by the syphilis spirochete to certain particular tracts of the spinal cord. But nail biting, or stuttering, or a fear of cats, or a feeling of inferiority, or an inability to control one's temper can only very rarely be attributed to actual damage of tissue anywhere in the nervous system. As a rule, there is no evidence in such cases that the nervous system is diseased or infected or in any way structurally damaged, although in some grave disorders, such as schizophrenia, detrimental biochemical conditions may be basically involved.[1] Hence, the treatment for such conditions usually consists of attempts to alter the undesirable behavior by purely psychological methods (*e.g.*, reconditioning), rather than by the employment of surgical or other medical remedies. Certain of these methods are described in Chap. XIX of this book.

---

[1] Hoskins, R. G. *The Biology of Schizophrenia.* New York, Norton, 1946.

CHAPTER XII

THE ELECTROPHYSIOLOGY OF THE NERVOUS SYSTEM

INTRODUCTION

Readers of newspapers and magazines are becoming somewhat used to the periodic appearance of articles headlined "Recently perfected device records man's thoughts electrically." Such reports leave one with the impression that the precise neural correlates of "thought" have been discovered, that means to record them have been devised, and that in order to find out what a person is thinking a skilled technician need only start his apparatus and analyze the resulting graphic records of "brain waves."

But psychology and neurology have not advanced quite so far as such articles suggest. Our knowledge of the modes of action of the nervous system is still very far from being complete. Just how the brain functions in thinking remains largely unknown. And although it is possible to record "brain waves," as the experiments reported in this chapter show, the "waves" that have been recorded most successfully do not seem likely to have a direct relation to thought processes.

Yet if the investigations of "brain waves" have not yielded the dramatic results claimed for them by some popular science writers, they already have added considerably to our understanding of a number of psychological phenomena and they offer hope of illuminating the still mysterious relationship between neural activity and overt behavior. The present chapter deals with a few recent studies which have been selected to indicate the number and variety of psychological problems which controlled observations of these neuroelectrical waves may help to solve.

One of the basic discoveries in the field of neurophysiology was Helmholtz's proof that nerve impulses travel at measurable speeds, far below the speed of electromagnetic impulses. Less than one hundred years ago Johannes Müller, the most eminent physiologist of his day, taught that the *velocity of conduction of the neural impulse* could never

215

be determined precisely, since its rate of propagation must approach that of light (about 186,000 miles per second). But by 1850 Helmholtz had shown by simple means that in the frog's sciatic nerve the velocity of propagation is only 28 m. (approximately 92 ft.) per second, and it was soon demonstrated that the speed of conduction is but 120 m. (about 394 ft.) per second in the most rapidly conducting medullated nerve fibers of the human nervous system. These and later investigations did much to remove the problem of the neural impulse from the realm of mysticism and to show that the phenomenon can be measured and described in terms of physicochemical principles. At the present time, there is considerable evidence in support of the view that the neural impulse may best be described as a wave of electrochemical change.

In the study of the electrical characteristics of neural functioning, the "action-potential" technique has been of very great service. Many years ago, it was discovered that if electrodes are placed in contact with active nerves, the changes in electrical potential involved in neural transmission can be made to bring about deflections in a sensitive galvanometer.[1] Recently several investigators have employed vacuum tubes to amplify the minute "action potentials," and elaborate oscillographs have been devised for graphic or photographic recording of the electrical changes. (The essential features of an apparatus for recording action potentials are shown in Fig. 24. In this particular circuit, the cathode-ray oscillograph replaces the galvanometer.) Such amplification and recording have made possible the study of numerous aspects of neural transmission which previously defied investigation. More accurate determinations have been made of the velocity of conduction in different fiber groups. For example, it has been shown that the fibers of relatively small diameter which conduct afferent impulses from "pain" receptors transmit their impulses at lower speeds than do those larger fibers which transmit

---

[1] A galvanometer is an instrument used to detect and to measure very weak electrical currents. While a nerve fiber is conducting an impulse, the surface of the fiber in the region where the impulse is passing at any given instant is at an electrical potential different from that of the surface in any other region of the fiber. Thus, waves of change of electrical potential sweep along the nerve fiber with the impulse, and it is these changes of potential that set up the weak currents which account for the deflections of the galvanometer. The currents are called "action currents," and the potentials causing the currents, "action potentials."

impulses from cutaneous pressure and temperature receptors. The rhythms of discharge of different groups of fibers can now be studied and compared. The well-known "all-or-none" principle of conduction[1] which Adrian originally demonstrated without the aid of the action-potential technique has now been verified through action potential observations.

These action-potential observations also indicate that when impulses are aroused through the stimulation of receptor mechanisms, the

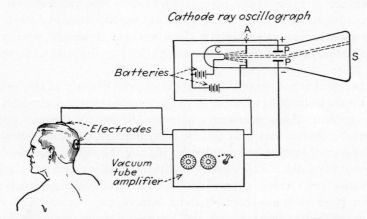

Fig. 24. Diagram of One Type of Circuit Used for Recording Cerebral Action Potentials.

In the cathode-ray oscillograph, C is the cathode, from which electrons are emitted. A beam of electrons passes through an opening in the anode, A, and falls on screen S. When changes in the electrical potential of plates $P - P$ occur, the beam of electrons is deflected, and when a succession of changes occurs, as in the case of brain rhythms, curves are traced on the screen. A camera, mounted to face this screen, will take permanent records of the waves (still or motion picture). Some investigators use a sensitive galvanometer instead of the cathode-ray oscillograph, in which case records are made photographically by having the galvanometer mirror reflect a beam of light upon a moving strip of photographic film or paper.

frequency of discharge (number of impulses conducted per second) along the afferent nerve fibers increases when the intensity of the stimulus is increased. (In a certain nerve in the frog the frequency of discharge has been found to vary from 5 to 100 impulses per second, depending upon the intensity of the stimulus.) The fact that the

[1] The nerve fiber, like a shotgun, operates on the "all-or-none" principle. If a sufficient force is applied to the trigger of the gun, the firing pin is released and the gun discharges completely. It is impossible to increase the magnitude of the discharge by increasing the force exerted upon the trigger. Likewise the nerve fiber does not transmit larger or more "vigorous" impulses in response to more intense stimuli. Each impulse is the same regardless of stimulus intensity, provided the latter exceeds the threshold value.

frequency of discharge is a function of the intensity of stimulation has come to be known as the "Adrian principle," since Adrian was the first to demonstrate this relationship.[1]

Much of the important recent work on the electrophysiology of the nervous system has involved the recording of action potentials from the cerebral cortex itself. The enormous complexity of cortical action and our ignorance of the precise mechanisms which control cortical functioning perhaps make it difficult for us to appreciate the full significance of these action-potential records. Nevertheless, various types of brain-wave patterns recorded and the variations which occur in these patterns under changing conditions are definitely worthy of our attention, even though we are not yet in a position to understand them fully.

Of course it is not possible to apply electrodes directly to the human cerebrum save in cases where severe injury to the skull has exposed the brain surface. Some years ago, however, Berger,[2] a German physiologist, discovered that with the use of appropriate amplifiers cerebral potential waves might be recorded by placing the electrodes upon the surface of the scalp. This record constitutes what is called an "electroencephalogram," often abbreviated E.E.G. Berger discovered two distinct types of brain-wave rhythms, and during the past 20 years other investigators have observed and recorded many other important kinds. A classification and description of the principal types follow, together with illustrations of them in Fig. 25.

TYPES OF BRAIN WAVE[3]

Type I. Berger's Alpha Waves. These are regular rhythms with definite frequencies, usually between 9 and 11 cycles per second, though some investigators report a range of 8 to 13 cycles in the normal adult. They appear in most adults, vary in amplitude (voltage change), and

---

[1] For summaries of many important neurophysiological studies, including some of Adrian's more important investigations, and a partial bibliography on the subject, see Evans, C. L. *Recent Advances in Physiology*, 4th ed., Chap. IX. London, Churchill, 1930; and Adrian, E. D. *The Physiological Background of Perception.* New York, Oxford, 1947.

[2] Berger, H. Über das Elektrenkephalogramm des Menschen. *Archiv für Psychiatrie und Nervenkrankheiten*, 1929, vol. 87, pp. 527–570.

[3] The description of all the types, except gamma, delta, and the "spike" variety, is taken from Loomis, A. L., E. N. Harvey, and C. G. Hobart, Electrical Potentials of the Human Brain. *Journal of Experimental Psychology*, 1926, vol. 19, pp. 249–279. (The original numerical designations have been altered.)

appear and disappear readily according to the subject's "mental" and emotional activity. Berger found that alpha waves may be observed in a normal adult, who is seated comfortably and has his eyes closed, if one electrode is placed in contact with the scalp in the occipital region and the other at some other point of the scalp surface

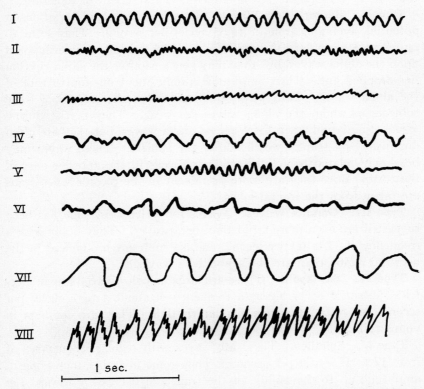

FIG. 25. Graphic Records of the Eight Types of Cerebral Action-Potential Waves
Described in the Text.

I, alpha; II, beta; III, gamma; IV, saw-tooth; V, spindles; VI, large "random waves"; VII, delta; VIII, spikes. As the length of the line labeled "1 sec." indicates, each of the above records covers a period of 3 sec.

(the exact location of the second electrode being immaterial if it covers a sufficient area.) However, if the subject opens his eyes to look at an object, or starts to read, these alpha waves disappear. Many investigators have verified these observations. The alpha waves have the greatest amplitude, *i.e.*, the greatest voltage change, of any of the several types of potentials which have been recorded from the surface of the scalps of normal awake subjects, and they tend to be strongest in the occipital regions. They first appear at the age of three to four months, at frequencies as low as 3 or 4 cycles per second; the frequency increases as the child develops, until it finally reaches the level of 9 to 11 per second which is characteristic of the adult.

Type II. Berger's Beta Waves. These are very rapid variations in potential, averaging from 25 to 35 cycles per second. They seem to represent a secondary series of waves which are often superimposed upon the alpha waves, but they may continue after the alpha rhythm has dropped out. Their amplitude is only about one-fourth that of the alpha waves. Beta waves predominate in the records of some subjects in whom the alpha waves are weak. They persist during visual stimulation when there are no alpha waves, but they are often diminished by stimuli which startle the subject. These waves may be closely related to activities of nerve cells in the anterior part of the cortex, since they are more prominent in the records when leads are taken from the frontal lobes.

Type III. Gamma Waves. Waves for which this name has been suggested are even more rapid than beta waves. They occur with a frequency of 35 to 60 per second, and are more often observed in the occipital region than are the slower beta waves.

Type IV. Saw-tooth. These are large and slow variations in electrical potential occurring at a frequency of about 4 to 7 cycles per second, but without a very regular rhythm. They are common in young children.

Type V. Spindles. These are waves with regular frequencies of from 12 to 15 cycles per second. They come in trains, increasing in amplitude up to the middle of the train and decreasing toward the end of it—a peculiarity which gives the whole train a spindlelike appearance on the graphic record. The spindle waves are observed only while the subject is sleeping.

Type VI. Large "Random" Waves. These waves recur irregularly at frequencies from 0.5 to 5 per second, and are characteristic of sound sleep.

Type VII. Delta Waves. These are large, slow waves having a frequency range of 0.5 or less to 5 or 6 per second. They have been observed in persons with epileptic tendencies, in other abnormal brain conditions, and in deep sleep. They are usually of the "flat-top" or "dome" variety, and they sometimes have smaller waves of higher frequency superimposed upon them.

Type VIII. Spikes. These are extremely pointed waves, often observed during epileptic seizures. During a *grand mal*[1] attack they may occur with increasing frequency, sometimes reaching a maximum of 25 per second at the height of the attack. This type of wave is shown in both Fig. 25 and Fig. 26. A typical *petit mal*[1] record shows alternate spikes and flat-top delta waves at a rate of about 3 per second, as shown in Fig. 26.

As the above classification shows, a considerable variety of different wave rhythms has been observed in the human cortex, and further-more, the kind of wave which is recorded at a given time is dependent upon many different factors, such as the age of the subject, whether the subject is being stimulated visually, whether he is asleep or awake, and so on.

During the past two decades, many investigations have been con-ducted with the aim of discovering the nature of the predominant brain rhythms under different conditions, and the effect of varying these conditions (*e.g.*, modes of stimulation) upon the wave forms. One of the best examples of such studies is the experiment of Loomis, Harvey, and Hobart already referred to.

I. Action Potentials of the Human Brain[2]

PURPOSE

The purpose of the experiment of Loomis and his associates was to record and compare action potentials from the brain under different conditions of stimulation and in subjects of different ages.

METHOD

The subjects of the experiment were 29 individuals who ranged in age from seventeen days to seventy-four years. The action potential records were obtained by means of the technique described above. The various specific conditions of stimulation which were employed are stated in the summary of results which follows. Records were

---

[1] See Part II of this chapter for a brief description of epilepsy, the nature of *grand mal* and *petit mal* attacks, etc.

[2] Adapted from Loomis, Harvey, and Hobart, *op. cit.*

obtained from each subject for a period of at least 2 hours, and one subject was studied continuously for a total period of 50 hours.

RESULTS

Alpha Waves: Brain Waves during Sleep. The findings of Loomis and his associates verified the conclusions of previous investigators that the *alpha rhythms* (Type I waves) appear in normal subjects who are at rest with closed eyes, and that they disappear when the subject opens his eyes to view an object, to read, or to react attentively in any way. It was further observed that, when the subject retired for sleep, the alpha waves continued as long as he was relaxing quietly, but that as he became drowsy they became less frequent, and were gradually replaced by the *random potentials* (Type VI), which are characteristic of sound sleep.

When subjects awakened during the night trains of alpha waves usually appeared at once and then changed gradually to the random type as deep sleep came on again.

In a number of sleeping subjects, trains of waves of the *spindle type* (Type V) appeared. Their frequency was from 13 to 15 cycles per second, and the individual spindles lasted from $\frac{1}{2}$ to 1 second. These spindles were recorded only during sleep and for the most part in adult subjects. Children and young persons in very deep sleep showed the *random* (Type VI) wave predominantly, with only occasional spindles.

The Effect upon Brain Waves of Auditory Stimulation during Sleep. Previous investigators had emphasized the fact that the *alpha waves* (Type I), which appear in a person at rest with his eyes closed, disappear when an object is viewed or when attention is concentrated upon any stimulus. Loomis and his coworkers observed that the alpha waves reappeared during sleep when certain auditory stimuli were presented. For example, in several subjects the rustling of paper, coughing by a person in the bedroom, closing a door at some distance from the subject, or low conversation initiated a train of alpha waves, which lasted from 5 to 8 seconds. The same sounds which initiated a train of alpha waves quite regularly during sleep failed to do so when the subjects were awake. Occasionally, trains of such waves appeared during sleep when there was no detectable external stimulation. It is quite possible that these alpha waves were aroused by internal bodily excitation, perhaps during dreams.

Brain Waves Recorded in Hypnosis.   As has been said, the trains of alpha waves appear in the normal subject most regularly and continuously when he is resting quietly and comfortably with his eyes closed.   Opening the eyes has no effect on the waves if the room is completely dark, but if the eyes are opened in a lighted room, the waves cease.   If the eyes are kept open in a dark room, trains of alpha waves will disappear and reappear as a minute point of light fixated by the subject is flashed on and off.   This reaction occurs even when the light is so faint that it can be seen only with a thoroughly dark-adapted eye.

A subject who had been hypnotized many times was tested in the normal waking state and during normal sleep.   Alpha waves at a frequency of 9.9 per second were recorded when the subject was awake, and the usual spindles at 12.5 per second while he was asleep. After the subject was hypnotized, the *alpha waves* characteristic of the waking state continued, and neither spindles nor random waves were recorded.   Hence, as far as the action potentials of the brain are concerned, hypnosis for this subject was like the relaxed waking state and unlike normal sleep.

To test the influence of hypnotic suggestion on the alpha waves, the subject's eyelids were fastened closed with adhesive tape.   Alternately, every 15 seconds, he was told, first that he could see, then that he was blind.   Whenever the suggestion that he could see was made, the alpha waves stopped.   When he was told that he could not see, the waves reappeared.   This happened both when there was a light in the room and when the room was in total darkness.

However, suggestion alone, without hypnosis, did not have exactly the same effects.

To study the effect of suggestion on individuals in the normal waking state, subjects who had never been hypnotized were tested in a totally dark room.   When it was suggested to a subject that he was seeing something (*e.g.*, a light or a face) the alpha waves disappeared, but when the room was lighted and the subject's eyes were open the experimenters were unable to start trains of alpha waves by suggesting to the subject that he was seeing nothing.   This finding indicates that although the alpha rhythm is influenced by suggestion in both the hypnotic state and the normal waking state, it is more susceptible to the effects of suggestion when the subject is under hypnosis.

Brain Waves in Alcoholic Stupor. One subject lapsed into a stupor after he had consumed a little more than a pint of gin within a half hour, as directed by the experimenters. During the stupor, he showed a marked *alpha rhythm with secondary potential waves superimposed upon it.* Not only were the superimposed rhythms different from those recorded before the alcohol was taken into the body, but the frequency of the alpha waves was reduced. The alpha rhythm began to disappear only after the subject had been asleep for an hour. It would appear that the electrical activities of the brain in alcoholic stupor, as in hypnosis, differ from those in normal sleep.

Brain Waves in Infants. Electroencephalograms were obtained from two babies every 2 weeks between the ages of seventeen and seventy-one days. *Random* and *saw-tooth* waves (Types VI and IV) were recorded in the infants, but no alpha waves were observed at any time during that period. (In fact, the alpha rhythm has been found to be absent in infants as old as four months.) The records were very similar, whether they were made when the infants were awake or asleep.[1]

II. Electroencephalographic Studies of Epilepsy

Introduction

It is perhaps surprising to learn that in most mental disorders, the brain waves are not consistently different from those found in normal people. Whatever may be the nature and the causes of these disorders, it appears that the brain activity is not usually disturbed in such a way as to produce an abnormal action-potential record.

However, in disorders in which structural brain damage is known to be present, abnormal brain-wave records are very often reported.

[1] Dr. J. R. Smith has recorded brain waves in babies on the first day after birth. The waves which he recorded seemed to originate in the motor area of the cortex (*i.e.*, in the pre-central convolution), and were of low frequency, occurring at the rate of about 4 or 5 per second. They were similar to those which have been observed in older infants during sleep, *i.e.*, the saw-tooth waves described by Loomis, Harvey, and Hobart. The occurrence of brain waves so soon after birth suggests that in all probability the rhythms have begun before birth, and that the brain is already functioning at that time. Smith, J. R. The Electroencephalogram during Normal Infancy and Childhood: I. Rhythmic Activities Present in the Neonate and Their Subsequent Development. *Journal of Genetic Psychology*, 1938, vol. 53, pp. 431–453; and II. The Nature of the Growth of the Alpha Waves, *ibid*, pp. 455–469.

Thus, various kinds of abnormal waves are frequently observed in cases of brain tumor, neurosyphilis, and the like.[1] These electro-encephalographic findings may aid in the diagnosis of such disorders, and in the location of the affected areas within the brain. It is believed that any kind of tissue destruction in the brain, however caused, may produce abnormal electrical potentials, usually of the *delta* type (Type VII). If the process of cell damage ceases, the electroencephalogram may return to a normal pattern, although if the destruction of nerve tissue has been sufficiently extensive, normal brain waves may never again be obtained.

It so happens that the most important, and most widely publicized, studies of brain waves in abnormal individuals have been carried out on epileptics. As a result of these investigations, new light has been obtained on the manner in which action-potential changes may be correlated with abnormal behavior. These studies have also yielded data which are helpful in the diagnosis of epilepsy, and which have contributed materially to current theory as to the causes of this disorder.

Epilepsy is a disorder characterized by recurrent seizures (or "fits"). In a majority of cases these seizures are of the *grand mal* type. The victim of the seizure falls to the ground and loses consciousness. Violent motor convulsions then occur, lasting for 5 to 8 minutes on the average, after which the patient regains consciousness. A brief period of stupor or deep sleep typically ensues. Many people have seen epileptic individuals undergoing attacks of this kind on the street, in restaurants, or in other public places. Another kind of seizure is the *petit mal*. This variety probably would not be regarded by the layman as being epilepsy at all, since the convulsive movements may be limited to a few spasms of the face or arms, and the patient loses consciousness for only a few seconds, or does not lose consciousness at all, experiencing instead only a momentary dizziness. Nevertheless, *petit mal* attacks are unquestionably epileptic in nature, and often occur in patients who have *grand mal* attacks also. Other kinds of epileptic seizure also exist, but they are relatively uncommon and need not be described here.

[1] See Hunt, J. McV., ed. *Personality and the Behavior Disorders*, Vol. II, Chap. 33, pp. 1033–1103. New York, Ronald, 1944.

Gilman, R. Electroencephalography: Review of 1942. *Psychological Bulletin*, 1944, vol. 41, pp. 416–432.

Electroencephalographic studies of epileptics yield several points of major interest. One finding is the striking changes in the action potentials of the brain which occur before and during a seizure. Figure 26 gives typical records for both the *grand mal* and *petit mal* types. These rhythms both show spikes (Type VIII), and the *petit*

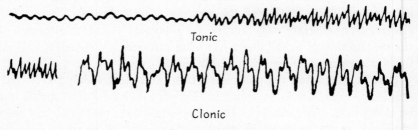

Tonic

Clonic

Grand mal seizure

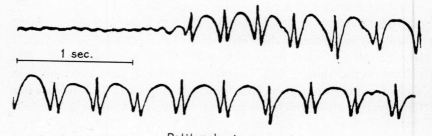

1 sec.

Petit mal seizure

Fig. 26. Representative Electroencephalograms of Two Epileptic Patients Taken before, and during, Two Types of Seizures, *Grand Mal* and *Petit Mal*.

The left of each tracing is a portion of the person's normal record. The rest of each tracing was made during a seizure. The record for the grand-mal seizure shows the characteristic fast spiked waves and the increased amplitude of the waves as the seizure passes from the initial phase (called "tonic") to the complete convulsive stage (called "clonic"). The record for the petit-mal seizure shows the typical alternation of spikes and flat-top delta waves. As the length of the line labeled "1 sec." indicates, each of the above records covers a period of 7 sec. (*Reproduced from F. A. Gibbs, E. L. Gibbs, and W. G. Lennox. Influence of the Blood Sugar Level on the Wave and Spike Formation in Petit Mal Epilepsy. Archives of Neurology and Psychiatry, 1939, p. 1112.*)

mal record characteristically shows spikes alternating with "flat-top" delta waves (Type VII). Inspection of these records shows that the motor convulsions are paralleled by cortical potentials of greatly increased speed and amplitude. Such records show how extreme abnormalities of behavior may be correlated with marked electroencephalographic changes.

An abnormal type of electroencephalogram also is found in 75 per cent or more of all epileptic individuals during the typically lengthy periods of time when they are "well," *i.e.*, not having seizures. This abnormality consists chiefly of slow, *delta* rhythms (Type VII), with frequencies ranging from 0.5 to 5 cycles per second. As we have said, these waves are of the "flat-top" variety, and they sometimes have smaller waves of higher frequency superimposed upon them. This particular phenomenon Lennox[1] calls "dysrhythmia."

Although a substantial majority of epileptics show dysrhythmia, by no means all persons who show dysrhythmia are epileptics. It is estimated that the encephalograms of approximately 10 per cent of the population—about 15 million Americans—possess this peculiarity, although only one-twentieth that number—about 750,000—ever have had epileptic seizures. The fact that an individual's encephalogram shows dysrhythmia is therefore not an indication that he either has or will have epilepsy. However, Lennox believes that cerebral dysrhythmia may indicate a *predisposition* to epilepsy, and he thinks that if an individual's encephalogram reveals dysrhythmia the chances that he has or will have epilepsy are greater than those of a person in whom dysrhythmia is absent. For this reason, during the war some neurologists advocated that candidates for admission to the air force who showed dysrhythmia should be rejected, since they might later develop epileptic seizures, particularly under the strains and hazards of flying. And recently, in an English law court, the presence of dysrhythmia in a murderer was accepted as evidence supporting his contention that he had committed the crime during an epileptic seizure and thus was not legally responsible for it.

Clinicians recognize two principal types of epileptic disorder: *essential epilepsy* and *symptomatic epilepsy*. In essential epilepsy the cerebral dysrhythmia is thought to indicate the presence of an inherent brain condition which functions as a predisposition to epilepsy. Given this inherent predisposition, the seizures may be brought about by various precipitating factors, such as a low concentration of sugar in the blood, kidney disease leading to toxemia (general systemic poisoning), disorders of the pituitary or parathyroid glands, emotional disturbances, and the like. In symptomatic epilepsy the dysrhythmia is not constitutional but results from cerebral damage due to such causes as accidental injury to the skull and brain, brain infections, the de-

[1] Lennox, W. G. *Science and Seizures*, 2d. ed. New York, Harper, 1946.

velopment of brain tumors, etc.   Here, as with essential epilepsy, the
seizures may be induced by various precipitating causes.   Symptomatic epilepsy is much less common than essential epilepsy.

The investigation now to be described was based upon the view
that cerebral dysrhythmia may be a predisposing condition in most
cases of epilepsy.   Its aim was to test the hypothesis that the disease
is a "familial" or heritable one—a hypothesis advanced by Hippocrates
2,300 years ago.

THE INHERITANCE OF CEREBRAL DYSRHYTHMIA AND EPILEPSY[1]

PURPOSE

The purpose of this investigation was to test the hypothesis that
hereditary factors operate in producing epilepsy.   Lennox and his
associates believe that various characteristics of the cortical potential
patterns of an individual depend upon heredity.[2]   If the cerebral
dysrhythmia typical of epilepsy is inherited, then it would be expected
that a large number of the near relatives of epileptics would exhibit the
phenomenon.   The specific object of the study was to discover whether
this expectation would turn out to be correct.

SUBJECTS

The subjects were: (1) 94 epileptics, all private patients of the
authors, and (2) 183 near relatives of these patients of whom 143 were
parents and 4 were children.[3]   A third group, (3), was a normal

---

[1] Adapted from Lennox, W. G., E. L. Gibbs, and F. A. Gibbs.   Inheritance of Cerebral
Dysrhythmia and Epilepsy.   *Archives of Neurology and Psychiatry*, 1940, vol. 44, pp.
1155–1183.

[2] Some important evidence bearing upon this point comes from the studies of identical
twins by Davis and Davis (Davis, H., and P. A. Davis.   Action Potentials of the Brain in
Normal States of Cerebral Activity.   *Archives of Neurology and Psychiatry*, 1936, vol.
36, pp. 1214–1224).   And by Lennox, *op. cit.*   These investigators obtained brain-wave
records from each member of several pairs of identical twins.   Davis and Davis present
records for 9 pairs of normal twins; Lennox for 7 pairs of abnormal twins, of which 6 pairs
had epilepsy.   In all 16 cases the brain-wave records were strikingly similar for both
members of each pair of twins.   Lennox, Gibbs, and Gibbs (The Brain Wave Pattern,
an Hereditary Trait.   *Journal of Heredity*, 1945, vol. 36, pp. 233–243) have more recently
reported observations of 71 "normal" twins, some identical and some nonidentical.   They
found that although the brain-wave records of the normal nonidentical twins were dis-
tinguishably different, those of the two members of identical twin pairs were indistinguish-
able.   These facts suggest that similarity of wave patterns is largely attributable to
similarity of hereditary factors.

[3] Parents are more likely than siblings to accompany patients coming from a distance
and patients do not often bring their children when they visit the physician, clinic, or
hospital.

group consisting of 76 physicians, technicians, and medical students, and 24 students attending a private school for boys. The immediate families of all the members of the normal group were free of epilepsy. The investigators suggest that in order to achieve a more nearly complete equivalence of the abnormal and control groups more subjects above forty years of age and more married couples should have been included in the latter group.

METHOD

The subjects were seated in easy chairs with eyes closed. The room was darkened and shielded to prevent extraneous electrical phenomena from influencing the records. Six electrodes were attached to the scalp in a bilaterally symmetrical placement, one over each of the two frontal, the two motor, and the two occipital areas, and "ground" electrodes were attached to the lobes of the ears. Leads were taken from the electrodes to six independent amplifiers, so that comparisons of waves from these various cortical areas could be made. Recordings were extended over periods of at least 20 minutes, because some subjects whose cerebral potentials are apparently normal when a diagnosis is based upon a recording of short duration may reveal abnormalities when observations are made over a longer time.

Interpretation of Records. A device known as a "frequency analyzer" was employed in reading and comparing the records. Any complex wave may be regarded as a combination of two or more simple waves, and the frequency analyzer makes it possible to determine the frequencies of the component waves.

In judging the abnormality of a record at least three characteristics of the wave tracing were considered: (1) the dominant frequency, (2) the constancy or regularity, and (3) the voltage (amplitude) of the record. Sometimes when the record presented a confused mixture of many frequencies, it was impossible to detect a dominant frequency. Where a dominant frequency was evident, it was considered to be abnormal in an adult subject if it was slower than 8 per second, or faster than 25 per second. Different criteria were used for children, in accordance with the slower normal frequencies typical of lower age levels. Elements weighing in favor of a "normal" judgment were the presence of regular 9 or 10 per second rhythms in the occipital or other leads, and the absence of sudden shifts in frequency. The degree of abnormality was indicated on a rating scale of four points.

RESULTS

Among the 183 relatives of the epileptic patients examined, 60 per cent had definite cerebral dysrhythmia, and 8 per cent had records which were classified as questionable. Thus only 32 per cent of these near relatives of epileptic patients showed brain waves which were found consistently and unquestionably normal. On the other hand, 84 per cent of the 100 normal control subjects gave records which were clearly normal. Only 10 per cent exhibited somewhat abnormal records, and only 6 per cent gave records which were questionable. Thus definite abnormalities of cortical rhythms were found to be six times as frequent in the relatives of patients as in the control group.

Encephalographic records were obtained from both parents of each of 55 patients. In 35 per cent of these the records of mother and father alike were definitely abnormal, and in 60 per cent the record of one parent was abnormal. In only 5 per cent were the records of both parents unmistakably normal.

In a later report,[1] based upon observations on a larger number of cases, similar findings are presented. Electroencephalograms were recorded for 470 near relatives of 140 epileptic patients, including in many cases both parents of the subject. Some kind of abnormality of brain wave was observed in 50 per cent of this group of 470 near relatives, in contrast to 16 per cent of an adult normal control group. Rhythms which were slightly slower or faster than the average were 2.6 times more frequent in relatives than in control subjects; very slow or very fast rhythms were 6 times more frequent than in the control group, and discharges of a seizure type were 8 times more frequent.

DISCUSSION

The results of these studies indicate that the cerebral dysrhythmia typical of epilepsy has a much higher incidence among the near relatives of the epileptics studied than it has among persons not related to epileptics. The authors conclude from this result that the brain condition which is responsible for dysrhythmia—and therefore, in their opinion, for a predisposition to epileptic seizure—is inherited.

However, caution must be observed in interpreting this conclusion. It should be emphasized, in the first place, that the findings of Lennox do not mean that epilepsy itself is inheritable. What the findings

[1] Lennox, W. G. Marriage and Children for the Epileptic. *Human Fertility*, 1945, vol. 10, pp. 95–105.

indicate, rather, is that an abnormal brain condition which is responsible for the dysrhythmia is inherited. This inherited brain condition may be conceived as constituting a predisposition to epileptic seizure. But the presence of dysrhythmia does not mean that epilepsy necessarily will develop in the given individual. The dysrhythmia may only indicate the existence of a condition that makes the individual more likely than the average person to develop seizures if the necessary precipitating factors are present.

In the second place, as has already been noted, dysrhythmia and epileptic seizures seem to appear, not only as a consequence of inherited brain conditions, but also because of environmentally caused accidents such as head injuries suffered either at birth or postnatally, neurosyphilis, and other organic nervous diseases. In most such cases, it may be presumed that the encephalogram of the patient prior to his injury was entirely normal. Only a few of the relatives of such patients show dysrhythmia.

In the third place, it is worthy of note that when treatment of epileptic patients—as by various special diets, and sedative drugs—succeeds in reducing the number of seizures, the dysrhythmia also tends to occur with lessened frequency. Hence in some clinics E. E. G. tests are made to obtain further indications as to the effectiveness of the treatments given. Even if the pattern of cerebral dysrhythmia is determined to some extent by hereditary factors, it appears that it may be altered by chemical means.

Finally, one must not assume that these discoveries of Lennox afford any hope for the elimination of epilepsy by eugenic means. The prohibition of the marriage of epileptics would have little significance. Since epileptics constitute only a small proportion of people with dysrhythmia, the restriction would have little effect on the transmission to offspring of a predisposition toward epilepsy. Widening of the marriage prohibition to include all those with dysrhythmia as well as actual epileptics is obviously impracticable since, as has been said, the brain-wave abnormality occurs in about 10 per cent of the population. The epileptic person who is contemplating marriage may derive reassurance from Lennox's assertion that the chances that the child of an epileptic parent will be an epileptic are no more than 1 in 40.[1]

[1] Lennox, W. G. The Genetics of Epilepsy. *American Journal of Psychiatry*, 1947, vol. 103, p. 458.

The conception of the inheritance of a predisposition may be applied in connection with a wide range of human traits. For example, few if any specialists in the field maintain that the various neuroses and psychoses are directly inheritable. A preferable view is that, by virtue of heritable characteristics transmitted through the germ plasm, an organic condition may arise in development, perhaps centering within the nervous system and especially the brain, which makes the individual relatively more likely than most people to have such disorders.

The correlation of cerebral dysrhythmia with epilepsy obviously encourages the expectation that similar correlations may be established between particular brain-wave patterns and other psychological and physiological conditions of the organism, both normal and abnormal. Of course it is possible that detectable brain-wave patterns represent such psychological and physiological conditions only incompletely and correspond to them only partially. But it is also very likely that the methods now employed in the study of brain waves are not sufficiently refined to reveal the extent to which a correspondence exists. Present techniques appear to record only the rhythmic discharges of large masses of cerebral neurones acting in unison. For example, investigators of cortical action potentials believe that the alpha rhythm, observed when a subject is at rest, reflects a massive discharge of such neurones, and that this mass action disappears when the subject becomes engaged in specific psychological activities. At such times definite waves disappear from the record, and it is quite probable that this disappearance is due to the fact that different groups of neurones now function in different rhythms, out of phase with each other, so that cancellation effects are produced as far as any obtainable records are concerned. A principal deficiency of the methods currently in use is that they do not reveal the minute potentials of single neurones or of small groups of neurones. Should it ever become possible to observe and record such potentials—and new technical discoveries may at any time make this feat possible—the scientist would have in his hands an instrument which might at last inform him as to what happens in the nervous system during thinking, learning, and the many other activities which constitute the subject matter of psychology.

CHAPTER XIII

THE EFFECT OF DISTRACTION UPON THE PERFORMANCE OF CERTAIN TASKS

INTRODUCTION

Of considerable practical importance are problems relating to the influence of distracting stimuli upon "mental" work and upon attentive attitudes or "mental sets" involved in the performance of tasks. Of especial interest is the problem of the effect upon such processes of auditory distractions, since noises are the most common and the most disturbing annoyances for most people. As Morgan[1] states,

> We know that in the reading of a particularly interesting book we can become entirely oblivious to everything about us, even severe noises. But not one of us will seek a particularly noisy place to take our reading, no matter how interesting it may be. When we enter a reading room we are confronted by the sign "Silence!" If we have some hard mental task, noise becomes really distasteful to us. It is then an important problem to determine just what effect a situation replete with irrelevant noises may have upon our performance. If it is merely a foolish fancy with which we are obsessed when we desire quiet, it is well that we know it. If noise is a hindrance, can it be overcome? If so, at what cost? These and many other questions are worthy of solution.

Perhaps some of these "many other questions" are the following: Does the effect of "distracting" noise depend upon what we are doing, *e.g.*, the complexity of the tasks, whether much or little in the way of thinking may be involved? Is the radio generally a help or a hindrance to study; or does its effect perhaps depend upon what the radio is playing at the time or upon the nature of the material which is being learned?

Many attempts have been made to determine experimentally the effect of noises upon the performance of various tasks. However, much of the earlier work in this field is open to criticism on several scores. For example, many of the tasks set for the subjects involved

[1] Morgan, J. J. B. The Overcoming of Distraction and Other Resistances. *Archives of Psychology*, 1916, No. 35, p. 2.

responses which, through practice, could be made automatic, that is, performed without thought or without need of continuous attention or concentration; such tasks are unsuited for use in experiments of this kind, since it has been shown that acts which have become automatic are relatively uninfluenced by "distracting" stimuli. Furthermore, in such investigations the sounds introduced were generally intermittent, and it is possible that under such conditions important parts of a task can be performed (for example, several sums can be calculated in a series of short addition examples) between the recurrences of the disturbing stimuli.

One of the first experiments to be planned in such a way as to remedy these defects was that of Morgan,[1] often quoted in psychological literature dealing with the effects of distraction upon behavior. Morgan's procedure was to have each subject perform a task alternately with and without noise distraction, beginning in each case with a period of performance in which there was no distraction. The task was a rather complicated one, in which the subjects were required to translate a series of letters into a series of numbers by means of a code which was given them and to respond by pressing keys marked with the numbers in question. The apparatus included an exposure device for displaying the letters and the code numbers, a row of 10 keys, and devices for recording which key the subject had pressed, his reaction time (the time between his seeing the letter and pressing the key), and the amount of pressure he exerted on the key. Breathing activities were recorded by means of a pneumograph.[2] Various noise-makers were employed, including bells, buzzers, and phonograph records.

The principal findings of Morgan's experiment may be summarized as follows:

1. With some subjects the initial effect of the noise was to retard the speed of work. With other subjects no such retardation was observed.

2. When an initial retardation occurred, there was usually an increase in speed during the noisy period, and frequently toward the end of the noisy period the subject exceeded the speed he had attained before the noises were introduced.

[1] Morgan, *op. cit.*
[2] See footnote on p. 93.

3. More pressure was exerted upon the keys during the noisy periods, suggesting that extra effort was put forth in order to overcome the effect of distraction. This increased effort was maintained with fair uniformity throughout the noisy period.

4. Spontaneous articulation, that is, whispering or saying the numbers and letters aloud, occurred during the noisy periods. These verbal activities may have helped the subject to overcome the effects of the noise.

5. There was no consistent increase in errors of performance during the noisy periods.

From these results it follows that records of speed and accuracy of performance of a task are not sufficient to show whether one condition is more or less favorable for "mental" work than another. Changes in an individual's energy expenditure are also significant in determining the relative advantages of different working conditions. Accordingly, it would appear that, after becoming adjusted to a noisy situation, a subject can perform tasks such as those set by Morgan as rapidly and as accurately as in a quiet situation, *but at the cost of a greater expenditure of energy.*

Additional evidence bearing upon the problem of auditory distraction was obtained by Ford, whose experiment is reviewed below.

I. FORD'S EXPERIMENT[1]

PURPOSE

In an experiment similar in many respects to that of Morgan, Ford endeavored to find out whether the introduction and the removal of distracting auditory stimuli would produce changes in efficiency of performance from problem to problem in a series. While Morgan had been able to show that often the first few problems in a series performed under conditions of distraction require a longer time for solution than do later ones, he had not made a complete study of the relationship between the position of a problem in a series and the efficiency with which it is solved under distracting conditions. The present experiment was designed to yield data which would make it possible to study solution time and accuracy, writing pressure, and

[1] Adapted from Ford, A. Attention-automatization: an Investigation of the Transitional Nature of Mind. *American Journal of Psychology*, 1929, vol. 41, pp. 1–32.

breathing changes as functions of the position of the problem in a series while the worker is subjected to distracting noise.

The Task. The subject's task was to note all of the numbers in a row of mixed letters and numerals, to add these numbers as he discovered them, and to write their sum on a strip of paper. The following is an example of one of the problems:

$$G \; d \; 7 \; F \; c \; 8 \; N \; f \; E \; a \; W \; 9 \; M \; B \; c \; O \; P \; T \; 5 \; F \; z \; A \; 4 \; N \; V \; c \; X \; z \; 6 \; M$$
$$k \; h \; g \; P \; 9 \; x \; t \; b$$

In each example, the numbers were scattered throughout the series of symbols without any predictable order. Sixty tasks of this type were devised.

The Distractions. Two methods of producing a noise distraction were used. In preliminary experiments, performed chiefly with the aim of improving the technique and perfecting the apparatus, a phonograph fitted with a loud needle was employed. Its amplifying horn was placed as close as possible to the subject's head. The record selected was a humorous monologue delivered in a male voice. In the later experiments, a Klaxon automobile horn placed about 2 feet from the subject's ear was used. The horn, which was sounded continuously, proved to be more satisfactory as a distractor than the phonograph record used in the earlier experiments.

Procedure. The subject sat alone in a room which was relatively free from extraneous and uncontrolled noises. A 60-watt incandescent lamp overhead gave a constant amount of illumination, while another 60-watt lamp on the table at the subject's side threw a bright light on the card of problems held in front of him in a rack. The electric wiring was arranged so that, without entering the room, the experimeter could turn on this table lamp as a signal for the subject to begin work, and turn it off as a signal for him to stop. All recording instruments and control switches were in another room, sound-insulated from the subject.

The entire series of 60 problems was placed before the subject on one card, and an endless belt was arranged for exposing the numbers indicating to him the problem which was to be solved next. The pushing of a lever by the subject brought a new number into view and at the same time moved to a new position the strip of paper on which he recorded his answers. This strip of paper was drawn on a spindle so as to run over a wooden plaque, fastened to a sheet of very stiff rubber which had been stretched over a large tambour (*i.e.*, a drumlike chamber). The tambour was connected by means of rubber tubing with a recording tambour in the experimenter's room, so that the subject's writing pressure could be recorded pneumatically on a kymograph drum. The arrangement for recording the subject's writing pressure is shown in Fig 27. A timing device made dots at 1-second intervals on the same kymograph drum, so that the time required for the solution of each problem could be measured by counting the dots between the mark indicating the presenting of the problem and the mark indicating its completion.

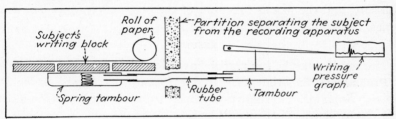

Fig. 27. Schematic Representation of Ford's Apparatus for Recording Writing Pressure.

The procedure involved first telling the subject the nature of the problems and then having him solve one sample problem, so that the process might be perfectly clear to him. After this, the noises were turned on for a moment, that the subject might also become acquainted with the nature of the distraction. The subject was told to work as rapidly as possible, to remember that both speed and accuracy records were being taken, and to try to resist interferences from any source until the signal to stop was given. After receiving the signal to start, the subject worked in succession upon eight of the problems. Then, as he began the next (that is, the ninth) problem, the noise was turned on. The noise persisted for exactly six problems, after which it was abruptly discontinued. Then the subject worked on six more problems under quiet conditions.

After the last problem had been solved, the subject was asked to describe his impressions during the work (his thoughts, feelings, etc.), and all significant "introspective" reports were recorded.

Subjects. Sixteen subjects were used for the preliminary experiments, and forty-one for the later (main) experiment. All were university students.

Treatment of Data. The measurements taken into consideration were those for the six reactions just prior to the introduction of the noise, the six during noise distraction, and the six during the quiet period following the discontinuance of the noise. (There were eight reactions in the first quiet period, but the results for the first two were discarded.) For each of these series of six problems the time scores, pressure values, and other data for the several subjects were averaged separately for each problem. That is to say, the average for all first problems was computed and recorded, then the average for all second problems, etc. This made it possible to study reaction time, writing pressure, and the like as functions of the position of a problem in the series.

RESULTS

The results may be summarized as follows.

Preliminary Experiments, *with the Phonograph Record as the Distracting Stimulus.* In these preliminary experiments it was found that

1. No practice effect was evident.

2. The initial problem in the distraction period required a conspicuously greater solution time than did any other in the series.

3. The six problems of the distraction period considered as a whole required a longer time than did those of either quiet period.

4. There was very little correlation between writing pressure and solution time.

Later Experiments, *with the Automobile Horn as the Distracting Stimulus.* These experiments yielded the following results:

1. A definite lengthening of solution time occurred at the beginning both of the noise period and of the following quiet period.

2. The initial retardation was more marked at the beginning of the noise period than at the beginning of the subsequent quiet period.

3. The fact that the cessation both of noisy and of quiet conditions seemed to function as a distracting occurrence was corroborated by the subject's introspective reports.

4. Under the conditions employed, the introduction of auditory distractions had little, if any, effect on the accuracy (that is, the number of errors committed) of the subjects' performance.

5. The reduction in speed of performance which resulted from a change of conditions endured longer for slow than for rapid workers.

6. Writing pressure increased during the period of noise and diminished from problem to problem during the following quiet period.

7. The breathing curves yielded the same evidence of verbal activity during auditory distraction as was found by Morgan.

DISCUSSION

One of the most conspicuous features of the records was the evidence of an initial lengthening of solution time, not only at the beginning of the noise period, but also at the beginning of the following quiet period. This result is interpreted by Ford as meaning that the onset of *both the noise and the quiet constituted distractions.* Since, when the automobile horn was used, the initial slowing was greater at the beginning of the noise period than it was at the beginning of the following quiet period, it may be concluded that the noise was more distracting than was the ensuing change to absolute quiet. Nevertheless, it is clear that the cessation of the noise was genuinely disturbing to most subjects. In this connection the introspective reports are very significant. For example, subjects reported that when the quiet period began they missed the noise and wished it had not stopped, or that when the horn stopped sounding they were astonished because they had forgotten it was in operation. Others said that they "missed the racket" and were bothered by the "uproarious quiet," that they could "hear the silence," etc. Often subjects would report that they wished the noise would stop, but when it did stop they then said they wished it had not done so. Some subjects reported that they had liked the noise because it produced an exciting effect. Most of the subjects were certain that they had worked more slowly during the noisy period and were equally sure that they had worked somewhat faster when the noise had stopped. However, the results showed that this had not been the case.

As we have pointed out, not only the noise but also the change from noise to quiet was distracting to the subjects. From this it may be inferred that any marked change in the general pattern of stimulation under which a person is working can constitute a distraction. Noises are commonly disturbing. But they are disturbing, not so much because they are noises, as because they usually occur intermittently and therefore continually alter the general stimulus pattern to which one is reacting.

Like Morgan, Ford found that auditory distractions had little or no effect on errors. Furthermore, he found that the effect of the distraction was about equal for fast and for slow workers in the first problem of the noisy and of the quiet periods. But the fast workers recovered very quickly from the effects of the distractions, whereas the slow workers did not recover until they had almost completed the entire series of six problems. Apparently, the slow workers had exceptional difficulty in building up a stereotyped, routine resistance to distraction, a disability which may well be one cause for their characteristically slow pace of performance.

We have in Ford's data evidence that the initial reactions of a series are highly susceptible to interference from new sources of stimulation, but that the later reactions of the series show recovery from the effects of such interference. Further analysis of these data shows that the solution time and the writing-pressure values changed from problem to problem throughout the series in such a way as to form definite gradients; that is to say, the pressure increased gradually during periods of noise and diminished gradually during quiet periods. This fact suggests that resistance to distraction is not based upon some change in the organism which occurs suddenly and all at once, but rather that it develops gradually, as if it were a process of habit formation and of learning.

II. FURTHER STUDIES OF ENERGY EXPENDITURE AND OF MUSCULAR TENSION UNDER DISTRACTION

The occurrence of increased energy expenditure, as evidenced by increased muscular tensions during periods of auditory distraction, is of course of great interest from a practical as well as from a theoretical point of view. Subsequent to the pioneer studies of Morgan and Ford, several investigators have attempted to study energy expenditure under distraction by measuring metabolic rate,[1] and to study muscular

[1] Metabolic rate is the rate at which nutritive substances are assimilated and built up into living protoplasm within the organism on the one hand, and the rate at which, on the other hand, living matter is broken down into simpler products. It is measured in terms of the rate at which oxygen is consumed by the individual. In order to make this measurement, the subject's nose is closed with a spring clip, and a special mouthpiece is provided through which oxygen is inhaled from a reservoir and carbon dioxide

tensions as recorded by action-potential techniques.[2]

In 1939 Freeman[3] published laboratory findings obtained through the use of both of these methods. Freeman had been impressed by an apparent incompatibility in the results obtained by different investigators concerning the energy costs of mental work performed under distraction. On the one hand, Morgan had reported *a sustained increase in muscular tension,* and Ford *a progressive increase in tension* under distraction. On the other hand, in another study, Davis[4] had found that although noise stimulation produced an increase in the magnitude of the action potentials recorded from the right arms of subjects who were solving problems, the tension thus indicated diminished as the noise continued, instead of increasing further or remaining at its initial high level. Harmon[5] had shown that the subject's metabolism per unit of work done increased when noise was first introduced, but noted that in a relatively short time the worker tended to return to the metabolic rate characteristic of work under conditions of quiet. A possible explanation of this seeming incompatibility of results was suggested by Poffenberger,[6] who said:

One might accept the increased tensions noted by Morgan as authentic, and interpret the reduced tensions demonstrated by Davis as a *shift of tensions* to new muscles with a reduction of tension only in those muscles on which measurements were being made at the time. The decreasing metabolic cost as adaptation to the distraction progressed would indicate merely that the later tension patterns functioned more economically than the earlier ones,—that is, with less expenditure of energy.

In Freeman's experimental situation, subjects solved problems in addition successively under conditions of quiet and of noise stimu-

---

and unused oxygen are exhaled into a chamber containing soda lime. The carbon dioxide is absorbed by the soda lime, and the unused oxygen is returned to the oxygen reservoir. Since metabolic rate is a function of rate of oxygen consumption, an index of metabolism may be obtained by determining the rate at which oxygen is drawn from the reservoir.

[2] Freeman, G. L. Changes in Tension-pattern and Total Energy Expenditure during Adaptation to Distracting Stimuli. *American Journal of Psychology,* 1939, vol. 52, pp. 354–360.

[3] See pp. 216–218 for a description of action-potential techniques.

[4] Davis, R. C. The Muscular Tension Reflex and Two of Its Modifying Conditions. Indiana University Publications, Science Service, 1935, No. 3, pp. 1–23.

[5] Harmon, F. L. The Effect of Noise upon Certain Psychological and Physiological Processes. *Archives of Psychology,* 1937, No. 147.

[6] Poffenberger, A. T. Some Unsolved Problems in Human Adjustment. *Science,* 1938, vol. 87, pp. 124–129.

lation, with rest periods preceding the work periods.   Records were obtained over a period of 12 days.   Determinations of oxygen consumption were made both during rest periods and during quiet and noisy work periods, and records of muscular action potentials were made independently for each of the subjects' four limbs.   As is usual in experiments of this kind, it was found that the introduction of a noise distraction was followed by a reduction in work output, but that this reduction was only temporary and that no decrease in accuracy occurred.   In addition, analysis of the action-potential records revealed evidence of shifting tension patterns, as Poffenberger had suggested in his interpretation of Harmon's results.   The indications were that the immediate effect of noise distraction was to bring about increased and widespread bodily tensions, and that this change was paralleled by an increase in oxygen consumption.   With continuation of the distracting noises, however, the tensions became more or less limited to the parts of the body used in the performance of the task, and as the tensions became less widespread, energy expenditure as measured in terms of oxygen consumption dropped to a lower level.

III. THE INFLUENCE OF MUSIC DISTRACTION UPON READING EFFICIENCY: FENDRICK'S EXPERIMENT

PURPOSE

While many investigations of auditory distraction have been carried out as laboratory studies, observations have also been made in the office, the classroom, and the factory.   Of especial interest to students is the experiment of Fendrick,[1] the aim of which was to determine the influence of radio or phonograph music upon reading speed and comprehension.   This investigator notes that both students and laymen express varying opinions concerning the way in which their reading comprehension is affected by the radio.   For example, Cantril and Allport[2] report that when 142 college students who owned radios responded to questionnaires, 68 per cent of them said that they *believed* that their study was less effective when the radio was "on." Most students reported, however, that music interfered with study less than speeches did, and that when they decided to have the radio on while studying they generally selected a musical program.   This is

[1] Adapted from Fendrick, P.   The Influence of Music Distraction upon Reading Efficiency.   *Journal of Educational Research*, 1937, vol. 3, pp. 264–271.

[2] Cantril, H., and G. W. Allport.   *The Psychology of Radio*.   New York, Harper, 1935.

precisely what one might expect, in view of the fact that the auditory language patterns of a radio speech probably interfere more directly than does music with the visual language patterns characteristic of reading.

The aim of Fendrick's investigation was to measure the difference in reading or study efficiency that might manifest itself when college students were asked to study a selected assignment in the classroom with and without distraction by phonographic music.

METHOD

Subjects. While Morgan, Ford, and Freeman had employed the single-group method of experimentation, Fendrick used the equivalent-group method.[1] The groups were two sections of college sophomores registered in a course in introductory psychology. One section containing 61 students served as the control group (the group which was to work without distraction); the other, composed of 62 students, constituted the "experimental" group. The two groups were equated with respect to chronological age, and their average scores on a test of intelligence were approximately equal.

Procedure. Each section was given as the study assignment a 12-page mimeographed chapter abstracted from a psychology textbook which the students had not seen previously. A period of exactly 30 min. was allowed for study of the chapter. While the control group worked under quiet conditions, music from phonograph records was used as the distractor for the experimental group, since it was not possible to get the desired kind of radio broadcast at the time chosen for the experiment. The records selected provided lively semiclassical music.

Promptly after the end of the study period a 60-item true-false test on the contents of the chapter was given. Fifteen minutes were allowed for the answering of the questions. Each student was asked

---

[1] The "single-group" method involves the use of one group of subjects. Each subject performs and is observed or tested under the two or more conditions imposed in the experiment, for example, with and without distraction. The "equivalent-group" method makes use of two or more groups of subjects so selected that if the groups were to perform under identical conditions, the averages and measures of variability would be the same for the groups. Equivalent groups must therefore be equal with respect to average age, intelligence, or any other factor which might be related to the performance or capacity being measured. One group then performs under one set of conditions while the other performs under different conditions. The results of the two groups are then compared.

to indicate on the test blank the number of pages he had read in the 30-min. period. He also was asked if playing the radio while he was studying usually annoyed, pleased, or made no difference to him.

The subjects in both groups were divided into five subgroups according to their quintile ranks[1] on the above-mentioned intelligence test, and the average "comprehension" scores on the true-false test for experimental and control subjects within each quintile intelligence group were compared.

RESULTS

Fifty per cent of the subjects reported that usually they did not like to study with the radio on; 25 per cent said they did like to study with the radio on; the remaining 25 per cent reported "indifference."

The results of the reading comprehension tests are summarized in Table I.

TABLE I

Average Comprehension Scores for Control and Experimental Subjects, Differences between Control and Experimental Averages, Standard Errors of the Differences, and Critical Ratios.

	Quintile rank, by intelligence					Total, all subjects
	I	II	III	IV	V	
Average scores in quiet condition........	22.50	30.54	35.25	36.00	38.63	33.69
Average scores in noise condition........	22.13	24.08	31.58	31.67	33.83	29.58
Difference between averages.............	0.37	6.46	3.67	4.33	4.80	4.11
Standard error of difference.............	3.56	3.58	2.77	2.32	2.21	1.57
Critical ratio..........................	0.1	1.8	1.3	1.9	2.2	2.6

It may be noted that, although some of the critical ratios[2] are small, the difference in every quintile group favored the nondistracted subjects. The difference of 4.11 points between the groups as wholes has a critical ratio of 2.6 and therefore possesses a considerable degree of statistical significance. Statistically speaking, the chances are about 97 in 100 that a repetition of the experiment would yield a difference in the same direction.

[1] If the members of a group are arranged in order of standing with respect to some trait, those in the lowest fifth of the group are said to fall within the first quintile, those in the second fifth are said to fall in the second quintile, etc.

[2] See footnote on p. 9 for a definition of "critical ratio."

The results also show that, with the exception of the difference for the second quintile subgroup, there is a gradual increase in the size of the differences between the average scores for distracted and non-distracted subjects as the level of intelligence becomes higher. This suggests that distractors of the kind employed in this experiment have a greater disturbing effect for subjects at higher levels of intelligence.

Although the average comprehension scores were higher for the nondistracted groups, the distracted subjects read a greater amount of material. Of the nondistracted subjects, only 17, or 28 per cent, read the entire assignment during the 30-min. study period, whereas 26, or 43 per cent of the distracted group, finished the reading. However, since the critical ratio of the difference was only 1.8, we cannot be confident that repetition of the experiment would not yield a difference in the opposite direction. Also, it is apparent that although the distracted group read more pages during the 30-min. study period, what advantage they gained thereby is not clear, in view of their inferiority in reading accuracy and comprehension.

DISCUSSION

Fendrick's experimental results indicate that auditory distraction of the kind employed by him does have an adverse effect, at least for most subjects, upon reading comprehension as measured by scores on an immediate true-false test. However, several questions remain unanswered. Is there an adaptation process in the "reading-with-distraction" situation, comparable to the adaptation observed by Morgan, Freeman, Ford, and others? It may be that the music exerted its greatest effect early in the period and that some adaptation occurred later on. The way in which the experiment was planned does not make it possible to answer this question. Furthermore, it is possible that the actual effects of the auditory distraction were quite different for different subjects of the experimental group. The music may have had little or no effect upon the reading comprehension of some of the subjects, a moderate effect upon that of some, and a relatively large effect upon that of others. The differences in the group averages for distracted and nondistracted subjects *may* be attributable largely to pronounced effects which the distraction had upon a few individuals, or it *may* be attributable to a moderate effect of distraction upon all or nearly all of the distracted subjects. Only a single-group method of experimentation could give us information concerning the effect of distraction in individual cases.

IV. NOISE IN INDUSTRY

Psychological literature contains many reports on observations concerning the effect of noise on work in offices and factories. For example, Kornhauser[1] compared the productivity of the same four typists when they were working in quiet and in noisy offices. No significant differences were observed with respect to errors, amount typed, or number of letters discarded because of numerous mistakes in them. In another office study, however, a noise reduction of 14.5 per cent brought about an increase of 8.8 per cent in the work output of typists and a decrease of 24 per cent in the number of errors committed. The noise reduction also decreased employee turnover by 47 per cent and absenteeism by 37 per cent. It is possible that in the latter situation the amount of auditory stimulation which prevailed before reduction was greater than the amount present under Kornhauser's noisy condition. In one factory study using as subjects workers assembling temperature regulators, it was found that moving their work from the vicinity of a boiler shop to a quiet area increased their production more than 37 per cent and decreased errors by one-eighth [2]

It would seem that, although in industry noise does not always diminish productivity, it *does not increase production*, as it did in some of the laboratory experiments after adaptation to noise had occurred. It has been suggested that this difference may be attributable to a difference in motivation. People are capable of working as well during noise stimulation as during a quiet period, but they must be strongly motivated to do so.

Various other reports[3] indicate that music has a favorable effect upon the productive efforts of factory workers when the tasks performed are simple and repetitive and have become automatized. It is even probable that in such a work situation, a limited distraction in the form of enjoyable music helps to lessen monotony and to maintain a more favorable attitude on the part of the worker.

[1] Kornhauser, A. W. The Effects of Noise on Office Output, *Industrial Psychology*, 1929, vol. 2, pp. 621–622.

[2] Anon. *Industrial Psychology*, 1928, vol. 3, p. 323.

[3] Smith, H. C. Music in Relation to Employee Attitudes, Piecework Production, and Industrial Accidents. *Applied Psychology Monographs*, 1947, No. 14.

Conclusions

Earlier we noted Morgan's question whether our desire for quiet is "merely a foolish fancy with which we are obsessed," and "If noise is a hindrance, can it be overcome? If so, at what cost?" The findings of his investigation and of the studies of Ford, Freeman, and Fendrick provide a basis for answering these questions. The normal desire for quiet conditions of work can scarcely be regarded as a "foolish fancy." Seemingly, noise is usually somewhat of a hindrance, at least at its onset. Its effects can be overcome, but only at the cost of what often is a considerable expenditure of energy. Furthermore, we must not disregard the possibility that the individual's increased tension in maintaining his habituated adjustment to an originally "distracting" stimulus may eventually be detrimental to health. Nevertheless, it is clear that if we become adjusted or adapted to a constant noise, its sudden termination may also constitute a distraction, at least temporarily. Hence the fundamental characteristic of a stimulus that we call "distracting" is that it constitutes a change with respect to previous conditions of stimulation.

The question whether or not the practice of studying to the accompaniment of the radio is a desirable one is difficult to answer at this time. An individual who had formed this habit would probably be "distracted" if the radio were turned off. However, it also seems very likely that studying under such circumstances usually requires a greater expenditure of energy and that the habit is therefore an uneconomical one for most people.

CHAPTER XIV

A COMPARISON OF THE INTELLIGENCE OF "RACIAL" AND NATIONAL GROUPS IN EUROPE

INTRODUCTION

The development of intelligence tests and their popular acceptance as a means of differentiating *individuals* of different levels or degrees of intellectual capacity have led to the attempt to employ these instruments for a variety of other specific purposes, among them the discovery of whether or not there are "superior" and "inferior" *races* of mankind. The hypothesis that some racial groups are inherently (*i.e.*, by heredity) more intelligent than others is commonly held. This hypothesis, however, is one which cannot easily be tested, first, because of the difficulty of securing a test of intelligence which will be equally valid as a measuring rod for individuals of widely different cultural backgrounds, and, second, because of the difficulty of identifying and isolating these so-called "races."

One obstacle in the way of securing a universally applicable measure of intelligence is, obviously, the language in which the test is constructed. For example, if the original Binet test is to be used with children in the public schools of Shanghai, it must first be translated into Chinese. The adequate translation into English of those parts of the test which were originally written in French presented certain difficulties. These difficulties are greatly increased when the translation must be made into a particular dialect of Chinese (or Aleut, or Bushman, or Fiji). But the difficulties of "translation"—if the test is to be equally fair[1] to the children of the various groups under comparison—go far beyond those dependent upon language differences alone. For example, in Shanghai the coins used in one part of the test can no longer be American ones. And even when we have selected

---

[1] A test may be said to be equally fair to the individuals or groups under comparison if performance on it is not significantly affected by *differences* among them in past experience, *i.e.*, in education, in culture, in socioeconomic status, etc.

Chinese coins for use with the Shanghai children, have we the right to assume that the test is now as fair for them as it is for American children, that is, that the familiarity of Chinese children with the Chinese money system, based on the frequency with which they handle and use Chinese coins, is as great as is that of American children with the American money system? And how is one to "translate" this test item for the children of a culture in which coins are not used at all? One encounters difficulties of equal magnitude in attempting to adapt many of the items included in any intelligence test standardized in a particular cultural group for use with the members of another. The specific objects pictured in an "object-recognition" test (*e.g.*, a bicycle, a glove, etc.) may be less common in one culture than in another, or familiar in *different* forms or shapes, or even completely unknown. The situations presented in a test of ethical discriminations may be susceptible of translation into the language of a particular group, but obviously, if the system of morality of that culture is a markedly different one, the test is simply not applicable. Furthermore, the validity of a given test item may vary considerably even for different groups of children who speak the same language and live in the same country. For example, the following incomplete sentence is an item in an intelligence test which has been widely used in the United States:

..... should prevail in churches and libraries.[1]

The expected completion is the word "Silence." This may be a fair question for twelve-year-old New York City children, but it is wholly unfair to Southern rural Negro children, many of whom have never seen a library, and many of whom are members of "revivalist" sects, who judge the "success" of a church meeting according to the amount of vociferous participation by the congregation.

There are other more deep-seated differences among various cultures which may render difficult or impossible a comparison of the intelligence of the different cultural groups on the basis of their performance on any given test. In certain societies, for example, great value is placed on the careful, meticulous execution of tasks, and there is little or no interest in the length of time taken to complete them, provided the product is of high quality. People of such cultures cannot validly

[1] National Intelligence Test, Scale A, Form 1, Test 2, item 20.

be examined by any of the many psychological tests in which speed of performance is a criterion of ability and constitutes one of the bases for computing the test score.[1]   Another deeply rooted cultural difference is in the degree of motivation (and therefore of effort one is willing to expend) in meeting such situations as intelligence tests present.   Children bred in societies in which the stress on the importance of winning the approval of adults which characterizes our society is less emphatic or virtually absent may be far more lackadaisical in their attitude toward the test situation.   Finally, there are cultures in which individual competitiveness plays a much smaller role than it does in the United States,[2] cultures in which group *mores* encourage a great deal more of mutual aid, consultation among individuals, and the cooperative performance of activities.   Psychologists and anthropologists who have attempted to test the intelligence of members of such societies have reported that the subjects were often surprised and disappointed that they were not permitted to help each other on the examinations. Confronted by a strange situation, and deprived of their habitual recourse to assistance by their friends and relatives, they tended to lose interest in the tests.[3]

Although the factors which have been discussed do not exhaust the list of culturally based differences among people which inevitably affect the nature of their performance on intelligence tests, they furnish sufficient evidence for seriously mistrusting the validity of any intelligence test standardized on a "population sample" of a given nationality or "race" for the members of any other national or "racial" group.

The second fundamental difficulty in the comparative measurement of racial intelligence is the problem of the identification of the races. Normally, it is relatively easy to determine the *nationality* of an individual: he is, usually, one of an aggregate of people living under a common governmental system and occupying a geographical area

---

[1] A culture in which speed in the performance of tasks usually is not deemed important, largely because time means little or nothing, is that of the Yakima Reservation Indians. See Klineberg, O. An Experimental Study of Speed and Other Factors in "Racial" Differences. *Archives of Psychology*, 1928, No. 93.

[2] An example of such a culture is that of the American Zuni, described in Chap. IV.

[3] A group of Australian aboriginals who behaved in this manner under test conditions is described in Porteus, S. D.   *The Psychology of a Primitive People: A Study of the Australian Aborigine.*   New York, Longmans, 1931.

which bears the national name.[1]   Nations, however, are not races, and the problem of the definitive designation of a given individual's *race* is a far more complex one.   Different groups of mankind, occupying various areas of the earth, exhibit obvious intragroup similarities and intergroup differences in certain traits of physique, primarily in color. Some ethnologists have differentiated "races" of men on the basis of skin color alone.   Others have attempted more elaborate "racial" differentiations—for example, distinctions between subdivisions of the white race (*i.e.*, the Mediterranean, the Alpine, and the Nordic "racial" types) on the basis of the principal geographic distribution of people who show differences in such traits as eye and hair coloration, head proportions, and stature.   Most scientists are agreed that such anatomical differences derive in large measure from inherent (*i.e.*, hereditary) factors.   But there is considerable disagreement regarding the validity of two inferences which some writers have drawn from the foregoing facts: first, that groups of people who show distinctive physical traits constitute different "stocks" or "strains" of mankind, analogous to different breeds of dogs, or of beef cattle, or of other infrahuman animals; and, second, that differences in significant psychological traits (*e.g.*, in intelligence) are associated with the observed anatomical differences.

Actually, throughout the period of recorded history, and doubtless also for the ages during which men lived on the earth without leaving chronicles of their existence, there have occurred countless invasions, migrations, and emigrations of people inhabiting certain terrestrial areas (and showing particular anatomical traits) to other regions, inhabited by people showing different physical characteristics.   Some of these migrations have involved very large, others smaller populations; some have occurred over vast distances, others over more limited ones.   Through the centuries Europe has undergone successive invasions, such as those by the oriental Huns, by the Mongolian followers of Genghis Khan, and by the Moors.   The ancient Greeks and Romans invaded Asia and Africa.   At different times, also, the Romans migrated into Gaul, Britain, western Germany, and Spain; north Europeans overran Greece, Asia Minor, and northern Africa,

---

[1] The definition of nationality (*i.e.*, of citizenship) is not always so simple, as, for example, in the case of the many thousands of "displaced persons" following the Second World War.

and spread westward to Italy and Spain; the Goths and other Germanic tribes, forced out of northeastern Europe by pressure from the Mongolians, spread into Italy and France, and into southern and western Europe generally.   England has been conquered and occupied at various times by the Romans, the Angles, the Saxons, the Danes, and the Normans.   Whether these great movements of men occurred by peaceful migration, by invasion and conquest, or by forced translocation (for purposes of colonization or of slave labor), intermixing of the alien with the native populations inevitably occurred.   Within the United States, for example, despite social and legal barriers of various sorts, there has been a continual interbreeding of Negroes and of Indians with each other and with the varied white and mongolian populations which have immigrated to this country from the beginning of its history.   In view of the fact that Asia and Africa, like Europe and the Americas, have been the scene of many similar migrations and invasions, it is not surprising to learn that in the opinion of almost all ethnologists the existence at present of any pure "racial stock" (apart from a few groups, such as the inhabitants of Iceland and the Australian Bushmen, that live in geographically isolated areas) is extremely unlikely.

Nevertheless, many people persist in thinking of mankind as composed of "pure racial types," and, moreover, consider that certain of these "races" are superior to others.[1]   Adolf Hitler, for example, was not the first and surely will not be the last person to assert the doctrine of the superiority of "the Nordic" to all other men.   The investigation presented below[2] represents an attempt to test the validity of allegations such as these.   Specifically, Klineberg's aim was to study the

[1] It is a "difficult task to establish any race as either superior or inferior, but relatively easy to prove that we entertain a strong prejudice in favor of our own racial superiority. . . ." (Kroeber, A. L. *Anthropology*, p. 85. New York, Harcourt Brace, 1923.)

"As one becomes immersed in the study of racial psychology one comes to realise that the significant factor involved is not by any means the psychical differences of the races, but rather the psychical unity of man. . . . What counts and demands attention is not the problematical difference in racial ability, but the disability of the genus Homo, however sapiens, to think intelligently and without prejudice in this field, so heavily charged with emotion, vanity, special pleading and still lowlier affects. . . ." (Goldenweiser, A. *Anthropology*, p. 36. New York, Appleton-Century-Crofts, 1938.)

See also Linton, R., ed. *The Science of Man in the World Crisis.* New York, Columbia University Press, 1944.

[2] Klineberg, O. A Study of Psychological Differences between "Racial" and National Groups in Europe. *Archives of Psychology*, 1931, vol. 20, No. 132.

intelligence of samples of the "Mediterranean," the "Alpine," and the "Nordic" divisions of the Caucasian race.

The *Nordic type* is said to be distinguished by a long head and face, light hair and eyes, and tall stature. The *Alpine type* is described as having a round head and face, brown hair, and as being medium in height. The *Mediterranean type* is described as having a long head and face, dark eyes, dark brown (or black) hair, and as being somewhat shorter in stature than the "Alpine." On the basis of the prevalence of these three types of physique in the population at large, the three European "races" are found to occupy roughly horizontal belts on the map of Europe. Individuals of the "Nordic type" are distributed principally around the North and Baltic Seas; "Alpines" predominate in the region of the Alps; individuals of the "Mediterranean type" live along the shores of the Mediterranean Sea. The "Nordic type" is found in relatively large numbers in the Scandinavian countries, in England and Scotland, Holland, northern Germany, and northern France. The "Alpine type" predominates in Switzerland, Austria, southern Germany, central France, northern Italy, Russia, and Poland. The "Mediterranean type" is most frequently found in the populations of Spain, Portugal, Greece, southern Italy, southern France, and northern Africa. Of course, many people who bear the physical characteristics of each of these "races" are found also in regions where the other "races" predominate.

KLINEBERG'S STUDY OF THE INTELLIGENCE OF NATIONAL AND "RACIAL" GROUPS IN EUROPE[1]

THE SUBJECTS

The Seven Rural Groups. Klineberg attempted to obtain as "pure" samples of the three European "races" as could be secured. France, Germany, and Italy were selected "because each one of these is made up of at least two of the three European 'races' (France of all three) so that comparisons might be made between different racial groups within the same nation, as well as between different [national] samples of the same racial group" (page 13). Because there is a greater mixture of "types" in cities, "racial" comparisons were made between rural groups only.

[1] Adapted from Klineberg, *op. cit.* See also the chapter by Klineberg in Linton, ed., *op. cit.*, pp. 63–77.

The subjects were all boys, ranging in age from ten to twelve years inclusive. In order to get the "purest" possible samples in sufficient numbers, the study was carried out in those places where individuals who possessed the physical characteristics which are attributed to the "race" under survey were found in greatest concentration. Furthermore, Klineberg selected only children who possessed the physical traits generally considered typical for the given "race," who had been born in the given area, and whose parents had been born there, also.

Three localities in France were selected: a northern district where the characteristics imputed to the "Nordic" are conspicuous in the population, one in the Alpine region, and one in southern France where the "Mediterranean type" prevails. In Germany, a section in the province of Hanover in northwestern Germany was selected for the "Nordic" area, and a section in the Black Forest of Baden for the "Alpine." In Italy, the "Alpine" sample was taken from an area near Turin, and the "Mediterranenean," from a region near Palermo, in Sicily.

In this way, seven "racial" groups were formed: two "Nordic," three "Alpine," and two "Mediterranean," with 100 boys in each group. None of the subjects came from a town with a population of over 3,000. For the selection of his subjects Klineberg adopted the following procedure. In the case of each community, he first collected all the boys who fell within the age range. He then eliminated boys who had been born outside the community or whose parents had been born outside the community, as well as all boys who did not possess the typical physical characteristics of the "race" in question. Every child who was finally placed in a "Nordic" group had fair hair, blue or light-gray eyes, and was long-headed (dolichocephalic) as determined by cranial measurements. Every boy included in the "Alpine" group was brachycephalic (round-headed), and was neither very light nor very dark in eye and hair coloration. Every " Mediterranean" boy had dark hair and eyes and was dolichocephalic. The investigator considered the criterion of stature inapplicable, since the subjects were not fully grown.

The fathers of the boys were, for the most part, peasants and farmers, laborers, wood-cutters, fishermen, and fruit dealers.

The Three City Groups. In each of the cities of Paris, Hamburg, and Rome, 100 boys were selected in order to compare the test scores of the urban with those of the rural children.   Four schools in each of the cities were visited.   From each school 25 boys falling within the required age range were selected at random.   These children did not have to belong to any "racial type," but merely had to be natives of the city in which the study was made.   The principal occupations of the boys' fathers were those of mechanic, clerk, laborer, merchant, factory hand, cabdriver, and waiter.

THE TESTS

Klineberg used six nonlanguage performance tests of the Pintner-Paterson series.   These were the Triangle Test, the Healy Puzzle *A*, the Two Figure Form Board, the Five Figure Form Board, the Casuist Form Board, and the Knox Cube Test.   All of these excepting the Knox test are form-board tests in which the task is to put blocks of wood together in such a way as to fill cutouts in the board.   There is a 5-min. time limit for each of these tests.   Records are kept of the time required to complete each form board and of the number of errors made.   The five form-board tests are shown in Fig. 28.   In the procedure for the Knox Cube Test the experimenter touches four cubes on a table with a fifth cube, in certain predetermined orders.   The subject attempts to repeat the series of movements exactly, and the number of his successes is recorded.

All of Klineberg's subjects were tested individually.   The writer himself gave all the tests, except for the work in Hamburg and Rome, where for a time he was assisted by university students.

RESULTS

The scores obtained on the six tests were combined for each child into a composite score, so that the "general intelligence" score of each child was indicated by the total number of points he received. Table I gives the average score for each of the 10 groups, arranged in order from highest to lowest.   The number of subjects in each group was 100.

City and Country Differences.   A marked and statistically reliable difference[1] was found between the scores made by the city and country children.   The three highest groups were the city groups.   Among

---

[1] The meaning of the statistical reliability of a difference is explained on p.9.

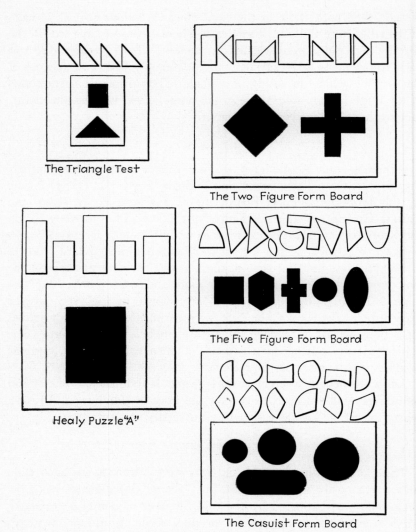

The Triangle Test

The Two Figure Form Board

Healy Puzzle "A"

The Five Figure Form Board

The Casuist Form Board

Fig. 28. Five of the Six Pintner-Paterson Nonlanguage Performance Tests Which Klineberg Used.

In each diagram, the darkened areas within the rectangular board are the cutouts, and the small geometrical forms above the board are the wooden blocks with which the cutouts are to be filled.

the city groups the differences proved to be small and unreliable, although the largest difference, that between Paris and Rome, has 87 chances in 100 of being a true one. On the other hand, the difference

TABLE I

Intelligence-test Scores of the Three Urban and the Seven Rural Groups

Group	Average score	Median score	S.D.[1]
Urban:			
Paris..................................	219.0	218.9	46.2
Hamburg............................	216.4	218.3	45.6
Rome................................	211.8	213.6	42.6
Rural:			
German "Nordic"......................	198.2	197.6	49.0
French "Mediterranean"................	197.4	204.4	45.6
German "Alpine"......................	193.6	199.0	48.0
Italian "Alpine"......................	188.8	186.3	48.4
French "Alpine"......................	180.2	185.3	46.6
French "Nordic"......................	178.8	183.3	56.4
Italian "Mediterranean"...............	173.0	172.7	54.2

[1] The standard deviation (S.D.) is a measure of variability which is computed by obtaining the deviation of every individual score from the average, then squaring each deviation, finding the average of the squares, and extracting the square root of that average.

between the poorest city group and the best country group was found to be highly reliable, the chances being 98 in 100 that there is a true difference.

TABLE II

Intelligence-test Scores of All the City and Country Children

Group	Average score	Median score	S.D.	Number
City.............................	215.7	216.9	45.1	300
Country..........................	187.1	187.0	50.9	700

This difference in favor of the urban over the rural groups becomes especially clear when all the groups of each type are combined. The averages for the combined groups are given in Table II.

The observed superiority of the city children in these six *performance tests* is in accord with the results of many other investigations in the

United States and in other countries in which urban children have regularly been found to excel rural children in standard *language tests* of intelligence. As will be seen later, this city-country difference is far more significant statistically than are any of the differences which the experimenter observed between "racial" and between national groups.

"Race" Differences. An examination of the data in Table I shows that of the seven national samples, the three which obtained the highest ranks comprised one "Nordic," one "Mediterranean," and one "Alpine" group. However, since the differences among the scores of these groups were very small and, moreover, proved to be statistically

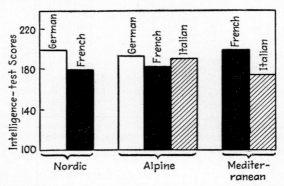

Fig. 29. A Graphic Presentation of the Average Intelligence-test Scores Obtained by the Various National Samples of Each of the Three "Racial" Groups.

unreliable, the groups may be considered about equal in their performance on these tests. Furthermore, it is to be noted that one sample of each of these three "racial" types also ranked relatively low. Finally, it is important to observe the wide differences among different national samples of the same "race." These differences are shown graphically in Fig. 29. From the data for the tests given in Germany, the superiority of the "Nordics" over the "Alpines" is negligible. In Italy, the "Alpines" appear to be superior to the "Mediterraneans"; but in France, the "Mediterraneans" are superior to the "Alpines" and both are superior to the "Nordics." In fact, in France the "Nordic-Alpine-Mediterranean" hierarchy which sometimes has been asserted to exist is completely reversed, and the difference in favor of the "Mediterranean" over the "Nordic" average is almost completely reliable (99.5 chances in 100); there is a completely reliable difference between the medians. In other words, there is no consistent superiority of one "racial" group over another; the hierarchy depends on the particular "Nordic," "Alpine," and "Mediterranean" samples studied.

If all the subjects are classified according to "race," without regard to nationality, the resulting averages and median scores for the different "racial" groups are as given in Table III.

TABLE III

Intelligence-test Scores of the Three "Racial" Groups

Group	Average score	Median score	S.D.	Number
"Nordic"........................	188.5	190.5	53.4	200
"Alpine"........................	187.5	190.2	48.4	300
"Mediterranean".................	185.2	188.5	51.8	200

A survey of Table III shows that the scores for the three "races" were practically identical. The differences are insignificant and "none of them even approach reliability." Klineberg concludes that, "As far as these results go, the quite insignificant differences between the 'races,' the wide variations found within the same 'race,' and the fact that a 'racial' hierarchy found in one nation does not hold for another, indicate that the concept of 'race' when applied to these European groups has no significance in relation to the kind of differences demonstrated by performance tests in this study" (page 31).

National Differences. If the three city groups are ranked in the order of scores obtained by the subjects selected from each, Paris is first, Hamburg next, and Rome last, with only slight and unreliable differences among them. If the rural groups are combined according to nationality, we find, as Table IV shows, that their rank is German first, French second, and Italian third.

The difference found between the scores for rural groups in Germany and for corresponding groups in France and Italy is almost entirely reliable, since there are respectively 99.9 and 99.4 chances in 100 that true differences exist. On the other hand, the difference between the French and the Italian rural groups is unreliable. Analysis of Klineberg's data discloses a considerable amount of variability within the French and within the Italian rural groups. As can be seen from Table I, the Italian "Alpines" score much closer to the two German groups and to the French "Mediterranean" group than they do to the Italian "Mediterraneans." Similarly, the French "Mediterranean" group resembles both German groups in intelligence much more closely than it does the other French groups. *It would seem, therefore, that the fact of nationality, as such, is not a factor determining the intelligence level of any national subgroup.* As Klineberg puts it, "There is so much variability between different samples of the same national group, and in many cases so much similarity between samples of

TABLE IV

Intelligence-test Scores of the Rural Samples of the Three National Groups

Group	Average score	Median score	S.D.	Number
German	195.9	198.4	48.6	200
French	185.7	191.0	50.4	300
Italian	180.9	179.8	52.3	200

different nations, that the evidence for national differences must be regarded as inconclusive" (page 34).

DISCUSSION

By using a nonverbal type of intelligence test, Klineberg avoided the difficulties inherent in the attempt to translate the same test with equal adequacy into several languages. The performance type of test which he employed required little more than the clear translation of the instructions for the subjects. However, whether the tests were equally valid as tests of "native" intelligence for the several groups investigated is not altogether clear. If they were valid tests of "native" intelligence, one would have to conclude from Klineberg's results that the urban children were superior in intellectual endowment to the rural children of this study.

One possible explanation for such a superiority in the intelligence of urban children is suggested by Klineberg. It may be that intellectually superior people are more likely than are the intellectually inferior to find or to make a superior environment for themselves and their children, to strive for better schools and homes, and for the achievement of such ends to seek residence in urban and industrial areas.   Insofar as one is impressed by this argument, he will be inclined to attribute the city-country differences, at least in part, to differences in the intellectual capacity of the ancestors of the subjects, and thus in the "native" intelligence of the children themselves.

An alternative explanation for the superiority of the scores of the urban children is that performance on these tests reflects not only native intelligence but environmental background as well.   In general, the living conditions of the groups which received high scores were superior to those of the low-scoring groups.   There was less poverty in the environments of the former groups; their means of communication were superior; their schools were better (by such indexes as discipline, attendance, educational methods, expenditures, etc.).   Moreover, it is highly probable that in tests of the kind used in this investigation, city children, as compared with country children, enjoy an advantage from the general emphasis which is placed upon a competitive attitude and speedy performance in industrial communities and from their greater ease in the presence of strangers (here, specifically, the foreign experimenter).   It may be that factors of this sort are responsible for the finding in this investigation, as in many others, that the average intelligence-test scores of urban children are higher than those of rural. Klineberg himself believes that cultural-environmental differences between the country and city samples offer an adequate explanation for the difference in their average test scores.

Klineberg's method of selecting representatives of the various "racial" and national groups to be compared eliminated certain ambiguities which other investigations of this question had presented. For example, prior to the publication of Klineberg's study, a number of investigations had been carried out, comparing the average intelligence-test scores (1) of native Americans and of various groups of foreign-born Americans (*e.g.*, French, Jewish, German, Armenian, etc.),[1] or (2) of the children of native Americans and of the children of

---

[1] The most comprehensive survey of the intelligence of immigrant groups resident in the United States was made by the Army testers during the First World War.   (Brigham, C.   *A Study of American Intelligence.*   Princeton, N. J., Princeton University Press, 1923.)   A few years after the publication of this study, Brigham completely repudiated the conclusion that it had disclosed true differences, biologically based, in the intelligence of various national and "racial" groups among immigrants in the United

various groups of foreign-born immigrants. In most of these studies differences, sometimes sizable, sometimes small, were reported in the average scores of the various groups compared. Where differences were found, certain writers did not hesitate to infer that the various European national groups from which these samples came differ in intelligence in much the same way that their representatives in the United States were found to differ. Apart from the fact that nationality is a legal characteristic, not a physiological or a psychological one, this inference may be challenged on two grounds. First, it is possible that various uncontrolled factors, such as differences in motivation, in cultural level, in social and economic status, in educational attainment, and in language facility, may be responsible for such differences as have been found in the average intelligence-test scores of the various samples. In the second place, even if the tests were equally fair to all the groups examined in the United States, it could not be assumed that the different groups of immigrants were *representative* samplings of their parent populations in Europe. People emigrate from their homelands for many and very different reasons. For example, they may emigrate because they are economic failures and therefore unable to survive at home, or, on the contrary, because they are economically successful and therefore have the means to reside in any country they choose. As Klineberg says, "If for example the Scandinavians who migrated were a superior group compared with those who stayed behind, while among the Italians it was an inferior group which migrated, the conclusion that the parent populations differed in the same way as did the respective immigrant groups in America would hardly be justified. . ." (page 8). From this discussion it should be clear that no valid generalizations as to national or "racial" differences in intelligence can be based upon studies of immigrants or of the offspring of immigrants in the United States or elsewhere. Whatever the findings of such studies, there will always remain the doubt as to whether the

States. In this later evaluation of the results of the Army study, he wrote: "Comparative studies of various national and racial groups may not be made with existing tests . . . ," and ". . . one of the most pretentious of these comparative racial studies—the writer's own—was without foundation." (Brigham, C. Intelligence Tests of Immigrant Groups. *Psychological Review*, 1930, vol. 37, pp. 158–165.)

At the present writing, no official publication has appeared which presents an analysis in terms of national or racial background of the psychological-test scores made by men in the armed services of the United States during the Second World War.

particular immigrant sample tested was truly representative of the parent population.

Klineberg avoided the pitfall inherent in the use of the questionably representative immigrant sample by two devices: (1) by testing French, Italian, and German boys in their own countries, and (2) by selecting subjects with the physical traits which characterize the "Mediterranean," the "Alpine," and the "Nordic types" living in regions where those types are most commonly found. His findings may therefore be taken as constituting significant evidence on the question of the existence of national or "racial" differences in intelligence.

So far as *national* differences in intelligence are concerned, Klineberg found a slight superiority of French urban over Italian and German urban groups, and a somewhat greater superiority of the German rural group over the rural groups of the other countries. These differences were much smaller than the differences between the rural and urban groups within each nation. They are probably to be explained in terms of differences in cultural-environmental background factors.

With regard to racial differences in intelligence, the results for the "Mediterranean," the "Alpine," and the "Nordic" samples warrant the conclusion that no significant differences in intelligence exist among the identifiable members of these three so-called "races."

CHAPTER XV

THE CONDITIONING OF VASOMOTOR RESPONSES

Introduction

When attention is called to some social lapse and a blush comes to the cheek of the indiscreet person, people ordinarily say, "Oh, he is embarrassed," and accept that as an explanation of the blushing. It is obvious that calling attention to the *faux pas* has somehow caused the blush, yet why should this particular effect have been produced rather than some other? The special problem of the present chapter concerns the manner in which such reactions come under the control of particular kinds of stimuli and become established as significant aspects of an individual's behavior.

Blushing or paling of the facial skin is called an "involuntary" response, since most people cannot say or think, "I will cause my cheeks to blush" (or to pale) and directly bring about the reaction. In contrast, after some training early in life, the individual can say or think, "I will move my finger," and thereupon produce that movement. The latter response is called a "voluntary" reaction because it can be regularly produced by the thought of making it. However, one cannot classify responses as being intrinsically either voluntary or involuntary. The term "involuntary action" is typically applied to responses which are not usually subject to control by words or thoughts or by any other stimulation which the individual can produce "at will." But it is possible that almost any such response can be made subject to this voluntary control if the person has had the appropriate combination of experiences or the right kind of training. For instance, only the exceptional individual can think, "I will move my ear," and directly do so. But through appropriate training, a number of subjects in an experiment by Bair[1] learned to make that response a

[1] Bair, J. H. The Practice Curve. *Psychological Review Monograph Supplements*, 1903, No. 19.

264

"voluntary" action. Not only such normally involuntary skeletal-muscle responses, but smooth-muscle responses as well, may become subject to a voluntary control which is effected through learning. This possibility raises many questions of psychological importance.

For example, some religious cults exploit the fact that thinking affects bodily activities and insist that this phenomenon proves the dominance of "mind" over "matter." Psychologists regard such an interpretation as both mystical and vague and raise the question whether such mysticism and vagueness cannot be replaced by a more lucid explanation. That thinking influences visceral activities is an indisputable fact, but the problem of showing how this influence is exerted is a difficult one.

Some tentative suggestions may be advanced on this point. Let us consider the case of a clerk who has frequently worried about losing his job and has repeatedly thought, "They're going to fire me and I can't help it." As is well known, worrying typically interferes with the normal functioning of the digestive organs. Hence the clerk soon develops digestive disturbances, and in time the mere mention of the boss's name may produce a digestive upset. In such cases, it is reasonable to suggest that, through experience, processes of a so-called "involuntary" nature have come under the control of various stimuli which originally could not elicit such responses. These new stimuli tend to become associated with the original cause of the anxiety and may be furnished by the environment (*e.g.*, mention of the boss's name by someone else) or through the individual's own activity (*e.g.*, thoughts such as, "He has it in for me!").

The possibility that certain environmental stimuli and also habitual activities, such as speaking and thinking, may acquire a specific control over visceral processes is of great importance for our understanding of the nature of the neuroses and their development in the individual. Many neurotic individuals seem to be able to produce "at will"—that is, whenever it suits their purposes—such reactions as heart attacks, vomiting, headaches, and other responses which are not ordinarily under voluntary control. Naturally the fact that such behavior is exceptional does not preclude the possibility that when better understood it may be accounted for in terms of established psychological theory, without invoking mystical or supernatural explanations.

For example, the arousal of contradictory motives, such as the duty of staying at home with an aged parent versus a desire to go out for the evening, frequently causes behavior difficulties, including emotional disturbances with their accompanying physiological disorders.　As the situation productive of conflict is repeatedly encountered, a habitually disturbed and unstable emotionalized behavior may develop, a condition which is commonly called "neurotic."　At length, merely thinking about the difficulty and the restrictions upon one's activities which it entails may arouse any or all of the symptoms which at first appeared only in the situation itself.　Much neurosis, according to this view, is basically a form of "habit sickness" in which both visceral processes and general behavior have come under the control of stimuli associated with some serious maladjustment.

The manner in which thinking and related types of behavior may lead to changes in the functioning of internal organs suggests to the psychologist that particular organic changes come to be elicited by particular stimuli as the result of learning.　If a reaction which is quite involuntary in most individuals can be trained ("conditioned") in the laboratory to previously ineffective stimuli selected by the experimenter, phenomena of the type we have mentioned lose much of their mystery.　The experiment to be described below represents a special investigation of this problem.

THE EXPERIMENT OF ROESSLER AND BROGDEN[1]

In two earlier experiments by Menzies[2, 3] vasomotor responses (changes in the diameter of small arterial blood vessels in the skin), in particular, vasoconstriction (decrease in the diameter of those vessels), were conditioned to various stimuli, including sounds, visual stimuli, and the whispering of a nonsense word by the subject.　Menzies used vasomotor reactions primarily because he wished to study a truly "involuntary" activity.　In addition, as we have seen, vasomotor responses are of interest in both normal and abnormal psychology. In everyday behavior, the flushing or paling of the skin, which indicates that vasomotor dilation or constriction has occurred, is a

[1] Adapted from Roessler, R. L., and W. J. Brogden.　Conditioned Differentiation of Vasoconstriction to Subvocal Stimuli.　*American Journal of Psychology*, 1943, vol. 56, pp. 78–86.

[2] Menzies, R.　Conditioned Vasomotor Responses in Human Subjects.　*Journal of Psychology*, 1937, vol. 4, pp. 75–120.

[3] Menzies, R.　Further Studies of Conditioned Vasomotor Responses in Human Subjects.　*Journal of Experimental Psychology*, 1941, vol. 29, pp. 457–482.

frequent and often a very noticeable response in emotionally excited individuals. Under unusual behavior conditions, such as the neuroses, peculiar vasomotor reactions are not uncommon, a fact which also suggests the importance of this type of response in emotion.

Like Menzies, Roessler and Brogden selected vasomotor responses for investigation because they are excellent examples of a normally involuntary activity. A further reason for selecting them was that Menzies already had shown that they could be conditioned to various external and internal stimuli, and therefore they seemed to be a suitable form of behavior for a conditioning study of a more elaborate type. The particular aim of the present investigation—aside from undertaking to test further how vasomotor responses are conditioned both to spoken words and to thoughts—was to establish a "conditioned differentiation." Specifically, it was to determine whether the response of vasoconstriction could be conditioned to the repetition by the subject of a particular nonsense syllable, either aloud or subvocally, and at the same time *not* be conditioned to the similar repetition of another, different nonsense syllable. An example of conditioned differentiation in daily experience would be to turn pale in response to certain thoughts (*e.g.*, "That pain is coming on again."), but not to give this response to other thoughts (*e.g.*, "I believe I'm feeling better."). Behavior of this nature occurs in many people. However, the means by which it is acquired is usually quite unknown to the individual concerned. It is of great psychological interest to find out whether vasomotor responses can become conditioned to certain verbal stimuli, but not to others, by regular laboratory procedures. Achievement of this result would furnish highly convincing evidence of the validity of the proposition that an involuntary reaction, through learning, can come under the control of words and thoughts as effective stimuli.

THE NEURAL CONTROL OF VASOMOTOR RESPONSES

Vasomotor reactions have two phases: *vasoconstriction*, which as we have said is the decrease in the diameter of blood vessels, and *vasodilation*, which is the enlargement in diameter of those vessels. Vasomotor changes may be produced by certain chemicals (*e.g.*, adrenin) in the blood, but our concern here is with their direct nervous control.

The principal nervous control of vasomotor reactions is effected through the autonomic nervous system.   Vasoconstriction is brought about by impulses transmitted through the sympathetic division of the autonomic nervous system, which discharges nervous impulses to the visceral organs from centers (*i.e.*, ganglia) lying in a double series parallel to the middle region of the spinal cord (see Fig. 30).   Vasodilaticn is thought to be produced by impulses transmitted to the blood vessels by way of fibers of the parasympathetic or craniosacral division of the autonomic system.   Most of the centers of this division are

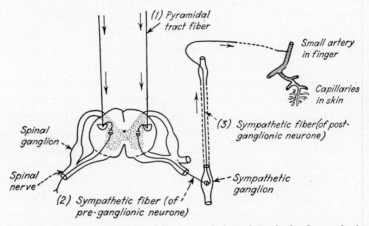

F ig. 30. The Neural Control of Vasoconstriction, through the Sympathetic Division of the Autonomic Nervous System.

Neural impulses from the brain (1) reach a level of the spinal cord in the thoracic region, then via preganglionic fibers of the sympathetic division (2) reach an adjacent sympathetic ganglion, and from the sympathetic chain are transmitted by a postganglionic fiber (3) to arterioles and capillaries in the skin, constricting these blood vessels. (The figure does not show the corresponding sympathetic ganglion on the other side of the spinal cord and the similar connections with the capillaries in the skin on the other side of the body.)

located in the medulla, though some are ganglia which lie in series parallel to the lowest (or sacral) region of the spinal cord.

APPARATUS AND EXPERIMENTAL SETTING

The experimenter chose vasoconstriction rather than vasodilation as the reaction to be conditioned.   The US (unconditioned stimulus) was a high-voltage electric shock which, like many intense stimuli, would ordinarily be expected to produce vasoconstriction.   The shock was delivered by electrodes strapped about 3 in. above the subject's left wrist.   Since vasomotor responses which are aroused in the skin of one arm typically occur almost immediately in the skin of the other, it was possible to use the subject's right arm to record and measure vasoconstriction produced by stimulation of the left arm. In order to make the vasoconstriction easily measurable, the blood vessels were kept in a state of dilation both by maintaining a high room

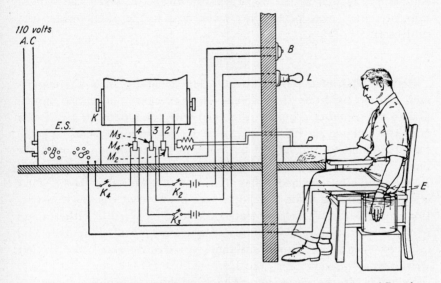

FIG. 31. A Schematic Representation of the Apparatus Used by Roessler and Brogden to Investigate the Conditioning of Vasoconstriction Responses.

P, plethysmograph; B, buzzer; L, lamp; $E.E.$, electrodes attached to subject's left wrist; K, kymograph; ES, electrostimulator; T, tambour; M_2, M_3, M_4, signal magnets; 1, stylus operated by tambour, recording vasomotor changes; 2, stylus recording auditory stimulus supplied by buzzer; 3, stylus recording visual stimulation furnished by lamp; 4, stylus recording electrical stimulation; K_2, key controlling buzzer; K_3, key controlling lamp; K_4, key controlling stimulator.

temperature (80°F.) and by keeping the subject's left hand immersed in very warm water.

The subject's right arm was strapped to an arm rest and fitted into an air plethysmograph[1] (see Fig. 31). The plethysmograph was con-

---

[1] A plethysmograph is an instrument designed to measure changes in the volume of a limb which are caused by changes in the amount of blood in that limb. In the more familiar type of plethysmograph, a cylindrical chamber is partly filled with water and the limb is suspended in it. If the volume of the limb changes according to variations in the amount of blood contained, more or less water is displaced from the chamber, and the air volume and air pressure in the rest of the system change proportionately. It is through changes in air pressure that the actual recording is done. In the air plethysmograph the water is replaced entirely by air, and changes in blood volume bring about changes in air pressure directly.

nected by glass tubing to an ink-writing tambour, which recorded vasomotor changes on an electrically driven kymograph. The operation of the buzzer, light, and electric shock used in the experimental procedure was also recorded on the kymograph. All the recording equipment, as well as the apparatus by means of which the stimuli were presented, was located in a room next to the one in which the subject sat.

METHOD

General Plan of the Experiment. The general plan of the experiment was to condition the response of vasoconstriction in the hands, first to the sound of a buzzer combined with the repetition aloud of a nonsense syllable by the subject, next to the same nonsense syllable repeated aloud by the subject but without the accompaniment of the buzzer, and then to the syllable repeated by the subject subvocally. In addition, a conditioned differentiation was to be established. That is, the subject was to be trained in such a way that the vasoconstriction would occur when he repeated the selected syllable, either aloud or subvocally, but would not occur when he repeated another and different syllable in similar fashion. An electric shock to the left wrist served throughout as the US.

Selection of the Subjects. The candidates originally chosen to serve as subjects for the experiment were 15 men, aged nineteen to twenty-two years, who were members of a class in elementary psychology at the University of Wisconsin.

In order to become a subject in the experiment a candidate had to satisfy two requirements. First, his initial (preexperimental) reaction to hand shock must be sufficiently reliable to provide a basis for the experiment. When an electric shock was applied to his left wrist, he had to react with vasoconstriction in the right hand in at least four out of five trials. Obviously, only subjects who reacted in this way would present a reaction which could be conditioned. Second, it was necessary that at the outset the candidate not react characteristically with vasoconstriction to any of the conditioned stimuli used in the experiment; that is, he must not respond with significant frequency to the sound of the buzzer, or to either of the nonsense syllables, whether repeated aloud or subvocally. The criterion of rejection of a candidate was a frequency of vasoconstriction to any

CS (conditioned stimulus) greater than one out of five trials. If a candidate gave more frequent responses to any of these stimuli, it was considered probable that he had somehow been conditioned to them (or to stimuli like them) already, and thus had acquired the very associations which were to be established by the experimental training.

In order to select individuals who could meet the above requirements, it was necessary to give a series of preliminary tests to the prospective subjects. Six tests of this kind were given, in the order in which they are described below. Each test consisted of five trials, that is, of five applications of the US, or of a given CS, or of some combination of conditioned stimuli. The interval between trials was varied in random fashion. Rest periods were introduced approximately every 25 min., their number and duration varying according to the subject's verbal expressions of fatigue. A record of whatever vasomotor changes occurred was kept at every trial. In each trial the experimental stimulus was not given until the vasodilation produced by the warm water and the high room temperature had reached its maximum. As has been said before, the purpose of securing a large initial vasodilation was to facilitate the measurement of any vasoconstriction that might occur later. The latency and the magnitude of the vasoconstrictions were carefully measured. "Latency" means the time in seconds for vasoconstriction to appear after the application of the stimulus. "Magnitude" means the amount of decrease in the volume of the right hand in cubic centimeters, a measurement which was obtained from the decrease in air pressure in the plethysmograph when the hand volume diminished.

In *Test* 1 the US, the electric shock, was given alone five times. Each shock lasted 5 sec. Nine of the fifteen candidates failed to give the response of vasoconstriction with sufficient frequency and so could not be used as subjects.

In *Test* 2 the buzzer was the stimulus. In each of the five trials it was sounded for 20 sec. One of the remaining six candidates showed vasoconstriction too frequently to the buzzer and had to be eliminated.

In *Test* 3 the candidate repeated the nonsense syllable "wek"[1]

[1] The experimenters used a nonsense syllable instead of an actual word in order to have a verbal reaction which would be equivalent to a spoken or a thought word but would be

aloud for 20 sec. A flash of red light provided the signal for him to begin the repetitions, and another flash the signal to stop them. One of the remaining five candidates responded too often with vaso-constriction to this stimulus and so was discarded.

TABLE I

For Each of the Four Subjects, the Number of Vasoconstriction Responses to Shock (the US) in Test 1, the Average Latency (in seconds) and the Average Magnitude (in cubic centimeters) of the Responses. Also, in Experiment I (Conditioning to Buzzer and "Wek" Spoken Aloud), the Number of Trials to Reach the Conditioning Criterion, and the Average Latency and Magnitude of the Conditioned Vasoconstriction Responses during the Five Criterion Trials.[1]

	Subjects			
	A	B	C	D
Test 1				
No. of vasoconstriction responses....................	4	4	5	4
Aver. latency[2].......................................	7.7	9.1	10.2	6.8
Aver. magnitude[2]...................................	0.12	0.20	0.16	0.29
Experiment I				
No. of trials to reach the conditioning criterion (excluding the criterion trials)......................	15	55	20	20
Aver. latency.......................................	5.1	6.1	5.3	7.0
Aver. magnitude...................................	0.06	0.07	0.06	0.06

[1] The "criterion trials" are the series of five successive trials during which the criterion of conditioning, to respond with vasoconstriction to the CS alone on at least four trials, was met.

[2] In this and the subsequent table the figures indicating the variability of the latencies and of the magnitudes of the responses have been omitted.

The four "surviving" candidates were given Tests 4, 5, and 6. In *Test* 4 the other nonsense syllable "zub" was repeated aloud under the same conditions and in the same manner as "wek" had been in Test 3. In *Test* 5 "wek" was repeated subvocally, also under the same conditions as in Test 3. Subvocal repetition meant that the subject was told to "think the word as actively as possible without whispering it or repeating it aloud." In *Test* 6 saying "wek" aloud was again used, this time in combination with the sounding of the buzzer for 20 sec. In this test the beginning and the end of the

devoid of any special or direct past associations for the subject. Since meaningful words already might have been associated with vasomotor changes in the subject, they were not suitable for use in an experiment of this type.

buzzer sound served as the signals for the subject to start and stop repeating the syllable.

All four individuals "passed" each of the above three tests and therefore became the subjects finally selected for the experiment. The latencies and the magnitudes of their vasoconstriction responses to the electric shock in Test 1 are given in Table I.

EXPERIMENTS AND RESULTS

In the experiment, each of the four subjects found suitable for the investigation went through two conditioning procedures, and two of the subjects went through five procedures. These procedures will be designated as Experiments I, II, III, IV, and V, respectively.

In all the experiments, the CS—whatever its nature might be— was 20 sec. in duration. In each trial the CS was presented first. After it had gone on for 15 sec., the US (the electric shock) was given for a period of 5 sec. Hence the CS and the US "overlapped," in that they were present simultaneously during the last 5 sec. of stimulation. The trials were given in series of five, with intervals of varying length between individual trials and between series of trials. As in the preliminary tests, rest periods were introduced about every 25 min. The criterion of conditioning was response by vasoconstriction to the CS alone in at least four out of five successive trials (*i.e.*, during one series). This response had to appear during the first 15 sec. after the application of the CS, and before the reinforcement of shock occurred. The criteria for the establishment of the conditioned differentiations in Experiments III and V are described below in connection with those experiments. The five experiments were carried out in the same order for all the subjects. As in the preliminary tests, the latency and the magnitude of each vasoconstriction were measured. It follows from what has been said above that a vasoconstriction response could not be regarded as a CR conditioned response) unless its latency was less than 15 sec.

Experiment I. The aim of the first experiment was to condition vasoconstriction to the combined stimulation afforded by the sound of the buzzer and the simultaneous repetition of the syllable "wek" aloud by the subject. As in all the experiments, the conditioned stimuli had a duration of 20 sec., that is, the buzzer sounded and the subject repeated "wek" for that length of time. As we have said, the shock was given after this stimulation had gone on for 15 sec., and continued during the last 5 sec. of combined buzzer sound and repetition of "wek."

All four subjects were readily conditioned to respond with vaso-constriction to this stimulus combination. As shown in Table I, the number of trials for conditioning the respective subjects to the criterion stated was 15, 55, 20, and 20. For three of the four subjects the average latency of the CRs was less than that of the unconditioned responses obtained in Test 1. In other words, vasoconstriction tended to appear more quickly after the presentation of the conditioned stimuli in this experiment than it had appeared in response to the electric shock given alone. However, the vasoconstriction reactions to the new stimulus combination were on the average considerably less in magnitude than they had been in Test 1.

Experiment II. The aim of Experiment II was to see whether vasoconstriction could be conditioned to "wek" alone, repeated aloud by the subject as before, but without the accompaniment of the buzzer. At each trial a flash of red light was the signal for the subject to start saying "wek." The shock began 15 sec. later, and its ter-mination was the signal for him to stop repeating the syllable.

As Table II shows, two of the subjects were conditioned in 25 and 5 trials, respectively. The latencies and the magnitudes of their CRs were not very different from those of the CRs obtained in Experi-ment I. The other two subjects, though they gave some evidence of conditioning, had not satisfied the criterion after 110 and 70 trials, respectively. Since they also had failed to show any improvement with respect to the number of CRs per series, their training was dis-continued and they were not used in the remaining experiments.

Experiment III. The aim in Experiment III was to develop a *conditioned differentiation*, that is, to find whether the subject could be made to react with vasoconstriction to the syllable "wek" repeated aloud but not give this response to the syllable "zub," also repeated aloud. The procedure was to alternate series of five presentations of "wek" reinforced (*i.e.,* followed) each time by shock, with series of five presentations of "zub" without shock reinforcement. "Presenta-tion" here means repetition of the syllable by the subject for 20 sec. The alternation of the two kinds of series continued until the subject reacted with vasoconstriction to "wek" in four out of five successive trials, and did not react with vasoconstriction to "zub" in more than one out of five successive trials. The flash of red light was the signal for the subject to repeat either "wek" or "zub." The signal to stop repeating "wek" was the end of the shock (as in Experiment II); the signal to stop repeating "zub" was a second flash of the light.

TABLE II

For Subjects A and D, in Experiments II, III, IV, and V, the Number of Trials to Reach the Conditioning Criterion, together with the Average Latency (in seconds) and the Average Magnitude (in cubic centimeters) of the Conditioned Vasoconstriction Responses during the Five Criterion Trials.

	Subjects	
	A	D
Experiment II. Conditioning to "wek" aloud		
No. of trials for conditioning..............................	25	5
Aver. latency..	7.0	6.6
Aver. magnitude...	0.07	0.15
Experiment III. Conditioned differentiation to "wek" and "zub" aloud		
No. of trials for the differentiation, with "wek"..................	0	25
No. of trials for the differentiation, with "zub"..................	0	30
Aver. latency, CRs to "wek"...............................	7.0	3.2
Aver. magnitude, CRs to "wek"............................	0.07	0.63
Experiment IV. Conditioning to "wek" subvocal		
No. of trials for conditioning..............................	5	25
Aver. latency..	3.5	5.0
Aver. magnitude...	0.11	0.67
Experiment V. Conditioned differentiation to "wek" and "zub" subvocal		
No. of trials for the differentiation, with "wek"..................	0	0
No. of trials for the differentiation, with "zub"..................	0	0
Aver. latency, CRs to "wek"...............................	3.5	5.0
Aver. magnitude, CRs to "wek"............................	0.11	0.67

As is shown in Table II, one of the two subjects (A) achieved the differentiation immediately; that is, he reacted with vasoconstriction at each of the first five trials with "wek" and reacted only once with vasoconstriction during the first five trials with "zub." The other subject (D) required 25 trials with "wek" and 30 trials with "zub" before the differentiation was regarded as established. For subject A the average latency and magnitude of the CRs were similar to those previously obtained. With subject D, however, the CR tended to be given with more rapidly (*i.e.*, with shorter latency) than before, and with much greater magnitude.

Experiment IV. In Experiment IV vasoconstriction was conditioned to "wek" repeated subvocally, in "thought." The procedure was exactly the same as in Experiment II except that the subject repeated the syllable "to himself" instead of aloud.

The conditioning was established rapidly in both subjects (see Table II), one subject requiring 5 trials, the other 25. For subject A the average latency of the CRs was less, and the average magnitude greater, than in any previous experiment. For subject D the latency did not differ greatly from speeds obtained in the previous experiments, but the magnitude was slightly greater even than it had been in Experiment III.

Experiment V. The purpose of this last experiment was to develop another conditioned differentiation, in this case between the two syllables repeated subvocally instead of aloud. The procedure was exactly the same as in Experiment III except for the difference in the manner of repeating the syllables. Both subjects exhibited the differentiation in the first series with each syllable and therefore required no additional training. The average latency and magnitude of their CRs were identical with those in Experiment IV.

DISCUSSION

These experiments by Roessler and Brogden, like the earlier work of Menzies, establish the fact that, through training, a vasomotor response of constriction may come to be evoked by a particular verbal stimulus, spoken aloud or merely "thought." They also show that a conditioned differentiation can be established, so that a subject may come to react with vasoconstriction to the repetition of a given word or thought but not give that response to the repetition of another word or thought. For the most part the CRs were not difficult to develop. Furthermore, as the training went on, there was a tendency for new conditionings to be acquired with increasing rapidity, and for the CRs to diminish in latency and to increase in magnitude. It is noteworthy that once a conditioned differentiation had been developed to the two syllables repeated aloud, it "transferred" or carried over immediately to the same syllables repeated subvocally, so that no specific training with the two "thoughts" was necessary.

The results suggest that in everyday experience the paling (and presumably the flushing also) of a part of the face when significant words are heard may well be a CR established as a consequence of specific past "training." The findings also indicate the possibility that if one repeatedly says or thinks certain embarrassing or disquieting words when vasoconstriction (or vasodilation) occurs in connection with some general emotional condition, paling (or flushing) of the face may become a direct and specific response to the words in question. Accordingly, it is clear that an important reason why a person's color "comes and goes" in the course of an ordinary conversation or argument may be that his vasomotor responses have become conditioned to different verbal stimuli in the course of his past experience.

Individuals differ widely in their vasomotor responses in ordinary social situations. Some people pale (or blush) intensely and often, others slightly and infrequently. Some people blush most easily when they say or think profane or obscene words, others when they are talking or thinking about personal failures and humiliations. For this reason one would expect to find rather wide individual differences in laboratory tests of vasomotor responses and in the acquisition of vasomotor conditionings. The outcome of the present experiments confirms this expectation. Most of the 15 men originally chosen as possible subjects did not respond consistently with vasoconstriction to an electric shock, although six of them did so respond. Among these six individuals, only two reacted originally with vasoconstriction to a buzzer sound or to the repetition of a nonsense syllable; the others had to be specifically conditioned to one or the other of these stimuli. Similarly, vasoconstriction in two subjects was conditioned successfully to a syllable repeated aloud, but in the other two this conditioning did not occur. Although the causes of such individual differences are not known with certainty, they may include such factors as physiological differences in the ease with which vasomotor responses can be elicited, the effects of possible previous conditionings (including inhibitory ones), and the attitude of the subject during the experiment itself.[1]

The results of Roessler and Brogden also show how so-called "involuntary" activities may be brought, through training, under the

---

[1] The results of Razran, among others, suggest that whether the attitude of a subject during an experiment is acquiescent, indifferent, or negative (*e.g.*, hostile) may determine whether or not a CR is established. (Razran, G. H. S. Conditioned Responses, an Experimental Study and a Theoretical Analysis. *Archives of Psychology*, 1935, No. 191.)

control of the individual's talking and thinking; that is, how involuntary responses may become "voluntary." Among other evidence for this statement is the fact that in Hudgins'[1] experiment the pupillary responses, both dilation and constriction, were separately conditioned to specific verbal stimuli, and that in Menzies' first experiment[2] vasoconstriction was conditioned to the whispering of a nonsense word. Such findings have great psychological significance, especially in the abnormal field. They suggest that in many abnormal individuals (*e.g.*, cases of hysteria and neurasthenia) the appearance of symptoms such as nausea, "nervous indigestion," fainting spells, and the like may be attributed to conditioning in connection with the repetition of certain emotional difficulties. For instance, many neurotics are able to bring on a headache when particular disturbing conditions arise. An example is the case of a mother whose "illness" has long prevented her son from marrying, pleading "One of my headaches has come on" when the son announces his intention of taking a girl out to dinner or brings up the subject of a home and family.

The fact that such behavior can be viewed as a learned response-process becomes more clear when we consider some features of the headache. Headache characteristically involves marked changes in brain circulation, and extreme vasomotor changes in the thick capillary network of the cerebral cortex appear to underlie the typical "heavy" pain. Such vasomotor changes are apparently subject to conditioning, judging from the manner in which many adults develop or recover from headaches in connection with specific types of stimulation. Just as subjects in the present experiments and in Menzies' investigations acquired the ability to give a specific vasomotor response to particular stimuli, the headache of the neurotic—and of many "normal" people also—may be regarded as a special learned response to the special stimulus situations which evoke it. At first, the headache may be only an incidental consequence of the individual's general disturbance when he is confronted with an emotional crisis (which functions as the US). But if this crisis is encountered often enough, if the individual has enough experiences in which the stimuli producing the emotional disturbance are followed by headache among other effects, the vasomotor changes which underlie the pain may come to be elicited

[1] Hudgins, C. V. Conditioning and the Voluntary Control of the Pupillary Reflex. *Journal of General Psychology*, 1933, vol. 8, pp. 3–51.

[2] Menzies, Conditioned Vasomotor Responses in Human Subjects.

by one particular stimulus alone. The individual who says, "Don't mention his name, or I'll have one of my headaches!" thereby discloses a CR which has a person's name as a CS; and the fact that the headache does not occur as a response to the names of other people reveals the existence of a conditioned differentiation. Such special habits persist and become stronger by virtue of the fact that they often help the individual to avoid or to escape from situations which he finds disturbing.

On the other hand, if the outcome of the experiments of Roessler and Brogden affords an explanation for the establishment of many neurotic symptoms, their results also suggest how special procedures for the removal of such difficulties may be devised. If an individual can learn to react with vasoconstriction to a particular stimulus by repeatedly pairing that stimulus with some US for the response, it should be possible to recondition him, to train him to lose the conditioned vasoconstriction, by pairing the CS with some stimulus that produces a different response, *e.g.*, vasodilation.

For this reconditioning in the case of headache, the CS might be paired with any stimulus that tends to have a "calming" effect, that tends to bring about a general relaxation of the musculature and a vasomotor condition different from that which underlies the headache. Such a stimulus might be listening to music, thinking of pleasant events in one's past, repeating a mystic formula such as "There is no pain," or listening to and later recalling the advice and encouragement of a psychiatrist or counselor. If the pairing in question occurs repeatedly under the proper conditions (among which may be a genuine desire on the part of the patient to get rid of his headaches), the former CS, *e.g.*, the mention of a disliked person's name, may cease to produce pain. In a similar manner, and in accordance with the same principle, various difficulties in individual behavior may be displaced by more desirable types of adjustment. A method of the above type, together with several related procedures, is described and discussed in detail in Chap. XIX.[1]

[1] The above comments should not be interpreted as an attempt to oversimplify psychotherapy along behavioristic lines. The reconditioning method suggested probably would be much more effective for eliminating a single localized symptom, such as a headache, than for alleviating a complex attitude, for example, a "feeling of inferiority." Also, though it is conceivable that a simple reconditioning might be effected without the active cooperation of the subject, it is very unlikely that it could be achieved against his actual opposition, whether the latter was openly displayed or existed more as an attitude of which he himself was perhaps unaware.

CHAPTER XVI

FORGETTING DURING SLEEP AND WAKING

INTRODUCTION

Recently, several psychological experimenters have undertaken to compare the amount of forgetting which takes place during sleep and during waking. In reality, all such experiments are primarily studies of retroactive inhibition. This term may be defined as the inhibitory effect exerted upon the retention of any activity (or material) by other activities intervening between the original learning and the retention test. The existence of such inhibitory effects was first demonstrated by two German psychologists, Müller and Pilzecker,[1] in 1900, but the importance of their discovery was so little realized that for 24 years the topic was relatively neglected in experimental psychology.

In 1924, however, there appeared the study of Jenkins and Dallenbach which is reviewed in this chapter. The results of their experiment were so striking as to give a new impetus to work in this field. At present, the investigation of retroactive inhibition has become one of the principal experimental problems in the psychology of retention and memory. Moreover, the phenomenon itself has been widely recognized as one of the most important causes of forgetting and, consequently, as the cause of much of our habitual failure to remember accurately the things which we have learned.

THE EXPERIMENT OF JENKINS AND DALLENBACH[2]

PURPOSE

The purpose of the experiment of Jenkins and Dallenbach was "to compare the rate of forgetting during sleep and waking." Their specific incentive for undertaking this problem derived from their desire to account for certain unexplained discrepancies in some of the curves

[1] Müller, G. E., and A. Pilzecker. Experimentelle Beiträge zur Lehre vom Gedächtnis. *Zeitschrift für Psychologie und Physiologie der Sinnesorgane*, Erganzungsband, 1, 1900.
[2] Adapted from Jenkins, J. G., and K. M. Dallenbach. Oblivescence during Sleep and Waking. *American Journal of Psychology*, 1924, vol. 35, pp. 605–612.

of forgetting reported by Ebbinghaus,[1] the pioneer in the experimental study of learning and memory. In one case, for example, Ebbinghaus found three times as much forgetting after 24 hr. as after 15 hr. Why should an increase in the time between learning and recall amounting to only 9 hr., or 60 per cent, produce a 300 per cent increase in the amount forgotten? If forgetting goes on more rapidly during waking than during sleeping, this discrepancy could be explained. For in Ebbinghaus's studies sleeping had filled a much larger proportion of many of the 15-hr. intervals than it had of most of the 24-hr. ones. Ebbinghaus himself suggested this explanation but finally discarded it in favor of the assumption that the discrepancy was due to some kind of accidental error in his work. Jenkins and Dallenbach, however, thought that his rejection of that explanation was premature, and decided to test the matter thoroughly themselves.

This, then, was their particular purpose. But the conclusions and implications which follow from their experiment go far beyond the relatively narrow aim set forth above.

METHOD

Subjects. The subjects were two senior college students. Both were without experience in psychological experimentation and were wholly ignorant of the purpose of the investigation. For the entire duration of the experiment they slept in an improvised room next to the laboratory, but otherwise they went about their daily affairs as usual.[2]

Material Learned. The material to be learned was typewritten lists of nonsense syllables of the usual three-letter, consonant-vowel-consonant kind (*e.g., baf, lum, sev*). Each list contained 10 syllables.

Method of Learning. The syllables were shown to the subjects visually by means of a special exposure apparatus. They were always shown in the same order. Each syllable appeared separately for a period of 0.7 sec. and the subject pronounced it aloud as soon as he saw it. After every presentation of the list, he recited as many of the syllables as he could remember. The list was then shown again,

[1] Ebbinghaus, H. *Über das Gedächtnis: Untersuchungen zur experimentellen Psychologie*, pp. 85–109, 1885.

[2] It is worth noting that, although most psychological experiments employ many more than two subjects, it often happens that an intensive study of a few individuals gives just as valuable results as are obtainable from a less intensive study of a large number.

and again he recited as much of it as he could. This procedure was continued for each of the subjects until he could recite the entire list once from the beginning to end in correct order. It was then considered to be learned. The subject was told not to try to read any meaning into the syllables, and not to use any special plan (mnemonic device) for remembering them.

Method of Measuring Retention. The subject's retention (*i.e.*, his memory for the list) was tested by the recall method, which means that after some prescribed interval of time he recited as much as he could remember of the list he had previously learned. The lengths of these prescribed intervals were different on different occasions and for different lists. Specifically, they were 1, 2, 4, or 8 hr. after the learning.

Activities between the Learning and the Retention Test. The crucial point in the experimental procedure was the difference in the kind of activities intervening between the original learning of a list and the later recall of it. The lists were learned either between 11:30 P.M. and 1 A.M., or between 8 and 10 A.M. (except for some sessions between 2 and 4 P.M., introduced as an additional check). For the learning at night the subject undressed and got ready for bed before the learning started, and went to bed, and usually to sleep also, just as soon as it was over. The daytime learning, however, occurred in the midst of and as a part of his normal waking activities. Hence, the learning at night was followed by sleeping, *i.e.*, by a minimum of general activity, whereas the daytime learning was followed by the customary routine of study, attendance at lectures, eating, conversation, sports, and the like.

With respect to the recall tests which were given after the 1- to 8-hr. intervals mentioned above, the following procedure was employed. If the learning was at night the subject was never told how soon he would be called upon to recite the list again. Instead, he was awakened by the experimenter during the night at the appropriate time, or summoned by him early the next morning, to recall it. The reason for not telling the subject beforehand after what interval his retention would be tested was based on the discovery that his attitude on going to sleep differed in accordance with whether he knew the interval before reproduction was to be short or long. It was noted, incidentally, that during many of these night recalls the subject was scarcely awake, and that the next morning he often could remember nothing about having had to recite the syllables. If the learning took place during the daytime, however, the subject was told to report back to the laboratory at a certain later hour for the recall. In all cases, the subjects were told never to repeat the lists during the interval.

Duration and Extent of the Experiment. The experiment lasted from April 14 to June 7. Records were taken on almost every day and night during that period, unless the subject's physical condition prevented. Each subject learned eight lists for each of the four intervals, and for both the sleeping and the waking conditions. The total number of lists learned and recalled by both subjects was 123 (there were five omissions in the above schedule).

RESULTS

The results of the experiment are shown for each subject individually in the following table and graph. The average number of syllables recalled is given for all four intervals and for both sleeping and waking

TABLE I

Showing the Average Number of Syllables Recalled by Each Subject after from 1 to 8 Hr. Spent in Sleep or in Waking Activities

| Subjects | Intervals | | | | | | | | Average for all intervals | |
| | 1 hr. | | 2 hr. | | 4 hr. | | 8 hr. | | | |
	Sleep	Waking	Sleep	Waking	Sleep	Waking	Sleep	Waking	Sleep	Waking
H	7.1	4.4	5.4	2.8	5.3	2.4	5.5	0.4	5.8	2.4
Mc	7.0	4.8	5.4	3.4	5.8	2.1	5.8	1.4	6.0	2.8

conditions. Ten syllables, it will be remembered, were learned in every one of the lists. Hence, a recall score of seven syllables, for example, shows that 70 per cent of the list originally learned was recalled or, conversely, that 30 per cent of the list was forgotten.

The results show very clearly that for both subjects retention after an interval during which the subject was asleep was far superior to retention after an equivalent interval during which he was engaged in his normal waking activities. For example, subject H after a 2-hr. interval spent in sleep recalled 5.4 syllables; but after 2 hr. occupied with waking activities, he recalled only 2.8 syllables—scarcely more than half as many.   This difference in favor of the sleep condition was found to be present for all of the intervals used.   Furthermore, the magnitude of the difference increased as the intervals became longer.

As the graph in Fig. 32 also shows, there seemed to be no decline in recall ability during the sleep condition after the 2-hr. interval; for the subjects recalled as many syllables after 8 hr. as they did after 2 hr. Under the waking condition, however, the recall score steadily decreased as the interval grew greater, so that the recall after 8 hr. was much less than it was after 2 or 4 hr.   In fact, after the 8-hr. interval,

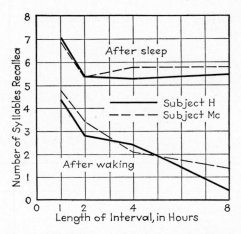

FIG. 32.   Retention after Sleep and after Waking.

the retention had diminished to scarcely 10 per cent of the list originally learned; *i.e.*, 90 per cent of the syllables had been forgotten.

The experiment was repeated with one other subject, for the 1- and 8-hr. intervals only, with results virtually identical with those reported above.

One question which might be raised is whether there was any difference in the difficulty of learning the lists under the night and the daytime conditions.   On the average, there was a difference; namely, that the night learning usually required from one to two more repetitions of a list than did the day learning.   However, this difference was not always present, nor was it found in the third subject mentioned above.   It is very unlikely, therefore, that it had any significant effect on the later retention.

CONCLUSIONS

The authors of the experiment conclude that, as their results clearly indicate, forgetting goes on at a slower rate during sleeping than it does during waking. Insofar as the discrepancies in Ebbinghaus's data are concerned, Jenkins and Dallenbach conclude that they were due simply to the fact that certain of his intervals (*e.g.*, the 15-hr. ones) tended to include more sleeping time than others did.

DISCUSSION

As we have seen, Jenkins and Dallenbach found that retention after sleep was far superior to retention after waking activities, when the time intervals between the learning and the recall test were identical. Five other experimenters also have compared retention after sleep and after waking and have obtained essentially similar results.[1] The most probable explanation of these findings is that during sleep almost all the activities of the organism are at a minimum, so that fewer reactions occur of a sort that might interfere with or inhibit the recall of what was originally learned. During normal waking activity, however, the number and variety of the responses which an individual makes are enormously increased. Hence, many reactions which can interfere with recall are almost certain to occur, even if the interval between learning and recall is as short as 1 hr.

As we have already said, this interference with the recall of something learned by activities occurring between the learning and the retention test is called "retroactive inhibition," and retroactive inhibition is now generally believed to be one of the principal causes of forgetting. Inability to remember something is not due to the mere lapse of time. If it were, then after any given period, *e.g.*, of 4 hr., one should remember just as much as he would after any other period of identical length. But this is precisely what did *not* happen in the experiment of Jenkins and Dallenbach. Their study showed that, in actuality, the nature of an individual's activities during a given interval greatly influenced his ability to recall what he had learned.

If retroactive inhibition is so important as a cause of forgetting one

---

[1] Three of these experiments are the following: Van Ormer, E. B. Retention after Intervals of Sleep and Waking. *Archives of Psychology*, 1932, No. 137; Graves, E. A. The Effect of Sleep upon Retention. *Journal of Experimental Psychology*, 1936, vol. 19, pp. 316–322; Newman, E. B. Forgetting of Meaningful Material during Sleep and Waking. *American Journal of Psychology*, 1939, vol. 52, pp. 65–71.

might inquire why anything at all was forgotten during the sleeping state in these experiments. To such a question two answers are possible: (1) Retroactive inhibition is not the only cause of forgetting; (2) even in the sleep condition some activity is present. In the study of Jenkins and Dallenbach, the subject did not always go to sleep the instant the learning was completed, and even during sleep numerous reactions undoubtedly occurred, such as various postural adjustments and dreaming. It is possible, too, that the retention of what had been learned was interfered with to some extent by the continuing vegetative activities of the body, such as respiration, circulation, and digestion.

In connection with the effect of sleep upon retention, the experiment of Newman[1] reveals a point of special interest. In this investigation the subjects learned "sense material" (specifically short stories of about three-hundred words each), instead of nonsense syllables, word pairs, and the like which had been used in all the earlier studies.

Each story was so constructed that it contained 12 items that were essential to the general meaning of the narrative, and 12 that were nonessential. The stories were read by the subjects in the morning, in the afternoon, or at night, and recall was required 8 hr. after the reading. Although recall was superior when the learning occurred at night and therefore was followed by sleep, the superiority of the night condition was pronounced only for the reproduction of the nonessential items. For the recall of the essential items, the night condition was only slightly more effective. Such a result is readily understandable. In general, material that is more meaningful, more related and organized, is better retained, *i.e.*, is less likely to be forgotten (see Chap. XVIII). One of the principal causes of forgetting is retroactive inhibition. Since meaningful material is less apt to be forgotten than nonsense material, it is presumably less susceptible to retroactive inhibition (*i.e.*, is more resistant to interference), at least from the various daily activities in which most persons are engaged. If the susceptibility of sense material to retroactive inhibition from daily waking activities is relatively small, it follows that the removal of such inhibition, by the substitution of sleep for waking during the intervals between learning and recall, would improve retention very little compared with the effect that would be expected if the material were of the nonsense

[1] Newman, *op. cit.*

type. In this way one can explain the very small superiority of the sleep condition which Newman found for the recall of the essential items in his stories, as well as its marked superiority for the recall of the nonessential items.

The explanation of retroactive inhibition, that is, the explanation of how activities which occur after learning can interfere with later recall of the material learned, is still a question of great interest to psychologists. Likewise, such problems as the variation of retroactive effect with differences in the nature of the activities learned, in the degree to which the activities are practiced, etc., occupy the attention of many investigators in the field of retention and memory. However, all of these topics lie beyond the scope of the experiment of Jenkins and Dallenbach and, except for the results of Newman cited above, beyond the scope of the present chapter as well.

CHAPTER XVII

THE EFFECT OF OVERLEARNING UPON RETENTION

INTRODUCTION

Among the important problems in the general field of learning and memory is the effect of overlearning upon retention. By "overlearning" is meant practicing an act to an extent greater than that necessary just to learn it. For example, if the act were memorizing a list of words, overlearning would mean going over the list more times than was necessary to repeat it just once correctly.

In general, everyone would agree that the more one practices anything, provided he works at it attentively and purposefully, the better he will be able to recall it later. Yet this, like many plausible notions in the field of psychology, must be experimentally demonstrated before it can be accepted as true. Furthermore, even if overlearning does usually result in improved retention, it is not certain just how great the benefits derived from different amounts of overlearning will be. Suppose it takes 10 repetitions to learn a list of words, which are to be recalled a week later. If the subject after learning the list had practiced it five times more, which would mean giving it 50 per cent more repetitions, would he remember 50 per cent more of it? Or, if he had given the list 10 additional repetitions, making 20 in all, would his recall be 100 per cent better? Likewise, the value of a given amount of overlearning might not be the same after different intervals had elapsed between the original learning and the retention test. If, for example, 50 per cent overlearning increased one's retention 60 per cent on a test given one day later, would its value be greater or less if the interval had been, say, four weeks instead of one day only?

For questions like these, common sense can give no clear answer. The last two problems, in particular, are of considerable practical significance, but they can be solved only by the carefully controlled experimentation which is exemplified in the studies reviewed in this chapter.

I. KRUEGER'S EXPERIMENT WITH WORD LISTS[1]

PURPOSE

The purpose of Krueger's experiment was to determine the effect of different amounts of overlearning upon the retention of lists of words after various prescribed intervals of time.

METHOD

Subjects. Twenty subjects were used in the experiment. (Presumably these were college students, although Krueger does not so state.)

Material Learned. The material to be learned was made up of lists of 12 nouns, each having one syllable only (*e.g.*, barn, lamp, tree, chair).

Method of Learning. Each list of nouns was shown visually, in a series, and always in the same order; each word was visible for 2 sec. The method of learning employed was the so-called "anticipation" method, a procedure which permits a high degree of control of the subject's behavior. This method requires that the subject try to "anticipate" each word in the list by saying it aloud when he sees the word which comes just before it in the series. The first time the list is presented to him he, of course, cannot do this, since all the words are strange to him. During this first trial, therefore, he simply looks at and pronounces each word as it appears. But on all later trials he tries to anticipate by giving the second word in the series when the first word appears, the third word when the second appears, etc. That is, he endeavors to make each successive word as it is presented to him a cue or stimulus for pronouncing the next word in the list. Krueger's method conformed to the above description, except that it was only on every other trial that the subject actually tried to "anticipate." On alternate trials, he merely observed the words as they appeared.

A list was considered just learned when the subject could go through it once without error; that is, when he could correctly anticipate all the words in it during a single presentation.

The Overlearning. The degree of proficiency represented by one successful anticipation of the entire list during a single exposure

---

[1] Adapted from Krueger, W. C. F. The Effect of Overlearning on Retention. *Journal of Experimental Psychology*, 1929, vol. 12, pp. 71–78.

Krueger called "100 per cent learning." Any practice beyond the amount necessary to achieve this result would then be overlearning. Krueger employed two degrees of overlearning, which he designated as 150 per cent learning and 200 per cent learning. In the former, the subject, after he had been given enough trials to learn the list according to the above standard, was given 50 per cent more trials. That is, if he had required 10 repetitions for the 100 per cent learning, he would now be given five overlearning trials. In the 200 per cent learning he was given 100 per cent more trials than were necessary to learn the list. Hence, if he had needed 10 trials to learn it, he would now be given 10 overlearning trials, making a total of twice as many as had been required just for learning.

The Retention Tests. The test of retention was given at a prescribed interval after the learning was finished. Six different intervals were used; 1, 2, 4, 7, 14, and 28 days. No list was tested for recall more than once; hence, if the interval was 14 days, the list recalled then would always be one which had never been tested at any previous time.

Each retention test was twofold in nature. First, the subject went through the list once by the same anticipation method that had been used for the learning, and the number of his correct anticipations was recorded. The number of words thus correctly anticipated, and the per cent which that number was of the 12 words originally learned, constituted the subject's *recall score*. (The recall scores are given in columns 3 and 4 of Table I.) Following this, the subject was given a sufficient number of presentations of the list for him to relearn it to the 100 per cent standard, *i.e.*, to anticipate correctly every word in it during one single exposure. The number of trials required for this relearning was then compared with the number necessary for the original learning. On the basis of this comparison the retention in per cent saved, called the *saving score*, was computed. The formula for this calculation is

$$\text{Per cent saved} = \left(1 - \frac{\text{number of trials for relearning}}{\text{number of trials for learning}}\right) \times 100$$

If a subject required 10 trials to learn a list originally and 4 trials to relearn it a week later, the per cent saved would be $(1 - \frac{4}{10}) \times 100$, or 60. In other words, he retained what he had learned sufficiently well to require 60 per cent fewer repetitions to learn the same material once more. (The saving scores are given in column 5 of Table I.)

It should be noted that these two methods of testing retention measure different aspects of it. The recall method takes account only of those responses which the subject can make without any additional practice with the material. The saving method, however, gives weight to any traces of the effects of the original learning which, though insufficient to make complete recall of a response possible, are still sufficient to make relearning of it easier. As one would expect, the per cent retained is in most cases greater by the saving method.

Amount of Data Obtained. As Table I shows, there were six retention intervals and three degrees of learning (of which two were degrees of overlearning) for each interval. Hence, in all there were 18 different conditions. Different groups of subjects were used for the different intervals, but the same group was tested for all of the three different degrees of learning for any one interval. Every subject learned a different list of approximately equal difficulty for each of his learning-retention records, but different subjects could, of course, use the same lists. The total number of lists learned, and so the total number of individual retention scores obtained, was 20 for each of the 18 experimental conditions, except that there were 40 for each of the three degrees of learning at the one-day interval.

RESULTS

Krueger's findings are presented in Table I. For the most part, the results given below are very clear-cut, and statistical treatment shows that practically all of the differences between the various retention scores are highly reliable.[1]

150 Per Cent versus 100 Per Cent Learning. Comparison of 150 and 100 per cent learning (*i.e.*, 50 per cent overlearning and bare learning) shows that in all cases the former was superior, since the retention score was higher for every interval and by both methods of measuring retention. Furthermore, it is evident that 50 per cent additional practice was in every sense worth while, since it always gave at least 50 per cent better retention, and in most cases produced an increase far exceeding that figure. After seven days, for example, it produced a recall score more than six times higher than the score for

---

[1] See Chap. I, p. 9, for an explanation of the reliability of differences.

100 per cent learning and a saving score more than 13 times higher. As for the relation between the value of 50 per cent overlearning and the length of the time interval, it is clear that as the interval increased in length the value of the overlearning increased also. For example,

TABLE I

The Average Number of Words Recalled, the Average Percentage of the Original List Recalled, and the Average Per Cent Saved, for Each of the Three Degrees of Learning after Each of the Six Intervals[1]

Length of interval, days	Degree of learning (per cent)	Average number of words recalled	Average per cent of the list recalled	Average per cent saved
1	100	3.10	25.83	21.73
	150	4.60	38.33	36.15
	200	5.83	48.58	47.10
2	100	1.80	15.00	13.40
	150	3.60	30.00	33.45
	200	4.65	38.75	42.05
4	100	0.50	4.17	3.40
	150	2.05	17.08	29.75
	200	3.30	27.50	32.30
7	100	0.20	1.67	1.75
	150	1.30	10.83	23.15
	200	1.65	13.75	27.55
14	100	0.15	1.25	1.65
	150	0.65	5.42	20.80
	200	0.90	7.50	25.45
28	100	0.00	0.00	1.70
	150	0.25	2.08	20.50
	200	0.40	3.33	25.10

[1] The average number of trials required for the original learning varied between 4.15 and 4.85 repetitions for the different lists. Since the variation was so small, the lists must have been approximately equal in difficulty.

after a one-day interval, 50 per cent overlearning was 67 per cent superior to 100 per cent learning by the saving method; after 2 days, it was nearly 250 per cent superior; and after 28 days, over 1,200 per cent.

200 Per Cent versus 150 Per Cent Learning. Comparing 200 and 150 per cent learning (*i.e.*, 100 per cent and 50 per cent overlearning), however, one obtains a somewhat different picture from that afforded by the comparison above. To be sure, 200 per cent learning gave the higher score at every interval by both the recall and the saving method. But since 200 per cent learning requires one-third (or $33\frac{1}{3}$ per cent) more repetitions than does 150 per cent learning, to prove itself *proportionately* superior to the latter it must give $33\frac{1}{3}$ per cent better retention. Inspection of the table shows that for the most part it did not have this value. By the recall method, 200 per cent learning was a little more than one-third superior to 150 per cent learning at three of the intervals, but less than one-third superior at the other three. By the saving method, it did not produce as much as $33\frac{1}{3}$ per cent better retention at any interval whatever. As for its value at different intervals, no consistent relationship was shown; by the saving method, it was 30 per cent superior after 1 day, 19 per cent superior after 7 days, and 22 per cent superior after 28 days.

CONCLUSIONS

Krueger draws the following conclusions from his data:

1. As the degree of learning was increased from 100 per cent to 150 per cent, the corresponding increase in retention for the one-day interval was approximately the same, and this ratio increased rapidly as the length of the interval between learning and recall was extended.

2. As the degree of learning was increased from 150 per cent to 200 per cent (that is by an additional $33\frac{1}{3}$ per cent), the corresponding increase in retention was usually less, and this proportion did not vary consistently with the length of the interval.

A certain degree of overlearning, at least 50 per cent, is highly economical from the standpoint of retention for intervals of 2 to 28 days, and the larger the interval, the greater is the economy. Further increases of overlearning, however, proved to be uneconomical for most intervals.

To the reviewers, the results suggest that although any and all amounts of overlearning may be expected to have value in the sense that they will produce some degree of improvement in retention, it cannot be expected that the betterment will continue to be proportional to the amount of extra practice involved. Diminishing returns are probably bound to show themselves sooner or later.

II. KRUEGER'S EXPERIMENT WITH MAZES[1]

Krueger subsequently repeated the entire experiment, using mazes instead of lists of words as the material for learning. The same three degrees of learning (100 per cent, 150 per cent, and 200 per cent) were employed, and retention was tested after intervals of from 1 to 28 days. The results of this second study were very similar to those of the first, except that with the mazes 150 per cent learning did not have quite its proportional value whereas, rather surprisingly, 200 per cent learning did. That is, the retention value of 200 per cent learning of mazes was always at least 33⅓ per cent superior to the retention value of 150 per cent learning.

Apparently for the purpose of finding whether with mazes, as well as with words, a sufficiently great amount of overlearning would produce diminishing returns, Krueger now had other subjects practice the mazes to the degree of 300 per cent learning. That is, after a subject had practiced a maze enough to enable him to traverse it once without error, he was then given twice as many additional trials. It was found that, although 300 per cent learning was superior to any smaller amount for all intervals, it was nevertheless not proportionately superior; *i.e.*, it was not so much as 50 per cent better than 200 per cent learning. Hence, the principle of diminishing returns which held for words was demonstrated to be true for mazes also.

Comparison of the two experiments shows, however, that the point at which the returns from overlearning begin to diminish is not the same with different activities and materials. With the word lists that point seems to have been somewhere between 150 and 200 per cent learning; with the mazes it probably fell between 200 and 300 per cent learning.

DISCUSSION

The practical implications of Krueger's work are fairly obvious. Practice beyond the amount necessary for just barely learning an activity may always be expected to improve one's retention of it to some extent (provided, that is, that the extra practice is carried out with proper attentiveness and with adequate motivation). However, no one can expect that this extra practice will continue to yield propor-

[1] Adapted from Krueger, W. C. F. Further Studies in Overlearning. *Journal of Experimental Psychology*, 1930, vol. 13, pp. 152–163.

tionate returns. The favorable effect of a little overlearning may be very great; but although very large amounts of overlearning will yield some further advantage, the gain may seem small in comparison with the additional time and effort expended. At least this conclusion seems warranted for the types of material used in Krueger's investigations.

This statement does not mean, however, that large amounts of overlearning are not worth while. Whether they are or are not depends solely on how important perfect retention is to the individual. If it is essential that his memory for some particular material be as accurate and reliable as he can possibly make it—which is the case, for example, when a pianist practices for a forthcoming concert—then, in spite of the principle of diminishing returns, very large amounts of overlearning will still be profitable to him. For there is no reason to suppose that even the last 100 trials out of 10,000 would not add something, however small, to the excellence of his subsequent performance.

Also it might be noted that the value of various amounts of overlearning for the retention of logically organized verbal material (such as a class assignment in psychology) may be different from the values found by Krueger for the retention of lists of unrelated words and of mazes. In general, it is not safe to assume that the efficacy of a given method of learning will be the same for different kinds of material. Such an assumption is especially insecure if the materials differ widely with respect to the complexity of their interrelationships and the nature of their organization.[1] Unfortunately, however, no experiments dealing with the value of overlearning for the retention of logical verbal material have yet been performed.

[1] See Chap. XVIII for a discussion of the effect upon memory of organizing the material to be learned.

CHAPTER XVIII

THE IMPORTANCE OF ORGANIZATION FOR RETENTION AND TRANSFER[1]

INTRODUCTION

One of the most important topics in the investigation of learning is the relation between the organization of the material or activity to be learned and the speed with which the activity is mastered, the degree to which it is retained, and the likelihood that transfer[2] to other situations will occur. Especially significant is the kind of organization which makes possible the development of a general principle, and the effect of such a principle—when acquired and understood by the learner—upon his retention of what he has learned and his ability to transfer it (or apply it) to a subsequent different situation.

Organization in its simplest form may be characterized as merely a sort of grouping. Thus, a subject who is trying to memorize the 12 digits 581215192226 may group them, say, by three's, and may therefore perceive and repeat the series as 581 215 192 226. If he says the series to himself he probably will employ rhythm also, perhaps accentuating the first of each group of three digits, either subvocally or aloud.

It has been demonstrated repeatedly that even organization of this kind, which Katona[3] terms "rudimentary . . . arbitrary and artificial," is superior to no organization at all, in that it leads to quicker learning of a series and to better and longer retention of it as well. Presumably the reason for its value is that it involves the establishment of relationships between the items of the material (here the different digits), and yields a kind of form, pattern, or "Gestalt" which confers some measure of unity upon the material. A series of 12 digits may become

---

[1] Based on Katona, George. *Organizing and Memorizing.* Copyright, 1940, by Columbia University Press, New York.

[2] "Transfer" or "transfer of training" means the influence of prior learning upon the learning of, or response to, new related material.

[3] Katona, *op. cit.*, p. 18; see also his discussion on pp. 165–192 and 283–287.

through rhythmic grouping a sequence of four groups of three digits each with the accent on the first digit of each group. The series now has more form, more pattern, than would be possessed by a 12-digit series in which each number was treated as separate and unrelated to any other.

There are many kinds and degrees of organization which may be employed in learning. Some of these are highly effective for the purposes of learning, retention, and transfer. Others by contrast are inadequate for such uses. In the above example the organization by arbitrary grouping is, as we have said, preferable to no organization at all. But it is very inefficient compared with the kind of organization which this particular number series permits. If the series is examined closely, it may be seen that the sequence of digits is by no means a chance one but proceeds according to a definite arithmetical principle. Actually the series is formed by beginning with the number 5, then adding alternately 3 and 4 to the last preceding number. Thus 5 plus 3 is 8, the second number in the series; 8 plus 4 is 12, the third number; 12 plus 3 is 15, the fourth number; and so on. Katona[1] reports that subjects who discovered or were told the above principle often learned the series at once, in a single repetition, and were usually able to recall it without error a week later. But those who memorized the series by the less adequate method of grouping by three's throughout often required several repetitions to learn it, and were seldom able to reproduce it correctly a week afterward.

It is obvious that the discovery of a general arithmetical principle in connection with the above series supplies it with an organization which is meaningful in high degree. It establishes relationships of a precise sort between the different numbers which comprise the series, so that if any particular number is forgotten it can readily be inferred or deduced in accordance with the principle. The series acquires a clear and definite pattern and becomes a meaningful unity.

Organization in different types of material can be achieved in many different ways. In memorizing a piano composition, for example, the rhythms, melodies, and harmonies of the music provide a basic organization of which virtually every learner takes advantage. However, the expert musician will perceive and utilize further organizing factors; for example, he will recognize the reappearance of a given

---

[1] *Ibid.*, pp. 11–20.

theme even though it is changed in key and tempo. His capacity to discern and profit by such relationships is one reason for his superiority in learning and remembering musical material.

In stylus maze learning, the mere association of each particular movement with the next, in terms either of successive kinesthetic stimulations or of guiding verbalizations, such as "left, right, forward, right," etc., yields little that could be termed "organization" in the sense in which Katona uses the word. However, a maze does possess a fairly definite structure or pattern, and the responses of the maze learner can become more or less organized in accordance with it. Thus a subject can group successive moves into small units, such as left-right-forward, or can be aided in learning specific groups of movements by a perception of their spatial relationships to other preceding and succeeding groups. Of special value to the maze learner is a comprehension of the general shape of the maze path as a whole, for example, that it approximates a circle, and first proceeds somewhat to the right, then turns and extends far to the left, and finally recurves and ends at a place near the starting point. Such an understanding of a maze path functions like a general principle, even though it may be applicable only to the particular maze in question. It helps to organize all the separate moves in the maze into an over-all form or pattern, and makes them meaningful by virtue of their relation to the general shape of the true path.

In most verbal learning—unless it be of the rote memorizing variety[1] —general principles are likely to be the preeminent organizing factors. When a student of psychology is reading about conditioning, he will encounter a number of general principles, for example, the basic principle that if two stimuli to which an organism is responsive are presented together, the reaction made to one stimulus may later come to be evoked by the other stimulus also. The student who understands these principles is likely to retain them long and well. Also, acquisition of the principles will make it easier for him to learn and remember the

[1] Rote memorizing means learning by repetition, with organization and understanding of the material at a minimum. Some materials, such as lists of nonsense syllables, telephone numbers, statistical and chemical formulas which are not understood, lack significant internal relationships and thus usually can be learned only in rote fashion. Most of what we learn, however, does possess inner relatedness, is meaningful, can be organized by the learner, and so can be acquired by what Katona calls "learning by understanding," a far more effective method.

various facts about conditioning which are presented in textbooks and lectures. But a student who did not learn and understand the principles might find it difficult to organize and relate the many factual details involved in the study of the topic. In consequence he might find the learning of this content an unduly difficult task, and his retention of it might be poor, as well.

So far we have discussed the value of organization, especially the organization afforded by the acquisition of general principles, for the learning and retention of a specific material or activity. Equally significant in the psychology of learning is the value of general principles from the viewpoint of transfer. One of the earliest investigations dealing with this problem is that of Judd.[1] In this experiment two groups of boys in grades V and VI practiced hitting with a dart a target submerged in water to the depth of 12 in. Both groups practiced hitting the target at that specific depth only, but one group in addition received an explanation of the principle of the refraction of light rays through water. During the practice the two groups were approximately equal with respect to the degree of accuracy they achieved. Then both groups were given a different but related task, namely, that of hitting the target when it was under only 4 in. of water. The group which had been taught the general principle rapidly adjusted to the changed condition and exhibited a large amount of transfer. The group which had had only the specific practice could not easily make the required adjustment and showed almost no transfer at all. Judd's experiment was repeated, with some modifications, by Hendrickson and Schroeder[2] in 1941. Their results were essentially the same as those obtained by Judd, although the difference in amount of transfer between the two groups was smaller.

Another experiment which demonstrates the transfer value of the acquisition and comprehension of general principles is that of Ruger.[3] Ruger had his subjects solve a number of mechanical puzzles, many of which were similar in construction. He found that a much greater amount of transfer from one puzzle to another was obtained by those subjects who discovered the general principle of solution of a particular

[1] Judd, C. H. The Relation of Special Training to General Intelligence. *Educational Review*, 1908, vol. 36, pp. 28–42.

[2] Hendrickson, G., and W. H. Schroeder. Transfer of Training in Learning to Hit a Submerged Target. *Journal of Educational Psychology*, 1941, vol. 32, pp. 205–213.

[3] Ruger, H. A. The Psychology of Efficiency. *Archives of Psychology*, 1910, No. 15.

puzzle, and who realized that many of the other puzzles could be solved by application of the same general rule.

Recently Katona[1] has published an extensive series of experiments dealing with the effect of different methods of learning on the acquisition, the retention, and the transfer of skill in performing a certain type of card trick, and in solving "match tasks" (matchstick puzzles). A primary aim of these experiments was to compare the value of (1) the rote memorizing of the solution of a specific trick (or tricks), and (2) the learning of the general principle by which a correct solution could be reached. Katona reasoned that the acquisition and understanding of a general principle should produce the kind of organization of the material which would improve the accuracy and duration of retention of a particular solution, and likewise facilitate transfer (application) of the learning to the solution of new but similar tricks. The remainder of this chapter will be devoted mainly to a presentation of certain of his many experiments.

KATONA'S CARD-TRICK EXPERIMENTS[2]

GENERAL PLAN

Katona's experiments with card tricks[3] have been selected for presentation in this chapter. The general plan of these experiments was as follows. The subjects were shown one or two versions of the type of card trick used. One group was told only the specific order in which the cards should be placed to do a particular trick (or tricks) and was instructed to learn that order. This group was called the "memorizing group." Another group was given an explanation of the general principle according to which the correct order of cards for a particular trick could be derived. This group was called the "understanding group." In many cases there also was a "control group," which was given tricks to solve without any practice or instruction whatever. Tests for the retention of the tricks learned were given after prescribed intervals of time. In addition, tests of transfer were made; that is,

---

[1] Katona, *op. cit.*

[2] Adapted from *ibid.*, especially pp. 32–54 and 263–268.

[2] In this chapter the card tricks were chosen for presentation instead of the more widely known match-task experiments because of their greater simplicity, the greater clarity of the experimental procedures used with them, and the more definite character of the results.

the subjects were given similar tricks to do without further aid from the experimenter.

The Card Tricks. Katona used eight card tricks in all, each of which was constructed according to very similar principles. The general nature of these card tricks was as follows. The experimenter took a prescribed number of ordinary playing cards and made a deck[1] of them, with the faces down and so invisible to him. He then laid out the cards, face up, on a table in a preannounced order, *e.g.*, alternately red and black, at the same time putting every other card, without looking at it, at the bottom of the deck from which he was dealing. This procedure was continued until the entire deck had been laid out on the table. Of course, such a trick is accomplished by making a specific prearrangement of the cards in the deck.

Thus, to quote the experimenter's oral description to his subjects of one of the tricks: "I take the top card" (of the prearranged deck) "and place it on the table. It is a red card. Then I take the next card and put it at the bottom of the deck without determining what it is. I place the third card on the table. It is a black card. The following card I put undetermined below the others; while the next card, which is red, I put on the table." The procedure of alternately placing one card on the table and one at the bottom of the deck was continued until all the cards of the deck were laid out on the table. The cards then appeared on the table in this order: red, black, red, black, etc.

According to Katona, a card trick of this type proved very satisfactory for experimental purposes. It was novel and was interesting to the subjects. Also this type of trick could be presented with many variations. It was possible to vary the number of cards, *e.g.*, to use a deck of 6, 8, or 13 cards. It also was possible to use a different order than that of alternating red and black. For example, in one case the trick was to make a deck of the 13 cards of the spade suit and to lay them on the table in sequence from the ace to king inclusive, always putting every other card at the bottom of the deck. Another

---

[1] The word "deck" does not refer to the whole deck of 52 cards. A deck might consist of only 6 cards, or 8, or 13, or indeed any number.

variation was to put two cards, instead of one card, at the bottom of the deck each time after a card was placed on the table.

Katona used eight card tricks of the type described above. The exact nature of each trick is shown in the accompanying table:

Trick	Number and kind of cards to be laid out	Order in which cards are to be laid out	Number of cards to be placed at the bottom of the deck after each card is laid out
A	4 red and 4 black	Red and black alternating	1
B	The 13 cards of the spade suit	In sequence from ace to king inclusive	1
C	The 8 cards of the spade suit from ace to 8 inclusive	In sequence from ace to 8 inclusive	1
D	3 red and 3 black	Red and black alternating	1
E	4 red and 4 black	Red and black alternating	2 (except only 1 after the 6th card is placed on the table)
F	8 spades, 4 of even and 4 of uneven denomination	Even and odd alternating	1
G	4 red and 4 black	4 red, then 4 black	1
H	3 red and 3 black	Red and black alternating	2

The reader may not find it easy to understand exactly how the tricks are done unless he practices with an actual pack of cards, although study of Katona's instructions to the "understanding" groups on page 303 should be helpful. Each of these tricks can be performed by prearranging the cards in the deck. It is possible to learn a specific order for each individual trick, or a general principle from which the solution of any one of the tricks can be deduced. The solution for each of the tricks (*i.e.*, the order in which the cards of the deck must be prearranged) is given on page 310.

The Learning Methods. After the subjects had seen the experimenter perform a "complicated version" of the card trick, they learned the solution of one trick (sometimes of two tricks) by one of the two methods described below.

1. *The Memorizing Method.* Each memorizing group received instructions, of which the following, for Trick A, is an example:

I suppose you would like to know how to perform the trick. I shall teach you a trick with four red and four black cards. We want to arrange these eight cards so that the uppermost card in the deck is red; it is to be placed on the table. The next card should be placed at the bottom of the deck without determining what card it is; then a black card should be placed on the table. In order to achieve this goal you must take in your hand: first, two red cards; then, one black card; then two red cards; and at last three black cards. [The last four phrases were written on a paper or on the blackboard.] You are to learn this order so as to remember it. We will, therefore, repeat three times: four red and four black cards are to be arranged as follows: first, two red cards, then. . . . [The experimenter pointed to the paper or the blackboard while the subjects read aloud.]

2. *The Understanding Method.* Each understanding group received instructions of which the following—also for Trick A—is an example:

We must arrange eight cards. We don't know in what order, therefore we put eight question marks on the blackboard. [See the schema below.] The first question mark represents the first card; the second question mark the second card; and so forth. The last question mark represents the last card. According to the task, the first card should be a red card. The second card should be placed below the others. We do not know what it is, therefore it is represented by a question mark. The third card must be a black card, while the fourth card is unknown (a question mark). [And so forth. The letters and question marks in the second line of the schema were written on the blackboard while these directions were being given.]

The four cards which are designated by letters on the blackboard are supposed to be on the table. The four cards designated by question marks are still in my hand. Now we must find out what cards these remaining question marks represent. My last two moves were to put a black card on the table and an unknown card at the bottom of the pack. The next card (that is, the first of the remaining question marks) must, therefore, be a red card. The following card, represented by the following question mark, has to be placed below the others and remains therefore a question mark. Then follows a black card and lastly a question mark. [Note the third line of the schema below.]

Two question marks remain, that is, I have two unknown cards in my hand. The first one, following a black card, must be a red card, while the next one remains a question mark. This one being the last card, following a red card, must be black.

Now we are ready to add up our findings. First we have a red card, then another red card. . . [reading the final line of the schema].

The schema which the experimenter put on the blackboard is reproduced herewith. "R" means red, "B" means black, "?" means color unknown.

?	?	?	?	?	?	?	?
R	?	B	?	R	?	B	?
	R		?		B		?
			R				?
							B
R	R	B	R	R	B	B	B

It should be noted that in a *memorizing group* the subjects were simply told the correct order of the cards and required to repeat it a given number of times. No explanation of the order was made to them, nor were they told why the prescribed order was the correct one. In an *understanding group*, however, not only was the correct order eventually given, but also a method of logically deriving it was fully presented. In a group of this type the subjects did not repeat the order aloud: rather their behavior throughout the explanation was that of attentive listening.

The teaching, and the learning and testing as well, were carried out with paper and pencil instead of with actual cards. When a subject was tested for his memory of any trick, or for his ability to solve a new and different one, he wrote on a piece of paper what he thought the order of the cards should be.

The procedure described above was used in all the five card-trick experiments presented below. The first three experiments were of a preliminary nature, in that they involved the use of only four subjects each. The remaining two experiments were more adequate quantitatively in that the subjects numbered 22 and 105, respectively.

THE FIVE EXPERIMENTS

Experiment I. The trick learned in this experiment was Trick A already described. The subjects were four college students. Two subjects were given, individually, the memorizing type of instruction and two the understanding type. The learning and instruction process required 1 min. for the memorizing and 4 min. for the understanding subjects. Immediately after this practice was finished, the subjects were tested for retention by being asked to write down the correct order of cards in the deck. They all succeeded in doing this, but the memorizing subjects recalled the order more quickly. Two weeks later another retention test was given. In this test one of the memorizers was unable to remember the correct order. The other wrote down the correct order after some hesitation, but then changed it to an incorrect one. In contrast, both of the understanding subjects gave the correct order in less than 2 min.

Experiment II. In this experiment the trick was to lay out the 13 spades in sequence (Trick B). As before, the subjects were four college students, none of whom had served in Experiment I. Two subjects were given the memorizing and two the understanding procedure. The memorizers spent 4 min. in learning the correct order of the cards, whereas the explanation given to the understanding subjects required 5 min. Two retention tests were given, one immediately and the other 8 days later. In the immediate test all four subjects correctly recalled the order of the cards, but the two memorizers did so more quickly. In the later retention test neither of the memorizers was able to remember the order, but both the understanding subjects recalled it without error.

Experiment III. As in Experiment II, the trick was the one employing the 13 spades (Trick B). As before, there were four new subjects, two for each type of learning procedure. In a retention test given immediately after the learning process, all four subjects correctly recalled the order of the cards. Then, instead of another retention test, a transfer test was given immediately. The subjects were asked to state (*i.e.*, to write down) how the cards should be arranged for Trick A already fully described. Neither memorizer was able to solve the problem within 5 min., whereas the two understanding subjects succeeded after 2½ and 3 min., respectively.

The results of these first three experiments suggest that (1) for immediate recall of the correct order of cards in a particular trick the memorizing method is equal to or superior to the understanding method; (2) for later recall—after 2 weeks in Experiment I and after 8 days in Experiment II—the understanding method is superior; and (3) for transfer, that is, for solving a similar card trick—as in Experiment III—the understanding method is likewise the better procedure.

Experiment IV. Katona next carried out a small group experiment. The *subjects* were 22 graduate students of psychology; all were entirely unfamiliar with card tricks of the type employed. These subjects were divided into three groups: a memorizing group, an understanding group, and a control group, which numbered nine, nine, and four individuals, respectively. The three groups were roughly equated for ability to solve these problems by having each subject classified by his instructor as very good or good, as average, or as poor, and by including within each of the three groups the same proportion of each of these classes. The *memorizing group* first learned the order of cards for Trick A already described, then the order of cards for the trick in which eight spades from the ace to the eight inclusive were

TABLE I

The Number of Subjects in Each Group Whose Solutions to Each of the Six Tasks Were Correct or False

Task and trick	Understanding group		Memorizing group		Control group	
	Correct	False	Correct	False	Correct	False
Task 1. Trick A............	6[1]	3[1]	8[1]	1[1]	0	4
Task 2. Trick D............	6	3	1	8	1	3
Task 3. Trick E............	5	4	2	7	0	4
Task 4. Trick F............	6	3	5	4	1	3
Task 5. Trick C............	6	3	7[1]	2[1]	0	4
Task 6. Trick G............	9	0	7	2	3	1

[1] Means that the particular trick had already been explained or practiced during the previous learning period.

to be laid out in sequence (Trick C). This learning was accomplished by having these subjects repeat the correct order of the cards five times for each trick, a procedure which required a total time of 4 min. The *understanding group* listened to the experimenter's explanation of how the order of cards for Trick A could be derived (given in full on page 303). This procedure also required 4 min.

The *test*, which began a few minutes after the completion of the learning period, consisted of six successive card-trick tasks. This test was given to both the above groups and also to the control group of subjects who had never before seen any tricks of this type. The subjects were allotted 4 min. to write down the solution of each task, and their papers were collected after each such time interval.

The results of the experiment are given in Table I. "Correct" means that the subject's solution was complete and without error.

"False" means that a solution was partly incorrect, or was incomplete, or that no solution at all was produced within the 4-min. time limit.

Of the above tricks, A and C already are familiar to the reader. Trick D was an easy variation of Trick A, employing only 3 red and 3 black cards instead of 4 of each color. Trick E was a difficult variation of Trick A, in that it required that (usually) two cards instead of one be put at the bottom of the deck after each card had been laid out on the table. Trick F was another easy variation of Trick A; in fact it was identical with A except for the substitution of even and uneven denominations for red and black. Trick G was sufficiently easy for intelligent persons to solve immediately, as a rule, without previous knowledge of these card tricks.

The results, like those of the first three experiments, indicate that for immediate recall the memorizing method is fully equal in value to the understanding procedure. This point is readily seen when we compare the number of subjects in the two groups who could remember the correct order of cards for Trick A already practiced. The data strongly indicate, however, that for the purpose of transfer—that is, the solution of new but similar tricks—the understanding procedure was definitely superior. In every instance in which both groups were required to solve a new trick, more of the understanding than of the memorizing subjects succeeded in doing so within the allotted 4 min. It is also worth noting that Trick C was solved by almost as many subjects of the understanding group, for whom it was a new task, as it was by subjects of the memorizing group, who had previously repeated five times the order of cards requisite for its solution.

Katona notes that the understanding subjects who were successful in the transfer situations usually did not recall the exact details of the schema according to which the correct order of cards for Trick A had been derived. Instead these subjects remembered, as they put it, "the general scheme" or "the principle" of the solving procedure. Katona also observed that the memorizing subjects who were able to solve the new tricks were successful largely because they happened to develop during the test an attitude of a "problem-solving" nature,[1]

---

[1] In this test, the development of a problem-solving attitude appears to be equivalent to getting the right "direction" in a problem situation requiring reasoning for its solution. See Chap. XXIII for a discussion of direction and its significance for thinking.

so that they searched for a formula or a principle instead of merely trying to use the specific card orders which they had memorized.

Experiment V. Katona's fifth experiment differed from the first four experiments in that the number of subjects was much greater, and the learning procedures were somewhat amplified. As in Experiment IV, the subjects were instructed and tested in groups instead of individually, and control groups were employed.

The *subjects* were 105 college students, divided into a memorizing group, an understanding group, and two control groups. The groups were approximately equated in the same manner as in Experiment IV.

The *experimental procedure* was as follows. First each group saw the experimenter perform the 13-spade trick (Trick B). Then the experimenter, without explaining the trick, asked the subjects if they knew or had seen this trick or any similar one. The few who answered in the affirmative were not used in the experiment. A learning period of 4 min. followed immediately. During this time the *memorizing group* repeated five times the correct order of cards required to perform Trick A, and similarly repeated five times the correct order for the eight-spade trick (Trick C). The *understanding group*, as in Experiment IV, was not given specific repetitions of any order of cards but simply listened to the experimenter's explanation of Trick A. The control groups had no learning or instruction period at all.

Immediately after the learning a series of three tests was given. The first was a transfer test utilizing Trick D, the easy variation of Trick A that also had been used in Experiment IV. The second test, too, was a transfer test, and consisted of Trick E, the difficult variation of Trick A that likewise had been employed in Experiment IV. The third test was simply a retention test of Trick A. In this experiment 2 min. instead of 4 were allotted for each solution. After the above tests had been given, the subjects were asked not to discuss the tricks or to show them to anyone.

Four weeks later the groups were given a second and entirely unexpected series of tests. This series was preceded by another demonstration of Trick B (as before without explanation). The subjects were asked whether they had thought of the tricks during the 4-week period, had tried them out, or had shown them to anyone. The test papers of those who answered any of these questions in the affirmative were not scored.   As the table shows, these stipulations resulted in a decrease of the number of subjects actually used in the second series of tests.

This second test series, like the first, consisted of three tasks, to be performed in 2 min. each.   The first of these was another retention test of Trick A.   The second was the eight-spade trick (Trick C). This was a retention test for the memorizing group, since these subjects had learned the order of cards for this trick during the learning period.   For the understanding group, however, it was a transfer

TABLE II

For Experiment V, the Percentages of Subjects in Each Group Achieving Perfect Solutions

Test	Understanding group		Memorizing group		Control group	
	No. of subjects	Per-centage	No. of subjects	Per-centage	No. of subjects	Per-centage
First series.................	25	..	26	..	32	
Trick D...................	..	44	..	23	..	9
Trick E...................	..	40	..	8	..	3
Trick A...................	..	44 [1]	..	42 [1]	..	9
Second series..............	21	..	22	..	22	
Trick A...................	..	48 [1]	..	32 [1]	..	9
Trick C...................	..	62	..	36 [1]	..	14
Trick H...................	..	52	..	18	..	9

[1] Means that the particular trick had already been explained or practiced during the learning period.

test, since they had never seen or attempted the trick before.   The last test was Trick H, which was a transfer test for both groups. Reference to page 310 will show that this trick was similar to Trick E, which had been used in the first test series.   Since a control group in an experiment of this type must be entirely unpracticed, the control subjects employed in the first test series could not serve again in that capacity and an entirely new group had to be selected.

The results of Experiment V are given in Table II.

The results of Experiment V are virtually identical with those of the other experiments.   As before, the two experimental groups were approximately equal with respect to their immediate memory for a trick previously presented.   This is seen when we compare the

percentages of subjects who succeeded in giving the correct order of
cards for Trick A in the first test series.   With respect to delayed
retention, the understanding group was superior to the memorizing
group, as a comparison of the percentages for Trick A in the second
test shows.   From the viewpoint of transfer, the understanding group
always was superior, as is disclosed by the results for Tricks D and
E in the first series, and for Trick H in the second series.   It is noteworthy that in the second series, 62 per cent of the understanding
group solved Trick C, which for them was a new task, whereas only
36 per cent of the memorizing group were able to give the correct
order of cards for this trick, even though they had learned the order
4 weeks previously.

Solutions of the Eight Card Tricks Described on Page 302, i.e., the Order in Which the Cards
Must Be Prearranged in the Deck

Trick	Solution
A	Red, red, black, red, red, black, black, black
B	Ace, queen, 2, 8, 3, jack, 4, 9, 5, king, 6, 10, 7
C	Ace, 5, 2, 7, 3, 6, 4, 8
D	Red, black, black, black, red, red
E	Red, black, black, black, red, black, red, red
F	Even, even, uneven, even, even, uneven, uneven, uneven
G	Red, black, red, black, red, black, red, black
H	Red, red, red, black, black, black

DISCUSSION

The experiments of Katona are unique in that, prior to his work,
no investigator had tried to compare directly the effects upon both retention and transfer of (1) the rote memorizing of a specific solution,
and (2) the learning and understanding of the general principle by
which the solution could be reached.

As the previous discussion has shown, the results of all of his five
card-trick experiments are in complete agreement.   They all point,
in direct and unambiguous fashion, to the conclusion that for delayed
retention and for transfer, learning the general principle by which a
specific solution is derived is superior to merely memorizing a specific
solution by rote.   Thus, his results clearly demonstrate the value,
for both delayed retention and transfer, of the kind of organization of
the material learned which a general principle furnishes.

With respect to the significance of organization for retention, there
are several studies other than those of Katona in the experimental

literature. Psychologists have long known that retention is better for material which is more meaningful, which embodies more relationships among its several items. For example, it has been amply demonstrated that poetry is better retained than are nonsense syllables,[1] that related pairs of words are better remembered than unrelated pairs,[2] that memory of the general substance or meaning of a prose selection is usually superior to that of a selection learned verbatim.[3] Such results are related to those obtained by Katona because the factors of meaning and relationship resemble general principles in their possession of organizing functions.

If one inquires why, in Katona's experiments, the rote memorizing of a specific solution should have been inferior for retention of that solution, over periods ranging from 8 days (in Experiment II) to 4 weeks (in Experiment V), the answer might be in part as follows. For Trick A (the one most frequently used for learning purposes) this type of learning consisted of the memorizing of the series "2 red cards, 1 black card, 2 red cards, 3 black cards." Such a series, in the absence of understanding of the principle according to which it is constructed, was almost entirely devoid of organization, *i.e.*, of significant inner relationships, and was meaningful only in the sense that it was known to be the solution of that particular trick. Being a short series of items, it could be learned quickly even by the rote method. But having little of an organized character, it was likely to be speedily forgotten. And once it was forgotten, even if only partially, it could not be reconstructed by the subject, since its deficiency in organization made it impossible for him to derive or infer any individual item from any other item. In contrast, the understanding method of learning yielded not only familiarity with a specific solution but also a comprehension of the general principle by which the specific order was derived. Like the arithmetical principle discussed earlier in this chapter, this principle functioned as

[1] Radossawljevitch, P. R. *Das Behalten und Vergessen bei Kindern und Erwachsenen nach experimentelle Untersuchungen.* Leipzig, Nemnich, 1907.

Whitely, P. L., and J.A. McGeoch. The Curve of Retention for Poetry. *Journal of Educational Psychology*, 1928, vol. 19, pp. 471–479.

[2] Key, C. B. Recall as a Function of Perceived Relations. *Archives of Psychology*, 1926, No. 83.

[3] English, H. B., E. L. Welborn, and C. D. Killian. Studies in Substance Memorization. *Journal of General Psychology*, 1934, vol. 11, pp. 233–260.

an organizing factor, which gave meaning to the individual details of the solution and made them parts of a unified pattern or whole. In addition, the principle itself was well retained, so that even if a specific solution was forgotten, it could be reconstructed with the aid of the remembered principle.

Why, in general, the retention of material learned by rote should be inferior to that of material learned with understanding is less easy to explain. Katona suggests that the "neural traces," which are theoretically basic to all retention, are less well organized when learning is of the rote variety and are therefore less durable and persistent. But whatever may be the explanation of these findings, there is no doubt as to their general validity. Material which is well organized and well understood does tend to be well retained for long periods of time.

Katona's findings with respect to the value of general principles for the production of transfer are similar to those of earlier experiments, e.g., to those of Judd and others already referred to in this chapter. However, few if any psychologists have laid as much stress as Katona does on the value of organizing the material of learning into meaningful patterns, and on the relative ineffectiveness for transfer of the rote memorizing of individual items. Few also have devised experiments whose results so clearly justify such emphasis.

From the viewpoint of transfer, the reasons for the superiority of the understanding method in the card-trick experiments seem very evident. Since the memorizing groups had learned only one or two specific solutions, and had learned these without understanding, they had acquired little that could be profitably applied to the solution of new tricks for which the correct sequences of cards were radically different. The understanding groups, however, had learned the principle by which the solution of a particular trick could be achieved. Since all the tricks were solvable by the same method, the principle involved actually was *general* for the tasks employed, and therefore could be utilized to solve each one of them.

In connection with the acquisition of general principles, Katona makes these further points, which are of considerable importance in the psychology of learning. As we have several times remarked, many specific facts or items cannot be adequately comprehended unless there is available a principle which can serve to organize or integrate them. But, according to Katona, what we call a "principle" must be actively derived and understood by the learner if it is to have much utility for him. If a principle is presented as a mere verbal formula which the subject is to memorize, it may be learned in a purely rote fashion, with no more understanding than usually attends the memorizing of a list of nonsense syllables or of telephone numbers. It should be noted that in these experiments Katona did not at any time present to the understanding groups a simple rule by which the card tricks could be solved, and which could be memorized verbatim. Instead he expounded a method by which the solution of a particular trick could be obtained. The subjects who genuinely profited from this procedure were those who themselves discovered and grasped the *general* principle while listening to the derivation of a *specific* solution. It seems probable that a procedure like this, in which a subject is led to discover a principle for himself, is the type most likely to yield that understanding of a principle which is essential for later productive use.

The question of why the acquisition of general principles usually produces more transfer than is yielded by the memorizing of specific facts suggests a brief consideration and comparison of the two most important contemporary theories of transfer. According to one viewpoint—the theory of identical elements expounded by Thorndike[1]— transfer depends on the number and importance of the elements which are present in both the training and the later transfer activities and situations. Thus learning one maze, or one arithmetic problem, or one card trick may aid in the learning of another insofar as the two activities have elements or items in common. This theory, which is presented in many textbooks of general psychology, has sometimes led to the conclusion that one can predict the probable amount of transfer from one activity to another by analyzing the two activities and noting what specific identities exist between them. Thus one might endeavor to predict the probable amount of transfer from one card trick to another by noting the exact orders of cards required to solve each trick and then computing the number of identical elements, *i.e.*, of cards which are identical in color (or denomination) and position in the two sequences. To illustrate, if the reader will turn to the

[1] Thorndike, E. L. *Educational Psychology.* New York, Teachers College, Columbia University, 1913.

solutions of the eight card tricks on page 310 and compare the order of cards required for solving Tricks A and E, he will see that the two orders contain four such identical elements, namely, the first, third, fifth, and sixth cards in each order.

Katona's interpretation, however, opposes the identical-element theory. He points out—as his results and those of other investigators clearly indicate[1]—that one cannot predict transfer in this simple fashion. In his experiments, transfer did not occur on any such basis as the identical-element theory would require. Memorizing a specific solution, a specific series of cards, did not carry over to other tasks in any rule-of-thumb manner. What was important for transfer was not identities in the position of specific cards but rather an understanding of the solution procedure *as a whole* in terms of the general principle which underlay it. Once this principle had been acquired, transfer occurred to other tasks on a considerable scale; but if it was not mastered, little if any transfer took place. Thus a comprehension of the *pattern* of relationships involved in solving Trick A enabled 40 per cent of the subjects in the understanding group, in the first test series of Experiment V, to solve Trick E. On the other hand, in the memorizing group only 8 per cent of the subjects could solve Trick E in spite of the fact that, as noted above, four of the eight "elements" in the two solutions are identical.

To those interpretations of Thorndike's theory which suggest that a general principle itself can be regarded as an identical element,[2] Katona would answer that a "principle" is not an "element," but is a complex and more or less highly organized pattern, which behaves in a very different way during transfer than do "elements" learned by rote. The critical factor for transfer, according to the Gestalt theories which Katona supports, is the *pattern* of relationship (*i.e.*, the organization) and not the number of identical elements.

Whatever may be the outcome of this theoretical controversy among psychologists, the fact remains that general principles are perhaps the most important of all acquisitions from the viewpoint of transfer. Katona, in discussing this point, says that "the material of learning is not necessarily the object of learning" and that "we do not learn

[1] For example, McKinney, F. Quantitative and Qualitative Essential Elements of Transfer. *Journal of Experimental Psychology*, 1933, vol. 16, pp. 854–864.

[2] See McGeoch, J. A. *The Psychology of Human Learning*. New York, Longmans, 1942, p. 439.

the examples; we learn *by* examples."[1]   If we apply these statements to the present chapter, we would conclude that the object of the reader should not necessarily be to memorize the details of the experimental procedures or of the tables which give their results. These are the "material of learning" and the "examples."   Although their presentation occupies the bulk of the chapter, they are set forth only to exemplify and make meaningful certain general principles in the field of learning, and in that respect they correspond more or less to the specific solutions of particular card tricks in the Katona experiments.   The goal of the reader should be to learn and understand these principles and to see how they may be deduced from the material given; the aim of the writer should be to present the material in a manner corresponding to Katona's procedures with his "understanding" groups. According to Katona, these final points concerning the objectives of students and the responsibilities of teachers are of vital importance in the entire educational process.   Only if such attitudes are present on the part of both students and instructors can knowledge be acquired which will be well retained, and which can be applied effectively to subsequent new situations.

[1] Katona, *op. cit.*, p. 125.

CHAPTER XIX

METHODS OF BREAKING UNDESIRABLE HABITS

Introduction

The question as to how an undesirable habit can best be eliminated is a problem which almost everyone encounters sooner or later. A person is likely to meet this problem first of all in his own behavior, unless he is one of those rare individuals who are either perfectly adjusted to their environment or wholly satisfied with their existing characteristics. If he escapes the problem in his own individual life, it is probable that he will meet it in connection with the troubles of some less fortunate friend or relative whom he is called upon to aid. If he becomes a parent, he will probably find that at times the undesirable habits of his children raise problems quite as crucial as their bodily health ever presents. And if he chances to become a psychiatrist[1] or a clinical psychologist, his lifework may consist largely of trying to change for the better the habits of his patients.

Since the problem of habit breaking is of such widespread importance, it is not surprising that psychologists have given great attention to it, especially in clinical work and in connection with their study of learning, inhibition, and forgetting. Their work and experience, together with the knowledge accumulated from psychiatric practice, have made possible the formulation of certain general methods of eliminating undesirable habits. It must be admitted that, since these methods are in the nature of general rules or principles, they cannot in themselves be expected to supply immediate solutions for all of the various specific difficulties that characterize each individual problem. Nevertheless, it is the general principles that furnish the essential basis from which one may develop detailed procedures adapted to varying individual needs.

A method of habit breaking is a method for bringing about the

---

[1] A psychiatrist is a medical doctor who specializes in the treatment of nervous and "mental" diseases and defects.

elimination of certain habitual responses. The elimination of a response can be accomplished only by subjecting it to inhibition. Inhibition, however, is not a passive but an active process. That is,

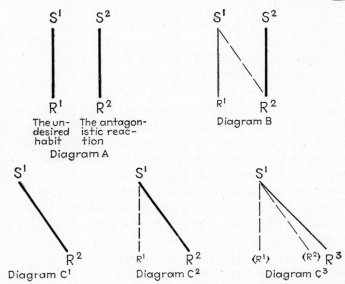

Fig. 33. Diagrams Representing Habit Breaking as a Process of Reconditioning.

In this and subsequent figures, S = stimulus, R = reaction, and a line connecting any S and R indicates the presence of an association between them. Heavy, light, and broken lines are used to indicate S-R associations of great, medium, and small strength, respectively.

Diagram A represents the circumstances prior to any reconditioning. The individual possesses the undesired habit (R') and also a reaction (R^2) which is antagonistic to it. Stimuli which evoke the two responses are designated by S^1 and S^2, respectively. Since the two reactions have never been associated, no reconditioning has occurred.

Diagram B represents the results of the performance of the antagonistic reaction in the presence of the stimulus for the habit. Since R^2 is stronger than R^1, the latter occurs only weakly if at all (as indicated by the small size of the letter). Thus an association between S^1 and R^2 begins to be formed.

Diagrams C^1, C^2, and C^3 represent three possible outcomes of the reconditioning process.

In Diagram C^1, S^1 no longer evokes R^1, but instead arouses the new reaction only. R^2 has not only completely inhibited R^1, but also has entirely displaced it.

Diagram C^2 represents an alternative possibility. Here R^1 is only partly inhibited, *i.e.*, it is still evoked by S^1 but at greatly reduced intensity.

Diagram C^3 represents another possible outcome. R^1 has been effectively inhibited but R^2 has not displaced it. Since R^1 and R^2 are mutually inhibitory, neither occurs as a response to S^1. In such cases, some new reaction (R^3) eventually may displace both R^1 and R^2.

an existing old response can be inhibited only by developing, through learning, a new reaction which is antagonistic to it, and which is superior (or at least equal) to it in strength. Therefore, any successful method of habit breaking requires the development of new reactions which are capable of inhibiting the undesirable habit.

Furthermore, for this inhibition actually to occur, it is necessary that the new reaction be aroused in situations which contain stimuli for the old response as well. Otherwise, the two reactions could not be stimulated simultaneously; and under ordinary conditions the development of a learned inhibition of one reaction by another requires that the two responses appear together during the training. Finally, if the new reaction is to inhibit the old response effectively and permanently, a process of *reconditioning* (or *inhibitory conditioning*) must take place. This reconditioning, as Fig. 33 shows, may have three possible outcomes. First, the stimulus which formerly produced the old, undesired response may elicit the new reaction only (Diagram C^1, Fig. 33). In this case, the new reaction *completely displaces* the habitual response. Second, the stimulus for the habit may arouse the new reaction strongly, but may also elicit the habitual response in a weakened or fragmentary form (Diagram C^2, Fig. 33). In this case, the new reaction *partially displaces* the habitual response (*partial inhibition*). Third, the stimulus for the habit may evoke neither the new reaction nor the habitual one. Instead, either it may produce no response at all (*i.e.*, the individual becomes "indifferent" or "negatively adapted" to the stimulus) or it may elicit some entirely different reaction (Diagram C^3, Fig. 33). In this case, the new and the old responses *mutually inhibit* each other (*mutual inhibition*).

The objective of any habit-breaking procedure, therefore, is to retrain the individual so that new and more desirable reactions may be aroused in situations which formerly elicited only the old, undesirable habits. The practical rule, as Guthrie states it in his *Psychology of Learning*,[1] is to "find the cues that initiate the action . . . and practice another response to those cues" (page 138).[2]

From the viewpoint of this rule, it may be said that the four general methods of habit breaking which we shall describe constitute four different ways by which Guthrie's prescription can be effectively followed.

[1] Guthrie, E. R. *The Psychology of Learning*. New York, Harper, 1935. Three of the four methods of habit breaking outlined below, together with many of the specific illustrations given, are taken from this book, especially from Chap. V, pp. 64–84, and Chap. XI, pp. 135–147.

[2] Guthrie, in his most recent work, states the general principle of reconditioning as follows: "When a stimulus is given and its response prevented, the stimulus loses its ability to call out that response." (Guthrie, E. R., and A. L. Edwards. *Psychology, a First Course in Human Behavior*. New York, Harper, 1949, p. 75.)

Before proceeding to a description of particular methods of habit breaking, it should be emphasized that the success of any of these methods depends mainly on the good judgment and perseverance of the individual himself. This statement holds true when an individual is trying to recondition himself, regardless of the amount of aid and guidance that he may be receiving. It holds equally true when he is attempting to retrain some other person. In particular, the importance of strong and enduring motivation cannot be overestimated. Reconditioning cannot be expected to occur "automatically" by virtue of the mere presence of the stimuli and the occurrence of the reactions described. Unless the establishment of the new S^1-R^2 association is in harmony with the individual's basic attitudes in the relearning situation, and contributes to the attainment of some goal toward which he is motivated, it is unlikely that the new association will ever be formed. Certainly no one can expect to break a long-established habit unless he is genuinely desirous of doing so, and unless he is willing to exert his utmost effort to check the undesired responses and to make vigorously the new reactions which are to displace them. Furthermore, the individual must avoid becoming discouraged by the difficulties and apparent failures which he may encounter, especially at the beginning of the reconditioning process, and must fortify himself with as much confidence in ultimate success as possible. Although it is true that effective methods of habit breaking are available, it is equally true that no easy methods exist.

It is also important to note that the habits of which we have been speaking need not be of the explicit, externally observable type. On the contrary, the responses to be corrected are very often undesirable thoughts or ideas. Similarly, the new inhibiting reactions are very frequently thought responses. Indeed, thoughts, especially those which take the form of "good resolutions," or those whose content is encouraging or reassuring in nature, are among the most effective of inhibitors. The individual who displays marked self-control is usually a person in whom thought responses are capable of preventing actions which he deems undesirable. Thus "right thinking," as the term has been traditionally used, may signify the formation of thinking habits which will be of great value in guiding conduct when some serious problem of habit elimination arises.

METHOD I. THE INCOMPATIBLE-RESPONSE METHOD

The most important and the most widely used of the methods of habit breaking described by Guthrie is one in which the undesired habit is eliminated by *"the action of incompatible responses"* (page 69). The objective of this method is to find and establish a new reaction (1) which is antagonistic to the habitual response, (2) which can be conditioned to stimuli that produce the habitual response, and (3) which can be made sufficiently strong to inhibit the habit when the critical stimuli are present. As will be evident later, this method differs from the others, in that the nature and the actual production of the new, inhibiting reaction are a matter of concern and careful planning from the very beginning of the treatment. (Figure 33, which represents habit breaking as a process of reconditioning in general, equally well illustrates the specific method of incompatible response.)

A simple illustration of this method may be found in the old advertising slogan, "Reach for a Lucky instead of a sweet" (a bit of advice which naturally did not please the candy manufacturers). In this example, eating candy is the supposedly undesirable response, and smoking a cigarette is the supposedly desirable one. Obviously, the act of smoking might come to inhibit candy eating entirely, if it were made the dominant reaction of the two, and if it became conditioned to the various stimuli which originally produced the response of candy eating.

Experiences in the field of child training offer innumerable illustrations of the use of the incompatible-response method. An example is the well-known experiment of Jones[1] in which the fear of rabbits in a thirty-four-months-old boy was eliminated by having him eat candy repeatedly while a rabbit was visible in a wire cage nearby. Since the positive reactions to the candy (*i.e.*, approaching and reaching, and a related positive emotional response as well) were stronger than the negative responses to the rabbit (*i.e.*, running away and the emotional reaction of fear), those positive reactions finally became conditioned to the rabbit, inhibited the negative responses, and so broke the undesired habit. Indeed, the treatment was so successful that the child actually came to like and to play with the rabbit.

Another example of the use of the incompatible-response method in

[1] Jones, M. C. The Elimination of Children's Fears. *Journal of Experimental Psychology*, 1924, vol. 7, pp. 382–390.

child training is the technique devised by Mowrer[1] for treating nocturnal enuresis (bed-wetting during sleep). In this technique the child
sleeps on a specially constructed pad which has fine wire inside it.
The wires in the pad are connected with a battery outside the bed.
If the child wets the pad, the wires are short-circuited and a bell
rings. The child then awakens, and, in conformity with the instructions he has received from his parents or other adults, gets up, breaks
the circuit by opening a switch, and goes to the bathroom whether or
not he needs to urinate further. When the procedure succeeds, the
response of awakening becomes conditioned to the stimuli arising from
the distention of the bladder, which have repeatedly preceded urination
and the consequent ringing of the bell. The above technique, together
with other ingenious reconditioning procedures for treating enuresis,
are fully described by Smith.[2] His discussion shows clearly, however,
that the full cooperation of the child, and therefore a strong favorable
motivation on his part, are essential for success, and that merely
having the child awakened at the appropriate time by the automatic
ringing of a bell will not effect a cure.

The incompatible-response method also is illustrated by the use of
punishment as a means of habit breaking. The term "punishment"
signifies a kind of stimulation which an individual finds disagreeable
or painful, or which he tries to avoid. Technically speaking, when
punishment succeeds it does so only by bringing about a new, often
negative reaction strong enough to inhibit the undesired response that
was punished. (Hence punishment has the function of S^2 in Fig. 33.)

One of the best known contemporary applications of a punishment
technique is the method for treating chronic alcoholics devised by
Voegtlin.[3] In each treatment by this method, an injection productive
of violent nausea is given in close conjunction with the presentation
of alcoholic liquors. Specifically, the procedure is as follows. The
patient must be in a hospital, and is given no solid food for at least
12 hr. before each treatment. The injection, the essential ingredient
of which is 50 grains of emetine HCl, is given hypodermically. Violent

[1] Mowrer, O. H., and W. M. Mowrer. Enuresis—a Method for Its Study and Treatment. *American Journal of Orthopsychiatry*, 1938, vol. 8, pp. 436–459.

[2] Smith, S. *The Psychological Origin and Treatment of Enuresis*. Seattle, University
of Washington Press, 1948.

[3] Voegtlin, W. L. The Treatment of Alcoholism by Establishing a Conditioned Reflex. *American Journal of Medical Science*, 1940, vol. 199, pp. 802–810.

nausea usually is brought about within 2 to 8 min.   A few seconds before the onset of the nausea, and likewise throughout its early stages, the patient drinks liquor (especially his favorite variety), inhales its odor deeply and repeatedly, and sees on a table in front of him a conspicuous array of liquor bottles.   Usually a total of four to seven treatments over a period of 3 to 7 days is administered.   In addition single treatments to the extent of one every 30 to 90 days throughout 1 year are commonly necessary to maintain (reinforce) the inhibitory conditioning.   The method apparently cures a consider- able percentage of cases.[1]   However, many psychiatrists[2] believe that its success requires favorable attitudes which are by no means present in all alcoholics, for example, the full cooperation of the patient and a strong desire on his part to be cured.   Furthermore, the likelihood of success is greatly increased by combining with the reconditioning technique various psychotherapeutic[3] procedures of the traditional types.

It is interesting to note that these traditional psychotherapeutic procedures also exemplify the incompatible-response method, in that they aim to develop in the patient new reactions which may inhibit and often replace the undesirable responses which constitute the ail- ment under treatment.   Thus, in the course of the lengthy conversa- tions which the psyciatrist has with his patient, the latter is led to speak freely about his symptoms and other troubles.   The psychiatrist explains the causes of these difficulties and designates the stimuli which produce the symptoms.   He also encourages the patient to believe that he can and will be cured.   In situations of this kind, the psychiatrist and his behavior (especially his actual words of explanation and encouragement) become stimuli for more favorable reactions on the part of the patient—more courage, for example, more self-confidence, and more understanding.   At the same time the patient is actually exhibiting his fears and other symptoms, or at least is thinking and talking about them.   Hence, an opportunity is afforded for the de-

---

[1] Voegtlin, W. L.   Conditioned Reflex Therapy of Chronic Alcoholism; Ten Years' Experience with the Method.   *Rocky Mountains Medical Journal*, 1947, vol. 44, pp. 807– 812.

[2] See, for example, Carlson, A. J.   The Conditioned Reflex Therapy of Alcoholic Ad- diction.   *Quarterly Journal of Studies of Alcohol*, 1944, vol. 5, pp. 212–215.

[3] "Psychotherapeutic" refers to "psychotherapy," a word which literally means "men- tal healing."   The term covers all psychological types of treatment.

velopment of an association between the more favorable reactions mentioned above and certain of the stimuli which evoke the symptoms. The psychiatrist hopes that in time the more desirable reactions will become strongly conditioned to the stimuli for the injurious habits and will finally inhibit the latter altogether. If this occurs, the patient is certain to be greatly benefited, and may even be permanently cured.

As we have said, all methods of habit breaking require the inhibition of the habit by some other reaction, and the conditioning of new responses to the stimuli for the habit. But, regardless of the method of habit breaking employed, difficulties arise which are not the fault of the method itself. As Guthrie points out (page 139), one cause for the difficulty which is often encountered during the attempt to eliminate an undesirable habit is the number and variety of stimuli to which the habit has been conditioned. Consider smoking, for example. One might suppose that the act of smoking was conditioned only to the stimuli furnished by the pipe, cigar, or cigarette itself. In actuality, the act of smoking can become conditioned to any stimulus which has ever been present while smoking was going on. Thus, the act may be conditioned to the situation of just having finished eating, to studying, to playing cards, to seeing other people smoke, to talking with friends or strangers, to all the various places where the person has smoked, to internal tension or "nervousness" from any source, to innumerable thoughts, feelings, and movements of the individual himself, and so on indefinitely. One reason why a well-established smoking habit is hard to break is that some kind of antagonistic reaction must be conditioned to every one of the stimuli which elicit smoking. Otherwise, some stimulus which evokes the response of smoking will fail to produce any antagonistic reaction and smoking, being now quite uninhibited, will naturally occur.

A further illustration of the difficulty created by a multiplicity of controlling stimuli is to be found in the case history of a certain drug addict. This patient, a middle-aged, married man, was sent to a sanatorium for treatment. While there he learned to do without the drug; that is, he learned to make reactions other than taking the drug in a great variety of situations characteristic of the everyday routine of living in the sanatorium. He was finally returned home as cured. However, he had not been home long before he had a quarrel with his wife, following which he at once resumed the drug habit. One reason for his relapse was that since his wife had not been present in the sanatorium he had not specifically learned to do something other than taking drugs after quarreling with her. Responses inhibitory to drug using had been conditioned to many of the stimuli for the habit, but no antagonistic reaction had been conditioned to the strong stimulus provided by domestic altercation.

This factor of stimulus multiplicity explains many "lapses" (*i.e.*, recurrences of some undesirable reaction), since these are often due to the accidental presence of some unsuspected stimulus which has been associated with the habit and for which no new response has been developed. For example, a particular fear or anxiety may disappear for a while, then suddenly reappear, thus refuting the belief that it had been entirely overcome. To anyone, and especially to the neurotic patient, these recurrences of the undesired response may seem very mysterious and are often productive of alarm and profound discouragement. Under such circumstances, the individual should remind himself of the fact of stimulus multiplicity, and should realize that, although this fact makes many habits hard to break, it does not change in any respect the methods of breaking them.

METHOD II. THE EXHAUSTION METHOD

Guthrie's second method of habit breaking involves the *exhaustion of the undesirable response* by continuous repetition of it. When a response is actually exhausted, it can no longer be aroused by its customary stimuli. But since an individual always continues to react in some way, he now makes a response which is different from the exhausted one, although the stimuli which initially produced the latter are still present. Hence, an opportunity is afforded for the conditioning of a new response to the stimuli for the undesired one. (This method is depicted in Fig. 34.)

As Guthrie points out (page 72), an excellent example of this method is to be found in the kind of "horse breaking" which is practiced on many Western ranches. The purpose of the horse breaker is to eliminate the responses of anger, struggle, and resistance on the part of the animal, and to substitute for them reactions of a docile and obedient type. In order to accomplish this, the horse is first roped and thrown and blindfolded. Then a heavy saddle is cinched tightly upon it and painful bits are forced into its mouth. The rider mounts, the blindfold is removed, and a struggle between horse and rider of the "let-'er-buck" variety ensues. If the horse fails to dislodge its rider, the animal sooner or later becomes exhausted. Its frantic struggles cease, and it either comes to a standstill, heaving and trembling, or trots off with its rider in quite docile fashion. In either case, new reactions have been produced; and since the saddle, bit, reins, rider, and other stimuli for the original fighting responses are still present, the new reactions can be conditioned to them.

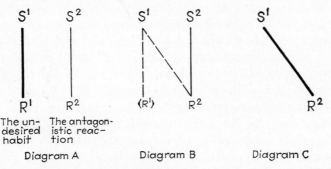

S^1 S^2 S^1 S^2 S^1

R^1 R^2 (R^1) R^2 R^2

The un-   The antagon-
desired   istic reac-
habit   tion

Diagram A   Diagram B   Diagram C

FIG. 34. Diagrams Representing Habit Breaking by the Exhaustion Method.

(The circumstances prior to any reconditioning are shown in Diagram A, Fig. 33.)

Diagram A represents the initial reaction in a given situation. A stimulus (S^1) produces the habitual response (R^1). However, the situation includes a stimulus (S^2) which would produce an antagonistic reaction (R^2) were it not for the greater strength of R^1.

In Diagram B, as a result of continuous repetition, R^1 has been so weakened (as the relative size of the letters indicates) that R^2 has become the stronger reaction of the two. Hence R^2 now occurs in the presence of S^1.

Diagram C represents the completion of the reconditioning. Instead of the undesired habit, S^1 now regularly evokes R^2.

An illustration of the use of the exhaustion method in child training is provided by a three-year-old girl who had developed the dangerous habit of striking matches and watching them burn. This she did with all the matches she could find in the house, in spite of scoldings and other punishments (using these devices would exemplify the incompatible-response method). One afternoon following a particularly flagrant instance of match burning, her mother decided to try a different mode of attack. She took her daughter into the yard, gave her six large boxes filled with matches, and forced her to strike every match in them. The child soon tired of this ordeal and was reduced to tears, outcries, and entreaties. But her mother was inflexible.   For two hours the child was compelled to stay there and to strike one match after another.   This emotionally arduous and physically exhausting experience is reported to have effected a permanent cure of the habit.

Methods of the exhaustion type are often used clinically.   For example, a neurotic young woman was afraid to ride in an automobile, except for a few miles over familiar roads, and had an especially intense fear of bridges and tunnels.   One day her doctor directed that she be driven from her home to his New York office.   The distance was nearly 50 miles, and the route involved crossing a number of high bridges and traversing the Holland Tunnel.   On the morning set for the ride the woman was in a condition of panic, with violent nausea, faintness, and an approach to hysteria.   Her terror persisted during much of the ride, but it diminished as she neared the refuge of her physician's house.   The return trip provoked little or no emotional disturbance, and subsequent journeys over the same route proved increasingly easy for her.   Apparently some measure of exhaustion of the fear reactions was induced, which permitted other more normal responses to appear while stimuli for the fear reaction were still present.

The exhaustion method, therefore, achieves exactly the same ultimate result as does the incompatible-response method.   The essential difference between the two methods lies in the practical procedures which characterize them.   In the incompatible-response method, the habitual response, however intense it may be, is inhibited by the presence of another even stronger reaction, which is antagonistic to it.   Hence, the person who is using this method must carefully select the new inhibiting reaction and contrive to have it occur when stimuli for the undesired habit are still present.   On the other hand, in the exhaustion method, the primary aim is to exhaust the undesired reaction by repetition.   It is true that when this exhaustion has occurred, some new response (which originally was weaker than the exhausted one) must be made, if the method is to be successful.   But the exact nature of this new reaction usually is left more or less to chance.

A further point in connection with the exhaustion method is that the exposure to a critical stimulus, which it requires, may have beneficial results other than those which devolve upon the actual exhaustion of the undesired response.   For example, it sometimes happens that a deliberate confronting of a feared stimulus reveals to the individual that the object is not nearly so frightening and terrible as he had thought. Under such circumstances, the fear reactions may abate quickly, and opportunity for the necessary reconditioning may be speedily afforded. Guthrie points out in his *Psychology of Human Conflict*[1] that the victim of a phobia[2] usually takes every precaution to avoid any encounter with the feared stimulus, and therefore deprives himself of any opportunity to be reconditioned. In such cases, exposure to the stimulus (either through self-initiated effort or under the direction of the psychiatrist) may bring about the favorable result described above.

The exhaustion method has been characterized as one of the "sink-or-swim" type. Many thoughtless and "nerveless" people regard it as the best possible method for ridding other individuals of what they term their "silly" fears and weaknesses. As a matter of fact, however, the method should be used only with caution. Obviously, one cannot always be sure that the undesired response will be exhausted. If it is not, then the habit may be fixated more strongly than ever, and the person's confidence in his ability to break it may become seriously impaired. In addition, the exhaustion of a response at a particular time does not preclude its reappearance on a subsequent occasion. Unless reconditioning occurs while the response is temporarily reduced or abolished because of exhaustion, the method cannot be expected to succeed. The exhaustion method of horse breaking often fails to eradicate the fighting reactions, and the horse may remain a "bucker" all its life. Similarly, forcing a child to go through with a public recitation or a musical performance which he dreads, without trying to diminish his fears beforehand by the incompatible-response method, may create a life-long horror of such situations.

METHOD III. THE TOLERATION METHOD

The third method described by Guthrie is one in which attention is turned primarily to the stimuli for the undesired habit, rather than to the response itself or to any possible substitute for it. It is a method in which the individual is led to develop a *slowly increasing toleration* for the stimuli for the undesired reaction. The procedure required

[1] Guthrie, E. R. *The Psychology of Human Conflict.* New York, Harper, 1938, p. 277.

[2] A "phobia" is a persistent and usually intense fear of something not commonly feared or regarded as dangerous.

by the toleration method is simply to present the stimulus for the habit at an intensity so slight that the undesired response is, at most, only very weakly aroused. Under these conditions, although the stimulus for the habit is at least partially or weakly present, the habit itself is not fully elicited by it. Hence, as in the first two methods, opportunity is given for making a new reaction which may be conditioned to the stimulus for the habit. As in the exhaustion method, the exact nature of this new reaction may not be predetermined. On later occasions, the strength of the stimulus is gradually increased, great

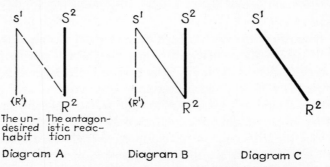

Fɪɢ. 35. Diagrams Representing Habit Breaking by the Toleration Method.

(The circumstances prior to any reconditioning are shown in Diagram A, Fig. 33.)

Diagram *A* represents the presentation of S^1 at such slight intensity (as indicated by the small size of the letters) that R^1 (the undesired habit) is aroused only very slightly, if at all. Hence another stimulus (S^2) can arouse an antagonistic reaction (R^2) in the presence of S^1, and reconditioning can begin.

Diagram *B* represents a later stage of the method. S^1 is presented at greater intensity, but the progressive conditioning of R^2 to S^1 prevents the appearance of R^1 in any but a very slight degree.

Diagram *C* represents the completion of the reconditioning. Now S^1, even when it is present at full intensity, arouses R^2 instead of R^1.

care being taken that it shall never be intense enough to arouse the undesired response too strongly. Finally, if the method succeeds, the original stimulus may be present at its full strength without exciting the undesired response. (This method is depicted in Fig. 35.)

Guthrie illustrates the method (page 71) by another type of horse breaking, the kind favored in the United States Army. Since the undesired responses are fear, anger, and resistance on the part of the animal, this method requires that the horse be adapted to the work of carrying a rider by a process so slow and cautious that those reactions are never strongly aroused. To this end the horse learns to tolerate a saddle upon its back by first having a light blanket laid upon it, then a sack with a little grain in it, and so on. Similarly, it is gradually accustomed to the bit in its mouth and to the presence of a rider.

Jones's treatment of the small boy who was afraid of rabbits (a study to which we have already referred) also illustrates the toleration method. In this particular case, it was soon found that if the rabbit in its cage was placed very near the child, it was a stimulus so intense that the boy cried and would not eat the candy at all. Hence, the experimenter was obliged to start the treatment with the rabbit so far away in the room that it was not a sufficiently strong stimulus to excite the undesired fear responses. When this was done, the boy would continue to eat the candy, though he also continued to be somewhat disturbed by the distant animal. At later sessions, the rabbit was gradually moved nearer and nearer, until finally the child would tolerate it very close to him and would even stroke and caress it without showing any fear.

Psychiatrists and clinical psychologists employ this toleration method very frequently. As Guthrie remarks (page 76), the fear of cats can sometimes be treated by giving the patient a kitten to bring up (provided, that is, that he is not equally terrified by kittens). If the patient can react more or less normally to the kitten in the course of feeding and caring for it, in time he may be able to react normally to the adult cat into which the kitten eventually grows. Similarly, if a neurotic patient fears to take a long walk alone, he may yet be able to walk a certain small distance—say, half a block—without too great an emotional disturbance. After having become accustomed to walking that distance, he can perhaps walk a full block alone, then two blocks, and so on.

Guthrie, in his *Psychology of Human Conflict*,[1] describes the treatment of a fear of mice by the toleration method. The patient was a woman whose phobia of the animal was so intense that she employed a skilled workman to "mouseproof" her house by blocking off or covering with wire netting every avenue (including the tops of the two chimneys) by which a mouse might conceivably get into her home. One result of these and other precautions was that it had been years since she had seen a mouse, or had actually been frightened by one. (As Guthrie points out, the skill with which an individual avoids the object of his phobia prevents him from being reconditioned by the

[1] Guthrie, *op. cit.*, p. 282.

incompatible-response or exhaustion methods.) Nevertheless, the mere mention of the animal at a social gathering was enough to cause her to leave the room. Guthrie's treatment for the elimination of the phobia consisted of the following series of steps. First she was inured to talking about mice with the psychologist. Then she got used to the presence in her room of a small china mouse. Next she became accustomed to the presence of a more lifelike mouse made of rubber. Presently she learned to tolerate a stuffed white mouse, and finally she learned to endure without distress a live mouse in a cage. Since in our culture the capacity to tolerate mice running freely about the house is not required, the patient was not subjected to this condition, and her fear was regarded as cured. Of course, the repeated conversations about mice and about the fear of mice throughout the treatment probably contributed materially to its success.

To some people this toleration method may seem too slow and tedious; to others of the "treat-'em-rough" school, it may seem a process too "soft" and too "gentle" to yield dependable results. However, it must not be thought that the method requires no effort on the part of the individual. On the contrary, the subject must be willing to try continually to make the stimulus as strong as he can stand it, *i.e.*, as intense as it can be without overstepping the limits of his toleration at the time. Patience, perseverance, and self-control are demanded by this method, just as they are by any other. Some methods of habit elimination perhaps are less painful than others but, as we have said, no really easy method of habit breaking exists.

METHOD IV.   THE CHANGE-OF-ENVIRONMENT METHOD

A fourth method of habit breaking, an important one though it is not mentioned specifically by Guthrie, is the *removal of the stimuli for the undesired habit*. Evidently, if these stimuli could be subtracted from the individual's experience, either partly or completely, the occurrence of the habit in question would be correspondingly reduced or eliminated. The removal of the stimuli, whether partial or complete, can be accomplished in either of two ways. They may be eliminated from the environment in which the person actually is living, or the individual may move to a different environment in which the stimuli may be less common, or even absent altogether.

How much benefit can be expected from changing the environment in which the person lives depends largely on whether the nature of the stimuli for the undesired habit is such as to make their removal feasible. If these stimuli—to recall some of the cases mentioned in this chapter—are such things as alcoholic liquors, tobacco, cats, or mice—it is evident that stimulus removal in the literal sense of the term would be virtually impossible. On the other hand, if the stimuli include such modifiable factors as, for example, the attitudes of other members of a person's family, then beneficial changes in that person's habits often can be effected.

Thus, if the person to be treated is a child, much good usually can be accomplished by persuading one or both parents to change certain of their attitudes toward him. The mother and father typically are the most important influences, *i.e.*, sources of stimulation, in a child's environment. If either of them has been, for example, overcritical, domineering, neglectful, or overprotective, a reform of such attitudes (and consequently a change in the parent's overt behavior toward the child) may aid greatly in modifying the child's undesirable responses. In the case of an adult also, it is frequently possible to effect useful changes in the home environment. For example, the departure of a mother-in-law often will remove the stimuli that have been primarily responsible for an adult's habitual tension or irritability and thus largely eliminate those reactions.

Usually, however, the critical stimuli cannot be effectively removed from the environment in which the individual is living. Hence, the change-of-environment method is likely to involve the removal of the person himself to new and different surroundings in which the stimuli for the undesirable habits will perhaps be less ubiquitous, less intense, or even absent entirely. Such devices as taking a trip or going to a sanatorium are familiar examples of this procedure. The method is widely recommended by physicians, who often advise a well-to-do patient to go on a sea voyage (as well as to take vitamins, change his diet, and abstain from coffee, tobacco, and alcohol). Clinicians also employ the method frequently, though usually with more discretion. To most people the method, if feasible, seems both easy and pleasant. Many of us often have felt that if we only could go to some new place, get a new job, or make new friends, our undesirable characteristics would be miraculously altered.

Sometimes, a radical change of environment undoubtedly is called for. An example is the case of a college student living at home who began to develop a speech difficulty. His parents not only were quite unsympathetic but even went so far as to laugh and jeer at his disorder. Unless the parents' attitude could be altered (a procedure which would change the environment in which he lived), it would clearly be desirable for the boy to go to a college away from home, where he would be free from daily contact with his family.

In many other cases, moving to a new environment can be helpful, provided the stimuli for the undesired habits are present less frequently or less intensely than they were in the individual's former surroundings. As we have said, if the critical stimuli can be thus reduced, the undesired responses will be aroused less often or less strongly, and the task of developing new reactions which are antagonistic to them may become less difficult. Thus one reason why the habit of drinking alcohol to excess can better be treated in a hospital or sanatorium than in a patient's home is that the new environment probably contains fewer of the many stimuli to which the habit has been conditioned.

However, the method of "going somewhere else" can rarely be depended upon as the sole means of cure. For one thing, most environments are fundamentally similar, and as a rule the so-called "new" environment also contains stimuli which arouse the undesired habits. Suppose, for example, that an individual is afraid of encountering certain people. If he moves to a new environment, he will of course meet new people. But some at least of these new people are likely to be so similar to those whom he feared that he may soon find himself just as apprehensive as before. In addition, the individual usually must return to his old environment sooner or later. Unless he has learned in the new environment how to adapt more successfully to the old one, he may gain no lasting benefit from the change. The case of the drug addict who was "cured" while he remained in the sanatorium but relapsed when he returned home illustrates this point.

In our opinion, the variety of change-of-environment methods discussed above might finally be evaluated as a procedure which may often be worth trying, but which is never to be relied upon as an instrument for permanent cure.

SUMMARY

The four methods of habit breaking which we have described may be briefly characterized as follows. In the *incompatible-response method* the individual consciously tries to devise, produce, and establish some new reaction suitable to inhibit the undesired habit.   In the *exhaustion* method the individual deliberately exposes himself to the stimuli which arouse the undesired response, in the hope that continued production of that response will exhaust it and so give opportunity for the occurrence of some more favorable reaction in the given situation.   In the *toleration method* the individual attempts, cautiously and gradually, to inure himself to some stimulus productive of undesirable responses by subjecting himself to that stimulus, at first at very slight, later at increasing intensities.   In the *change-of-environment method*, the individual tries to remove the stimuli for the habit from his present surroundings or, more usually, removes himself to a different locality in which those stimuli may be less frequent.   Each of these methods, of course, can be employed either by a person who is seeking to effect changes in his own behavior or by a psychologist or a psychiatrist who is trying to cure a patient.

The question as to which of these methods is the best cannot be answered in any simple or categorical fashion.   For one thing, the value of a given method depends on the nature of the habit to be eliminated, on the characteristics of the person in whom the habit is established, and on the various attendant circumstances which are involved in every individual case.   Furthermore, the use of one method in no way precludes the use of other methods also.   Even the exhaustion and the toleration methods, which might seem to be mutually exclusive, can be used with the same individual on different occasions.   Hence, psychologists and psychiatrists often employ all four methods in the treatment of a single patient.

In general, however, the incompatible-response method appears to be the most widely useful and the most reliable.   It is suitable for the treatment of virtually any type of habit.   It has the further advantage of including, as an intrinsic part of the method, a definite plan for the production of the indispensable inhibiting reactions.   Its principal drawback is the difficulty often encountered in finding a new reaction which is desirable and which can be made sufficiently strong to overcome the habit.

The exhaustion method is best adapted for the treatment of reactions which can be exhausted through repetition with a reasonable degree of probability and within a reasonable length of time.   Hence, it is better suited for the elimination of intense emotional responses, for example, than for the abolition of undesirable habits of thought. Moreover, as we have pointed out, the practice of this method usually is fraught with certain dangers, and the occurrence of the necessary reconditioning can in no sense be guaranteed. (The toleration method is used primarily for the elimination of undesirable negative or avoiding responses, such as fears, aversions, and the like.) The principal hindrance to the use of this method is the difficulty of controlling the intensity of the stimulus for the habit. When the stimulus intensity can be suitably regulated, however, the method is usually a desirable one. As to the change-of-environment method, we already have pointed out that to bring about the necessary changes in the environment in which the person lives often is not feasible, and that to move to a new environment can never in itself be depended upon to effect a permanent cure.

There are methods, other than those which we have described, for eliminating undesirable habits. However, our account of these four methods may be regarded as illustrative of the manner in which psychologists, especially those of the objective school, commonly view the problem. Many special books and treatises are available on psychotherapy and on various aspects of the psychology of learning, of which habit elimination is a part. It is to such sources that those who desire further information should refer.

CHAPTER XX

CONFLICT AND EXPERIMENTAL NEUROSES IN CATS

INTRODUCTION

One of the most important types of research in the fields of animal and abnormal psychology is the investigation of the effects of conflict on animals, with particular emphasis on the appearance of abnormal behavior. This abnormal behavior frequently reaches the degree of "experimental neurosis," a term which means behavior disturbances, produced in an animal by experimental procedures, which resemble the symptoms of human neuroses.

The significance of this type of study to psychology and psychiatry is evident. Controlled experimentation enables us to find out what kinds of situation will bring about behavior disorders in animals. Since human beings are similar to dogs, rats, pigs, sheep, goats, etc., in many important respects, such discoveries may be of aid to us in understanding the causes of similar disorders in ourselves.

The first investigator to produce an experimental neurosis was Pavlov.[1] In the study most often cited, a dog was repeatedly shown a luminous circle, immediately following which it was always fed. It also was repeatedly shown a luminous ellipse, after which no food was ever given. It soon mastered the required discrimination, learning to salivate (and get ready for food) whenever it saw the circle, and not to salivate, to remain "indifferent," whenever it saw the ellipse. Then the experimenter presented a series of ellipses, in which the figures became progressively more and more like circles. Eventually the figure became too ambiguous for the discriminative capacity of the animal. The dog became unable to react to it either as to a circle (and thus a food signal) or as to an ellipse (and thus a stimulus for a negative response). Furthermore, the dog was held on a platform by a harnesslike contrivance, so that no escape from the predica-

---

[1] Pavlov, I. P. *Lectures on Conditioned Reflexes.* New York, International Publishers, 1928.

ment was possible. A "breakdown" now occurred. The dog, hitherto docile and quiet, began to squeal, struggle, bark, and bite. Moreover, this behavior persisted, so that when it was later brought back to the laboratory situation it again reacted in this "neurotic" fashion.

Other experimenters have obtained similar results with many other species of animals. For example, Anderson and Liddell[1] and Anderson and Parmenter[2] have subjected sheep to situations such as the following. Like Pavlov's dog, the animal is held in a constant position on a platform. The stimuli used are metronome beats, at two different frequencies. When the metronome rate is 120 per minute an electric shock is given to a foreleg; when the rate is 50 per minute no shock is given. The sheep learns to withdraw its foreleg when it hears the faster rate and to remain quiet in response to the slower one. Then the animal is subjected daily to such pairs of rates as 120 and 60, 120 and 72, 120 and 84, 120 and 92, 120 and 100. Eventually the discrimination of the sheep breaks down, just as did the discrimination of Pavlov's dog; and, like the dog, the sheep is unable to escape from the experimental situation. The result is, as in the case of the dog, an experimental neurosis. The nature of the behavior disturbance varies greatly in different sheep (and also in different pigs, goats, dogs, etc.). In the laboratory, the disturbance usually involves fear, struggling, irritability, and "nervousness," and may include a loss of excretory control, rigidity or spasmodic movements of the reacting leg, and various other abnormal responses, e.g., increase of respiration and heart action. In addition, "neurotic" behavior may be exhibited outside the laboratory. This behavior may include such reactions as jumping and trembling at a slight touch or a sudden noise, general shyness and timidity even toward other animals, insomnia, disturbances in breathing and heart action and, in the case of one male dog, absence of any sexual response to a female in heat.

The current explanation of these results involves the concept of conflict and its effects upon behavior. In the training situation the animal learns to make a specific kind of response to one stimulus, and a different, antagonistic response to another stimulus. Accurate discrimination between the two stimuli is necessary for this learning.

[1] Anderson, O. D., and H. S. Liddell. Observations on Experimental Neurosis in Sheep. *Archives of Neurology and Psychiatry*, 1935, vol. 34, pp. 330–354.

[2] Anderson, O. D., and R. Parmenter. A Long-term Study of the Experimental Neurosis in the Sheep and Dog. *Psychosomatic Medicine Monographs*, 1941, vol. 2, Nos. 3 and 4.

Then, in the neurosis-producing situation, the animal is subjected to stimuli which are so similar to both the training stimuli, or so similar to each other, that it is unable to discriminate between them. Therefore the stimuli tend to arouse both of the antagonistic reactions. But both of the responses cannot appear; *e.g.*, an animal cannot both escape and remain quiet. A conflict between the opposed reactions develops. Emotional disturbances occur; and if the animal is repeatedly presented with the conflict-producing situation, neurotic behavior finally appears.

In studies of the kind so far described, however, the means by which the experimental neurosis was produced may seem rather different from the causes of neurosis in human beings. To be sure, conflict seems to be an indispensable factor in both cases, a conclusion which is derived from the controlled experimentation with the animals and from analytic, clinical study of human cases. But in the animals the conflict usually has occurred between two fairly simple responses such as *salivation* versus *"indifference,"* or *leg withdrawal* versus *remaining quiet*. In human neurotics, by contrast, the conflicts typically appear to be between *major human motives, between whole areas of behavior associated with such motives and their goals*. Also, with the animals, the conflict usually has developed because of inability to discriminate between two external stimuli. In human cases, however, the person's difficulties do not commonly arise from inability to discriminate. Instead they derive from inability to resolve conflicts between powerful antagonistic motives, *e.g.*, between socially tabooed sexual impulses and moral considerations, between love for a father and hatred of him, between a need for prestige and a fear of failure. Finally, the experimental animals usually have been placed in very confining situations in which their movements have been greatly limited by harnesses and similar devices, whereas the human neurotic is not subjected to such external restrictions, and moves and acts with relative freedom in his ordinary environment.

A kind of experimental situation with animals which would more closely resemble the conditions productive of human neuroses therefore would have to meet the following requirements: (1) the conflict would have to be between two strong drives or motives, as between hunger and fear, (2) the conflict would have to be based on factors other than inability to discriminate, and (3) the animal's responses would have to be reasonably unrestricted (although complete escape from the laboratory situation of course could not be allowed).   Maier[1] with rats and Masserman with cats have performed several experiments which apparently fulfill these requirements.   Masserman's experiments were selected for detailed report in this chapter because both his study of external frustration (*i.e.*, the blocking of goal-seeking behavior by an external obstacle) and his investigation of various curative methods are in many respects unique, and of major interest to students of abnormal behavior and its treatment.

EXPERIMENTAL NEUROSES IN CATS[2]

PURPOSES

The principal aims of Masserman's experiments were: (1) to observe the effect of external frustration upon the behavior of cats; (2) to study the effect of conflict, especially in connection with the development of experimental neuroses in these animals; (3) to investigate the effect of certain variations in experimental conditions upon the neurotic behavior; and (4) to ascertain the curative value of several kinds of therapy or treatment.

SUBJECTS

The subjects of the experiments to be reported were 82 cats.

APPARATUS

The apparatus used is shown in Fig. 36.   The cage, in which the cat was placed for the experiment, measured 40 by 20 by 20 in. and had a sliding door and two top hatches for the entry of the animal.   Its side walls and top were of glass; its floor was an iron grid.   The fan at the right provided ventilation.   In the middle of the floor there was an "escape" platform on which the cat could take refuge if the grid was electrified.   In the box there was a glass barrier, framed in wood, which could be moved to the left or right by the cords which can be seen emerging at the upper right-hand corner of the cage. In this way the cage could be divided into two compartments of any desired size.   There were spaces between both the front and the back

---

[1] Maier, N. R. F.   *Studies of Abnormal Behavior in the Rat.*   New York, Harper, 1939.

[2] Adapted from Masserman, J.   *Behavior and Neurosis; an Experimental Psychoanalytic Approach to Psychobiologic Principles*, Chaps. II and IV.   Chicago, University of Chicago Press, 1943.

of the barrier and the corresponding walls of the cage. These two spaces usually were blocked; however, they might be left open, in which case the cat could pass freely between the two compartments. Also the glass of the barrier might at times be covered with an opaque

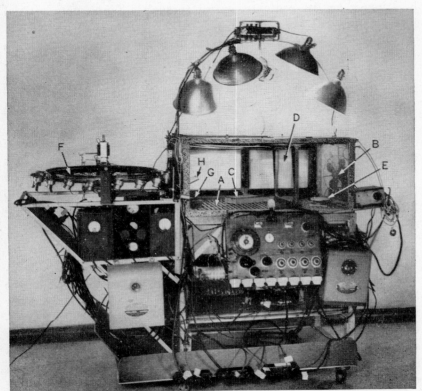

FIG. 36. Masserman's Apparatus for His Investigation of Experimental Neuroses in Cats.

A, iron grid; *B*, fan; *C*, escape platform; *D*, glass barrier; *E*, disk control switch; *F*, rotary feeder with cups; *G*, food box; *H*, hinged lid of food-box. (*Reproduced by permission of the University of Chicago press.*)

screen so that the cat could not see from one compartment to the other. On the floor at the extreme right of the cage just below the ventilating fan there was a disk-control switch. This the cat could learn to press and thereby activate the signals and the rotary feeder described below.

To the left of the cage there was a rotary feeder, provided with numerous cups containing food. Inside the cage, at the extreme left, there was a food-box with a hinged lid (shown raised in the figure). The apparatus was so contrived that when desired, *e.g.*, at the production of the feeding signals, the feeder would rotate until one of the food cups was directly opposite the food-box. The cup would then be tripped and its contents poured through a funnel (not visible) into the box.

On the arch above the cage there were lights of various intensities, together with bells and buzzers. These provided the feeding signals.

In the lower rear left-hand corner of the cage there was an air vent (not visible) which when opened threw a blast of air across the food-box. Both the grid floor and the escape platform could be made to provide an electric shock to an animal in contact with them.

The various other parts of the apparatus not specifically noted above were designed and used for the automatic production of the various signals, the air blast and the electric shock, and for the movement of the rotary feeder. In addition a motion-picture camera was used to photograph the subjects at appropriate times. Some of these photographs are reproduced in Fig. 37.

THE DEVELOPMENT OF CONDITIONED FEEDING RESPONSES

In order to investigate the effects of frustration and conflict on the behavior of cats, it was first necessary for them to learn the behavior which was to be frustrated, or subjected to conflict-producing situations. This learned behavior consisted of "conditioned feeding responses." Two different conditioned responses were established in all the cats, and a third type was developed in many of them. These responses, and the methods by which they were established, were as follows:

1. The cat first learned to associate the feeding signals with the delivery of food into the food-box. These signals usually were the simultaneous occurrence of a light flash and a ringing bell, which lasted for about 2 sec. To establish this conditioning, the cat was first accustomed in its living cage to a daily ration of a specific type; namely, a mixture of solid "Kiblets," "Ideal" dog food, and salmon. After 24 hr. without food it was put in the experimental cage, the lid of the food-box was opened, and the familiar food placed in it. The cat learned almost at once to eat its ration from the food-box. Then, sometimes on the third experimental day, the feeding signals were

given and—at the same time or a second or so later—some food was put in the box. The cat learned quickly—in one case in 12 trials—to go to the food-box (the lid of which was always open) when the feeding signals were presented, and get the food or wait briefly for it.

2. The cat next learned to open the food-box when the lid was down by raising the lid with its head or paw. This response was developed by having the lid put lower and lower on successive signal-accompanied feedings. The cat thus gradually learned to get at the food by lifting the lid, at first a little, then more, until finally it could lift it from its fully shut position. Now the animal, in response to the light and sound signals, would at once go to the food-box, raise the lid, and get the food. An additional stimulus for the animal was provided by the sound of the movement of the rotary feeder, which was synchronized with the signals and automatically delivered the food.

By this time most of the cats eagerly jumped into the cage when allowed to do so, resisted removal from it, and seemed to wait for the feeding signals with avid anticipation. In many cases the responses were given a very large amount of practice, since the animals obtained all their food in the cage and the small size of the food cups might make 30 to 50 feedings a day necessary for the maintenance of normal weight and physical condition.

3. Many cats also learned to get food by depressing the disk-control switch, which could activate the feeding signals and the delivery of food by the feeder. This learning typically required 10 to 60 trials over a period of 1 to 6 days. In some cases the cat learned to depress the switch by accidentally rubbing against it, following which the light flashed, a bell or buzzer sounded, the feeder rotated, and food appeared in the food-box. In other cases the cat was "taught"; that is, a large and conspicuous platform was put on the switch disk and the experimenter placed the animal's paw on the platform many times in succession. In other instances a small cup filled with salmon juice was attached to the disk, so that the cat would necessarily depress the switch by chin or mouth pressure while lapping the juice. The animals varied in their manner of pressing the switch, some using the paw, others the head, depending on which way of responding they had first employed. Once a cat had learned the reaction it would press the switch, go to the food-box, eat as much as it could get from it, return to the switch, press it again, and so on until the feeding was stopped or the cat was satiated.

After the cats had acquired these two or three "conditionings," they were ready to be tested for the effects of external frustration and of conflict.

THE EFFECTS OF EXTERNAL FRUSTRATION

An important section of Masserman's experiments deals with the effects of external frustration upon the behavior of cats. As we have said, external frustration means the blocking of goal-seeking behavior by an external obstacle. In the present instance the goal was to feed in the food-box. The principal external obstacles employed are described below.

1. Presence of a Barrier. In some cases the glass barrier was placed in such a way that the food-box was on one side of it while the cat was on the other, able to see the box but unable to reach it. When the feeding signals were given and the food was deposited in the box, the animal clawed at the barrier, mewed, and paced about. However, it gave no evidence of anxiety, fear, or conflict, and after about 8 to 20 trials stopped responding at all to the signals (experimental extinction[1]).

2. Closing of the Food-box. Another external obstacle was provided by locking the lid of the food-box. This procedure was used with 12 well-trained cats. Typical reactions were scratching and prying at the lid following the feeding signals. After a few trials— in two cases, seven trials—the animals simply stopped responding to the signals (again, experimental extinction). No neurotic behavior was ever produced.

3. Failure of the Control Switch to Function. Still another kind of external frustration was used with some of the cats that had learned to manipulate the control switch. The current was turned off, so that pressure on the switch was no longer followed by the feeding signals. The animal became markedly disturbed, refusing to feed, mewing almost continually, pacing about, energetically pressing on the switch, and even attacking it with teeth and claws. Nevertheless, no actual neurosis developed, and when the current was restored the cat at once resumed its normal behavior.

---

[1] "Experimental extinction" means the elimination (often only temporary) of a conditioned reaction by repeated presentation of the conditioned stimulus (here, the feeding signals) without reinforcement by the unconditioned stimulus (here, accessible food in the food-box).

4. Irregular Feeding. Eight cats were subjected to the partial frustration produced by irregular feeding; that is, sometimes food would appear in the food-box following the signals and sometimes it would not. Under these circumstances some restlessness was observed, but there was no evidence of any marked disturbance, and the normal reaction to the signals persisted even though it was often quite unrewarded.

DISCUSSION

So far as Masserman's cats are concerned, the results of the frustration of feeding behavior by means of external obstacles were definite and consistent. The most frequent effect of such frustration was to bring about an adaptive cessation—a temporary extinction—of the food-getting responses. No behavior that could be called "neurotic" was ever produced by it. It is uncertain to what degree one can draw analogies between these few cats in these specific laboratory situations and human beings in the complex vicissitudes of their daily living. However, the negative results of external frustration in this experiment contribute some additional support to the belief, widely held by psychologists and psychiatrists, that external frustration alone does not commonly produce "mental" disorders; that human beings do not usually break down merely because external (environmental) obstacles block them from obtaining the money, prestige, sexual satisfaction, etc., that they desire; and that for frustration to be causative of neurosis, goal-seeking behavior must be blocked through internal sources, typically by some sort of internal conflict. Thus if a young man's proposal of marriage meets with rejection—which is here the external obstacle—although he may be deeply affected, he does not commonly develop a neurosis; but if his sexual desires are frustrated by an internal struggle between them and fear of the opposite sex, a "breakdown" frequently results.

THE EFFECTS OF CONFLICT: THE PRODUCTION OF EXPERIMENTAL NEUROSIS

Masserman produced experimental neuroses in his animals by a very simple method. After a cat had learned to secure food in the food-box in response to the feeding signals, it was subjected to an air blast, a grid shock, or both, *at the moment of feeding*.

The air blast was delivered across the food-box just as the cat opened the lid or was about to feed. The blast usually lasted 1 to 2 sec. The typical reaction in 52 of the 58 cats subjected to this stimulus was a sudden rush to the far side of the cage and a crouching there, the behavior being suggestive of intense fear. The animal usually refused to make any further attempt to feed in spite of the repetition of the feeding signals and the presence of food in the box. This fear response seems to be an unlearned or reflex reaction in the cat. (However, six animals reacted less vigorously than the others. They cowered only momentarily, withdrew only slightly from the food-box, and soon began to reexplore the latter.)

The grid shock, delivered through the floor of the cage to the animals' feet, was used with 24 cats, and also was given at the moment of feeding. Usually two or three shocks were given in rapid succession. The typical response was a startled jump at each shock, followed by a slow retreat from the food-box after the shocks ended. In other cases the cat would remain for a time near the box in a crouched position with tensed muscles, closed eyes, and curled paws. Occasionally the shock produced the same "precipitate scramble" as the air blast did, and eight animals were so excited by it that they dashed about the cage seeking escape. Some snarled, mewed, and yowled also. Feeding of course ceased entirely in every case. Seven cats were given an opportunity to avoid the shocks by going to the escape platform and quickly learned that response.

Twenty-four cats were subjected both to the air blast and the grid shock. Their reactions resembled those to the air blast alone.

Thus far the typical result of these procedures has been as follows: The cat, having been subjected, at the very moment of feeding, to stimuli that are terrifying, painful, or both, has stopped its food-getting responses and exhibited marked fear behavior. In spite of its hunger, the continued presentation of the feeding signals, and the presence of food in the food-box, it refuses to make further attempts to eat and persists in its fear responses.

Eventually the cat was removed from the cage, and its first conflict-producing experience was over. Twenty-four hours later it was again placed in the cage. It now had eaten nothing for two days, since, as was stated earlier, all feeding took place in the experimental situation. Many cats now responded to the feeding signals with the fear behavior they had shown during their initial experience with the air blast or shock. If a cat made any attempt to feed normally, the air blast or shock was repeated with the behavior effects already described. In either case the cat again was removed from the cage, and after another 24 hr. was returned again to it. Now, in spite of its extreme hunger, the fear behavior almost always recurred without further stimulation and the cat would eat nothing.

Aside from the fear and the refusal to eat in the cage described above, these blast and shock experiences also produced an experimental neurosis. It may be presumed that a severe conflict was brought about in the animal. On the one hand it was hungry, often extremely so, and food was there for the taking by means with which the cat was thoroughly familiar. On the other hand, it feared the blast, the shock, or both. Thus the animal in the cage was simultaneously under the stress of the two incompatible motives of hunger and fear, and was simultaneously impelled to the incompatible actions of feeding and escape. In a sense it was driven to make two antagonistic responses at one and the same time, much as a human being is when fear competes with anger, or with sexual desire, or with a sense of duty.

In almost every cat one or two such experiences were enough to produce some sort of "neurotic" behavior. The symptoms shown by different animals varied greatly in kind, in degree, and in the number of stimuli which would elicit them. Some animals showed *changes in spontaneous activity*, *i.e.*, previously quiet, placid cats tended to become restless and "nervous," while previously active ones tended to become passive and inert, lying immobile in the cage for long periods. Many displayed *chronic anxiety*, both in the cage and outside it. They were restless, trembled frequently, often crouched or hid themselves, gave startle reactions to minor stimuli in the environment, and showed recurrent or chronic disturbances of pulse and respiration. *Phobic responses* also were very common. In the experimental cage the cats usually reacted to the feeding signals with fear amounting to panic, and with efforts to escape which sometimes became frantic. Animals that had learned to use the control switch often avoided it, as if it had become dangerous, or "ignored" it, behaving as though it were not in the cage at all. Others continued to press it, but would make no attempt to get the food. Some starved themselves into a condition of severe weakness and malnutrition, even

FIG. 37. Examples of Various Types of Neurotic Behavior in Masserman's Cats.

  a. A marked fear reaction in a cat prevented from escaping from the cage.   The animal showed erection of the hair and a considerable pupillary dilation.

  b. Continued refusal of nearby food by a cat which has starved itself for two days.

  c. A cat snarling at the signal for food.

  d. Hiding the head in the food-box in response to the feeding signals.   Despite several days of starvation the animal remained fixed in this position for from 5 to 30 min. without touching the food in the box.

  e. Marked fear reaction accompanied by frantic attempts to escape, made by a hungry cat kept close to the food-box by the movable barrier.   The food signals are being given.

  f. Persistent pressing of the switch which activated the feeding signals, but with no attempt to walk around the barrier and get the food.   (*Reproduced by permission of the University of Chicago Press.*)

though food was in the cage and readily available.   One cat would not feed in the cage for 16 days, though given only one-tenth of its normal ration outside the cage, and thus lost one-third of its weight. Some animals developed a kind of generalized fear of food and of eating.

They would eat very little food anywhere, in or out of the cage; or would eat only food different frcm that provided in the cage, or food given them by the experimenter's hand. *Stereotyped nonadaptive responses*, often of a peculiar nature, were exhibited by some animals. An example is that of a cat that ran to the food-box, put its head under the lid, and remained fixedly in this position but without eating in spite of many days of starvation. Another cat crouched in a fixed position behind the food-box on the side of the air blast. Many animals showed what Masserman calls "regressive behavior,"[1] that is, responses assumed to be more characteristic of earlier periods in their lives. Thus some cats became unusually playful and affectionate, like young kittens, and seemed to want to be petted and fondled. Others seemed to lose their tameness, becoming aggressive and vicious, and attacking their cage mates and even anyone who offered them food. Many animals exhibited several kinds of symptoms, either simultaneously or at different times during their "neurosis." Some of these and other neurotic reactions are shown in Fig. 37.

The above brief description shows that the cats developed behavior which was definitely abnormal and maladjustive when compared with their previous well-adjusted reactions, and which also was similar to that commonly observed in human neurotics.

It should be noted that these neurotic reactions were not just ordinary fear responses to the air blast, and apparently were not due to the fearsome qualities of the blast alone. In a control experiment, six cats were subjected repeatedly to the air blast without any connection with feeding. All of these animals quickly became accustomed to the blast and ceased to show their initial fear. Also, the effects on the cats in the main experiment went beyond those characteristic of ordinary fear reactions, especially in that they were not confined to stimulation by the blast itself but pervaded the animal's whole behavior.

FACTORS TENDING TO ACCENTUATE THE NEUROTIC BEHAVIOR

Two factors were found to accentuate the neurotic behavior. One was an increase of hunger to the point of about 72 hr. of starvation. It will be remembered that normally the cats were fed only in the ex-

---

[1] It is possible that, from a strictly factual viewpoint, this "regressive behavior" consisted only in a change of emotional responses on the part of certain cats.

perimental cage, and that after they had undergone the fear experience and had refused to eat there, they were brought back on later days for repeated observations. It was found that up to and including the third day, as their hunger increased, their behavior grew increasingly disturbed also, until on the third day, when they had been without food for 72 hr., it usually reached a kind of climax. After this third day many animals had to be given small feedings outside the cage to maintain health and life. In other cases, further starvation apparently produced such an accentuation of the hunger drive that the fear was overcome and, if no further "punishment" was given, the cat began to eat again in the cage. This result is described in connection with the curative procedures discussed below.

Another factor which accentuated the neurotic behavior was restriction to a small space in the cage. This restriction was readily accomplished by moving the barrier to the left (see Fig. 36e) and putting the cat in the compartment thus created, a space which was not only very small but which also contained both the food-box and the place where the air blast or shock had been experienced. Sometimes the glass barrier was made even more confining in its effect by placing the opaque screen over it. In this situation the feeding signals usually brought about more violent clawings and attempts to escape than any that had been shown previously.

Both of these experimental procedures augmented the stress to which the animal was subjected, by increasing the intensity of its hunger in the one case, and the intensity of its fear in the other. The effects resemble those which might be produced in a human conflict situation if the intensity of one of the motives involved, such as sexual desire, hatred, or fear, became strengthened. However, as the results of Masserman's curative methods will show, if the intensity of a drive or other motivation is increased sufficiently, it may bring about such overt action as will break the impasse and terminate the conflict.

METHODS OF ALLEVIATING EXPERIMENTALLY INDUCED NEUROTIC BEHAVIOR

An interesting and valuable part of Masserman's experiments is his use of various procedures designed to alleviate or "cure" the experimental neuroses, and his observations as to their effectiveness. These methods resemble in many ways those employed with human neurotics, and in a sense may be regarded as methods of "psychotherapy."

One method was that of *rest*. Thirty-seven neurotic cats were returned to the experimental cage after "rest periods," *i.e.*, absences from it and the fears and conflicts it had induced, of from 2 weeks to 5 months. Thirty of these animals displayed almost the same neurotic reactions as before to the feeding signals and to the cage in general, refusing to feed there and still showing marked fear. In seven cases, however, a "prolonged" rest did result in some alleviation of the neurotic behavior; the cats seemed less afraid, and sometimes ate a little in the cage. The failure of the rest method for the great majority of the subjects with which it was used has considerable psychological interest. In general, it indicates that reactions once formed tend to persist unless definite reconditioning processes like those described in Chap. XIX have taken place in the meantime. Other experimenters working with other species of animals similarly have found that rest, in the sense of absence from the conflict situation, was of little or no curative value. In some instances the neurotic behavior has even been more pronounced after such a "vacation."

Another method was *reduction of the hunger drive.* If a cat was fed just before being placed in the cage, it usually showed diminished neurotic behavior. The explanation seems to be that reduction of one of the antagonistic motives lessened the conflict. However, few if any animals were actually cured by this means.

A third method is termed *reassurance* and *persuasion.* In this procedure a neurotic cat might be induced to eat from the food-box by handling, stroking, and petting by the experimenter. However, the cat tended to remain dependent on the latter, and might stop feeding the moment the experimenter's hand was withdrawn. Also, this kind of "therapy" could not be used if the animal had become distrustful or fearful of human beings.

Another method was that of *forced solution*, in which the intensity of the cat's desire for food was increased to such a degree that the food-getting reactions came definitely to prevail over the fear behavior. At first it was thought that this method required only that the cat not be fed at all outside the cage, the assumption being that its increasing hunger eventually would compel it to eat from the dreaded food-box. Actually, however, the intensity of the animal's hunger seemed to diminish from the third day on,[1] and many cats refrained from eating

---

[1] It is interesting to note that according to Cannon stomach contractions and hunger pangs cease in human beings after a few days of complete fasting. (Cannon, W. B. *Bodily Changes in Pain, Hunger, Fear and Rage,* New York, Appleton, 1915.)

for such long periods that only forced feedings outside the cage kept them alive. Hence, for most of the cats treated by this method, the intense hunger had to be combined with other stimuli highly conducive to eating. Among these stimuli were providing very attractive food, including catnip, in the food-box, keeping the lid of the box open so that the food in it was clearly perceptible, and forcing the animal close to the box by using the glass barrier in the manner already described. Under such conditions most cats finally started to eat, at first in a very hurried and fearful way, later in an increasingly normal fashion.

A fifth method was *social example*, that is, the effect of seeing the normal feeding behavior of a nonneurotic cagemate. This method was tried with nine animals, each of which was placed in the cage with its normal mate and saw the latter get food in response to the signals. The results were highly variable. Some cats learned to feed normally again after such an experience, whereas others were quite unaffected by it and remained as neurotic as before.

A final method was one involving *partial control of the situation* by the animal subject. This procedure could be used only with those cats that had learned to manipulate the control switch. When these animals were exposed to the blast or shock, they developed neurotic behavior like the others, though usually in a milder form. However, their ability to control the production of the feeding signals themselves (by pressing or not pressing the switch) seemed to give them a marked advantage over the other animals. Usually, with or without the stimulus of increasing hunger or spatial constriction, they would begin spontaneously to approach the switch again, to reexplore it, and finally to manipulate it once more. Then, with behavior that suggested increasing self-confidence, they reestablished their former normal behavior and their neurotic reactions vanished. This sixth method was the most effective of all.

It is noteworthy that once the cat was "cured," the air blast which had occurred at the moment of feeding—but apparently not the electric shock—might become an "eagerly awaited signal for feeding," a remarkable reversal of response which testifies to the malleability of cat behavior.[1]

[1] It should be pointed out that Masserman did not use the same procedure with all his animals. As we have said, some learned to manipulate the switch control, others did not. Some, but not all, were subjected to external frustrations and to conditions intended to

Masserman is not the only psychologist who has experimented with various curative procedures for neurotic animals. For example, Anderson and Parmenter,[1] using sheep as subjects, tried such methods as rest, which was not particularly effective, making the problem (in this case, one of discrimination) easier, using various drugs and hormones (which varied in their effects but in general were of little value), etc. Possibly, however, Masserman has explored the therapeutic possibilities of psychological (reconditioning or retraining) methods with animals more thoroughly than most other investigators.

Although no one can infer directly from these results with cats what methods would be most effective for the treatment of disturbed human beings, certain comparisons seem possible. The slight value of *rest* for cats, for example, appears to have some analogy with its similarly dubious effectiveness for human beings. (See the discussion of the change-of-environment method in Chap. XIX.) As is generally known, *reassurance and persuasion* of a verbal type are extensively used with human cases. Usually, these devices are more likely to make a patient feel better, to relieve his symptoms for a time, than they are to cure him. However, as reference to Chap. XIX will show, reassurance and persuasion may play the role of S^2 in the "incompatible-response" method. The *forced solution* method also has its analogies in human psychotherapy. It resembles somewhat the "exhaustion" method of reconditioning also described in Chap. XIX. Its effects also are like those of an inescapable emotional or other crisis, or a huge accentuation of some drive or dominant motive, which sometimes seems to force a behavior change in the human patient. The *social example* method is likewise similar to conditions which may benefit human subjects. Thus, as Masserman points out, civilians made

---

accentuate neurotic behavior. For the production of an experimental neurosis, the air blast alone was used with some animals, with others the grid shock or a combination of blast and shock. After a neurosis had been established, both the kind of curative method and the exact way in which it was used varied considerably with different animals. Many cats were treated almost as if they were human cases, in the sense that several types of therapy were tried with them and tests of their value made. Hence it is impossible to express the results of the many experiments in tabular or statistical form. In addition, Masserman does not always state the exact numbers of animals that were subjected to the various experimental procedures, nor does he give such data as the average numbers of trials required for the establishment of the three conditioned responses, for the development of the neurotic behavior, etc.

[1] Anderson and Parmenter, *op. cit.*

temporarily hysterical during a bombing raid were helped to recover by seeing their more stable fellows going about their work with relative calmness.   The last method of Masserman, in which the animal could *exert some control over the situation*, could "work through" it himself, seems to be an excellent device whenever it can be applied.   Masserman compares it to the behavior of the airplane pilot who forestalls a neurotic breakdown after his plane has crashed by at once flying another plane and thus reasserting his "accustomed and reassuring mastery."   Indeed, the method is similar to the creation of any circumstances which allow a person some control over conflict situations. The stutterer would have much less difficulty with his speech, might in fact be able to reduce or eliminate his disorder, if he could himself choose just when he would speak, to whom he would speak, and what he would say.

Summary and Conclusions

Masserman's work shows that experimental neuroses can be readily produced in cats by subjecting them to a situation which brings about a conflict between two presumably powerful motives, hunger and escape from terrifying or painful stimulation.   A conflict of this type seems to resemble closely the conflicts basic to human neuroses, such as those between sex urges and moral considerations, between fear in a soldier and his sense of duty to his unit, between resentment toward one's parents and affection for them.   The relationship shown to exist in cats between conflict and neurosislike behavior adds further cogent support to the principle that conflict probably is an essential factor in producing functional mental disorders, *i.e.*, disorders of behavior not attributable to organic brain damage, infections, toxins, and other physiological agencies.[1]

Masserman's finding that external frustration alone did not produce any neurotic disturbances is of special interest.   Many students of mental disorders have long agreed with Freud[2] that although frustra-

[1] A somewhat different explanation of the behavior of both Masserman's cats and of human neurotics is given by White, who believes that the essential factor in producing neurosis is not conflict, but fear or anxiety and the efforts to diminish or eliminate it and prevent its recurrence. See White, R. W. *The Abnormal Personality.* New York, Ronald, 1948.

[2] Freud, S. Types of Neurotic Nosogenesis. In *Collected Papers*, vol. 2, pp. 113–121, London, Hogarth Press, 1921.

tion in the sense of the blocking of strongly motivated behavior is essential to neurosis, the blocking must be due to conflict, must come from internal sources. The present experimental results appear to bear out this view, as we have seen.

As we have pointed out, the various curative methods which Masserman employed are similar in many ways to those used with human beings. The failure of rest to "cure" the abnormal behavior, and the success of forced-solution and partial-control methods are especially noteworthy. Of course Masserman could not try all possible procedures, and did not experiment specifically with the toleration, exhaustion, and other methods described in Chap. XIX. In this connection it might be noted that Masserman has recently tried still other kinds of treatment with neurotic cats, notably the administration of alcohol[1] and cerebral electric-shock therapy.[2] Lack of space prevents us from saying more than that as a rule both of these procedures were successful.

Psychologists and psychiatrists have long been interested in the production and study of abnormal behavior in animals, and this kind of research is certain to continue. One reason for the general belief in its importance is the significant advances in our knowledge and control of various physical diseases which have resulted from experimental work with animals. The utmost value may accrue to the discovery of animal species which are susceptible to human diseases, and which therefore can be utilized in controlled experimentation designed to discover the causes of a particular disease and methods of treating it. Observations made upon cows were of vital importance in the discovery of vaccination as a preventive of smallpox; experiments with dogs contributed greatly to the discovery of the specific cause of diabetes and of the insulin treatment. Similarly, in the psychological realm, in the field of functional mental disorders, our ability to create what seem to be analogous disturbances in animals amounts to a genuine scientific achievement. Our understanding of the causes of human disorders already has materially benefited from

[1] Masserman, J. H., and K. S. Yum. An Analysis of the Influence of Alcohol on Experimental Neuroses in Cats. *Psychosomatic Medicine*, 1948, vol. 8, pp. 36–52.

[2] Masserman, J. H., and M. G. Jacques. Effects of Cerebral Electroshock on Experimental Neurosis in Cats. *American Journal of Psychiatry*, 1947, vol. 104, pp. 92–99.

these investigations, and the further testing of various therapeutic methods with animals may greatly facilitate our search for the most desirable procedures to be used with human beings. Certainly psychologists and psychiatrists will neglect no promising source of helpful evidence in their efforts to deal with the tremendous personal and social problems created by mental disorders in modern society.

CHAPTER XXI

PROBLEMS IN THE PERCEPTION OF THE VERTICAL IN SPACE

INTRODUCTION

The subject of perception, which involves the study of the organized impressions we form of the world around us, deals typically with phenomena that every person has often experienced. Such phenomena are exemplified by our perception of the vertical and the horizontal. Usually we are able to identify these main dimensions of space with accuracy. Almost from moment to moment we make judgments about the position of surrounding objects and of our own bodies which indicate an effective mastery of the location of the true vertical in space. Nearly always we can tell readily and without deliberation whether or not a picture on the wall is straight, whether the road on which we are walking has a slope or is level, or whether we are leaning backward or forward when sitting in a rocking chair. These operations in the perception of space are so smooth-running and reliable that they occasion little notice in everyday life. It is only when "something goes wrong" that it becomes difficult to tell whether we are right side up or not. This may happen at times during an airplane ride, or in such amusement-park devices as the roller coaster or the "haunted swing."[1]

The capacity to perceive the vertical and the horizontal is basic to our everyday dealings with objects in the environment and to the "handling" of our own bodies. Experiments designed to discover how this kind of perception takes place may therefore cast light on pro-

---

[1] In the "haunted-swing situation" studied years ago by Wood in connection with problems in space perception, the subject is strapped into the seat of a chair suspended from a horizontal bar running the length of a large barrel-shaped canvas room. He believes that the "swing" is to be set in motion, but instead, the canvas room is turned forward and backward through a limited distance as though it were an oscillating drum. Under these conditions there results a most compelling illusion that the "swing" itself is being moved back and forth and that the room is stationary. (Wood, H. S. The "Haunted-swing" Illusion. *Psychological Review*, 1895, vol. 2, pp. 277–278.)

cesses which are vitally necessary to our effective everyday perceptual adjustments.

For one thing, we find in the perception of the vertical and horizontal a striking example of what is known as "perceptual constancy." The meaning of this term is readily illustrated by the fact that one can tilt his head, lie on his side, or even stand on his head without having the walls of the room and objects in the room cease to appear "upright" while these postural changes are occurring. A moment's consideration will show that what happens in such cases is far from simple. Actually, tilting the head causes reflected light from objects to be projected upon the retina at very different angles than is the case when the head is erect. Notwithstanding such changes in the specific stimulative effects provided by surrounding objects, these objects continue to retain their upright character for the perceiver. It is in this sense that such phenomena are said to exemplify "perceptual constancy."

There is another problem of general psychological importance which is involved in studying perception of the vertical and horizontal. Perception of this aspect of the environment depends not only upon vision but also to a great extent upon the stimulation of several other types of receptors, such as the kinesthetic and the static. Furthermore, the fields of sensitivity involved do not usually function separately but rather as a total system in which the parts are closely interrelated and form organized patterns. The integration of different types of sensory impressions plays a far more prominent role in space perception than in cases such as color vision which involve only a single sense modality.

Let us consider further the statement that perception of the vertical and horizontal depends upon the integration of several different kinds of sensory stimuli. Basically these stimuli fall into two main categories, the visual and the postural. Now "space," as it is visually perceived, may be described as having a frameworklike composition, the main axes of which are set by the vertical and horizontal directions. This "framework" was described by the late Max Wertheimer, a noted Gestalt (or "configurational") theorist in psychology, as an organized, patterned visual field distinguishable from the postural and the more subjective factors influencing perception. In this "field" the separate components (*e.g.*, the vertical and horizontal lines in a given situation, as furnished by the corners of walls and floor in a room) have a combined patternlike effect attributable to their presence together in a system under given conditions.

The verticals and horizontals which abound in almost every situation provide us with a "standard" against which the position of any object—including one's own body—may be perceived. In addition to the visual basis for judging the vertical and horizontal, the gravitational pull on the body, a force which corresponds in direction to the true vertical (*i.e.*, to the drop of a plumb line) provides a further basis for judgment. Although normally we are not aware of the fact, the body is constantly adjusting itself to this pull, and the sensory effects that result from our postural adjustments enable us "automatically" (*i.e.*, without thinking about it) to determine the direction of the pull, and thereby to determine the upright. Thus, with eyes closed, it is possible to determine whether one's body is upright or is tilted left or right, and any perceptual adjustment of this kind reflects an effective knowledge of the direction of the true vertical and horizontal. The specific sensory data available to the mammalian organism in adjusting to gravity include kinesthetic impulses from muscles and tendons, a complex pattern of tactual impulses from the skin, and impulses from the viscera and from the semicircular canals of the inner ear.

Although two main sources of "information" (visual and postural) are available for determining the vertical and horizontal in almost any situation, we do not experience two separate sets of verticals and horizontals, one visual and the other postural, which we must then somehow put together. Rather, our experience is unified to such an extent that it is very difficult to determine the separate contributions of visual and postural factors to the adjustment. A principal reason for its unified character is the fact that the vertical of the visual field and the gravitational vertical coincide perfectly in direction. This intimate and orderly relation between visual and postural factors is invaluable in helping us to determine our own position and the position of other objects quickly and easily, and therefore aids us greatly in coping with our environment.

However, the very closeness of the relationship between these two factors makes it impossible to study the problem of how we perceive the vertical (*i.e.*, the upright) aspect of space adequately under everyday conditions. The separation of visual and postural factors so that their characteristic individual contributions to space perception may be discerned can be accomplished only by experimental means.

The investigation to be described in this chapter represents such an undertaking. Some of the specific questions on which these experiments throw light are the following: how is one's perception of body position and the position of the surrounding field accomplished? What is the relative importance of visual and postural factors in such perception? How is the constancy of the perceived vertical and horizontal ordinarily maintained? How do people differ in the way in which they integrate the visual and postural experiences which underlie the perception of the upright?

WITKIN'S INVESTIGATION[1]

The problem of the experiments to be reported in this chapter was to investigate the conditions which determine the perception of the upright when the position of the subject's body itself, the position of the visual field, or both of these are subjected to systematic changes.

APPARATUS AND SITUATION

The subject in the present experiments was seated in a specially constructed chair within an experimental room, in a situation so arranged that either the room or the chair could be tilted to right or to left as the procedure required. The tilting-room and tilting-chair setup used in this investigation is shown in Fig. 38. The room was made of plywood and was 6 ft. long, 5 ft. wide, and 5 ft. high. In order that the experimenter could observe the subject at all times and speak to him when necessary, the back of the room was left without a wall. The entire room was mounted on stands, with a worm-gear arrangement in the mounting which permitted the experimenter to tilt the room through a predetermined angle up to 35 degrees to either side from the true vertical, simply by turning a crank, and which also permitted the subject to tilt the chair, when procedure required.

The experimental room was lighted from within by a 25-watt fluorescent lamp. The outer laboratory was kept fairly dark so that no visual cues would be available to the subject from shadows outside his room.

---

[1] Adapted from Witkin, H. A.   Perception of Body Position and of the Position of the Visual Field. *Psychological Monographs: General and Applied*, 1949, vol. 63, No. 302, pp. 1–46.

In this way, effective cues for judging the upright were confined to the tilting room itself. To provide a well-defined visual framework within the room, the entire inside of the room was painted gray and the

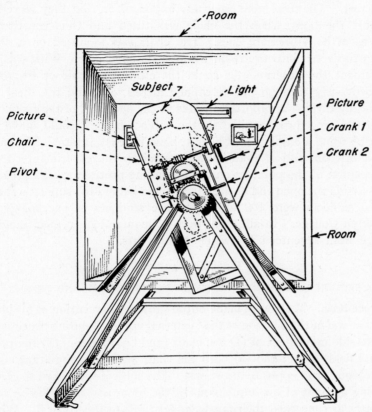

FIG. 38. Sketch of the Tilting-room and Tilting-chair Apparatus as Arranged for Situation F, Series II, in Which the Room is Upright and the Subject's Chair is Initially Tilted 22 Degrees to the Left.

In this test the subject (while blindfolded) is to bring the chair to a position which he perceives as "upright." The various arrangements of room and chair used in these experiments are described in the text, and those of series II are shown graphically in Fig. 39. Crank 1, experimenter's crank for changing angle of chair tilt; Crank 2, experimenter's crank for changing angle of room tilt; Pivot, axis about which room and chair are turned.

borders of the walls were marked boldly with white paint; also two pictures in rectangular frames were fixed to the wall in front of the subject's chair.

The subject sat in a high-backed chair which was placed in the middle of the tilting room and was provided with arm rests, foot rests, and a head rest.   The rests were especially important in that they served to support the body when the chair was tilted and thus constituted sources of body-pressure cues.   The chair was mounted on a shaft which projected into the room through its open rear.   With this arrangement the experimenter could tilt either the chair or the room independently through predetermined angles, or could tilt them together, by turning appropriate cranks at the open end of the room.   Or when the procedure required it, the subject himself could move his chair by using a crank placed near at hand in front of him.   The angle of tilt of room and of chair could be read by the experimenter from the position of the pointers on corresponding protractor scales placed just outside the open end of the tilting room behind the subject's chair.

The subjects were 100 undergraduate students of psychology at Brooklyn College.   In all, there were 22 men and 78 women, ranging in age from seventeen to twenty-three years.

The Experiments

SECTION I: CHANGING RELATIONS BETWEEN BODY AND FIELD

Procedure.   Tests were made of the subject's perception of his body position and of the position of the "external upright" during continuous side-to-side movement of (1) the chair (and body) alone; (2) the room (visual field) alone; and (3) both the chair and room simultaneously, in the same or in opposite directions.   The subject was asked to give a running account of his impressions of the room and of his body, particularly as concerned their apparent relations to the vertical.   When the subject happened to stop talking for any length of time, the experimenter would ask, "What is happening now?"

Results.   Under *condition 1*, when the chair alone was moving, with the room stationary and upright, the situation was always correctly perceived, *i.e.*, the subject reported the different tilt-positions of the chair with considerable accuracy.

Under *condition 2*, in contrast, radical perceptual errors occurred when the room alone moved while the chair remained stationary.   In such cases, an illusory body movement was experienced in a direction *opposite* to that of the room movement, while the room movement was either underestimated or was not perceived at all.   Thus either all or part of the changed relation between body and field, actually due entirely to room movement, was attributed to body (*i.e.*, chair) movement.   When the *entire* change was attributed to body movement, the room was reported as completely stationary, even though it had been moved from extreme right to extreme left.   When the change was attributed only *partially* to body movement, the subject reported some movement of the room, but referred this to some extent at least to body movement.   In such cases, the room was perceived as moving in the direction it was actually taking, and the body was perceived as moving in the opposite direction.

Under *condition 3*, when body and field moved simultaneously but in *opposite* directions, the effect on the subject's perception was complex.   He perceived correctly that his body was moving in a given direction but experienced the illusion of a faster movement than actually was the case.   In tests under condition 3 in which body and field moved in the *same* direction, the subject also perceived correctly that his body was moving, but now the movement seemed to him to be slower than it really was.

From the results obtained under conditions 1, 2, and 3, it seems clear that the perceived speed and direction of body movement depends upon whether the relation between body and field changes, and if it does, what the nature of the change is.   If the body alone is moved, with the field stationary, the body movement is correctly perceived.   If the field alone is moved, with the body stationary, an illusion of body movement occurs in varying degrees.   If both body and field are moved, the body movement is always perceived, but it appears to be faster or slower than actually is the case, depending upon whether the body and field move in the opposite or in the same direction.   Hence these tests demonstrate the important part which the "visual framework" may play in the perception of body movement.[1]

[1] One of the special tests under condition 2 indicated how the illusion of movement changes in dependence upon the effective stimulative field.   For instance, a complete illusory body movement was much more likely to occur when the subject (himself stationary while the room moved) was instructed to look toward the floor of the room than when he looked toward the ceiling.   A difference in the complexity of the visual field (*i.e.*, the number of "reference points" in it) in the two cases evidently was responsible— *i.e.*, the "floor view" included glimpses of the subject's own body and of the chair and its fittings, whereas the "ceiling view" involved only features of the room itself.

Under all of these test conditions there were marked individual differences in the extent to which the condition of the visual field influenced the perception of body movement. Under condition 2, in which the body was stationary and only the room moved, most of the subjects experienced a body movement which seemed so real that its illusory character was seldom even suspected. However, a few of the subjects reported no illusion of body movement at all in this situation. Similarly, under condition 3, where both chair and room actually moved, some of the subjects were more affected by displacement of the visual field than were others. There appear to be significant differences among people in their susceptibility to illusions of body movement in relation to visual perception.

Just as in many other perceptual illusions (*e.g.*, the Müller-Lyer illusion), knowledge of the actual situation does not eliminate the induced illusion, although such knowledge may reduce the effect. On certain trials under condition 2, after the subject had reported illusory movement, he was instructed to turn around and look into the main laboratory through the open rear wall of the experimental room. But even after he had thereby established the fact that only the experimental room had been moved, he again experienced the illusion that his body had moved when he faced back into the small room.

During some of the tests of Section I, the subject was given a plumb line to hold and was asked to view it in front of him while chair and room were moved and perceived in various positions. Under condition 1, when chair movement stopped with chair tilted and room upright, all of the subjects perceived the plumb line as hanging straight down. However, under conditions 2 and 3, when room movement stopped with the room tilted, there occurred a very strong and persistent illusion that the plumb line was suspended at an angle, in a direction opposite to the tilt of the room and to an extent corresponding to the angle of room tilt. This illusion occurred regardless of whether the body was tilted or upright at the time. So vivid was the illusory effect that the subject rarely considered the fact that a plumb line hanging freely from his own hand must of necessity represent the true vertical. Instead, a variety of alternative explanations was offered. Some subjects thought that an invisible wire must be pulling the plumb line to one side, others said that its position was controlled by a magnet outside the room, and others suggested that a blast of air was being directed at it. Many simply stated that this apparent violation of the laws of gravitation was beyond their comprehension.

It is significant for understanding the relative importance of body cues and visual cues that the apparent position of the plumb line remained the same (*i.e.*, vertical) when its relation to the body was changed, whereas its apparent position was radically affected when its relation to the visual field was changed. As long as the visual field actually remained upright, the plumb line continued to appear vertical whatever the position of the body; but, if the visual field was tilted, the plumb line appeared slanted regardless of possible cues from an erect body position. The illusion evidently depends upon displacement of the visual perceptual field from the upright, and occurs regardless of what the position of the body may be.

SECTION II: QUANTITATIVE TESTS OF THE PERCEPTION OF FIELD AND BODY POSITION

Procedure. In these experiments the subject was required to adjust the controls of room or of chair so that, following a displacement of room or chair, according to instructions he returned either the room or the chair (*i.e.*, his body) to what he perceived as the true vertical.[1]

The room and the chair were first brought to one of the positions listed below. The subject then was instructed to operate the control at his chair so as to straighten the room (tests A, B, and C) or his chair (tests D, E, and F) to what he perceived to be the true upright. The test situations were as follows:

Test	Condition	Subject's task
A	Chair upright; room 35° L or R	To adjust *room* to the "upright"
B	Chair 22° L, room 35° L	To adjust *room* to the "upright"
C	Chair 22° L, room 35° R	To adjust *room* to the "upright"
D	Chair 22° L, room 35° L	To adjust *chair* to the "upright"
E	Chair 22° L, room 35° R	To adjust *chair* to the "upright"
F	Subject's eyes closed	To adjust *chair* to the "upright"
(control)	Chair 22° L, room upright	

[1] This set of procedures represents an adaptation of the psychophysical Method of Average Error, in which the subject himself operates the changing of the variable stimulus (here his apparent position or the apparent position of the room) until it is equal for him to a standard stimulus (here, the true vertical). The difference between his judgment and the standard value (*i.e.*, the actual vertical) thus is a measure of the illusory effect on a given trial, and the average of such "errors" expresses the magnitude of the typical illusory effect in his case.

The conditions of the respective tests in section II are represented graphically in Fig. 39.   It will be noted that the room had to be straightened while the body was upright (test A), tilted with the room (test B), and tilted opposite to the room (test C); and that the body had to be straightened while the visual field was tilted with it (test D), tilted opposite to it (test E), and absent, in effect (test F).   The trials of tests B and C were alternated, as were the trials of tests D and E.

Fifty-four subjects were given the first five test conditions.   Twenty-three of these subjects were given test F as well.

The standard procedure on each trial was as follows: After the subject had closed his eyes, the experimenter brought chair and room to their required initial positions.   Upon opening his eyes, the subject was asked to describe his position and the position of the room.   Then the subject himself straightened the chair or the room, according to instructions, by turning the appropriate control.   In every test, while the room or the chair was being adjusted, the other (*i.e.*, chair or room) remained in its initial position throughout.

The tests involving adjustment of the room depended upon the assumption that the degree of tilt of the room (*i.e.*, the angle it forms with the true vertical) when the subject perceives it as upright provides a measure of his "extent of acceptance" of the visual framework.   A subject who perceives the room as straight when its initial tilt is 35 degrees thus shows a larger error (*i.e.*, a greater acceptance of the field) than one who must move it to a point only 10 degrees tilted before he perceives it as straight.   Similarly, in the tests requiring adjustment of the chair, the assumption is that the farther the body is tilted toward the prevailing field when it is finally perceived as upright, the greater is the subject's dependence on the visual framework in his perception of body position.

Results.   The average amounts (*i.e.*, "Average Errors") by which the adjustment of room or chair differed from the true upright under each test condition are given in Table I.   To show the magnitude of the individual differences in these tests, frequency distributions of the results for room adjustments are presented in Fig. 40 and for the chair adjustments in Fig. 41.

From Table I it will be seen that under the conditions of Test A, the room was still tilted by 11.7 degrees on the average when per-

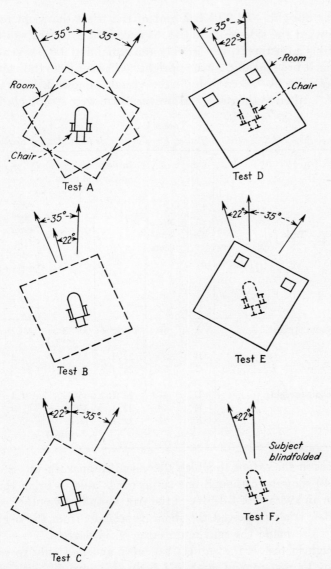

FIG. 39. Schematic Representation of the Initial Positions of Room and of Chair in the Six Tests of Section II.

The one (*i.e.*, room or chair) to be made "upright" by the subject in each test is indicated by dotted lines in the figure. The amount by which each is initially displaced from the vertical is also indicated.

ceived as upright.   In 90.4 per cent of the trials the room remained tilted toward the side of its initial displacement after the subject had finished his adjustment, and in only the remaining 9.6 per cent of the trials was it brought to the true upright.   The subjects thus tended to accept (*i.e.*, to be "taken in by") the visual framework in its original terms, *e.g.*, tilted to the right.   However, there were striking individual

TABLE I

Average Errors of Subjects in Adjusting Room and Chair in the Tests of Section II

Task	Test	No. of subjects	Initial positions of chair and room		Average error (in degrees)	Percentage of trials chair remained on side of its initial tilt after subject's adjustment
			Chair	Room		
To make room upright..........	A	50	Upright	35° R or 35° L	11.7	90.4
	B	55	22° L	35° L	12.2	76.8
	C	53	22° L	35° R	22.3	90.1
To make chair upright...........	D	47	22° L	35° L	9.4	97.0
	E	48	22° L	35° R	5.9	66.3
	F	23	22° L	(eyes closed)	2.4	—

differences in the extent to which the visual framework was accepted, as Fig. 40 shows.   Although one subject was able to bring the room to within an average of 1 degree of the true upright, two other subjects on all their trials perceived the room as straight from the beginning, and therefore made the maximum error of 35 degrees.[1]

Although in test A the subject sat erect and had only to readjust the room to realignment with his body, his upright position, surprisingly enough, did not lead to a more accurate adjustment of the

[1] In further experiments it has been found that some subjects perceive the experimental room as upright at tilts even greater than 35 degrees, and as great as 60 degrees in some cases.

room. The reason is that perception of the body itself was usually affected by the tilted framework, so that most subjects perceived the body as tilted in the opposite direction to the room. Although some of the subjects recognized the illusory character of the experience, for

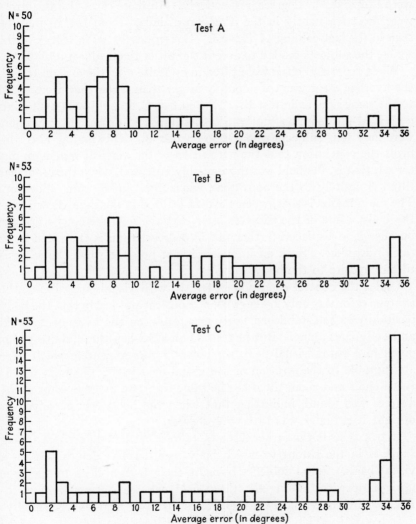

FIG. 40. Distribution of Individual Scores for the Room-adjustment Tests (Tests A, B, and C) in Series II.

The initial setting in each test is given in FIG. 39.

others the illusion was strong enough to induce false chair-pressure effects. Consequently the upright body was not too useful as a source of cues for perceiving changes in room position.

In tests B and C of section II, the averages of the subjects' errors were 12.2 and 22.3 degrees, respectively. In these cases also the errors were most frequently in the direction of initial room tilt, as may be seen in the last column of Table I. Consequently, as in test A of the series, the subjects tended to accept the tilt of the field as presented.

When room and chair were tilted in opposite directions, as in test C, the average error was considerably larger than when they were tilted to the same side, as in test B. Thus in test C, 16 subjects on all trials perceived the room as "upright" at its initial 35-degree tilt, but there were only four subjects who did so on test B. This finding also confirms the conclusion that the perception of the vertical was more distorted, that is, the field was more readily accepted, when the room was tilted oppositely to the body than when tilted in the same direction. The main reason is that, when the field is tilted in the same direction as the body, some of the subjects infer that the field cannot be upright because it is displaced farther (at 35 degrees) than is the tilted body (at 22 degrees). Such an inference is not possible when the room is tilted opposite to the body.

Under the control condition in test F, with visual cues absent, the average error was only 2.4 degrees, demonstrating clearly that the body position can be established fairly accurately on the basis of postural and body cues alone. But in tests D and E when the same task was given in a tilted visual field, significant errors appeared which were attributable to the position of the visual field itself. Thus in test D (with chair and room tilted to the same side), an average error of 9.4 degrees was found, indicating that when the body was perceived as upright it actually was tilted 9.4 degrees.

In test D, as in the earlier tests, there were marked differences among subjects in the extent to which body position was determined on a visual basis. Some subjects brought their bodies close to the true upright notwithstanding the tilted field, whereas others were so influenced by the visual field that errors up to 31 degrees were made.

In test E, in which chair and room were tilted oppositely, the average error for all subjects was 5.9 degrees, definitely smaller than in test D. With the room now tilted to the right, only 66.3 per cent of the errors in making the body upright were in the same direction, in contrast to

97 per cent in test D. Clearly, the judgment of body position was more strongly influenced by the tilted field in test D than in test E. It is suggested that in test E, with the subject initially tilted 22 degrees

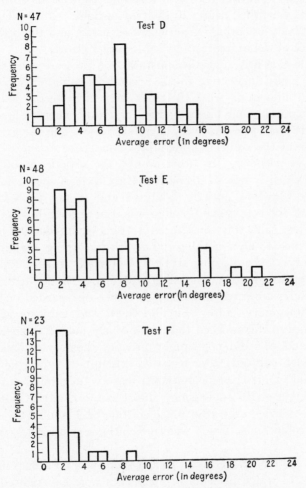

Fig. 41. Distribution of Individual Scores for the Chair-adjustment Tests (Tests D, E, and F) in Series II.

The initial setting in each test is given in Fig. 39.

left and the room 35 degrees right, he not only felt his body as tilted to the left but also *saw* it tilted to the left, so that it had to be moved toward the right to be perceived as straight. However, in moving the body toward the right there occurred a shift in weight (hence in pressure) from the left side to the right as the chair passed the upright position.   This shift called attention to the body and emphasized body cues, thereby reducing the effect of visual impressions and leading to judgments which fell nearer to the true upright.   In test D, however, no such "body-orienting" experiences occurred, and the resulting predominance of visual impressions led to larger errors.

The question arises whether postural and pressure effects from tilting were really ineffective in the visually dominated subjects, or if they were influential, what their role may have been.   How could a subject maintain that his body was "upright" when he was actually tilted, with chair pressures very asymmetrical?   The case reports show that some of the subjects under these conditions *actually experienced no pressure whatever*.   In other words, the experience of *appearing* straight evidently was so strong that the effects of contradictory body cues were somehow entirely inhibited and so not perceived at all. With other subjects, some pressure was experienced; but, as one practiced subject said, this constituted a "remote, intellectual awareness, which seemed to have nothing to do with the strong, certain, and immediate experience of being straight."   Usually in such cases specific questioning was necessary to elicit statements about pressure effects. The pressures appeared to have been either disregarded or attributed to some imaginary cause.   Finally, there were subjects who experienced pressure effects when they erroneously judged themselves to be upright, and who did not simply discount them or rationalize them away.   Such subjects, after repeated attempts to find a normal position, would report that for unknown reasons they could not *feel* erect and *look* erect at the same time.   For them, a choice of position generally was reached only after much shifting back and forth, and represented a compromise which was frequently very unsatisfactory to the subject.

In this section of the investigation there was no actual measure of the extent to which pressure or body cues were experienced.   To investigate this matter, tests A to F were repeated under two conditions, in both of which the experimenter moved the chair in 2-degree steps until the subject reported himself in an upright position.   The difference between the conditions was that for the *experimental* group of this series the *elimination of pressure inequalities* through chair adjustments was emphasized in the instructions as the task to be accomplished, whereas the *control* group was required only to report when an (apparently) upright position had been reached, with no mention of equalizing pressure effects.

Notwithstanding the difference in instructions about pressure, the results for the two groups were much the same. In both groups, the body was usually still tilted when perceived as upright, and by similar amounts, *i.e.*, the average errors were similar. For example, under the conditions of test D the Average Error was 13.3 degrees for the control group and 15.9 degrees for the experimental group; under the conditions of test E the Average Error was 7.8 degrees for control and 10.4 degrees for experimental subjects. Thus the results were much the same whether or not the instructions emphasized pressure effects.

The results of tests D, E, and F indicate that the perception of body position depends not only on how the body feels, but to an even greater degree on how it looks to the subject in relation to his surroundings. If the subject is to perceive his body as upright, when he is in a tilted field, he must be moved toward alignment with the field. These tests also disclose that some people seem to rely primarily on the visual relationship between the body and its surroundings, presumably either suppressing contradictory body effects or perceiving them as remote from their experiences. In contrast, other subjects are less affected by visual impressions and seem able to make good use of body cues in judging their position. The ranges found in the amount of error (from 0 to 31 degrees in test D, and from 1 to 24 degrees in test E) reflect the magnitude of such individual differences. The cause of some of these variations will be investigated in the next section of this chapter.

SECTION III: QUALITATIVE DIFFERENCES IN PERFORMANCE

An examination of some of the case reports, especially those of subjects whose orientation was very poor, will offer a basis for understanding the nature of the different adjustments to these situations. The following excerpts are taken from the protocols (case records) of a set of experiments already referred to in which the experimenter made the adjustment for the subject by moving room and chair in small steps until the subject reported them to be straight.

Protocol for Subject A. Under conditions equivalent to those in test B of Section II (with the difference in procedure noted above), this subject, in accepting the experimenter's adjustment of the room to the upright from 35 degrees right or left on successive trials, made error scores of 18, 31, 32, 32, 7, and 35 degrees, indicating a marked acceptance of the visual field.   Although on the first trial (under condition B) she was able to accept an adjustment within 9 degrees of the true upright, on the next two trials she was in error by 32 and 24 degrees, respectively.   In test C, when the room was initially at 35 degrees right and the body at 22 degrees left, she accepted the room as straight at once on the first trial, and on the next two trials she was off by 37 degrees each time.

On the second trial of tests D and E, where the chair was initially tilted 22 degrees left and the room 35 degrees right, very severe disorientation developed, as the following excerpts from the protocols show very clearly:

First the subject had herself moved past the upright in the direction of room tilt, until she was tilted 24° right.   Then she said: "No, I'm at an angle.   There are difficult things to decide.   I feel by my weight that I'm thrown to the right. Move me to the left.   No, to the right.   No, maybe more to the right.   No, I wish I could tell you; move me more to the right.   That's it."—Her difficulty was that when her body looked straight to her in relation to the room, she felt tilted, and when she felt straight she looked very tilted. . . .

At 26° right, later: "I feel cockeyed.   Go to the left.   I'm sorry if I sound dumb, but I can't get myself straightened out."—At 24° right: "I'm beginning to be on my head.   (Excitedly) Turn me to the right.   I've never been on my head before. I'm almost on my head now.   No wonder I couldn't tell." . . .   At 40° right: "I'm approaching being on my head.   Let's experiment some more.   Move me to the left."—At 26° right: "If you want to, you can say I'm on my head now. I can't say definitely, but let's say I'm fairly sure I'm on my head.   I feel very stupid.   Move me to the left."

—Considerably later, at 18° right: "I'm going back on my head.   Ah, I know. The walls are moving too."   When asked whether it was possible to get straight, she replied: "Not by moving left and right.   Move the walls back (pointing to the front wall of the experimental room); we're both oriented down.   The front wall is becoming the floor.   If you tipped it over a little (pointing upward) it would become the floor."   When asked where the floor was, she replied: "It's where you are."   (Here she judged the open back wall of the room to be the floor, —a plane at right angles to the true floor of the experimental room!)

The trial was discontinued soon after this, since it was clear that this subject would not be able to regain her bearings sufficiently even to approach making herself straight.   When returned to the actual upright, she exclaimed: "Oh, it's wonderful!   I was hanging like a crescent moon."

This performance has many interesting features. First with rather slight tilts of the chair and room, and these in the right-left direction only, the subject experienced extreme changes in her own perceived position and in that of the field. Concerning her own body she experienced the illusion of tilts in the front-back direction, as well as spiraling movements, and during a considerable part of the last trial she felt herself to be on her head. With respect to the room, at one point she perceived its *front wall* as the ceiling, and at another point as the floor. These shifts in the perceived orientation of the room occurred while the room remained in the same position and came about quite suddenly. Thus on one occasion, after reporting that the front of the room was becoming the floor, she exclaimed, "Now I have a completely different orientation. We're climbing, and the front wall is nearer to the ceiling." Of importance also is the severe disorientation suffered by this subject. At many points her perceived upright was far from the true spatial upright. At times she became extremely confused about where the upright was, so that on the last trial she failed to find a position where her body seemed upright, after trying for 50 minutes. Such experiences proved very disturbing to the subject throughout most of the test.

The difficulties experienced by this subject undoubtedly resulted from a strong tendency to perceive the upright primarily on the basis of visual impressions, and an insufficient reference to the body. Thus she accepted the tilted room as straight, even when she sat erect and had maximal use of body cues.

Protocols for Subjects B and C. Another example of disoriented performance in these tests, associated with poor scores, was provided by subject B. On the three trials of test A in which the room was tilted 35 degrees left with the chair upright, she perceived the room as straight at the very outset, and accordingly reported that her erect body was tilted far to the *right*.

On trial 2, with chair 22° right, room 35° right, she said: "Ah, me, the floor is the left wall and the ceiling is the right wall. (When asked if the room was straight—) I can't decide. (After a long pause—) I'm trying to figure it out. I'm tilted to the *right*, and if I were straight how would it look? It's down to the left."

On trial 5, with chair 22° left, room 35° right: "The room is straight. It's again in order. The chair is slightly to the *right*. Then why don't I fall to the right? There is something very mysterious. You must have magnets."

The difficulties of subject B, as with A, depended upon the fact that her perception of the visual field was dominant. Her confusion became so great that even after detecting the tilt of the room she could not tell which way it had to be moved to become straight. Closing her eyes to eliminate the confusing influence of the field did not help her, for as soon as she looked again at the room she came so strongly under its influence that the impression of body position established with eyes closed was obliterated. Not only did she have gross misconceptions about the position of her body and of the field, but she experienced difficulty in making her judgments. She was hesitant and unsure throughout; each decision required a great deal of time and then was often made quite without confidence. Like subject A, she was markedly disturbed, often emotionally agitated.

Subjects A and B were both very intelligent, but neither was successful in overcoming her strong visual impressions through an intellectual treatment of the situation. Another very intelligent subject, C, had the technical knowledge concerning sensory mechanisms necessary to deal with such conflicting experiences. Yet despite his knowledge, and his effort to "figure out" each situation, he gave a highly confused performance similar to that of subjects A and B, as the following excerpt from his protocol shows:

On one trial, with the chair initially 22° left and the room 35° right, his comment was, "I'm on the left side and the room is a little to the right." (When the chair had been moved toward the right to a point where it was 14° right, he said:) "Wow! I'm upside down. I feel suspended from the floor position. I have a hunch, though, that objectively I'm still a little to the left; yet when I look it seems the right wall is the bottom, even though I know it is not so. I'm jutting out like a branch from the floor part, that is now the left wall; but I know it's not true.—I could find out by spitting."

Thus the subjects who were very strongly influenced by visual impressions in this situation were not assisted much by their intelligence, or even by technical knowledge, to counteract these impressions and achieve a satisfactory integration of visual and postural experiences.

Comments such as the above occurred almost exclusively among subjects who made very large errors in judging the upright. Confusion among other poorly performing subjects usually was milder, more transitory, and limited to a part of the test. As a rule, the judgments of subjects with large errors were made rapidly and without evidence of conflict, with a rather "glib, unquestioning acceptance of the visual field." As difficulties arose, this type of subject as a rule soon gave up trying, often with the assertion that she had done her best.

SECTION IV: SYMPTOMS OF EXTREME DISORIENTATION IN AN UNSTABLE VISUAL AND POSTURAL SITUATION

In the course of the above experiments, some of the subjects complained of "illness" and reported symptoms which usually included (in order of prominence) dizziness, sweating, headache, and nausea. To investigate this reaction to the experimental conditions, tests consisting of special combinations of room-and-chair movement (as in Section I) were given, each of them presented ten times to each subject. The following combinations were used:

1. The subject was tilted through an arc from 10 degrees left to 10 degrees right of the vertical, first with eyes closed, next with eyes open.

2. While the subject remained upright in the chair, the room was tilted from 10 degrees left to 10 degrees right, then from 35 degrees left to 35 degrees right.

3. The subject and room were moved together, from 15 degrees left to 15 degrees right; then oppositely—for example, chair to 15 degrees left, room to 15 degrees right.

The results consistently showed that body movement, whether with eyes open or closed, produced no ill effects whatever. When body movement was combined with room movement, some "illness" appeared, but it was only occasional and usually was mild. However, severe discomfort and "illness" appeared with room movement alone, and particularly with the 35-degree room displacement.

In connection with tests A to E of section II, discomfort and "illness" were frequently reported when a subject opened his eyes at the beginning of a trial and found the room and chair in very different positions. The speed with which the illness developed and the circumstances of its occurrence strongly suggest that it was a consequence of being confronted suddenly with a very unstable situation. In agreement with this interpretation, the results show that motion of the visual field when the room was tilted set up an illusory body movement which was inconsistent with actual body pressures, and therefore very confusing and disturbing. In the tests involving a back-and-forth tilting of the room with the body stationary, some of the subjects experienced severe discomfort at the moment when the room movement was reversed in direction. It was also at that moment that the subject had their greatest difficulty in perceiving what was happening.

The reason for such difficulties seems to be that a change in body movement draws attention to the body, thereby reinstating a conflict between visual and postural cues—a conflict which is stilled by the dominance of visual impressions during continuous movement. When there is marked disorientation and uncertainty as to whether the room, the body, or both room and body are moving, and the disparity between visual and postural sensory effects is at its height, the organic symptoms of "illness" characteristically appear. Thus when the room was tilted, although it was stationary at the time, some of the subjects complained of lost bearings and a "topsy-turvy impression," accompanied by dizziness and nausea. When orientation is relatively secure and there is no sensory conflict, "illness" does not develop.

A somewhat comparable situation, very disturbing to some people, is the experience of being momentarily disoriented when sitting in a moving train that is passed by another train. An experience of dizziness and nausea is not uncommon under such conditions. Such effects are accentuated when a sudden shift occurs in the field of moving objects, as when a train on a nearby parallel track begins moving in a direction opposite to that in which one's own train has been moving. In these circumstances, it is even possible to refer the experienced nausea and organic discomfort to an attitude of emotional apprehension (*i.e.*, anxiety) which is a typical reaction to very unstable situations. In fact, some of the subjects in these experiments, who asked that the movement of chair and room be stopped immediately after it had begun, described their distress as "anxiety" or "anxiousness," and seemed to perceive the situation as a threatening one. This type of "illness" is somewhat different from the "motion sickness" (*e.g.*, seasickness) sometimes experienced in body-movement situations, which is more dominantly physiological in nature and commonly involves actual vomiting as a symptom.

A situation comparable to that described above is involved in a common form of "airsickness" likely to be met with by inexperienced pilots undertaking somewhat abrupt and difficult maneuvers. Under such conditions, when the plane banks suddenly, the pilot is likely to perceive the earth's surface precipitately turned on its side, as it were, and sharply inconsistent with his body position at the moment. Then a condition of acute disorientation and anxiety may seize him, which often immediately involves symptoms of illness such as those we have described.[1] The individual's distress may be increased by an added organic upset attributable to a direct stimulation of the viscera and of static receptors by the radical bodily displacement itself.

DISCUSSION

The experiments of Witkin show that perception of the position of the body at any given moment typically depends more upon visual impressions than upon postural cues. The results show that to understand the specific way in which visual impressions help to determine our perception of our body's position, it is necessary to consider not just the body itself, but also the body in relation to its surroundings. When the subject's body was aligned with the vertical axis of the visual field he reported that his body looked straight to him, and when it was displaced from this axis his body tended to look tilted. The subject's judgment of his own position often seemed to be a very strange one, until the specific manner in which he saw the field surrounding his body became known.

These findings support the generalization that the perception of an object is influenced greatly by the surrounding field (*i.e.*, the field of which the object is a part), and because objects rarely occur for us in isolation, the results apply to the perception of most objects in the environment. In fact, the surrounding field may be expected to exert an even greater influence on the perception of external objects than on the perception of the body, for the body provides sensory cues useful in judging its position—cues which arise independently of the field. Other experiments, in which subjects determined whether an external object was upright or tilted, provide further examples of the way in which the surrounding field influences the perception of objects within it. Thus, most subjects standing erect in a dark room tended to view a

---

[1] Armstrong, H. G. *Principles and Practice of Aviation Medicine.* Baltimore, Williams & Wilkins, 1939.

luminous straight rod (placed vertically in all trials) as tilted or as upright depending upon whether a luminous square frame surrounding this rod was tilted or upright.[1] Also, as would be expected from the foregoing discussion, whatever tilt was perceived in the rod seemed to be in the direction opposite to the tilt of the field.

Other cases of perception provide further examples of the principle that the perception of objects depends upon their specific relation to the field in which they are viewed.   Thus a medium-gray object will appear brighter in a field of dark gray than in a field which is light gray. It is mainly the brightness of an object in relation to brightness of surrounding surfaces, rather than the absolute brightness of that object, which is important.   As another example, the apparent distance of an object from us depends not merely upon stimuli from the object itself but to a large extent on the relation of the object to other objects in the surrounding field.   Thus, a distant house which is partially blocked from our view by another usually is perceived as farther off than one actually at the same distance but in unobstructed view.   If an object, especially one that is familiar, seems smaller than other objects of the same class and size (*e.g.*, a row of oak trees on a hill), or is less clear than other objects, it is likely to seem more distant.   If, while one moves his head, an object remains stationary while other objects seem to move across the field in relation to it, the still object will be perceived as more distant.   Innumerable examples may be found to demonstrate that the perception of an object and its qualities depends not simply on the object itself but also on its context—that is, on its background and its relations to its surroundings.

An important question attacked in the present studies was the basis of the constancy of the perceived vertical and horizontal in everyday experience.   Notwithstanding many variations in our specific postural orientation, we normally continue to perceive the vertical and horizontal accurately.   The results of the described experiments suggest that this perceptual constancy depends primarily on the highly stable visual field about us.   For example, when the room was tilted, subjects tended to accept its upright as the true upright.   They were likely to underestimate the tilt of the field more or less—for example, in straight-

[1] Witkin, H. A., and S. E. Asch.   Studies in Space Orientation: IV. Further Experiments on Perception of the Upright with Displaced Visual Fields.   *Journal of Experimental Psychology*, 1948, vol. 38, pp. 762–782.

ening the body they tended to displace it toward the perceived vertical of the field, as in readjusting a picture on the wall of a room, one tends to move it into line with the room's main axes.

Any characteristics which tend to emphasize the visual field (*e.g.*, pictures on the wall in front of the subject's chair) also tend to accentuate the extent to which the perceived vertical and horizontal shift with the field as the latter is moved. The perceived vertical and horizontal seem to be "anchored" to the visual field, and with a field as "strong" as that provided by our everyday surroundings, these perceptions are almost certain to depend upon its dictates. Not only is the normally prevalent visual field a strong one in this sense, but it is also highly stable in that it represents the vertical and horizontal correctly, *i.e.*, in accordance with gravity. In view of these facts, the constancy with which we perceive the spatial planes is not surprising.

The important role of the visual field in the adequate perception of the upright is shown by the very limited effect of changes in head or body position when a visual field is effective. In the present experiments, changes in body position in the presence of an upright visual field were without effect in producing perceptual errors, whereas changes in the field (even with the body upright, as in test A, Section II) led to marked illusions.

It is clear that *constancy in our adult perception of the upright must depend for its development on the presence of a stable visual field of the kind normally provided by our surroundings, and on the effect of a gravitational force which is consistently related to the principal visual axes as encountered in everyday life.* That is to say, *a consistent set of relationships between body position and environmental circumstances influences the basic development of our processes in space perception.*

Ordinarily it is not possible to determine whether the perceived upright is based more upon postural factors or upon visual. This is because the gravitational factor and the verticals of the visual field coincide in direction, so that the result is the same whether judgments are based upon one or the other. However, these experiments, by providing unusual situations involving variable displacements of the visual field and of body position, afforded a means of separating the roles of visual and postural factors. From the results, it is clear first of all that when the visually and posturally indicated uprights are in conflict, the subject's perception of "upright" generally is not based simply on the one or the other but represents a compromise between the two. The findings show that this compromise depends mainly on the "strength" (*i.e.*, detail, extent of accentuation) of the visual field. Similarly, a visual field of the kind predominant in everyday life dictates the accepted "upright" in perceptual situations more effectively for most people than do postural factors.

However, it is imperative to recognize that people differ from one another with respect to the relative importance of these factors. In a given situation, although most people favor the visual field as a basis, others rely more on postural cues derived from the body itself. The point may be emphasized by inspection of the individual differences represented in Figs. 40 and 41.

Furthermore, in perceiving the upright some individuals tend to be more consistent than do others in their degree of dependence on the visual field as it appears in different situations. However, it may be said that on the whole the characteristics of a particular individual in perceiving the upright in one kind of situation also appear definitely in other and different situations. For example, supplementary to the tests of Section II, one group of subjects was given a test in which a previously viewed simple figure was to be identified in a larger complex figure designed to "hide" or "embed" the simple figure. Success in this type of perceptual task requires that the subject not "go along with" the total visual field provided by the complex figure, but deal with its constituent parts in a somewhat flexible and independent manner. It is not surprising that a fairly high correlation ($r = +.61$ for men; $r = +.51$ for women) was found between the results for the same subjects in the "hidden figures" test and those for tests involving adjustment of chair and room to the vertical, for analysis reveals that a similar process is involved in the two situations. Thus, subjects who have difficulty separating their bodies perceptually from the surrounding field also find it difficult to discern the simple figure when it is "embedded" in complex surroundings. Individual characteristics in perception thus appear to be somewhat generalized, so that they are revealed in recognizably similar ways even in situations where the specific perceptual tasks are quite different.

It is clear that a knowledge of the field conditions (*i.e.*, the stimulus objects) alone, important as these conditions are, cannot provide an adequate understanding of how a given person will perceive a particular situation.   If field conditions were the sole determinants of perception, then, notwithstanding individual differences in sensory and neural equipment, people would be expected to perceive much more similarly than they do.   The fact that marked individual differences in perception appear under equivalent external conditions, and furthermore that most individuals tend to show fairly stable and consistent perceptual characteristics, emphasizes the presence of further internal determinants of perception which are unique to the individual and which influence his perceptual organization of a particular situation.   Further experiments now in progress suggest that at least some of these highly individualized determinants of perception are related to and dependent upon the motivational characteristics of the person.

CHAPTER XXII

PERCEPTION AND MEMORY AS INFLUENCED BY ATTITUDE AND EXPERIENCE

INTRODUCTION

A camera is a mechanism by means of which patterns of light chemically transform a sensitive film and leave lasting traces upon it. In much the same manner, living organisms are affected by the stimuli which impinge upon them, and the effects of these stimuli persist often over long periods of time. This persistence of the effects of stimulation is what is meant by retention, or memory.

Although the impression left on a photographic film bears a close resemblance to the object which was photographed, it is not a precise copy of that object. A photograph of a tree is smaller than the tree; it commonly lacks the tree's colors; and, unless the camera lens is exceptionally good, the edges of the picture are blurred. What is impressed upon the sensitive film, therefore, is determined not only by the character of the object producing the impression, but also by the structural characteristics of the recording mechanism itself (primarily of the lens and the film). The differences between the object photographed and the resulting photograph depend upon the deficiencies of the camera mechanism.

In some respects, the functioning of the human memory mechanism resembles that of the camera. As a rule, what we remember has a definite similarity to the pattern of stimuli which furnished the basis for the memory. But we do not remember perfectly. Memories are generally incomplete and defective in the sense that they do not reproduce in a literal way the past objects or events which they represent. If you were asked to recall the first paragraphs of this chapter, you might be able to state their general import, perhaps reproduce some of the exact phrases, but it is very doubtful that you could achieve a letter-perfect copy. The fallibility of our memory processes is brought home to all of us many times each day. We are frequently confident

382

that we are recalling an object perfectly, yet our recollection generally proves very defective when compared with the actual object.

Certain of the factors which make the memory of an object deviate from that object are similar to the factors which limit the accuracy of a camera. With respect to visually perceived objects, for example, faulty eye structure, like faulty camera construction, causes distortion of what is seen, and consequently of what is remembered.[1] However, the analogy between photography, on the one hand, and human perception and memory, on the other, is a very incomplete one. Whereas the aberrations in a camera record result from faults in the mechanisms of lens and sensitive plate, the discrepancies between the visual perception and memory of an object, and the object itself, are chiefly attributable to factors other than the eye alone.

The human organism is an inconceivably more complex instrument for the reception and recording of impressions than is any camera. In photography, the character of a particular picture on a roll of film is not affected by the nature of the pictures taken previously. But in human perception and memory, what one perceives at a given time may be greatly influenced by what one has perceived at an earlier period. A very simple illustration of this fact is furnished by the phenomenon of "successive contrast" (*e.g.*, the unusual brilliance which bright objects appear to possess when they are viewed after dark ones). But the fact that our perceptions and memories are influenced by antecedent events is true in a very wide and complex sense, as well. We see particular groupings of black marks on white paper as letters and words, only because our training has provided the foundation for that observation. The patterns of light and shade that we see, the sounds that we hear—in fact, everything that enters the channels of sense—are perceived and remembered in terms of experiences prior to the perception.

A second point of difference between the functioning of the camera and of the human organism is the fact that, unlike the photographic record, the perception and memory of an object are affected by the nature of the situation in which the object appears. The photo-

---

[1] Here belong such defects as disproportions in the shape of the crystalline lens or in the length of the eyeball (which produce nearsightedness or farsightedness), imperfections in the curvature of the cornea, lens, or eyeball (which result in astigmatism), inadequate ocular coordination (which causes the seeing of single objects as double), and peculiarities in retinal structure (*e.g.*, those which underlie color blindness).

graphic image of a given tree would be exactly the same, regardless of whether the tree were flanked by other larger trees or stood alone on a grassy bank. But our impression of the size and shape of an object may be influenced by almost any irrelevant stimuli which are simultaneously present. Thus, a tree of a given height would be perceived and remembered as shorter if it stood beside a number of taller trees than if it were surrounded only by low shrubbery. Similarly, if two black circles of equal size are drawn, one in a small and the other in a large white square, it is the circle in the smaller square that is perceived and remembered as definitely the larger.

The influence of stimulus setting and background upon perception is especially apparent in illusions such as the Müller-Lyer illusion and the size-weight illusion. In our everyday experience, illusions due to this factor of context occur quite frequently. However, it is only when a particularly obvious error is made (*e.g.*, when one boisterously greets a stranger whom one has mistaken for a friend) that such false perceptions are identified as erroneous or illusory. Because of this fact, we ordinarily do not realize that our perception of a given object may vary greatly from one occasion to another, as a result of differences in the settings in which the object appears. Although we may think that we are attending exclusively to certain items in a complex of stimuli, our perception of these items is influenced by other factors in the situation.

Finally, the memory of an experience may be affected by subsequent experiences. In photography, the seventh picture on a roll of film is not changed by the later exposure of picture number eight. But a particular painting in a museum may be remembered as exceptionally beautiful, or as merely mediocre, depending on the reactions which were evoked by the pictures seen after it. Similarly, one's ability to recall something he has learned may differ greatly in accordance with whether he has spent the time between the learning and the recall test in sleeping or in pursuing ordinary daytime activities.[1]

Evidently, therefore, both the perception and the memory of a given experience are influenced by previous and by contemporaneous experiences, and the memory of an experience is likewise affected by events which follow it.

[1] For a report of experimental studies on this subject see Chap. XVI.

The various ways in which a person's past experience may affect his perception and memory of things and events have been the object of many recent psychological studies. In all these investigations, each stimulus presented is the same for all the subjects; the experimental variable is the background of experience of the subjects themselves. If these identical stimuli are perceived and remembered in different ways by different subjects, such variations must be the result of differences in the subjects' past experiences.

In certain investigations of this problem, the experimenter himself produces the differences in the experiences of his subjects by varying the instructions or suggestions that he gives to them. The experimental "creation" of such differences is analogous to many familiar occurrences in everyday life. For example, a number of people may happen to see a man lying prostrate and apparently unconscious on a city sidewalk, and later observe an ambulance arrive and take him away. If one of the group chances to hear someone say, "He's drunk," whereas another happens to overhear the remark, "He's had a heart attack," and if each person accepts the characterization he hears as correct, it is virtually certain that the two persons will differ considerably in both their perceptions and their memories of the incident. Such remarks constitute verbal experiences, and differences in them tend to produce corresponding differences in our perceptions and memories of the objects and events to which they refer. An excellent example of an investigation in which the experimenter presented different verbal experiences to different subjects, with the aim of ascertaining the effect of these differences upon the subjects' perceptions and memories, is the study of Carmichael, Hogan, and Walter[1] which forms the principal basis of the present chapter.

In another type of investigation, the experimenter does not "create" differences in the past experiences of his subjects but rather selects subjects who already differ in ways which he conceives may affect their perceptions and memories, for example, in their attitudes[2] toward various aspects of their environment. To these subjects he presents

---

[1] Carmichael, L., H. P. Hogan, and A. A. Walter. An Experimental Study of the Effect of Language on the Reproduction of Visually Perceived Form. *Journal of Experimental Psychology*, 1932, vol. 15, pp. 73–86.

[2] An attitude may be defined as a state of readiness to react in a characteristic way to specific objects or situations on the basis of factors related to the experience and the motivation of the individual.

selected stimuli and observes such differences as may occur in their perceptions and memories of them. Individual differences in perception and memory arising from this source are a matter of common observation. Suppose, for example, that a group of people strolling on a country road includes a painter, a botanist, and an architect. The color masses of flowers and foliage, the contours of hills, the interplay of light and shadow, are likely to constitute the high spots of the day for the artist. As for the botanist, it may be the discovery by the roadside of an obscure lichen, not even seen by others of the group, which makes this day a memorable one for him. And the architect may remember vividly only one thing about the excursion: an old cottage skillfully modernized. Studies of differences in perception and memory deriving from differences in vocation, race, economic status, attitude on social issues, and other factors stemming from the personal history of the subjects belong to this class of investigation. Several experiments of this type are briefly reported in Part II of this chapter.

The experiment by Carmichael, Hogan, and Walter was designed to investigate the effect exerted by certain previous experiences of the subject upon his perception and memory of visual designs. These previous experiences consisted of various familiar words which were presented to the subject by the experimenter. We are justified in speaking of the presentation of words as the giving of "experiences" to the subject. Each individual has learned in the past to connect particular words with corresponding experiences, with the result that, when a specific verbal expression is presented, it serves as an effective stimulus for the recall of certain related experiences. In this sense, the expression functions as a symbol for previous experience, and this experience constitutes the meaning of the expression.

It is obvious that our memory of a given event may be greatly influenced by subsequent verbal experiences, *e.g.*, when we converse with others about some previous event, or when we think (in words) about it. Similarly, it is clear that the preconceptions and expectations which color our impressions of the world about us become established largely through verbal means, *e.g.*, the advices and suggestions which we receive from reading or from communication with others. What is not so apparent, however, is that our perception of simple, concrete objects and our immediate recollection of them may be profoundly affected by the words which we have associated with the objects. It is this phase of the effect of language experiences upon perception and memory which was investigated in the experiment reviewed below.

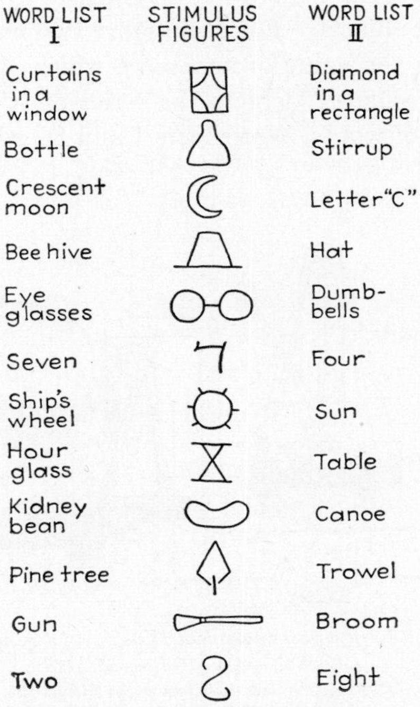

WORD LIST I	STIMULUS FIGURES	WORD LIST II
Curtains in a window		Diamond in a rectangle
Bottle		Stirrup
Crescent moon		Letter"C"
Bee hive		Hat
Eye glasses		Dumb-bells
Seven		Four
Ship's wheel		Sun
Hour glass		Table
Kidney bean		Canoe
Pine tree		Trowel
Gun		Broom
Two		Eight

FIG. 42. The Stimulus Figures and Word Lists I and II Which Were Presented Together with the Stimulus Figures.

I. THE EXPERIMENT OF CARMICHAEL, HOGAN, AND WALTER[1]

PURPOSE

The present experiment was designed to investigate the influence of verbal symbols upon the recall of visual patterns. Specifically, the aim was to discover whether the suggestion of an object-name for a visually perceived geometrical figure may affect the subsequent reproduction of that figure.

METHOD

Subjects. The subjects were 60 women and 35 men. All were college students or college instructors.

[1] Adapted from Carmichael, Hogan, and Walter, *op. cit.*

The Stimulus Figures and the Word Lists. The stimulus figures were a series of drawings representing 12 simple geometrical forms. Although none of these figures was a complete or accurate representation of any object, each of them was so constructed that it resembled at least two actual objects. For each figure two names were devised, each of which was the name of an object which that figure more or less resembled. Figure 42 depicts the series of stimulus figures and gives the two lists of words, Word Lists I and II, which were assigned to them.

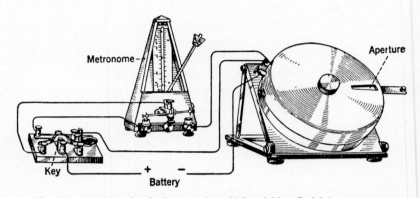

Fɪɢ. 43. Apparatus for the Presentation of Material in a Serial Arrangement.

In using the instrument illustrated (the Ranschburg memory apparatus), the experimenter marks off a circular card in radii and writes in successive or alternate sectors the stimuli (*i.e.*, syllables, words, or figures) which are to be serially presented. The card is then placed upon a revolving platform under the circular cover of the apparatus. This cover is stationary and contains an aperture through which a single sector of the card can be seen. The card rotates with the platform, and the stimuli inscribed upon the card are thus brought one at a time under the aperture. By means of a metronome or some similar regulating device, the rotation of the platform (which carries the card) is electrically controlled, so that it remains stationary for a predetermined period when each stimulus item appears in the slit. Each exposure is a "still," and the shift from one exposure to the next occurs by a rapid jerk.

Apparatus. The apparatus for presenting the stimulus figures was essentially the Ranschburg memory apparatus, illustrated in Fig. 43, although certain modifications were introduced. A white cardboard disk, 19 cm. in diameter, was divided by radial lines into 30 equal sectors. The disk contained the series of 12 stimulus figures, each figure separated from adjacent ones by blank sectors. A space of seven empty sectors followed the twelfth figure of the series. The mode of operation of the Ranschburg apparatus is described in connection with Fig. 43. The stimulus figures were shown in a regular series, probably at a rate of 2 sec. for the exposure of each figure and 2 sec. for each blank sector between adjacent figures.

Procedure. Experimenter and subject sat opposite each other at a laboratory table. The exposure apparatus was placed before the subject and the illumination was arranged so that each successive figure was clearly visible to him as it appeared in its turn in the exposure slit.

Before beginning the experiment proper, the subject was told that he would be shown a series of figures, and that after the completion of the series he was to try to draw them as accurately as possible. He was further instructed that he might make his drawings in any order he wished; that is, it was not necessary for the sequence of his reproductions to correspond to the serial order of the presented figures.

The subjects were divided into three groups. All three groups were shown the same series of 12 figures. For the 48 subjects of Group A, and for the 38 subjects of Group B, the figures were designated by the object-names of one or the other of the word lists. Thus, for these subjects, each time that an empty sector appeared in the exposure slit, the experimenter said, "The next figure resembles . . . ," giving one of the two names of the figure about to appear. For the subjects of Group A the experimenter pronounced the word of List I which was appropriate to the figure in question. For the subjects of Group B the word was the corresponding one from List II. For the nine subjects of Group C the experimenter simply exposed the series of stimulus figures without giving any names in connection with them. The tests with Group C represented a control experiment.

When the presentation of the series of figures had been completed, the subject was requested to draw all the figures which he had just been shown. If he failed to produce a recognizable representation of all 12 figures, the series was shown again in the exposure apparatus, and for Groups A and B the experimenter used the same words to suggest the resemblance of each figure to the concrete object named during the original presentation. Following this second exposure, the subject again attempted to reproduce the figures. This procedure was continued until a recognizable reproduction of all 12 forms was secured.[1]

The Scoring of the Drawings. After the completion of the experimental work, the papers containing the subjects' reproductions were

[1] For the achievement of this criterion, the subjects of Groups A and B required an average of three trials; the subjects of Group C, four trials.

studied independently by two of the three authors serving as judges. The judges ranked each drawing on a five-point rating scale according to the degree of resemblance between the drawing and the figure which it was intended to reproduce. The rating scale was as follows:

Grade 1. Drawings that were approximately perfect reproductions of the stimulus figures.

Grade 2. Drawings "with very slight changes from the original." These changes usually took the form of "slight shortenings or lengthenings of lines, slight changes in curves or angles, or slight changes in the proportion of one part of the figure in relation to some other part of the figure."

Grade 3. Drawings which showed "a noticeable change in the original figure, but which did not mark a complete distortion." Such figures were characterized by definite increases or decreases in the length of lines, or by pronounced alterations in curves, angles, or proportions. "These figures were in all cases, however, still quite satisfactory reproductions of the original."

Grade 4. Drawings "showing marked changes such as additions or omissions, and marked changes in proportion. The figures in this group, while still somewhat resembling the original, were changed considerably from it."

Grade 5. Drawings "which were almost completely changed from the original. Here were included inverted figures, and those hardly recognizable in relation to the stimulus-figure."[1]

In the rating procedure, the judges considered each reproduction without reference to the particular word which had been associated with the figure at the time of the original presentation. After all of the reproductions had been independently rated by the two judges, their estimates of the rating-scale position appropriate to each drawing were compared. When it was found that the ratings of the two judges differed, the reasons for the difference were discussed and an attempt was made to arrive at an agreement. If, as occasionally happened, a conclusion could not be reached in this way, the third experimenter was consulted and his verdict was accepted as final.

In the opinion of the authors, the influence of any factor which

[1] The authors recognize that inadequacies must be present in a rating-scale method of measurement when the steps of the scale represent qualitative rather than quantitative units. Because of the nature of the data obtained in the present experiment, however, the authors considered the rating plan which they adopted to be the most reliable scoring device available under the conditions.

tended to produce discrepancies between the objective appearance of a stimulus figure and the reproduction of it would be most clearly revealed in the most discrepant drawings. A close study of the drawings which were judged as Grade 5, therefore, was considered the best means of discovering the effects of the experimental factor being investigated, *i.e.*, the names of objects which the stimulus figures were said to resemble. Such an analysis might have two different outcomes. One possibility was that the Grade 5 drawings might show no consistent resemblance to the typical visual form of the objects which the experimenter had named. In this event, one would have to conclude that, under the conditions of the experiment, the accompanying verbal stimulus was not the factor responsible for the errors in the reproductions of the visual patterns. On the other hand, a greater resemblance might consistently be found between the reproductions of Grade 5 and the objects named than existed between the stimulus figures themselves and those objects. Such a finding would enforce the conclusion that language may bring about modifications in the memory of visually perceived figures (to the extent, that is, that memory is measured by reproductive accuracy).

The drawings of Grade 5 were studied with the specific purpose of determining which were more similar to the objects named by the experimenter: (1) the stimulus figures to which those names had been applied, or (2) the drawings which the subjects had made of the figures. For example, which was more like a hat, the figure which the experimenter had said resembled a hat, or the reproductions which the subjects had made of that figure? Similarly, which looked more like a ship's wheel, the figure to which the experimenter had applied that name, or the drawings which the subjects had made of it? When the two raters failed to agree in their judgments of a given drawing, recourse was had to the third experimenter, whose decision was accepted.

In the same way, the drawings assigned to Grades 2, 3, and 4 were studied, in order to determine whether these reproductions were more or less similar to the objects named than were the stimulus figures themselves.

RESULTS

1. Table I gives the number and per cent of the drawings, made by the subjects of Groups A and B, which the experimenters assigned to each of the five grades of the rating scale.

Thus, 26 per cent of the 3,495 drawings were classified in Grade 5, and 91 per cent were referred to the three lowest ranks of the rating scale. Grades 4 and 5 together received 62 per cent, whereas Grades 1 and 2 together received only 9 per cent.

2. When the 905 reproductions of Grade 5 were studied for the degree of their resemblance to the objects named in Word Lists I and II, the results presented in Table II were obtained.

As Table II shows, almost 75 per cent of these drawings looked more like the objects named than did the original stimulus figures. It is of especial interest to note the manner in which the different names given by the experimenter in Word Lists I and II produced corresponding differences in the reproductions. When figure 10 had been called a "pine tree," 86 per cent of this group of drawings resembled a pine

TABLE I

The Number of Drawings Assigned to Each of the Rating-scale Divisions, for Groups A and B

Scale of grades	Number of reproductions	Per cent of the total number
1	26	1
2	285	8
3	1,011	29
4	1,268	36
5	905	26
Total..........	3,495	100

tree more than the stimulus figure did. But of the reproductions which were made of the same figure after it had been called a "trowel," 100 per cent were more trowellike than the stimulus. In the same way, the proportions of the Grade 5 drawings of stimulus figure 2 which resembled a "bottle" or a "stirrup" more than did the figure were 100 per cent and 69 per cent, respectively, depending upon which of these names the experimenter had applied to the figure. A study of Table II reveals comparable findings for each of the other 10 stimulus figures. It is, therefore, clear that when a subject reproduced a stimulus figure very inaccurately, his drawing tended to be similar to the object which the experimenter had named when the figure was presented. Figure 44 shows a number of examples of the way in which the drawings distorted the stimulus figures in the direction of those objects.

Of the Grade 5 drawings of the Group C subjects (to whom the experimenter had given no names in connection with the stimulus figures), 45 per cent showed a fairly marked resemblance to the objects named for Groups A and B. This percentage is considerably smaller than the corresponding percentages for Groups A and B (74 and 73, respectively).

The authors report that a subsequent study of the reproductions ranked in Grades 2, 3, and 4 revealed similar relationships, although in a less marked degree, between the character of the drawings and

TABLE II

The Per Cent of the Reproductions of Grade 5 Which Surpassed the Stimulus Figures in the Degree of Similarity to the Objects Named (Groups A and B)

Stimulus figure	Per cent of reproductions	
	Word List I	Word List II
1	47	78
2	100	69
3	65	48
4	69	75
5	45	81
6	87	94
7	54	47
8	83	100
9	90	63
10	86	100
11	76	85
12	87	40
Average.........	74	73

the objects named by the experimenter. (The percentage values for these three grades are not presented in the original report of the experiment.)

DISCUSSION

The results of the experiment by Carmichael, Hogan, and Walter clearly demonstrate how language may influence the reproduction of visually perceived forms in striking ways. This finding is in agreement with the results of previous experiments[1] in which it was discovered

[1] Wulf, F. Beiträge zur Psychologie der Gestalt. VI. Ueber die Veränderung von Vorstellungen (Gedächtnis und Gestalt). *Psychologische Forschung*, 1921, vol. 1, pp. 333–373.

Gibson, J. J. The Reproduction of Visually Perceived Forms. *Journal of Experimental Psychology*, 1929, vol. 12, pp. 1–39.

that subjects often *spontaneously* identified the stimulus figures with various concrete objects, that this identification involved naming the objects, and that this naming apparently influenced the character of the subsequent reproductions.   Furthermore, it had been found that, even when the stimulus figures did not suggest concrete objects, the figures frequently were verbally described by the subjects "to them-

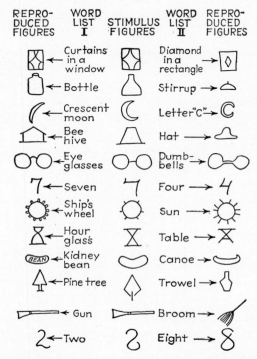

Fig. 44. The Stimulus Figures and Examples of Reproductions Which Conformed to the Visual Representations of the Object-names of Word Lists I and II.

selves," and the later reproductions showed changes in harmony with the descriptions.   Thus, if the subject himself had termed a stimulus figure "symmetrical," or "rounded," or "Gothic," the drawing which he made commonly exaggerated the trait.[1]   In this connection it is

---

[1] Gibson writes that alterations in the reproductions often seemed to be determined by "cues from a verbal analysis which was made of the forms [by the subjects] during perception." *Op. cit.*, p. 39.

interesting to consider the fact that 45 per cent of the Grade 5 reproductions of Group C resembled the objects named in Word Lists
I and II more than did the stimulus figures. It is highly probable that
a considerable number of these reproductions were influenced by spontaneously perceived and named similarities between the stimulus figures
and the objects which they resembled (the objects which were ex-
plicitly designated for Groups A and B by Word Lists I and II, respectively).

Evidence from many sources suggests that the influence exerted by
language on memory and perception is not restricted to such material
as visual diagrams. The lawyer's trick of asking uncertain witnesses
leading questions is a familiar application of the principle. "What
color was the overcoat which the accused was wearing?" may cause a
witness to "remember" a coat which in actual fact never existed.
Similar instances in direct perception might be cited. For example,
the excited whisper, "There's a deer. I can see him move!" may cause
the hunter to take careful aim at a motionless stump. Such facts
provide reason for wondering whether Shakespeare's opinion that "A
rose by any other name would smell as sweet" is a valid dictum.
Surely, it is not substantiated by experiences such as the shift in a
person's feeling tone as he realizes that what someone has pointed out
to him as a large and luminous "moon" is merely a prosaic street lamp.
Without question, the word which is applied to a stimulus object
strongly influences the nature of the perceptual response to that object.

The conclusion that words influence what we perceive and what
we remember is of great importance for the study of man's thought
processes. No normal person creates his own words in order to sym-
bolize his own experiences. For such purposes, we accept the words
of the particular language we speak and interpret new experiences in
terms of those words. In consequence, everything we perceive is
influenced, not only by what *we* have previously perceived, but also
by what *the society into which we are born* has perceived and has formulated into language symbols. People of some nationalities are taught
that a certain group of stars is the "Great Bear"; others are informed
that the same constellation is the "Big Dipper." If the results of the
present experiment are generally valid, it must be supposed that those
who call it "The Bear" see and remember it as more like a bear than
do those who call it "The Dipper."

In our own society there are many instances in which different kinds of behavior are aroused toward an object when different words are applied to it. The recognition of this fact is exemplified by the attempt to "dignify" certain vocations, *i.e.*, to win an attitude of greater public respect toward them, by the simple expedient of changing their names. One does not regard a house handyman with the awe which a "dwelling engineer" elicits; one is more likely to engage a room in a "hotelette" than in a rooming house. Similarly, we now have "sanitary engineers" (garbage men), "appearance engineers" or "tonsorial artists" (barbers), "demolition engineers" (house wreckers), "sleep engineers" (bedding manufacturers), "morticians" (undertakers), etc. If we had never encountered either flower and were given the choice of planting a "thorn apple" or a "stinkweed" in our garden, most of us would unhesitatingly select the former, although both are names for the same plant.

The comparative study of languages strengthens this argument. In many cultures there exist language distinctions which to us seem unnecessary or even unintelligible. Eskimo languages contain separate words for "snow on the ground," "snow heap," "falling snow," "drifting snow," "soft snow," etc. The fact that we have but one word for all these varieties of snow may be the reason why we often fail to perceive slight differences in snow which would be immediately obvious to Eskimos and which they would designate by different words. Conversely, language distinctions which seem inevitable to us may be ignored in languages which reflect a very different type of culture. Thus, in some languages, it would be impossible to express the difference which we perceive between "manslaughter" and "murder," because the underlying legal philosophy which determines our use of these terms is wholly absent in certain societies.

In other words, if we used a different vocabulary or if we spoke a different language, we would perceive a somewhat different world.

Of course, the distinction which we draw between the concepts "manslaughter" and "murder" was not created because of the existence of different words. The different words were themselves created because as a society we had come to differentiate and had taught our children to differentiate between these modes of inflicting death. If we should cease to respond in different ways to these two types of situation, it is probable that one of the words would sooner or later disappear from general use. The people of the sixteenth century were tremendously interested in hawking, and, in order to aid themselves in distinguishing different types of hawks, they used such terms as "peregrines," "tercels," and "merlins," to designate the varieties of the bird. The sport has passed out of fashion, and, although we still see the same birds, the one word "hawk" suffices for them all.

Conversely, the inception of a new activity or interest which demands a more delicate perceptual analysis is accompanied by an increase in vocabulary. Even though such interests or activities may *create* no new objects, every such development carries with it a multitude of new words, not because of an increasing keenness of sense, but because of the need for making finer discriminations. One must learn many new names of colors if one is to become a clothing stylist; many new names of trees to become a forester. Lack of the words operates as a positive hindrance to the performance of the necessary perceptual processes, in the sense that numerous and fine distinctions are missed if one does not have the words with which to label them. Possession of the different terms, on the other hand, helps to make the distinctions obvious and easily remembered.

Thus, the demands of the society in which we live have created a language to which our perceptions, memories, and thoughts must be adapted. Hence, our perceptual, memory, and thought responses are poured into the mold of a system of symbols which has been imposed upon us by society. That we rarely, if ever, have thoughts which transcend the confines of our vocabulary is a tribute to the efficacy of the binding and congealing power of language, as expressing a particular culture pattern.

II. INVESTIGATIONS OF THE EFFECT OF ATTITUDES UPON PERCEPTION AND MEMORY

The experiment discussed above provides a clear demonstration of the general proposition that the way a person perceives and remembers things depends not only upon the characteristics of the things themselves and of the person's recording mechanisms but also upon the particular psychological condition of the person at the time the perception takes place. This study shows that the language symbols used in designating an object of perception, by setting up a specific expectation in the subject, can influence the way in which he remembers that object.

More recently, numerous investigations have been directed at a study of various other factors stemming from the individual's past experience which may affect his perception and memory, especially the attitudes which he has developed as consequences of this experience. Among the factors which have been studied are the individual's wants and "values," his conception of his place in the world, his ideas of prestige, his racial prejudices, his attitude toward religion, and so on. These factors can be subsumed under such terms as "attitudes," or "frames of reference."[1]

Bruner and Goodman,[2] for example, attempted to discover whether the perception and memory of the size of an object are affected by the value or desirability of the object to the person seeing and remembering it. These investigators made use of an apparatus designed to permit the subject to adjust the size of a circular patch of light appearing on a ground-glass screen so as to make it equal in size to any one of a number of objects which the experimenter successively named for him or showed him. The objects which the subjects were asked to match in size were the United States coins of the five denominations from the cent to the half dollar inclusive. The subjects of this research were ten-year-old children, one group consisting of 10 children of poor socioeconomic background (drawn from a settlement house in a slum area), another group consisting of 10 children of relatively wealthy families (selected from a school attended by the children of prosperous business and professional people). Each child of these two groups was tested individually. He was asked to estimate from memory, one after the other as the experimenter named them, the sizes of a cent, a nickel, a dime, a quarter, and a half dollar. The subject made each estimate (or judgment) by adjusting the circular patch of light until he was satisfied that its size was the same as that of the designated coin. It was found that the "poor" children tended to overestimate the size of the coins to a significantly greater degree than did the "rich" children; that is, the "poor" children tended to make the matching circular patches of light larger than the "rich" children did.[3]

---

[1] The term "frames of reference" means the *standards of judgment* by which we perceive and interpret particular situations and events.

[2] Bruner, J. S., and C. C. Goodman. Value and Need as Organizing Factors in Perception. *Journal of Abnormal and Social Psychology*, 1947, vol. 42, pp. 33–44.

[3] This finding of Bruner and Goodman has been confirmed in a more recent experiment by Carter and Schooler on a larger number of subjects, in which a similar apparatus and

This more emphatic tendency on the part of the "poor" children to overestimate the size of the coins is interpreted by Bruner and Goodman as deriving from the fact that the "want" or "need" of these children for the coins was more intense than was that of the well to do. The more the children wanted the coins, the larger they remembered them to be.   According to these authors, if we value an object, one result is that our perception and memory of it are accentuated, or characterized by an increased vividness.   In other words, our attitude (our "state of readiness to react") toward a highly valued object tends to magnify it in recollection, and perhaps in direct perception as well.

Perhaps a similar psychological principle lies behind the tendency of painters and sculptors to portray heroic characters in "heroic" proportions—that is, as large as possible—as though that which is grand inevitably is huge as well.   The use of the expression "great" as equivalent to "good" or "excellent" is probably another illustration of the principle.   In other words, our very language "magnifies" what we approve of.   If certain of the conclusions of the Bruner and Goodman study, as confirmed by that of Carter and Schooler, are generally valid, the fisherman who exaggerates the size of the trout he has caught may not be "lying" but rather giving an accurate report of his memory—even if not of the fish.

Another experiment on this general subject is that of Marks,[1] who investigated the influence on perception exerted by the individual's attitude toward his own place in the social environment.   Negro students were asked to rate their own skin color and that of their classmates on an eight-point scale, from 0 (very dark) to 7 (very light). They were also asked to indicate on the scale the color which they themselves would prefer to be.   The results showed that the students'

---

procedure were used.   (Carter, L. F., and K. Schooler.   Value, Need, and Other Factors in Perception. *Psychological Review*, 1949, vol. 56, pp. 200–207.)   However, the results of this later study do not corroborate another finding reported by Bruner and Goodman, namely, that the *direct perception* of the sizes of the coins also was more exaggerated by the poor than by the rich children.   That is, in the experiment of Bruner and Goodman—but not in that of Carter and Schooler—the poor children tended to make the matching circles of light larger than the rich children did, even when *the coins were actually present* so that the sizes of the circles and the coins could be directly compared.   Further investigation of the problem should reveal the basis of this difference in results.

[1] Marks, E. S.   Skin Color Judgments of Negro College Students. *Journal of Abnormal and Social Psychology*, 1943, vol. 38, pp. 370–376.

judgments of the color of others were markedly influenced by their own colors. Typically, the dark student tended to exaggerate the degree of lightness of classmates who were lighter skinned than he, just as the light student tended to exaggerate the degree of darkness of companions who were darker than he. Hence, the darker students tended to perceive a given classmate as lighter than did the lighter students, and vice versa. In their rating of their own skin color, the subjects generally judged themselves to be either the shade they had stated they wanted to be, or a shade between that preferred shade and the shade assigned to them by the other subjects. In the latter case, the response appears to represent a compromise between the individual's desires and the objective fact. This study demonstrates how differences in an individual's attitude, in this case toward skin color, can actually bring about differences in the manner in which he perceives his own skin color and that of other persons.

The effect exerted upon perception by ideas of prestige is shown in an experiment in which the investigator asked a number of college students to describe 6 of the 10 standard Rorschach ink blots.[1,2] To half of these students he had given the spurious information that professional men and businessmen tended to interpret the blots as wholes and frequently saw animals in them, while skilled laborers and workers on government relief projects analyzed the blots into details and tended to see inanimate objects. Information, equally spurious, ascribing the opposite tendencies to the two occupational groups had been given to the other half of the subjects. The results plainly showed that the two groups of students reacted to the blots very differently, since the members of each group described them in the manner they believed characteristic of the members of occupations which they held in high social repute and to which they evidently wanted to belong. Thus, the experiment shows that another variety of attitude—in this case, toward certain kinds of occupation—can modify what subjects perceive in the ambiguous Rorschach ink blots.

Other studies show that prejudicial attitudes of various kinds, including racial, religious, and political ones, also affect perception and

[1] Coffin, T. E. Some Conditions of Suggestion and Suggestibility: A Study of Certain Attitudinal and Situational Factors Influencing the Process of Suggestion. *Psychological Monographs*, 1941, vol. 53, No. 241.

[2] The Rorschach test is briefly described in Chap. XXV.

memory. For example, one investigator,[1] by means of a questionnaire, ascertained the nature of attitudes toward Negroes of a group of 400 students in two New York colleges. The 200 subjects who revealed the most extreme positive or negative attitudes were shown 15 photographs of Negroes and 15 of white people. After an interval, the subjects were given the task of trying to pick out the 30 photographs which they had already seen from a total of 46 pictures. The results showed that the "anti-Negro" group in both colleges recognized significantly fewer pictures of Negroes than did the "pro-Negro" group. The author concludes that "Unfavorable attitude toward the Negro tended to obliterate recognition of individual differences among Negro pictures, whereas favorable attitude tended to heighten recognition of these differences" (page 61). In another part of the same study, Seeleman showed her 200 subjects 28 new photographs, half of them representing Negroes and half white persons. Each photograph had a caption, briefly characterizing the persons pictured, either in complimentary or in uncomplimentary terms (*e.g.*, "always a good sport," or "conceited and always boasting"). The "anti-Negro" group remembered significantly more unfavorable characterizations of Negroes, and remembered them in more correct association with individual Negro photographs than did the "pro-Negro" group. The results of this experiment strikingly demonstrate how the kind of attitude that we term "race prejudice" can both reduce one's ability to recognize individual members of the less respected race, and increase one's ability to recall facts which are unfavorable to them and therefore harmonious with the prejudicial "frame of reference."

Other studies have demonstrated that women tend to remember more items favorable to women, while men tend to remember more items favorable to men;[2] that a person's theological attitudes in part determine what he will remember of material concerning atheism and theism;[3] that the political sympathies of college students affected their ability to recognize items in a speech they had heard about Roosevelt's

[1] Seeleman, V. The Influence of Attitude upon the Remembering of Pictorial Material. *Archives of Psychology*, 1940, No. 258.

[2] Zillig, M. Einstellung und Aussage. *Zeitschrift für Psychologie*, 1928, vol. 106, pp. 58–106.

[3] Watson, W. S., and G. W. Hartmann. Rigidity of a Basic Attitudinal Frame. *Journal of Abnormal and Social Psychology*, 1939, vol. 34, pp. 314–336.

domestic program.[1] It has also been demonstrated that perception and memory vary with such influences as reward and punishment,[2] emotional stress,[3] and various kinds of experimentally induced suggestion.[4]

Conclusions

The experiments described in this chapter tend to support the popular observation that people tend to "see" what they expect to see, or what they want to see. Their perception, and consequently their memory of events, is clearly influenced by their expectations, their habitual modes of thought, their backgrounds, prejudices, estimates of themselves, and so on. Indeed, one means of recognizing individuals with unusual systems of habits and ideas, in particular, the extreme types possessed by psychotics, is by the deviation of their perceptions and memories from those of normal people. The psychotic, though enjoying normal auditory capacity, may not hear what other people hear; he may hear what other people do not hear (for example, angels talking to him); he may hear things in ways very different from those of most ordinary people (for example, he hears behind him the footsteps, not of another pedestrian, but of an unknown enemy who seeks his life).

Among normal people, however, there are evidently limits to the influence which an individual's own personal experiences and attitudes can exercise upon his perceptions. Cherished pet to the child, common cur to the dog fancier, the same animal is perceived as "dog" by both. It should be recalled that the chief object of the investigations reported in this chapter was to study the influence of individual experience upon perception and memory, and that most of the studies were ac-

[1] Edwards, A. L. Political Frames of Reference as a Factor Influencing Recognition. *Journal of Abnormal and Social Psychology*, 1941, vol. 36, pp. 34–50.

[2] Proshansky, H., and G. Murphy. The Effects of Reward and Punishment in Perception. *Journal of Psychology*, 1942, vol. 13, pp. 295–305.

Shafer, R., and G. Murphy. The Role of Autism in a Visual Figure-ground Relationship. *Journal of Experimental Psychology*, 1943, vol. 32, pp. 335–343.

Haggard, E. R., and G. J. Rose. Some Effects of Mental Set and Active Participation in the Conditioning of the Autokinetic Phenomenon. *Journal of Experimental Psychology*, 1944, vol. 34, pp. 45–59.

[3] Postman, L., and J. S. Bruner. Perception under Stress. *Psychological Review*, 1948, vol. 55, pp. 314–323.

[4] Sherif, M. A Study of Some Social Factors in Perception. *Archives of Psychology*, 1935, No. 187.

cordingly planned so as to give the greatest possible scope to such influence. For example, the Carmichael figure that was remembered as a "7" or as a "4," depending upon which word was associated with it, was objectively a compromise between a "7" and a "4." There is evidence that, had the figure not been a compromise, *i.e.*, had it been unmistakably a "7" or a "4," Carmichael's results would have been less striking.[1] Yet studies such as those reviewed in the present chapter provide convincing evidence that the differences in past experiences, which differentiate people either momentarily or characteristically, bring about corresponding differences in their perceptions and their memories.

It is also worth pointing out that studies of this type are of especial interest to the social psychologist. In any complex society, significant differences in the life histories (*i.e.*, the previous experiences) of its members are likely to result from differences in racial and national origin, socioeconomic status, political and religious affiliations, and so on. It is evident that such differences in experience intimately influence the development of differences in attitudes, in wants, needs, interests, prejudices, and the like, so that large groups of persons within the population may differ from other groups in these respects. What psychologists have recently discovered is that the attitudes characteristic of different groups within a society tend to produce measurable differences in the perceptions and memories of the individuals who belong to them. Thus, whether a person is white or colored, rich or poor, Democrat or Republican, communist or anticommunist, religious or atheistic, tends in some measure to affect—to alter or even to distort—his perception and memory of objects and events in the world about him.[2]

[1] See Luchins, A. S. Social Influences on Perception of Complex Drawings. *Journal of Social Psychology*, 1945, vol. 21, pp. 257–273.

[2] The influence of attitudes and similar psychological processes in producing individual differences in behavior has been noted in several other chapters of this book; *e.g.*, in connection with a person's belief or nonbelief in the occult (Chap. I), his susceptibility to motivation by competitive and by cooperative incentives (Chap. IV), the probability that he will be able to recall more tasks that he has finished or more that he has had to leave unfinished (Chap. V), his behavior in intelligence-test situations (Chap. XIV), the likelihood that he will be conditioned (Chap. XV), the nature of his perception of the vertical (Chap. XXI), and the character of his projective responses (Chap. XXV).

CHAPTER XXIII

"DIRECTION" AND THE "SOLUTION CONSCIOUSNESS" IN REASONING

INTRODUCTION

Many psychologists who have studied human behavior in problem situations conceive of the problem-solving process as one which requires the proper *selection* of the element or elements necessary for the accomplishment of a given task. Suppose, for instance, that a camper must light a fire but can find no matches. Solution of the problem requires that he *select* for performance one particular group of actions rather than another. Praying for matches to rain down from the skies will not get him very far, nor will going to sleep or walking around in circles. But if he thinks of using his flashlight lens to focus the sun's rays on some inflammable material, he has selected a very promising set of elements for the solution of the problem.

The process by which the correct selection is made is commonly understood to involve two mechanisms: (1) *trial and error*, and (2) *association by similarity*. By *trial and error* is meant the random movements of a baffled organism, "random" in the sense that they are inefficient and unregulated so far as the problem is concerned. The organism is forced into action by the stimulation of a need (*e.g.*, hunger). If in this crucial situation food is not available, the organism responds first in one way and then in another, each "try" being followed by failure. Eventually, however, a movement or group of movements may be made which results in the removal of the stimulus (in our example, cessation of the hunger pangs). Here the correct selection has occurred by a chance discovery. If the situation should recur, and if the animal is capable of learning or thinking, the successful response is likely to appear more readily. After many repetitions of the situation, such an animal will make the proper response promptly. *Association by similarity*[1] means the reproduction in a new situation

---

[1] Many psychologists regard association by similarity as an instance of stimulus gen-

of responses formerly made in another situation to which the new one is similar. The camper in the illustration given above may never have used his flashlight in order to make a fire. But if, in his present need, he thinks of the physics class exercise of using a magnifying glass to create a hot point, and sees how the same end may be attained by means of a flashlight lens, he has made the correct selection through association by similarity.

In their application to problem solving, trial and error and association by similarity provide two ways in which the proper selection of responses may be achieved. Either the solver makes many random movements which fail and eventually hits upon the right ones by chance, or he recalls the responses which he made to a similar situation in the past and applies them in the present setting.

However, Maier,[1] one of the leading investigators of problem-solving behavior, is of the opinion that *selection* of the proper responses is not the whole, nor even the most essential, part of problem solving. Maier does believe that in order to solve a difficult problem, the right part-responses must be selected. But, in addition, one must have the right slant, or approach, or as Maier calls it, *direction*. If the right direction is lacking, the correctly selected part-responses alone cannot furnish the solution. For example, one may know the English equivalents of every word in a Latin sentence and still be unable to translate the sentence as a whole. One has all the necessary part-responses, but the problem cannot be solved because of the absence of the right direction. Under these circumstances, however, the reading of the sentence or two preceding the difficult one may furnish a general way of understanding, *i.e.*, a direction as to the general meaning of the problem sentence. If this direction is the right one, the part-responses will be integrated into the correct pattern and the translation will now be possible. According to Maier, it is the right direction which furnishes the means for making the proper arrangement and organization of the correctly selected responses. So long as the subject working on a problem has no direction, or a wrong one, he cannot reach a solution.

---

eralization, a concept discussed in connection with conditioning in most textbooks in introductory psychology.

[1] Maier, N. R. F. Reasoning in Humans. I. On Direction. *Journal of Comparative Psychology*, 1930, vol. 10, pp. 115–144.

I. "DIRECTION" IN HUMAN REASONING[1]

PURPOSE

The aim of the present experiment was to find out whether or not the selection of the correct part-responses alone is sufficient for the solution of a problem.

METHOD

The Problem to Be Solved. The subjects were given four poles, a number of clamps, lengths of wire, and pieces of chalk. They were asked to construct with these materials two pendulums which might be swung in such a way as to make chalk marks at specified points on the laboratory floor. The only solution which would actually work was the following. The two pieces of wire were attached to opposite ends of one of the poles. To the free end of each of the pieces of wire was tied a clamp. Each clamp grasped a piece of chalk. Two other poles were clamped together to form a single length, a fraction of an inch less than the length necessary to span the distance from floor to ceiling. The pole carrying the two wire-clamp-chalk appendages was laid flush with the ceiling and was held in place by the double pole pressing up against its center. The double pole was thus wedged between the floor and the center of the pendulum pole. The completed structure looked like a T with the pendulums hanging from the tips of the horizontal bar.

The experimental materials presented to the subject are shown in Diagram *A*, and their correct combination for the solution in Diagram *B* of Fig. 45.

The Part-responses and Direction. This solution process Maier divided into three parts: (1) the chalk-clamp-wire arrangement, (2) the process of making a long pole by means of two short ones clamped together, and (3) the wedging of the horizontal bar against the ceiling by the vertical bar. To certain subjects he accordingly gave the following *preliminary demonstrations* which were designed to supply the three part-responses necessary for the solution of the problem. He showed the subject (1) how to make a plumb line out of a cord, a clamp, and a pencil; (2) how to make a long rod out of two short rods and a clamp; (3) how to hold a bar against the vertical edge of a door-

[1] Adapted from *ibid.*

way by wedging against the middle of the bar another bar which reached exactly to the opposite vertical edge, the completed structure resembling a T laid on its side.   The proper application and combina-

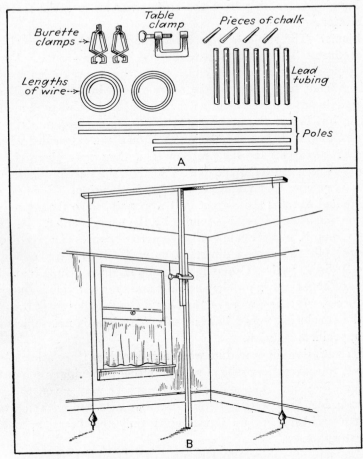

Fig. 45. The Pendulum Problem.

Diagram *A*, the materials available to the subject.   Diagram *B*, the correct solution.

tion of the three demonstrated principles should provide the solution of the pendulum problem.

When the *proper direction* was to be given, the experimenter said, "I should like to have you appreciate how simple this problem would be if we could just hang the pendulums from a nail in the ceiling. Of course, that is not a possible solution, but I just want you to appreciate how simple the problem would be if that were possible." By this observation Maier hoped to direct the subject's attention to the fact that hanging something from the ceiling was an essential feature of the solution.

Subjects. The subjects were 84 college students.

Procedure. The subjects were divided into five groups. Each of these groups received from the experimenter its own set of instructions, which differed from those of the other groups in some critical way. The experimenter gave these instructions after he had presented the problem but before the attempts at solution were begun. The subjects of Group A, before they began their task, were provided with the right part-responses for the problem (*i.e.*, they were given the preliminary demonstrations) and were told that the part-responses comprised everything that was necessary for the solution. None of these subjects had to *select* the correct part-responses, since the appropriate selection was determined in advance by the experimenter. A second group, Group B, was given not only the part-responses (*i.e.*, the demonstrations) but the correct direction, as well. If it were found that Group A did as well as Group B, then one might conclude that direction is not important in problem solving, and that selection is the essential process. If many more of the Group B subjects solved the problem, the conclusion would be that selection alone is not sufficient to explain problem solution.

Other variations in procedure were introduced for three other groups. Group C was given the problem without either preliminary demonstrations or direction. The subjects of Group D were given the part-responses, but they were not told that the parts had anything to do with the problem. Group E was given only the direction, and not the part-responses.

There were 62 subjects in Groups A, C, D, and E combined, and 22 in Group B.

RESULTS

Only 1 of the 62 subjects in Groups A, C, D, and E reached the solution, but of the 22 subjects in Group B, 8 were successful.

CONCLUSIONS

Neither the selection of the proper part-responses alone (as given to Group A) nor the selection of the right direction alone (Group E) was sufficient to bring about a solution of the problem. Solutions occurred when both the proper part-responses *and* the proper direction were present (Group B). Maier suggests that the effect of a given direction is to enable only *certain* groupings of the part-responses to appear. In this way, a correct direction acts to *organize* the part-responses correctly, *i.e.*, in a way which makes possible a solution of the problem.

DISCUSSION

This experiment proves conclusively that problem-solving behavior cannot be explained by a mere *selection* of the correct response units. In addition to selection, the factor of *direction* plays a critical role. This conclusion fits in perfectly with everyday observation of the difficulties we encounter while trying to solve problems. Everyone knows enough arithmetic to solve this problem: "A frog is trying to climb out of a well 30 ft. deep. It manages to jump up 3 ft. every day, but slips back 2 ft. every night. How long does it take the frog to reach the top?" Although the mathematics involved is very easy, it may take the reasoner a long time to reach the correct solution. He fails because he has developed a habitual mode of procedure, *i.e.*, a direction, for problems of this sort, largely as a result of much school training and exercise in solving similar problems. This habitual direction involves a mechanical application of the principle that to discover how long it takes to progress a specified distance, one divides the total distance to be covered by the distance traversed in a given unit of time. Reasoning in accordance with this direction, the solver calculates that if the frog climbs a distance of 1 ft. a day, it will take him 30 days to climb 30 ft. But the spontaneous and habitual way of approaching this problem happens to be wrong, and therefore the solution achieved as a result of this erroneous direction is also wrong. In order to solve the problem, it is necessary for the individual to realize that once the frog has reached the top of the well he will no longer fall back. The right direction therefore involves the understanding that by the end of the twenty-seventh day the frog has climbed to a height of 27 ft., and that he spends the twenty-eighth day in climbing to 30 ft. and to freedom.   Until the thinker realizes that a direct application of the method in which he has been so thoroughly drilled does not satisfy the conditions of the problem, he will not be able to reach the solution.

And so it is with many problems.   The individual knows all there is to know in order to solve a given problem, but he cannot immediately do so, either because he has no direction (no idea or "slant" as to how to combine the part-responses correctly), or because he has an erroneous direction, *i.e.*, he can see a way which *ought* to solve the problem, but for some reason which he cannot understand, the solution will not come that way.   We have all had the experience of feeling particularly foolish when the solution of a problem we have given up is demonstrated to us.   We say it was really very simple; we knew everything that was necessary for the right answer, yet somehow we were unable to put the pieces of our knowledge together into the correct pattern. Maier would say that we lacked the right direction which would have brought about the proper organization of the items of knowledge.

On the other hand, although the correct direction is essential, it alone will not provide all the conditions for the solution of the problem. The part-experiences must also be available to the subject.   None of the subjects of Maier's Group E, who received the direction but not the part-experiences, was able to solve the problem.   This point is corroborated in an experiment by Birch.[1]   He found that chimpanzees, who had been carefully observed from the time of their birth and had never made any spontaneous use of sticks as reaching tools, were unable to solve a problem which required such a use of sticks for its solution.   But after a period of three days, during which they were given sticks, played with them spontaneously, and in the course of such play came to use them as a prolongation of the arm, they were able to solve the problem without difficulty.   Not only the direction, therefore, but the part-experiences as well were necessary for solution to occur.   As Birch states,

Once the animal has learned to use the stick as an extension of its arm-reach, it is capable of utilizing this knowledge in a wide variety of ways.   *This ability to reorganize previous experiences in accordance with the requirements of a new*

[1] Birch, H. G.   The Relation of Previous Experience to Insightful Problem-solving. *Journal of Comparative Psychology*, 1945, vol. 38, pp. 367–383.

problem-situation is the essential feature of problem-solving.   The ability to select from the available repertoire of recall and reorganize into new patterns of response previously learned . . . items of experience, makes possible an enormous expansion of the adjustive possibilities of an organism (pages 381–382).

But Maier does not attempt to tell us under what conditions the correct direction appears.   If, as he says, one may have a right or a wrong direction in any problem, then one must be able to select the right one in order to be successful.   How *this* selection is achieved Maier does not explain.   It is difficult to believe that the factor of direction itself is independent of selection through trial and error, or through association by similarity.[1]

II. THE ROLE OF WRONG DIRECTIONS IN HUMAN REASONING[2]

PURPOSE

In the first section of this chapter we explained the meaning of Maier's concept of *direction*.   The results of Maier's first experiment showed that, in many cases, the subjects failed at first to solve the problem because they started out with the wrong direction; *i.e.*, they approached the problem from the wrong angle.   The results also showed that subjects often adhered obstinately to a wrong direction, in spite of their repeated failure to solve the problem under its guidance.

In the present experiment, Maier's purpose was to find out whether this wrong direction is an active factor which *prevents* the appearance of the right one, or whether it persists merely because the right direction does not appear.

[1] An experiment in which Maier's pendulum problem was presented to a group of college students has been performed by Weaver and Madden.   Perhaps because of certain differences in conditions, the authors of this investigation obtained results which differentiate less clearly than those of Maier's study between subjects who had received the part-experiences plus the direction, and subjects who had received the part-experiences only.   Ten of the fifty-four subjects of this investigation succeeded in solving the problem.   Of these ten solutions, four were achieved by subjects who had received the part-experiences but not the direction.   In interpreting these results, the authors do not claim that these solutions occurred without direction.   Rather, in accordance with Maier's theory, they suggest that the solutions were arrived at through the integration of the experimentally given part-experiences in terms of the correct direction, and that this direction was selected by the subjects on the basis of their past experience.   (Weaver, H. E., and E. H. Madden.   "Direction" in Problem Solving.   *Journal of Psychology*, 1949, vol. 27, pp. 331–345.)

[2] Adapted from Maier, N. R. F.   An Aspect of Human Reasoning.   *British Journal of Psychology*, 1933, vol. 24, pp. 144–155.

The method involved observing the effectiveness, as an aid to problem solving, of advice calculated to make the subjects hold less firmly to their first assumptions concerning the solution of a given problem. If the advice actually helped to produce solutions, this result would show that the pursuit of a wrong direction is in itself a factor which interferes with successful problem solving. If, on the contrary, such advice failed to prove helpful, this finding would indicate that a wrong direction does not inhibit the appearance of the right one, but continues to operate only because the right direction is not present.

The Problems to Be Solved. The subjects were given the following three problems:

1. *The Two-cord Problem.* In this problem the subject was required to tie together the free ends of two cords hanging from the ceiling to the floor. The distance between the cords was such that it was impossible to reach one if the other was held. Various solutions of the problem were possible. One cord might be lengthened. One cord might be tied to a chair between the two cords. One cord might be pulled in with a pole, while the other cord was held. If the subject solved the problem in any of these ways, he was told to look for another solution. The solution which the experimenter arbitrarily designated as "correct" was to tie a weight (*e.g.*, a pair of pliers) to one of the cords and swing it as a pendulum. Then the subject would be able to hold the stationary cord with one hand, and with the other hand to reach the swinging cord on its approach movement.

2. *The Problem of Making a Stable Hatrack by Means of Two Poles and a Clamp.* The solution was to clamp the two poles together so as to make one long pole reaching from floor to ceiling. This long pole could then be wedged between floor and ceiling, and the clamp used as a hook.

3. *The Problem of Putting Out a Lighted Candle 8 ft. Distant from the Subject.* Sections of rubber and glass tubing had to be fitted together and the whole kept from sagging by clamping it to a rod. The subject would then be able to blow at the candle through the 8-ft. tube.

The initial arrangements of the experimental materials and their combinations into the correct solutions are shown for problems 1, 2, and 3 in Figs. 46, 47, and 48, respectively.

Subjects. The subjects were 384 students in an introductory course in psychology. The subjects were divided into an experimental and a control group.

General Procedure. The three problems were presented together at the beginning of the experimental period. The subjects worked

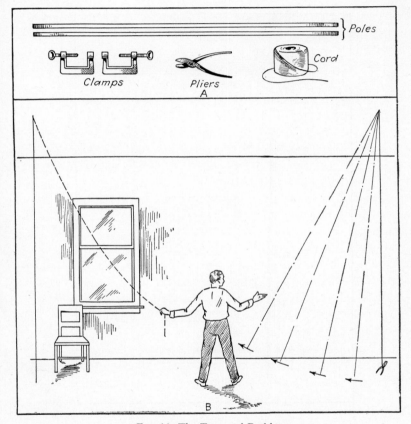

FIG. 46. The Two-cord Problem.

Diagram *A*, the materials available to the subject. Diagram *B*, the correct solution.

individually. They were permitted to attack the problems in any order and to study the materials for solving them for as long as they wished. Each student continued to work until he had achieved an acceptable solution for each problem, or until he had worked for a total period of 1 hr. The subjects did not actually manipulate the materials but described their suggested solutions in writing.

Procedure for the Control Condition.   The 206 subjects who worked under the control condition were presented with the three problems but were given no preliminary instructions.

Procedure for the Experimental Condition.   The 178 subjects who worked under the experimental condition were given a preliminary

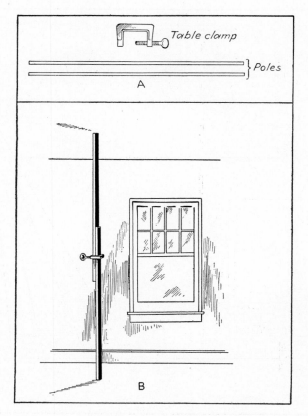

FIG. 47. The Hatrack Problem.
Diagram *A*, the materials available to the subject.   Diagram *B*, the correct solution.

lecture, lasting 20 min., on the solving of problems, which was then summarized in these hints: "(1) Locate a difficulty and try to overcome it.   If you fail, get it completely out of your mind and seek an entirely different difficulty.   (2) Do not be a creature of habit and stay in a rut. Keep your mind open for new meanings. (3) The solution-pattern appears suddenly. You cannot force it. Keep your mind open for new combinations and do not waste time on unsuccessful efforts" (page 147). The problems were then presented.

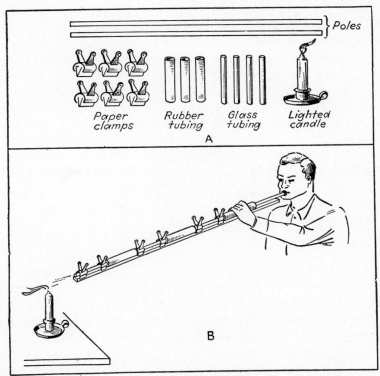

FIG. 48. The Candle Problem.

Diagram *A*, the materials available to the subject. Diagram *B*, the correct solution.

RESULTS

The findings are presented in Table I, page 416.

As the table shows, more experimental subjects than control subjects solved each of the three problems. The difference was greatest for problem 3, the candle problem.

CONCLUSIONS

The only difference in the procedure for the experimental and control groups was the introductory instructions which were given to the experimental subjects. As a consequence, those instructions must have been responsible for the better showing of the experimental group, unless that group was naturally superior to the control in ability to solve problems. In order to test the latter possibility, Maier ran a check experiment in which he compared, not the performance of one group with another group, but the performance of a single group of 169 subjects with and without the preliminary general instructions, on two problems of equal difficulty. Since this group as a whole scored twice as many solutions *after* it was given the instructions as before, there seems little doubt that the superior performance of the experimental group in the main experiment can be explained in terms of the effects of the experimenter's lecture warning against a "one-track" approach.

TABLE I

Showing for the Control and for the Experimental Conditions the Percentage of Subjects Solving Each of the Three Problems

Condition	Number of subjects	Per cent of subjects solving		
		Problem 1	Problem 2	Problem 3
Experimental........	178	50.6	28.7	68.3
Control.............	206	49.0	22.3	47.8

Maier concludes that (1) " ... persistent [wrong] directions which accompany problem-solving actually prevent solution-patterns from appearing." (2) " ... reasoning is, at least in part, the overcoming or inhibiting of habitual responses" (page 153). By "habitual responses" Maier means the wrong direction which the solver first pursues.

DISCUSSION

The foregoing experiment emphasizes the danger of remaining too stubbornly fixed in a single direction when one is trying to solve a problem. Sometimes, the solution to a problem lies under one's very nose, so to speak, yet it is not grasped because one is intent on something else (*i.e.*, one has organized the field in an incorrect way). Although a flashlight lens, a blazing sun, and dry tinder may all be present, it is possible that a concentration on the search for matches occupies the camper so completely that he never thinks of lighting a fire by means of the lens. Maier's preliminary instructions to his subjects made them somewhat skeptical of the directions from which they first attacked the problems and made them more receptive to new angles of approach. The instructions were, therefore, helpful in the solution of such problems as Maier presented, since in each of them, the usual (*i.e.*, the "habitual") direction was a wrong one, and the solution came easily and immediately when the right direction was taken.

But it must be pointed out that Maier's instructions may not prove helpful in *all* task situations. In some situations, the "habitual" direction may be the right one, even though it does not immediately lead to the solution. Perhaps the camper's matches are actually to be found in some obscure corner of his knapsack. If the camper gives up the search too quickly, he may never find them, and if, in addition, he fails to think of using the lens of his flashlight, he may have to eat his food raw.

Maier probably would not call the process of finding the hidden matches "problem solving," since he believes that only situations which require the arousal of new (*i.e.*, "unhabitual") directions for solution may properly be described as "problems." Nevertheless, discovery of the matches adjusts the camper's difficulties and satisfies his need. However, the question as to what is and what is not a "problem" is irrelevant to the value of Maier's instructions in *task* situations. A motivated individual does not know beforehand whether the direction which he first follows, if pursued assiduously enough, will lead sooner or later to the goal, or whether in order to achieve it he will have to abandon the original direction and adopt a new and unusual one. If the situation happens not to be of the kind which Maier calls a "problem," the pursuit of Maier's instructions, instead of aiding, might actually interfere with the attainment of the goal. In such situations, an individual who remained intent on his first and "habitual" direction would do better than one who was too ready to shift his method of approach. However, it is surely true that the following of Maier's instructions in situations which he characterizes as problems would facilitate the achievement of the solution.

III. THE APPEARANCE OF PROBLEM SOLUTIONS IN CONSCIOUSNESS[1]

PURPOSE

In the investigation of human reasoning it is frequently found that, when subjects have completed the solution of a problem, they are

[1] Adapted from Maier, N. R. F. The Solution of a Problem and Its Appearance in Consciousness. *Journal of Comparative Psychology*, 1931, vol. 12, pp. 181–194.

unable to tell the experimenter just how the solution was attained. In fact, they are often unable to supply any information at all about the processes which led to the solution. In response to questions, all they can say is, "I was entirely baffled one moment, and the next moment I had the right idea," or, "The solution just seemed to pop into my head."

Maier wished to discover why people cannot reconstruct the stages by which they achieved the solution of a difficult problem. He therefore states the aims of the present investigation in these terms:

1. "Does the solution develop from a nucleus or does it appear as a completed whole?" (That is, does the solution pass through a process of development, or, as subjects' introspections suggest, does it appear suddenly and completely formed?)

2. "What is the conscious experience of an individual just before the solution is found?"

3. "Is the reasoner conscious of the different factors which aid in bringing about the solution?" (Page 181.)

METHOD

The Problem to Be Solved. The problem was *the two-cord problem*, described in the report of the second experiment. Only the "pendulum" solution was accepted. The room in which the experiment was carried on contained many objects, such as pliers, clamps, pieces of cord, poles, tables, and chairs. In Fig. 46, Diagram *A* illustrates the initial arrangement of the experimental materials, and Diagram *B* their combination into the "correct" solution.

Subjects. The subjects were 116 men and women who were graduate and undergraduate university students. These subjects were divided into two groups.

Experimental Condition. (61 subjects) If the subjects who worked under the experimental condition failed to solve the problem within 10 min., the following "hints" were given:

Hint 1. While walking to the window, the experimenter "accidentally" brushed against one cord, thereby starting it into slight motion. If it was noted that the moving cord was not in the subject's line of vision, the action was repeated.

Hint 2. The experimenter gave the subject a pair of pliers and told him that with the aid of that tool alone the problem could be solved.

Hint 1 was given first.   If the solution failed to follow within a few minutes, Hint 2 was given.   If the solution still did not appear, Hint 1 was repeated.   If this hint failed to prove effective, the subject was shown the solution.

Control Condition.   (55 subjects)   The group which worked under the control condition was not given the hints.   The subjects worked on the problem for at least 30 min. before they were permitted to give up.

RESULTS

Experimental Condition.
  A. 24 subjects (39.3 per cent) solved without the aid of the hints.
  B. 23 subjects (37.7 per cent) solved after the hints had been given.
  C. 14 subjects (23.0 per cent) failed even after receiving the hints.

Maier chose subgroup B for analysis, because only in that subgroup could he analyze the role of the artificial aids in producing solutions. For 19 of the 23 subjects of subgroup B, the solution followed Hint 1 and not Hint 2.   For the 23 subjects the average length of time between the last hint and the solution was 42 sec.

According to their statements, the solution appeared *in parts* for 7 of the 23 subjects who solved with the aid of hints.   For these subjects, the idea of swinging the cord and the idea of attaching a weight to it appeared separately.   The other 16 subjects produced the solution *as a whole*; that is, these subjects first thought of the pendulum principle and then proceeded to "weight" the cord and to swing it.

Of the 7 subjects who solved *in parts*, 6 ascribed the solution to Hint 1.   Of the 16 who solved *as a whole*, 15 failed to report the occurrence of Hint 1; when they were specifically asked whether or not they had seen the cord swaying, most were very vague in their answers but insisted that they were unaware of having been helped by the hint.

Control Condition.   Of the subjects who solved the problem under this condition, 80 per cent solved within 10 min.   Only 20 per cent of the solutions occurred after that time.

CONCLUSIONS

1. In the experimental group, 47 per cent of the successful subjects solved the problem after the initial 10-min. period had elapsed.   In the control, only 20 per cent of the successful subjects solved it after

10 min. This difference shows that the extra working time after the giving of the hints could not have accounted for the increase in solutions following the hints. The short time intervening between hint and solution (an average of 42 sec.) also indicates the efficacy of the hint. Maier concludes that the hints were effective aids, and describes them as " . . . added elements which make the pendulum organization more readily experienced, just as additional points represent the organization of a circle more readily than three points" (page 191).

2. Those subjects who solved the problem in two steps recognized the aid given by the hint. But those who solved it in a single step denied that the hint had helped them. The conclusion Maier draws from these reports is that, when the solution appears gradually, the subject experiences the steps by which it comes about; when the solution occurs in but a single step, the subject cannot recognize the process by which it is established. Thus, according to Maier, the subjects were not aware of Hint 1 because the sudden appearance of the solution dominated consciousness.

Maier summarizes: "The perception of the solution of a problem is like the perceiving of a hidden figure in a puzzle-picture. In both cases (a) the perception is sudden; (b) there is no conscious intermediate stage" between fruitless efforts directed at solution and the dawn of the solution idea (page 193).

DISCUSSION

This study of Maier's touches on issues which have been little explored by the experimental psychologist. It provides a particularly interesting demonstration of the untrustworthiness of introspective reports. Maier proved that his hints were a substantial aid to the subjects in achieving their solutions. Yet many of the subjects denied that they were helped by the hints, and some were even unable to recall that any hints had been given. This observation is corroborated by common experience. Ideas which "pop" into our heads without seeming to undergo any growth or development may often be accounted for by some occurrence in the environment which serves as a "cue" or "hint." We can think of the event responsible for the "explosion" of a new idea as a sort of fuse; but the fuse may be blown up in the explosion which it starts, and it may never be found.

Everyone has had the experience of struggling long and fruitlessly toward the solution of a problem which suddenly seems to solve itself. If, after the solution has been achieved, we try to recall the way in which we arrived at it, we are frequently unable to shed any light on the process. All we can say is that we were pursuing a false "hunch," were "barking up the wrong tree," and that then, all of a sudden, the solution or the way of achieving the solution flashed into being. We cannot recapture the steps which intervened between our last futile efforts and the birth of the right idea. We can only say that the solution idea was wholly absent one moment and present the next, that at first the various parts or aspects of the problem would not hang together correctly but that this confused state then shifted to an "insight" in which all the parts appeared in their proper interrelationships.

Introspection or "self-observation" by adult human subjects in experiments like those by Maier bears out the thesis that the solution of a problem often occurs in a flash (that is to say, by insight), and that such insight frequently appears suddenly and comes about through a process of development which cannot be detected by means of introspection. But the fact that one cannot remember what it was that led to the "insight" certainly does not mean that no causal process preceded it. To assert that a problem was solved because an insight occurred leaves entirely unsettled the crucial question as to what processes produced the insight.

By supplying his subjects with hints, Maier enabled them to produce solutions which they could not have reached without assistance. For a large number of the members of the experimental group, the utilization of the hint was the turning point from the pursuit of incorrect efforts at solution toward the dawn of the solution idea. Yet few of these subjects acknowledged that they had been aided by the hints, and the majority of them actually appeared to have been unaware of their occurrence.

The results of Maier's experiment add to the already considerable fund of evidence which proves that we are entirely unaware of many of the factors which influence our behavior. The stimuli, both internal and external, which act on the human being from moment to moment are exceedingly numerous and complex. Of these stimuli, we are usually conscious at any given moment of but very few, and sometimes of none at all. The result is that when an individual is questioned as to the causes of some given action on his part, he may be quite unable to explain the behavior in terms of antecedent stimulating factors.   Or if he thinks he can give a retrospective account of the origin of his actions, his description may deviate widely from the sequence of events which actually occurred.   Such unconscious falsification may arise in either of two ways: (1) the report may be incomplete in the sense that the subject is able to recall some, but not all, of the stimulating factors which actually controlled his behavior; (2) the subject's report may describe only incidental stimuli which had little or no directive effect on the course of his activities, and thus may omit the crucial behavior determinants altogether.[1]

The fact that our awareness of why we act as we do is characteristically vague and incomplete constitutes a fundamental objection to the method of introspection in psychological research.   Many psychologists believe that even in the study of the simplest processes the method of self-observation gives at best but a partial account of the behavior under investigation.   For example, in one study,[2] subjects were required to determine whether a visually presented symbol was $\times$ or $+$.   As part of the procedure, the intensity of the illumination of the symbol was at times reduced to a point at which the subject claimed that he could not determine which figure he was seeing, and that his judgments as to its nature were therefore pure guesses.   One would expect that the percentage of correctness of the subjects' responses under these conditions would be only 50, *i.e.*, the proportion which would be correct by chance alone.   But the investigator found that at these levels of stimulus intensity, and even at somewhat lower levels, the percentage of correct judgments was considerably above chance.   It was only when the intensity of the stimuli was reduced to a point much below the first "guesswork" level that the proportion of correct judgments fell to 50 per cent.   The same results were obtained when auditory stimuli were used.   Since all the subjects denied having been aware of stimuli which were proved to have affected their behavior, the study shows how unreliable is the method of verbal report (introspection), even for the study of so relatively simple a process as discriminating between two familiar symbols.

[1] As pointed out in Chap. I of this book, the field of the "occult" is replete with examples of such errors.

[2] Baker, L. E.   The Influence of Subliminal Stimuli upon Verbal Behavior.   *Journal of Experimental Psychology*, 1937, vol. 20, pp. 84–100.

When we are concerned with processes as complex as those involved in problem solving, the reliability of results which are obtained by the introspective method alone is very questionable. Some of the most enthusiastic advocates of introspection have cautioned us not to rely too much upon it as a means of investigating complex forms of behavior. Although there are not many psychologists who would repudiate self-observation entirely, it is also true that the great majority insist upon supplementing or replacing it, whenever possible, by observational methods of a more objective sort.

CHAPTER XXIV

IMPLICIT MUSCULAR ACTIVITIES DURING THINKING

INTRODUCTION

There are two general theories concerning the physiological basis of thinking. According to the older of these theories, which we may term the "central" theory, processes of thought, reasoning, imagination, or ideation depend upon or are aspects of complex brain activities. The implied assumption is that motor processes are not a necessary condition of thinking, and that thoughts and ideas may run their courses, even in the absence of all motor activities. On the other hand, the somewhat newer "motor" or ("peripheral") theory assumes that processes of thinking, reasoning, or imagining are as much dependent upon motor responses as upon brain action. Thinking, so viewed, is not a correlate or aspect of cortical brain activity alone but is intrinsically a reaction which functions in terms of complete sensorimotor patterns, with the motor part of each circuit just as essential to the process as the central segment is.

A few adherents of the motor theory of thinking have insisted that thought processes are to be identified with activities of the speech mechanisms. According to this view, when a person is thinking, he is "talking to himself" and his vocal organs are active, even though the movements are microscopic and are detectable only with the aid of sensitive instruments. Thinking and imagining are merely "subvocal" talking. Other exponents of the motor theory have proposed broader interpretations, suggesting that thinking may be based upon implicit muscular contractions involving many other muscle groups as well.

Early Experimental Investigations. Prior to the studies which will be described in the following pages, several attempts had been made to test experimentally the role of motor processes in thinking, but the results obtained by different investigators had been somewhat contradictory. Some of the reported results favored the motor theory, but quite as many findings were of a negative sort. In all probability,

424

these inconsistencies are attributable to the crudity of the instrumental techniques employed and to the lack of adequate experimental controls.   In one experiment, for example, a rubber bulb was placed in the front part of the mouth between the teeth and the tip of the tongue and was connected to a recording tambour.   By this arrangement, slight movements of the tongue exerted pressures on the bulb and such pressures were recorded graphically.   It was reported that every record obtained during "silent thinking" revealed some movement, and the conclusions drawn was that unconscious movements of the tongue[1] actually take place during thinking.   But the technique was imperfect, in that the apparatus attached to the tongue was activated by respiration and by swallowing, as well as by tongue movements. Therefore, the seemingly positive results cannot be accepted without question, since we have no guarantee that the movements recorded were essential to, or even directly associated with, the thought processes.

In another study[2] in which tongue and lip movements were recorded by mechanical means, the response patterns obtained were not the same when the subject was thinking in words "to himself" and when he was saying the same words aloud.   Moreover, some records showed no lip or tongue movements during silent thought.   The experimenter concluded that, since lip and tongue movements are not universal in internal speech, and since, when they do occur, they are not always identical with the movements made in pronouncing the same words aloud, thought activities do not necessarily involve motor expression and are probably "intraneural."

However, in criticism of the above experiment and its conclusions, it may be said that mechanical recording systems are not sufficiently sensitive to respond to all the minute components of an implicit pattern of response, and because of their inevitable inertia they are not capable of following effector changes which occur in rapid succession.   It may be said that many of the weaker elements of a pattern of vocal organ response which would be recorded if the response were overt would lie below the threshold of the instrument's sensitivity when the pattern

[1] Courten, H. C.   Involuntary Movements of the Tongue.   *Yale Psychological Studies*, 1902, vol. 10, pp. 93–96.

[2] Thorsen, A. M.   The Relation of Tongue Movements to Internal Speech.   *Journal of Experimental Psychology*, 1925, vol. 8, pp. 1–32.

is reduced to the implicit level.   Thus, the records would be different even if the patterns of response were actually similar.   Furthermore, when vocal behavior is reduced to the implicit level, it may become much abbreviated and "short-circuited"; that is, it may require a much shorter time and its pattern may be considerably altered in form.   If this is true, the record of an implicit thought pattern would not be simply a reproduction in miniature of the record of an overt speech pattern, even when the two patterns represented equivalent verbal processes (*i.e.*, thinking silently in words or saying the same words aloud).   Such complex relations between the two records could not be identified by their crude, mechanically registered representations on the smoked drum.

Within recent years, however, new *electrical* methods of recording implicit muscular activity have been utilized in the investigation of the motor theory of thinking.   Certain of the results obtained appear to be somewhat more significant than those secured through the use of less sensitive mechanical devices.   The experiments of two investigators who used the electrical recording technique will be described in the following pages.

I. JACOBSON'S EXPERIMENT[1]

PURPOSE

The aims of Jacobson's experiment were: (1) to learn something specific about what takes place in the nervous or neuromuscular system during the process of thinking, and (2) as far as possible, to represent these processes in quantitative terms.

METHOD

Apparatus.   All muscular activity involves changes in electrical potential.   The electrical changes which occur, even in minute implicit muscular contractions, may be detected and recorded by means of a system involving electrodes attached to the subject's body in the neighborhood of the muscles concerned, and connected with a very sensitive galvanometer.   (A galvanometer is a delicate instrument which detects and measures very weak currents of electricity.)   The currents

[1] Adapted from Jacobson, L. E.   The Electrophysiology of Mental Activities.   *American Journal of Psychology*, 1932, vol. 44, pp. 677–694.

set up by the electrical potentials involved in muscular and neural action are called "action currents."

In the present experiment, an extremely sensitive galvanometer was used in conjunction with vacuum tubes, the latter being employed to amplify the weak action currents. Means were provided whereby all deflections of the galvanometer were recorded photographically on a moving film, as a kind of shadowgraph. So sensitive was the apparatus that changes in electrical potential as small as one-millionth of a volt could be recorded.

Subjects. All of the subjects employed had been trained to proficiency in the act of relaxing the skeletal muscles to an extent such that little more than the minimum tonic tension remained. This training in relaxation was very important for the purposes of the experiment because restless movements of subjects who had not been trained to relax would have confused the interpretation of the records. We are not informed as to the number, age, or sex of the subjects.

Procedure. During every test, the subject's eyes were closed and he lay upon a couch in a darkened, quiet, partially soundproof room. All possible sources of distraction were carefully excluded. The subject was instructed to engage in some stated type of imaginative activity (*i.e.*, thinking about or performing a particular movement or imagining some specified situation) as soon as he heard the click of a telegraph sounder, and to discontinue the "mental" activity and to relax any muscular tensions present when he heard a second signal click. The exact instant at which each click occurred was indicated photographically on the same film upon which the muscular activity was recorded. This was accomplished by having an electrically operated bar cast a shadow upon the film each time the sounder was activated.

RESULTS

Imagination of Arm Movements. In one series of tests the electrodes were connected with the flexor muscles of the right arm. The relaxed subject was told that when he heard the first signal he was to *imagine* bending his right arm and when he heard the second signal he was to relax any muscle tension which might be present. During the period of general relaxation preceding the first signal no muscular activity was recorded; the galvanometer recording was a straight line,

Within a fraction of a second after the first signal, however, the record began to show large galvanometer swings which persisted until soon after the signal to relax was given. The results were the same for 20 subjects tested under these conditions.

Six control conditions were imposed. With electrodes attached to the *flexors of the right arm*, the subject was instructed, in different tests, (1) to imagine bending the left foot; (2) to imagine bending the left arm; (3) actually to bend the left arm; (4) actually to bend the left foot 1 in.; (5) to imagine the left arm perfectly relaxed, or to imagine it paralyzed; (6) to imagine extending the right arm.

Negative results were obtained under all the control conditions outlined above; that is to say, no electrical changes in the flexors of the right arm were recorded. These negative results ruled out the possibilities (1) that the deflections observed during the imagination of the right arm flexion are due to the effects of the signal sound upon the subject; (2) that the act of imagination which was tested involved action currents all over the body.

In other test series, the electrodes were attached to the muscles of the right arm and the subjects were instructed to imagine various acts involving activity of the arm muscles. When the instructions were to imagine lifting a 10-lb. weight with the right arm, electrical fluctuations were found to occur in that arm during the process of imagining but not during the foregoing and the succeeding periods in which the subject was instructed to relax. Positive results were recorded, similarly, when the instructions were to imagine the following acts—acts which the subjects agreed invariably involved the right hand: (1) lifting a cigarette to the mouth; (2) pulling a microscope toward one; (3) pulling up one's socks.

Positive results were also obtained for the imagination of rhythmical acts, such as climbing a rope, pumping up a tire, grinding coffee, or turning an ice-cream freezer. In these tests, the galvanometer showed rhythmical alternations of the presence and absence of action currents. Thus, when the instructions were to imagine performing an act involving a relatively brief muscular action (*e.g.*, throwing a ball), only a single brief series of long deflections was recorded, but when the subject was told to imagine throwing a ball three times, three distinct series of deflections were recorded, with rests between.

Do the muscle fibers actually contract during imagination? Or is there merely physiological activity involving electrical changes without any actual shortening of the fibers? In investigating this problem a lever was arranged so that the flexion of the right arm could be magnified eightyfold and recorded photographically along with the action-current record. By means of this device, microscopic arm movements were found to occur when action currents were detected. These findings are in accord with other evidence which indicates that the occurrence of action currents always signifies the shortening of muscle fibers to some extent.

Is motor activity a necessary condition for imagination? The data reported above indicate that implicit muscular activity accompanies the imagining of overt motor acts. But they do not force us to the conclusion that a subject cannot imagine an act without engaging in microscopic movements (that is, that motor activity is necessary if imagination is to occur). Certain tests were made, in an attempt to investigate this fundamental question. The tests and their results were the following:

1. In one test the subject was instructed to cease imagining when he heard the second of the two signals. In a second test he was told to "relax any muscular tension present," at the second signal.

The photographic records were found to be identical in type in both cases. Ceasing to imagine seems to be the same process as relaxation.

2. The subject was given two tests, in both of which he was told to keep the arm completely relaxed at the first signal, and simultaneously to imagine bending the arm or lifting a weight. In one of these tests, the subject was told that in case it was impossible for him to do both, he was to imagine only. In the other test he was instructed that, if he was unable to relax and to imagine simultaneously, he was to keep all muscles relaxed.

Action currents were recorded under the first of these conditions but not under the second. This result suggests that the subject either imagines or relaxes. At any given time he cannot do both simultaneously.

Visual Imagination. Tests of visual imagery were also made with the electrodes placed near the eyeballs. The subject was instructed to imagine visually certain stipulated acts and objects. The records indicated that the eye muscles were implicitly active during the acts of imagining but were relatively inactive before and after the period of imagining.

Verbal Thinking. Positive results were likewise obtained when the electrodes were attached to the tongue or lip muscles and the subjects were instructed to imagine counting or telling a friend the date, or to think of abstract matters such as "eternity," "electrical resistance," "Ohm's law," etc. Marked galvanometric deflections followed the first signal but ceased soon after the second signal. In further tests, as in these, it was found that the deflections of the galvanometer during implicit speech corresponded with those recorded during audible speech.

CONCLUSIONS

According to Jacobson, the results of his experiments lend support to the views that:

1. Processes of imagining or thinking involve implicit motor activity.

2. The motor activity associated with imagining and thinking is an essential condition for such processes, and is not a mere incidental accompaniment of their occurrence.

3. The implicit activity involved in imagining a motor act is for the most part confined to the muscles which would be employed in the overt execution of the act, except in cases in which the act is described verbally or is imagined visually. In such cases, implicit movements of the speech mechanisms or eye muscles occur.

THE RELAXATION METHOD

It is worth noting that Dr. Jacobson's interest in the motor theory of thinking derives largely from his advocacy of the so-called "relaxation method" of treating neurotics and other persons who exhibit excessive muscular tension. In the full "progressive relaxation" procedure described by Jacobson,[1] the patient learns to relax completely all the skeletal muscles of his body, by carefully planned and directed practice for 1 to 2 hr. a day over a period of approximately 75 days. He commonly begins by learning to relax the right arm, then the left arm, then the legs, then the trunk, neck, forehead, and so on. Of especial importance is the fact that during the last 30 days of the program there is intensive practice in relaxing the eye muscles, and finally

[1] Jacobson, E. *You Must Relax*, rev. ed. New York, McGraw-Hill, 1942.

the cheeks, jaws, lips, tongue, and the rest of the speech apparatus. One of the general behavioral principles which can be advanced to justify the method is the fact that most "nervous" people are habitually in a condition of abnormally great muscular tension, largely because of their susceptibility to disturbing emotions of which such tension is a virtually invariable component. If a nervous individual can learn voluntarily to relax all of his skeletal muscles more or less completely (there is always, in the healthy individual, the normal residual of muscular tonus), his "nervous" tension will be eliminated or greatly reduced. Hence, the emotions themselves will be largely dissipated, at least so long as the relaxation can be maintained. Similarly, if thinking typically requires—or is normally accompanied by—contractions in the muscles of the eyes or of the speech apparatus, it follows that if these muscles can be kept relaxed, thinking, at least in terms of visual imagery or subvocal speech, will become impossible. This "elimination of thought," as Jacobson calls it, can be of great practical value for neurotics. Much of their thinking is of such a nature that it readily induces distressing emotional reactions, and these in turn lead to a variety of bodily disturbances. The method is widely used by psychiatrists and psychologists as a specific treatment for insomnia, a condition in which widespread muscular tension and disturbing thoughts are particularly obvious. Jacobson reports it to be of great value for the alleviation of many other neurotic symptoms as well.

II. MAX'S EXPERIMENT ON THE "MOTOR THEORY OF CONSCIOUSNESS"[1]

INTRODUCTION

The investigations of Max have produced further evidence for an appraisal of the validity of the motor theory of thought and imagination.

The question whether thinking necessarily involves motor responses is closely related to the broader problem of the physiological basis of consciousness in general. Normally, thought and imagination are conscious processes; *i.e.*, they are activities of which the individual is aware. If it were shown that there are action currents from muscles

---

[1] Adapted from Max, L. W.   An Experimental Study of the Motor Theory of Consciousness.   III. Action-current Responses in Deaf-Mutes during Sleep, Sensory Stimulation and Dreams. *Journal of Comparative Psychology*, 1935, vol. 19, pp. 469–486.

during all consciousness, even when the subject's experiences are too simple or too fragmentary to be termed "thoughts" or "imagination" the motor theory of thinking would receive strong support. For if such relatively obscure phenomena were invariably accompanied by muscular movements, there would be every reason to believe that the much more vivid experiences which we term "acts of thought" or "imagination" would likewise involve muscular action.

For similar reasons, further support would be given to the motor theory of thinking if it were shown that action currents tend to disappear in sleep (except when the individual is dreaming), to reappear as traces of consciousness reappear, and to become progressively more intense as conscious activities become more complex. Moreover, if we may regard dreaming as thinking during sleep, then evidence of muscle-action currents while a subject is dreaming would be of considerable significance to the motor theory. For these reasons, Max's experiments are highly pertinent to the specific problem treated in this chapter, even though their author terms them more generally studies of the "motor theory of consciousness." The first is reviewed below.

PURPOSE

The aim of the experiment was to test the "motor theory of consciousness" (and therefore the motor theory of thinking) (1) by comparing action-current records obtained when a subject was awake and when he was asleep, (2) by comparing such records when a subject was dreaming and when his sleep was dreamless, and (3) by determining whether action currents occur following the application of stimuli during sleep.

METHOD

Apparatus. The apparatus consisted of two extremely sensitive string galvanometers, each operating in conjunction with a set of vacuum-tube amplifiers. The two amplifier-galvanometer circuits were independent, making it possible to record action currents from two different muscle groups simultaneously. (In most cases one galvanometer was attached to the right arm and the other to the left arm.) Photographic records were made of galvanometer deflections by means of an electrocardiograph camera. The apparatus is represented in Fig. 49.

Subjects. The subjects were 19 deaf-mutes.

Plan of the Experiment. Totally deaf subjects were used because the hands of the deaf are the seat of both their "oral" and written speech, and therefore the speech musculature of such subjects is far more accessible to experimental investigation than is the speech musculature (larynx and pharynx) of normal hearing subjects. Max

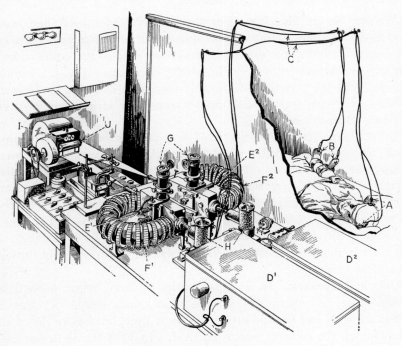

FIG. 49. Max's Apparatus.

This is a duplex apparatus which makes it possible to record action potentials from two parts of the body independently, or to record muscular action potentials and cerebral action potentials simultaneously, as in the case illustrated.

A, brain electrodes; *B*, arm-muscle electrodes; *C*, shielded wires connecting electrodes with amplifiers; D^1D^2, amplifiers; E^1E^2, string galvanometers; F^1F^2, the powerful horseshoe electromagnets of the galvanometers; *G*, housings of the quartz filaments of the galvanometers; *H*, projection lamps; *I*, camera; *J*, narrow window through which shadows of vibrating quartz filaments are cast upon moving photographic film or paper. (*Adapted from a drawing supplied by courtesy of Popular Science Monthly.*)

thought that any records of implicit hand or arm movements obtained from deaf-mutes would be especially significant for the motor theory of consciousness. Furthermore, records taken from the hands or arms of normal hearing subjects would provide an excellent control, since normal subjects do not think or speak with their hands.

Procedure. All the tests were made when the subject was asleep or preparing to go to sleep on a bed in the laboratory. Action-current records were obtained from the subject under both waking and sleeping conditions, and after the application of certain stimuli during sleep.

RESULTS

Waking versus Sleeping. For a time after the subject had been told to go to sleep, a considerable amount of action-current activity was recorded, but as the subject became more relaxed and comfortable, the action currents fell to a low level or disappeared entirely. Among the different subjects there were wide variations in the magnitude of initial action currents, but in all cases the currents showed a progressive decrease as sleep came on.

Quiet Sleep. In the records of 134 sleep periods for which no dreams were reported and during which there were no overt movements, there were 41 instances (31 per cent) in which action currents disappeared entirely during sleep. In 83 records (62 per cent) the action currents did not disappear altogether, but diminished progressively to a minimum of 0.9 to 0.1 microvolts. In 10 records (7 per cent) the response in quiet sleep was above 1 microvolt. In 69 per cent of the records, therefore, muscular activity was not entirely absent during dreamless sleep.

Dream Responses. In 33 cases, series of large action potentials (mean value, 3.67 microvolts) were recorded during sleep. After such action currents had been in progress a short time, but before they had disappeared, the subjects were awakened. In 30 of the 33 cases, subjects reported that they had just been dreaming, and in accordance with the experimenter's request, they proceeded directly to write out accounts of their dreams. In 6 cases, although introspective reports indicated that the dream content was primarily visual, the record showed definite action currents from the fingers. It was inferred, therefore, that verbalization processes may be involved in many "visual" dreams.

In one case, the experimenter pressed upon a subject's chest at a time when there had been no action-current activity for a considerable period. Following this stimulation, strong action currents were recorded from both arms. The subject was then awakened. He reported a dream of a barbecue party, at which he was excitedly arguing with a fellow deaf-mute as to how best to insert the iron spit on which the meat was to be roasted. The argument had been carried on by means of sign language.

To see whether dreams ever occurred without action-current activity in the arm muscles, the subjects were awakened on 62 occasions during periods of electrical quiescence. In 53 of these cases the subjects reported no dreams, but in 9 cases they claimed to have been dreaming. However, these 9 cases were not definitely negative, for in 5 of them the content of the dream was primarily visual, and the seat of the motor activity may have been the eye muscles, which were not in the galvanometer circuit at the time.

Duration of Dreams. The duration of the action-current activities in dreaming subjects is of interest in relation to the problem of the duration of dreams. Many psychologists have held the view that even those dreams which seem especially long to the dreamer are in reality compressed into the brief period of a few seconds. However, the periods of action-current activity which seemed to be definitely related to dream experiences were usually 2½ min. or more in length.

Response to Stimulation during Sleep. At various times, the experimenter presented auditory, tactual, and other stimuli to the subjects while they were asleep. Care was taken not to use stimuli so intense as to awaken the subject. Under these circumstances, action currents were recorded in 122 out of 187 cases. Hence, even weak sensory stimulations normally aroused definite, though implicit, motor responses.

Control Observations on Normal Hearing Subjects. During 33 tests on normal subjects during sleep no instance of action-current activity in either arms or legs was noted. But when the subjects were awakened during these periods of electrical quiescence, 10 dreams were reported. It is unfortunate that eye and vocal-organ records were not obtained for these subjects. However, the absence of arm and finger activity in hearing subjects during dreams suggests that the manual-action currents recorded during the dreams of deaf-mutes are primarily linguistic in origin. An attempt was made to find out whether similar action currents would be detected in the tongue and lip muscles of normal hearing subjects during dreams. However the discomfort induced by the apparatus was so great that only four subjects were able to fall asleep under these conditions, and in those four cases, even during dreamless sleep, the minimal response registered by the tongue was 6 microvolts, compared with an average of 1 microvolt from the arms of the same subjects.

SUMMARY

Max summarizes the results of his experiment as follows:

1. The transition from the waking to the sleeping state was accompanied by a progressive diminution of action-current responses from the peripheral musculature of both deaf and hearing subjects.

2. In deaf subjects, sleep resulted in the complete absence of action-current activity in only a small proportion of the cases. In the majority of cases, the action currents persisted but at a markedly diminished intensity.

3. The onset of dreams in deaf subjects could be detected in most cases by the appearance of large action-current responses in the arm and finger muscles. Such currents were unaccompanied by overt muscular movements and were distinguishable from those due to motility changes (restless movements of hands, etc.). Dream responses were sometimes induced by special sensory stimulation and were of longer duration than the few seconds frequently ascribed to dreams.

4. External stimulation introduced during sleep frequently evoked action currents in the peripheral musculature of the deaf.

Max points out that several questions call for further investigation. Among them are the following: What is the significance of the slight amount of residual muscular activity recorded during dreamless sleep? Is the quantity of residual action-current activity an index of depth of sleep? Is there a relation between depth of sleep and the latent period of action-current response to sensory stimulation? How much of the motor response observed originates in speech mechanisms, and how much in the musculature generally? Is the demonstrated motor activity an essential concomitant or a mere by-product of conscious experience? Does the magnitude of the action-current response vary with the intensity of consciousness?

III. FURTHER STUDIES OF THE "MOTOR THEORY OF CONSCIOUSNESS"[1]

A second series of experiments was later conducted in which Max obtained action-current records from the hands of deaf-mute subjects

* [1] Adapted from Max, L. W. Experimental Study of the Motor Theory of Conscious-

during the transition from sleep to the waking state, during periods when the subjects reported kinesthetic imagery, and during thinking. As before, control tests were run with normal subjects. The apparatus and general method were identical with those of his earlier study. The results of this second investigation may be summarized briefly as follows.

Awakening. When a sleeping deaf-mute subject was suddenly awakened by the experimenter, there was always a violent onset of action-current activity. Much of this activity could be attributed to the overt limb movements connected with waking. But in 20 cases in which no visible movements occurred, there was, nevertheless, a steady increase in the amplitude of action-current response as the subject gradually awakened. In all subjects, a maximum of electrical response was reached soon after awakening. Then, as the subject relaxed, preparatory to the experimenter's presentation of a thought problem, the amount of electrical activity diminished.

Kinesthetic Imagery. The subjects were told to imagine such acts as holding a wriggling snake behind the head, holding a squirming fish in the hands, telegraphing an S O S signal, typewriting, etc. Under these circumstances, the electrical records showed that the subjective experience of a kinesthetic image as reported by the subjects was usually accompanied by actual contractions of the muscles which would be active in the performance of the acts imagined. In fact, the muscle contractions were sometimes large enough to be detected without any amplification. It was also found that below a certain microvoltage, the magnitude of which varied with different individuals, the subjects did not kinesthetically perceive muscular contractions, which, although feeble, were definitely present.

Abstract Thinking. Abstract thought problems, such as adding, multiplying, and dividing mentally, reading, and selecting appropriate sentences in multiple-choice tests, etc., were given to the subjects. During the solution of these problems, action currents of hand and finger muscles occurred in 84 per cent of the cases with 18 deaf subjects, as compared with only 31 per cent of the cases with 16 hearing subjects. (Such action currents as were recorded from the finger muscles of hearing subjects may be at least partially explained by the

ness; IV. Action-current Responses in the Deaf during Awakening, Kinaesthetic Imagery and Abstract Thinking. *Journal of Comparative Psychology*, 1937, vol. 24, pp. 301–344.

fact that many normal individuals perform arithmetic calculations with the aid of the fingers.)   The two groups differed also with respect to the average amplitude of reponse, which was 3.4 microvolts for the deaf and only 0.8 microvolt for the hearing subjects.   But when the subjects were instructed to imagine that they were performing tasks which would involve the use of the arm muscles, the percentage of positive arm responses from deaf and hearing subjects was substantially the same.   *Hence*, during thought problems the arms and hands of the deaf yielded larger and far more frequent responses than did the arms and hands of the normal subjects.

Discussion

In this chapter we have described several investigations upon the motor theory of thinking and of consciousness.   The results of the experiments both of Jacobson and of Max lend substantial support to the motor theory.

Jacobson found that implicit motor activity occurred during think-ing and imagining.   He found, moreover, that motor activity was most intense in the limb muscles which would be activated if the imagined act were actually being executed or, in the case of visual imagery and verbal thinking, in the eyes and speech mechanisms, respectively. On the basis of these findings, Jacobson concluded that motor activity is an essential condition for thinking.

In his investigation of the motor theory of consciousness, Max dis-covered that dreamless sleep was normally accompanied by a cessation or a diminution of muscle-action currents, but that in dreaming an increase in the currents generally occurred.   Like Jacobson, he found that imagining the performance of an action produced responses in the body parts which would be involved in the overt commission of the act.   Max also found that when deaf-mute subjects were dreaming (which may be regarded as thinking during sleep), or were solving abstract problems in the waking state, action currents were usually recorded from the arm muscles, whereas in normal hearing subjects very little activity in this part of the body was detected.   According to the motor theory of thinking, the thinking of deaf-mutes should often involve activity in the manual organs which they use in their "sign language," just as the thinking of hearing subjects should often in-volve activity in the vocal mechanisms.   The results of Max's investi-gations, therefore, are in accord with the postulates of the motor theory.

However, it cannot be inferred from these results that the motor theory of thinking is to be regarded as fully substantiated. Although the above data constitute strong *supporting* evidence, they are not *conclusive* evidence. The data show that muscular activity is usually, if not always, correlated with thinking. Moreover, to many psychologists Jacobson's results prove that motor response is an essential condition for thought. However, it remains to be demonstrated that the motor response is the most essential process of thought itself.

CHAPTER XXV

PROJECTION AND THE THEMATIC APPERCEPTION TEST

INTRODUCTION

Projection is one of the most common and one of the most important ways in which human beings perceive and think about objects in the external environment. According to Symonds[1] it may be defined as "the reference of impulses, thoughts, feelings and wishes originating in the person himself to persons and objects in the outside world." The process is usually (some say always) unconscious, in the sense that the individual does not know that he is coloring and perhaps distorting his apprehension of external objects and people by imbuing them with his own characteristics.

Most accounts of projection emphasize the point that we typically tend to project our undesirable traits.[2] Thus a low-grade workman may blame his tools for his poor work, instead of himself, which means that he projects his own inefficiency into the instruments he uses and perceives them rather than his own clumsiness as at fault. An individual who is a habitual cheater may console himself with the reflection that everyone cheats anyway. Bernard Shaw is said to have remarked that the chief punishment of a liar is that he cannot believe others. The paranoiac projects his feelings of hatred and suspicion of other people and develops delusions of persecution, that is, convictions to the

---

[1] Symonds, P. M. *The Dynamics of Human Adjustment*, p. 296. New York, Appleton, 1946.

[2] According to some definitions, projection always is defensive and involves the ascription of only undesirable traits to objects and to other persons. Thus Healy *et al.* define projection in psychoanalytic terms as a "defensive process under the sway of the pleasure principle whereby the ego thrusts forth on the external world wishes and ideas which, if allowed to penetrate into consciousness, would be painful to the ego." (Healy, W., A. F. Bronner, and A. M. Bowers. *The Structure and Meaning of Psychoanalysis*. New York, Knopf, 1930.) To the reviewers, such an interpretation seems unduly narrow. Indeed, Freud himself came to use projection in the broader sense in which it will be employed in this chapter. (See *Totem and Taboo* in *The Basic Writings of Sigmund Freud*. New York, Modern Lib., 1938.)

effect that other persons hate him and are trying to do him harm. This projection of undesirable traits into the environment is typically a kind of defense reaction, in that we thereby protect ourselves from having to recognize our own faults—or find excuses for our own short-comings—by perceiving the very same defects in other things and people.

However, it also is possible to project desirable characteristics, or for that matter, traits which are not commonly judged as being either good or bad in any definite sense of the words.   Thus children, and individuals from primitive cultures, tend to project many of their own traits into inanimate objects, and animistically endow hills, streams, the sun, the wind, and the rain with characteristics which only living organisms like themselves possess.   Similarly, children—and many adults also—project their own traits into animals and perceive and think about animals anthropomorphically, that is, as feeling, thinking, and desiring in an altogether human fashion.   Poets and novelists fre-quently project their own emotions and conflicts into their characters and create individuals whose traits and experiences reflect—and thus often strikingly reveal—the authors' own feelings and desires.

Projection was first described by Sigmund Freud, the founder of psychoanalysis, in 1894.[1]   It is very unlikely that Freud was the first observer of human nature to realize that the tendency to interpret external objects in terms of ourselves is a conspicuous and ubiquitous human characteristic.   However, he was the first person in the field of psychology to give the process a name, to define it, and to make clear its importance.

During the past 50 years, psychologists and psychiatrists have be-come increasingly aware of the significance of the projection process. They have come to realize that this process is typical of much of the perceiving and thinking of normal individuals, and that it is also re-sponsible for many of the gross misinterpretations of the external world which characterize serious mental disorders.

Furthermore, in recent years psychologists and others have de-veloped a number of different projective tests, in which the test situa-tion and the instructions to the subject are so designed that the lat-

[1] Freud, S.   The Justification for Detaching from Neurasthenia a Particular Syndrome: The Anxiety Neurosis. *Collected Papers*, International Psychoanalytical Library, No. 7, Vol. 1, pp. 76–106.   London, Hogarth, 1924.

ter's responses tend to be projections of his feelings, attitudes, thoughts, and desires.   The administration and interpretation of these projective tests have become the most widely used method for discovering certain more or less hidden aspects of a subject's personality and for obtaining a rapid appraisal of his personality as a whole.

The first important projective test, and the one still in widest use, is the Rorschach.   This test is described in most textbooks of general psychology.   It may suffice here to say that it consists of a standard series of 10 different ink blots.   These are shown to the subject, one at a time, and for each the subject is asked to state what he sees, what it might be, what it makes him think of.   Since each ink blot is an essentially meaningless figure, different people perceive it very differently and are led to think of very different things when they observe it. Thus projective reactions are very apt to occur.   Examples of such reactions are given by Lindner,[1] who finds that to see "eyes looking at me" in either of two of the Rorschach cards is a typical paranoid[2] reaction, and that to interpret the "human figures" which many see in a certain ink blot as "puppets or marionettes" is characteristic of schizophrenics[3] who feel themselves directed, influenced, and manipulated by other persons who are hostile to them.   In this way the Rorschach test may reveal aspects of a subject's feeling and thinking of which the subject is quite unaware, and which could be discovered only with difficulty, if at all, by any sort of direct questioning procedure.[4]

Another widely used projective test, and the one with which the present chapter is primarily concerned, is the Thematic Apperception Test (the TAT) devised by Morgan and Murray and first mentioned

[1] Lindner, R. M.   Some Significant Rorschach Responses.   *Journal of Criminal Psychopathology*, 1944, vol. 5, pp. 775–778.

[2] As we have said, a paranoiac perceives in other persons the malice and hatred that actually are within himself.

[3] Schizophrenia, like paranoia, is one of the most serious types of psychosis, *i.e.*, of severe mental disorder.

[4] Actually, the content of a subject's Rorschach responses, *e.g.*, whether a particular ink blot suggests a human being to him and, if so, what he imagines the latter to be doing, is only one of his reaction characteristics which is regarded as important.   Even more significant are certain general aspects of his responses, such as the total number of things the ink blots suggest to him, whether his response is determined more by the ink blot as a whole or by some detail of it, how he is affected by color (in those cards in which it appears), and so on.

in the literature in 1935.[1]   This test consists of a standard series of 20 pictures, each of which depicts some event, usually of a dramatic nature.[2]   For example, in one picture a woman is clutching the shoulders of a man whose face and shoulders are averted as if he were trying to pull away from her; in another a boy is huddled on the floor against a couch, with his head bowed on his right arm and a revolver on the

Fig. 50. One of the TAT Pictures. (*Reproduced by permission of the Harvard University Press.*)

floor beside him.   The subject is shown the pictures one at a time and is asked to make up a story about each of them.   The objective characteristics of the picture, of course, set some limits to his narrative. For example, any story about the last-mentioned picture normally would include reference to the boy and to the weapon.   However,

[1] Morgan, C. D., and H. A. Murray.   A Method for Investigating Phantasies: The Thematic Apperception Test.   *Archives of Neurology and Psychiatry*, Chicago, 1935, vol. 34, pp. 289–306.

[2] One of these pictures is reproduced in Fig. 50.

within these limits, a very wide range of interpretations is possible. Thus, in the above picture, the boy may be viewed as struggling against the temptation to kill someone, as having done so already, as having witnessed a murder the perpetrator of which has escaped leaving his weapon behind him, etc. His emotional state may be characterized as one of remorse and guilt, or terror, or anger. If the subject conceives that it is anger, he may describe the object of the boy's hostility as being his father, his mother, a brother or sister, a girl, a male acquaintance, etc. Naturally further details of the story, such as the events which led to the tragic situation and what the final outcome will be, may vary endlessly.

Since the stimulus situation, and the experimenter's instructions, permit the subject to read into the picture almost anything he happens to think of,[1] opportunity for projection on a considerable scale is afforded. The subject can invent almost any story he pleases. The narrative which he does invent is regarded as being expressive of his own personal feelings, motives, and problems. Thus, for example, if a subject's story is analyzed for indications of aggressiveness, it is often found that the degree of aggressiveness which is suggested by this analysis is corroborated by evidence obtained through clinical and biographical study of the subject. Hence the subject appears often to project his attitudes into his stories and to reveal in this way significant personal traits of which he himself may be unaware. (There are several other important types of projection tests. Discussion of these, however, is beyond the scope of this chapter.)

The discussion so far probably has given the impression that (1) projection is a type of reaction the existence of which is completely substantiated, and that (2) the so-called "projective tests," especially the TAT, have been proved to yield projective responses capable of a clear and direct interpretation. According to certain psychological viewpoints, this impression might be regarded as entirely correct. However, experiments which actually attempt to produce and study the phenomenon of projection have been very few in number. Most psychologists, although they may be inclined to accept the concept of

[1] It is instructive to compare the wide latitude of responses permitted in the TAT with the restriction of reactions characteristic of most intelligence-test questions, *e.g.*, in such a question as, "Which of the following words is the opposite of loyal: enemy, treacherous, thief, coward, jealous?"

projection on the basis of general psychological theory and of clinical evidence from individual case studies, would welcome *experimental demonstrations* of its occurrence. In addition, psychologists who use projective tests as one of their clinical procedures would appreciate *actual proof* that a subject's feelings and attitudes do influence his test responses, even though they may regard the existence of such a relationship as highly probable. Among the very few investigations in which an experimental control of projection has been attempted are the studies of Bellak which constitute the principal basis of this chapter.

BELLAK'S EXPERIMENTS ON PROJECTION AND THE THEMATIC APPERCEPTION TEST[1]

PURPOSE: GENERAL PLAN

The aims of Bellak's experiments were to "test the existence of the hypothetical process of projection," and to find out whether projection actually occurs in responses to the TAT.

The general plan of the experiments was to obtain a subject's responses (*i.e.*, his stories) to a number of TAT pictures under normal conditions, then to obtain his responses to an equivalent series of TAT pictures after an emotional attitude of resentfulness and hostility (in one experiment, of depression) had been aroused in him. If people do tend to project their emotions, and if the TAT provides an appropriate situation for such projection, the subject's responses after the arousal of the emotion should contain more indications of agressiveness (or of depression) than they did before the emotion was present.

EXPERIMENT I

Subjects. The subjects of Bellak's first experiment were seven Harvard University students, all members of the Reserve Officers' Training Corps. They were met by the experimenter in connection with a personality examination, and were entirely ignorant of the purpose of the experiment.

Material. The material consisted of 10 of the 20 TAT pictures, divided into 2 sets of 5 pictures each. The pictures selected were as

[1] Adapted from Bellak, L. The Concept of Projection, an Experimental Investigation and Study of the Concept. *Psychiatry*, 1944, vol. 7, pp. 353–370.

follows:

Set A
    (*a*) A surgical operation with a young man in the foreground
    (*b*) A man on a couch, with another man bent over him
    (*c*) Cowboys at rest
    (*d*) A man with raised fist
    (*e*) Two boys standing in an archway
Set B
    (1) A mother and son
    (2) A boy on a couch with a revolver on the floor (the picture previously described)
    (3) A nude man and a nude woman faced by a clothed woman holding a baby
    (4) An older, gray-haired man facing a younger man
    (5) A man gripped from behind by several disembodied hands

Three subjects were given Set A first, then Set B; the remaining four subjects received Set B first and Set A second.

Method. The method was as follows. Each subject was interviewed individually, in a room which, in order to minimize distractions, contained little more than a couch, a chair, and a table lamp. A microphone concealed in the lamp transmitted the subject's oral story, in some sessions to a stenographer, in others to a recording device, each located on another floor of the building. During the interview, the subject was asked to lie down on the couch; the experimenter sat behind him.

The subject received these standardized instructions:

This is an opportunity for free imagination. I want you to make up a story. Tell me what has led up to the situation shown in the picture, describe what the characters are feeling, and tell me what the outcome will be. Speak your thoughts out loud as they come to your mind. Use your imagination and make up anything you please.

After these instructions, the subject was given the first picture. As soon as he had completed his story about it, he returned the picture, was given the next one, and so on. If a subject asked whether he should stop or should continue his narrative, he was told that this was always for him to decide, and that whenever he felt he had said all he wanted to say he was simply to hand back the picture. The experimenter made no comments whatever on the subject's stories until the response to the fifth picture had been made.

After each subject's fifth story, however, and also after his sixth, seventh, eighth, and ninth stories, the experimenter criticized his production sharply, using a caustic tone of voice. The criticisms, which were identical for all subjects, were as follows:

[After the fifth story], "These stories are about the worst I ever heard. They are illogical and unstructured. Could you try to get some better ones?" [After the sixth story], "There are still no ideas in it, no life, no nothing. Could you try some more?" [After the seventh story], "This is some of the damnedest stuff I have ever got. Try this one." [After the eighth story], "You are pretty hopeless. See what you can do with this one." [And after the ninth story], "Well, this is your last chance to show if you have anything in you. Go ahead."

After a subject had responded to each of the 10 pictures, the session was ended. His stories, which had been recorded either in shorthand or mechanically, were now typewritten. Next they were carefully analyzed by the experimenter and also by two other psychologists who were unacquainted with the aims of the investigation. The analysis was for the express purpose of detecting evidence of aggressiveness in the subject's stories, and was accomplished by counting every word of an aggressive nature in them. It was found that the three counts of aggressive words made independently by the three judges differed only slightly; hence the figures presented under "Results" in Table 1 are the averages of the three counts.[1]

In order to illustrate the difference between stories containing a relatively small and a relatively large number of aggressive words, two narratives given by two different subjects in response to picture 2 in Set B are reproduced below.[2] In each story the words scored as aggressive are italicized. The aggressiveness scores for the two stories are 2 and 8 words, respectively.

(1) I'd say that he was a boy, probably in high school or perhaps just in high school, that, ah . . . he's been disappointed by his latest report card and he had received a *scolding* from his family . . . a little bit disappointed but possibly more disappointed in the fact that he was being *punished* by getting a bad mark . . . very unhappy at the time and, ah . . . and he probably feels at the moment that life

[1] In addition, each judge rated each story, considered as a whole, on a five-point scale for aggressiveness. The results obtained by this method were judged to agree closely with those obtained by the method of counting aggressive words and are not presented by Bellak in his published article.

[2] These two stories, not presented in the published article, were kindly furnished by Dr. L. Bellak.

is pretty dreary and bitter and he doesn't have much to look forward to . . . thoroughly unhappy but seems to me to be rather passing. He will probably get over it and he will go back to school, maybe work a little bit harder and probably next time he will get a little better marks.

(2) Well, just like this young fellow, this is his *gun* down there. I will tell it like this. This young fellow has led an unhappy life. His father and mother have been *mean* to him. He's led an unhappy home life. He is about ten years old. He comes home from school and things have been going badly. He comes home and his father is *threatening* his mother. He sees his father's *gun* lying there and rushes over and gets his father's *gun* and he *kills* him, *kills* them both, and after he's done that and sees what he's done and that he has *killed* them he leans over and cries and then he calls up the police and they take him away. The next one I'll make up a happy story.

Results. Table I gives the results of the experiment.

TABLE I

The Total Number of Aggressive Words Given by Each Subject, for Each Set of Pictures, under the Two Conditions, without Criticism and with Criticism

Set and condition	Number of aggressive words				
	Individual subjects				Total
	Ma	Fr	Am		
Set A, without criticism..............	0	3	2		5
Set B, with criticism.................	12	11	9		32
	Mc	Ha	Go	De	
Set B, without criticism..............	8	4	3	4	19
Set A, with criticism.................	6	1	2	4	13

The results show that the group which had Set A without criticism and Set B with criticism gave more than six times as many aggressive responses (words) to Set B than they did to Set A. However, the group which had Set B without criticism and Set A with criticism made somewhat fewer aggressive responses to the latter set. In all probability, the reason for these apparently inconsistent results is that the pictures of Set B were intrinsically more likely to elicit stories containing an aggressive content than were those of Set A. Hence, for the second group, even the experimenter's criticisms could not produce more aggressive responses for Set A.

However, if one compares the number of aggressive words given for each set with and without criticism, the effects of the criticism become more evident. Set A without criticism yielded a total of 5 aggressive words, an average of 1.67 per subject, but with criticism it yielded 13, an average of 3.25. Similarly, Set B evoked 19 aggressive words without criticism (average, 4.75), but with criticism it elicited 32 (average, 10.67).

Discussion. The interpretation of these results would appear to be as follows: The subjects usually gave evidence of being disturbed by the criticisms, even though some of them denied that they were much concerned. One subject said he felt completely discouraged; another, who stuttered, had more difficulty in speaking when criticized. A few subjects exhibited hand tremors and paling or blushing of the face. Two subjects expressed their resentment openly by blaming the poor quality of the pictures; one blamed the experimenter for the vagueness of his instructions. The subjects, therefore, tended to become disturbed, angry, and resentful. They could not express their resentment fully and directly, since the experimenter was to them an "authoritative person." Hence they tended to express it, at least in some degree, by projection. That is, after having been subjected to criticism, they tended to invent stories involving more aggression on the part of the characters in them.[1]

However, the results also show that the nature of a picture, as well as the feelings and attitudes of the subject, influences the story which a subject devises; witness the considerably greater number of aggressive responses elicited by Set B than by Set A under normal conditions. This finding suggested to Bellak a second experiment, in which the two sets of pictures would be equated beforehand for the number of aggressive reactions which they normally produce.

EXPERIMENT II

Purpose. The aim of Bellak's second experiment was to determine the effect of criticism by the experimenter upon a subject's responses to TAT pictures, when the pictures used under the "without criticism" and the "with criticism" conditions are equated for the number of aggressive responses which they evoke under normal circumstances.

---

[1] In Table I this conclusion is directly confirmed only for subjects Ma, Fr, and Am, who had Set A without and Set B with criticism. However, additional evidence for the conclusion is derived from a comparison which Bellak made between the stories told for Set B with criticism, in the present experiment, and the stories told for the same pictures by 25 individuals who took the entire test for another purpose and under normal conditions (*i.e.*, without criticism). The stories obtained in the present experiment contained on the average almost three times as many aggressive words.

Subjects.   The subjects were 10 Harvard University students, who were sent to the laboratory by the Student Employment Office and who were paid for their services.   None of them had studied psychology, and all were ignorant of the purpose of the experiment.

Material.   The material consisted of two sets of five TAT pictures each.   The pictures in the two sets (C and D) were matched for the degree to which they suggested aggressive stories by counting the number of aggressive responses (words) made to them by about 50 subjects in other investigations.   These subjects had taken the test under normal conditions; that is, the experimenter had listened to and recorded their stories with no comments of any sort, critical or otherwise.

The two sets consisted of the following pictures:

Set C
    (*a*) A man with upraised arm and open mouth
    (*b*) A rural scene
    (*c*) A man gripped from behind (also used in Experiment I as picture 5 of Set B)
    (*d*) An operation (formerly picture *a* of Set A)
    (*e*) A man shaking his fist
Set D
    (1) A young woman clutching a young man
    (2) A boy on a couch with a revolver on the floor (formerly picture 2 of Set B)
    (3) A man's silhouette against a window
    (4) Two boys standing in an archway (formerly picture *e* of Set A)
    (5) A gray-haired man facing a younger man (formerly picture 4 of Set B)

Five subjects were given Set C first, then Set D.   For the remaining five subjects the order in which the sets were given was reversed.

Method.   The method was exactly the same as in Experiment I, except for some minor changes in the precise wording of the instructions to the subjects.   The criticisms were identical with those of Experiment I, and the analysis of the stories was made in the same way as it was in the first experiment.

Results.   Bellak does not give the results of his second experiment in the detailed fashion that he did for his first experiment.   However, he reports that the average number of aggressive words per subject before criticism was 12.6, and after criticism 23.7, giving a statistically reliable difference of 11.1 words.[1]

---

[1] For a definition of statistical reliability of a difference, see Chap. I p. 9.

Although data are not presented for each set of pictures separately, it is stated that the two sets proved to be about equal in their capacity to evoke aggressive responses after criticism. These results are interpreted as providing further evidence for the occurrence of projection in TAT responses. The reasons for this interpretation are identical with those already presented in connection with the discussion of Experiment I.

EXPERIMENT III[1]

Purpose and General Procedure. Bellak continued his study of projection and the TAT with a third experiment in which he used post-hypnotic instructions or suggestions,[2] instead of criticism of his subjects in the normal waking state, to induce a mood of anger and hostility. It is well known that feelings and attitudes of virtually any desired kind can be induced readily by an expert hypnotist in a good hypnotic subject. Bellak's plan was to have his subjects give stories as responses to TAT pictures, first under a control condition (*i.e.*, under normal circumstances), and second under the experimental condition, which in this investigation was a condition of hypnotically induced anger.

Subjects. This experiment was performed at St. Elizabeth's Hospital, in Washington, D.C. The subjects consisted of a group of five Navy corpsmen assigned to the hospital as male nurses for psychiatric patients, and a group of five male theological seminary students, who were being given clinical training and doing nursing duty at the hospital. The motive of the subjects for volunteering was primarily an expressed curiosity about hypnosis, as well as a desire to find out whether they personally could be hypnotized and to learn how it felt to be hypnotized. All of them were quite unaware of the purpose of the experiment. However, they were fully informed of its purpose and results after their work in it had been completed. The 10 men

---

[1] Adapted from portions of Dr. L. Bellak's doctoral dissertation (as yet unpublished) at Harvard University.

[2] In posthypnotic instruction, or posthypnotic suggestion, a subject is directed while in the hypnotic condition to respond in certain prescribed ways at some specified time after he has been awakened from that condition. Usually the subject also is told that he will be amnesic for the instructions, that is, that he will not remember having received them. Hence a good hypnotic subject, given the posthypnotic suggestion that he will take a drink of water at exactly 3 P.M., will get the water at the stipulated time when he is no longer in the hypnotic state, but will not have any knowledge of why he performs the act.

used as subjects were chosen from among a total of 50 volunteers as being in the experimenter's judgment those most capable of deep hypnosis and most able or willing to comply in full with the posthypnotic instructions.

Material. The material was the same two sets of TAT cards that had been used in Experiment II, except for the substitution of another TAT card for one of the cards of Set D.

Method. The control condition was given first for all the subjects. In this condition the subject was presented in succession with the five pictures of one set, in the same manner and with essentially the same instructions as had been used in Experiments I and II for the first five pictures before criticism. The five corpsmen received Set D under this condition, the five theological seminary students received Set C.

Each subject was then hypnotized deeply and was given the following posthypnotic instructions:

> After you have awakened you will feel tremendously angry inside; you will be boiling and awfully angry without realizing that you are angry and without remembering that you are angry because I told you to be.
>
> After you awaken you will not remember anything that went on in hypnosis, but you will be angry inside, without realizing it.
>
> You will tell stories about five pictures. After you have finished the fifth story about the fifth picture, you will suddenly say that you were awfully angry inside. You will suddenly remember everything that went on in hypnosis, and at the same time your anger will cease and you will feel very happy, relaxed, and comfortable.[1]

It should be noted that the subjects were told to be angry, yet at the same time were told to be unaware of the emotion. The reason for this stipulation was that Bellak thought that the clinical significance of responses to the TAT would be particularly well demonstrated if projection of feelings of which the subject was unaware could be produced. In order to find out whether the posthypnotic instructions were being followed, the subjects were closely observed and carefully questioned before they were given the first picture of the experimental

---

[1] The last sentence of the instructions is typical of the way in which posthypnotic instructions usually end. Its primary aim was to make certain that none of the subjects would suffer any harm from the experience—for example, that none would be left with any permanent amnesia for the events of the hypnotic condition, or would be subject to any bewilderment, confusion, and the like. Such precautions are necessary, especially in view of the common belief that being hypnotized may constitute an injurious experience.

set, and after they had finished their stories for the third and fifth pictures of this set.   The records of any individual who did not comply fully with all the instructions were discarded, and not considered in the results.   As one evidence of the success of the posthypnotic suggestions with the subjects used, Bellak notes that frequently he observed in them such evidences of anger as fast breathing, a flushed face, and strong pencil pressure (while writing their stories).

The five stories given in the experimental condition are designated as "stories with hypnosis," since the subjects produced them under the influence of the posthypnotic instructions.   These stories were

TABLE II

*The Total Number of Aggressive Words Given by Each Subject, for Each Set of Pictures,
under the Two Conditions, Normal and with Hypnosis (Control and Experimental)*

Subjects	Number of aggressive words					
	Individual subjects					Aver-age
Corpsmen:						
Set D, normal condition..............	20	17	21	21	17	19.2
Set C, with hypnosis..................	37	41	60	56	39	46.6
Seminary students:						
Set C, normal condition..............	3	22	19	9	12	13.4
Set D, with hypnosis..................	42	49	32	21	33	35.4

not given orally by the subjects, as was the case in the control condition (and in Experiments I and II), but instead were *written* by them. This variation in the procedure was introduced because it was felt that the subjects would be more apt to comply fully with the instructions if they could work by themselves without having to face, and talk to, the experimenter.

All of the stories were carefully analyzed, as in the previous experiments, in order to determine the number of aggressive words which they contained.   In the present investigation the analyses were made by a doctor stationed at the hospital, who was unfamiliar with the nature of the experiment.

Results.   The results of Experiment III are given in Table II.

Discussion.   The results show clearly that in the experimental condition, under the posthypnotic instructions to be "tremendously angry" though without awareness of such an emotion, the subjects told stories which contained a much larger number of aggressive words than did their stories told in the control condition. This result was obtained for both groups of subjects and for both sets of pictures, and is reported by Bellak to be statistically reliable. Comparison with the results of Experiment II (in which virtually the same sets of pictures were used) shows that the average number of aggressive words under the control condition was approximately the same for the seminary students in the present study and for the 10 subjects in the former experiment, the averages being 13.4 and 12.6, respectively. However, the average number of such words given by the corpsmen in the control condition was considerably greater than the above figures. This result suggests to Bellak that the personalities of the corpsmen tended to be more aggressive than those of either the Harvard University students of Experiment II or the theological seminary students of the present investigation. Also, under the hypnotic condition, both groups of subjects in the present experiment gave a larger average number of aggressive words than had been obtained in either of the earlier studies, with any group or any set of pictures. In explanation of this difference, it is very probable that the posthypnotic instructions were more effective for inducing anger than were the personal criticisms used in Experiments I and II. It also is conceivable that the instruction to remain unaware of the anger resulted in a more extensive projection of the emotional attitude.

Experiment IV

Bellak also performed a fourth experiment[1] which will be reported briefly. The subjects were 12 of his acquaintances. Posthypnotic suggestions again formed the basis for the experimental condition. In this investigation the subjects first reacted to five TAT pictures in a normal state. The procedure was identical with that used in the control condition in the first three experiments except that the subjects *wrote* their stories instead of relating them orally. The subjects were then hypnotized (as in Experiment III) and were given posthypnotic instructions calculated to arouse *depressed* feelings. Specifically they were told: "After you have awakened, you will feel awfully unhappy and depressed inside, without being aware of it. You will feel as if somebody very dear to you were seriously ill, or had died."

---

[1] Bellak's fourth experiment also is an unpublished part of his doctoral dissertation.

Otherwise the instructions were essentially the same as in Experiment II. As before, the subjects, upon awakening from the hypnotic condition, were presented with five TAT pictures and wrote a story about each of them.

The principal result was that a much greater number of depressed words and phrases was given under the hypnotic condition than under the normal one. The average number of such items, for all five pictures taken together, was 10.4 for the 12 subjects in the normal state and 26.2 for the subjects in the hypnotic condition. The difference of 15.8 is statistically reliable. Furthermore, every one of the 12 subjects gave more depressed words and phrases under the hypnotic state than under the control condition. In some cases the differences were striking. For example, two subjects gave a total of 3 and 4 words, respectively, in the normal state, but gave totals of 44 and 33, respectively, while under the influence of the posthypnotic instructions.[1, 2]

DISCUSSION

In this chapter, projection has been dealt with from two viewpoints: (1) as a way of perceiving and thinking about objects and people in the external environment, and (2) as a kind of reaction which projective tests—among them the TAT—are believed to induce in significant fashion and degree.

The results of the experiments of Bellak support the conclusion, favored by clinical evidence and psychological theory, that human beings do project their "impulses, thoughts, feelings and wishes" into external objects. For in these studies the subjects projected the resentment and aggression resulting from personal criticism, and anger or depression hypnotically induced, into a selected series of pictures about which the subject could invent any stories he pleased.

As we have said, projection is both a way of perceiving external objects and a way of thinking about them. According to Bellak, the projective process may be regarded as arising from a readiness, a set,

[1] However, it must be noted that no attempt was made to equate the pictures used in the two conditions.

[2] Bellak also reports the results obtained by hypnotizing a female nurse and giving her posthypnotic instructions to feel "extremely happy." This subject, in response to TAT pictures, "gave stories full of happiness to the extent that even a horse in one of the pictures was said to have a happy expression."

to react in accordance with some feeling or attitude.[1] A vindictive person tends to perceive most other people as malicious and hostile, and in his thinking about them he is apt to imagine them as acting in accordance with those characteristics. These reactions are due to his own attitudes of hatred and hostility, which keep him continually ready or set to make such interpretations. The tendency often is protective or defensive, in that it may help to prevent an individual from recognizing his own undesirable traits and thus aid him in maintaining his self-esteem.

However, as Bellak demonstrated in his first experiment, as a rule, projection does not occur without reference to the objective nature of the stimulus. An individual who tends to project his hostility will not do so in equal degree into all other persons. Some of the people he meets may display a friendliness so patent that even he will find it difficult to perceive them as hostile (though if he is an actual paranoiac he may construe their friendliness as designed to hide their evil intentions). But if the behavior of another person is ambiguous, in the sense that it does not exhibit clear indications of either hostility or friendliness, then the individual who is characterized by many animosities and who habitually projects his hatreds is very likely to regard him as an enemy.[2]

Bellak's results also indicate that the TAT really is a projective test in that the subjects tended to devise stories which contained more aggressive (or depressed) words after feelings of resentment (or sadness) had been aroused in them. Hence Bellak's data provide important experimental evidence for the opinion prevalent among psychologists who use the test, that the TAT pictures are well designed for the purpose of eliciting projective responses.[3]

It is worth reiterating that the attitudes, etc., which the subject projects may be only partly known, or at times quite unknown to him. Thus a subject in his various stories may repeatedly introduce the theme of a father's mistreatment of his son and the consequent resentment and antagonism of the latter. Even if the subject asserts that his own attitude toward his father is one of affection and gratitude,

---

[1] For a definition of "attitude" see Chap. XXII.

[2] For a brief discussion of the effects of attitudes on the perception of objects of different degrees of clarity or ambiguity, see Chap. XXII.

[3] This statement does not in any sense imply that the TAT is the only test which elicits significant projective reactions.

the clinician would be likely to conclude that the subject's narratives offered strong evidence to the contrary, or at least evidence of ambivalence[1] and conflict. If this viewpoint is correct, then a principal value of the TAT is to reveal motives and attitudes of which the subject is ignorant (often through repression[2] and rationalization), or which he refuses to admit are his characteristics. As we have said, another value of this test (and of many other projective tests as well) is that the experimenter, through his analytic study of the subject's responses, may obtain clues to the probable personality traits of the subject more quickly than can be accomplished by any other available means.

Finally, one might note a rather obvious point, namely, that projection typically is a fault, a deficiency, rather than an asset, in that it tends to produce misinterpretations of external objects and people. It is apparent that this process may corrupt in some degree the perceiving and thinking of almost everyone even if it is desirable rather than undesirable traits that are projected. And in some gravely disturbed neurotics and psychotics it acquires a magnitude, grossness, and persistence that seriously impair their adjustment to their environment, especially their social adjustments to other people.

[1] "Ambivalence" means the simultaneous existence of contradictory or antagonistic emotions or attitudes (for example, love and hate) toward the same person.

[2] For a definition of repression, see Chap. V.

CHAPTER XXVI

THE OPINION-POLLING TECHNIQUE AS USED IN A STUDY OF THE EFFECTS OF BOMBING ON JAPANESE MORALE

INTRODUCTION

The sensational failure of the public-opinion polls to predict the election of Harry Truman in 1948 brought the beanstalk growth of sampling techniques forcibly to public attention. During the period of 15 or 20 years before that date, the notion that one could tell what all of the people thought by asking some of them what they thought had developed into a flourishing and lucrative enterprise. Entrepreneurs of the most varied sorts came to rely upon public-opinion polls to determine what the country would buy from them. Candidates for political office wrote speeches, manufacturers changed the shape of ironing boards, movie and radio magnates discarded productions, and public relations experts mounted million-dollar campaigns, all in accordance with the decision of "the sample."

Basically, the method of the sample is one which is made use of in almost every branch of scientific investigation. In order to find out the effect of a newly compounded drug on diabetes the physiologist tries it on a limited number of those afflicted with the disease. The artillery officer fires a few shells from a new shipment. The chemist tests several fragments of a vein of ore-bearing rock. In each case, the assumption is that if the sample is a true sample—that is, chosen without bias, completely at random—what is found out about the sample will be true of the whole also.

The novelty of the sampling technique is therefore not in its principle, but in its specific application to social situations. In this application, as the interpretation of the preelection polls of 1948 made clear, the technique is open to serious error. How the numerous possibilities of error and distortion can be eliminated or minimized, and in general, the nature of the limitations of sampling methods in social

458

situations, are matters that have received a great deal of study. As an illustration of some of the techniques that have been devised for the purpose of increasing the reliability of the method, we have selected an investigation of "the effects of strategic bombing on Japanese morale." This study is considered significant because it represents a use of the method of the random sample in an especially difficult and complex situation.

With the heated arguments which have been carried on as to the social value of opinion polling, the present chapter has nothing to do. Nor is it especially concerned with the errors in application of method or in interpretation of results that gave rise to the gross miscalculation of the 1948 election. It is the opinion-sampling method itself which is the principal subject of our study.

THE EFFECTS OF STRATEGIC BOMBING ON JAPANESE MORALE[1]

PURPOSE

It was the task of the Survey to discover whether changes in the morale of individual Japanese civilians were related to the series of low- and high-level, day and night, incendiary, high-explosive, and atomic bombings of the Japanese home islands which began in earnest in June, 1944.

PRELIMINARY CONSIDERATIONS

Definition of Morale. The first step was necessarily a definition of morale, the characteristic to be measured. Most authorities, according to the authors of the Survey report, agree that "morale of a group in wartime is as 'good' as its consistent long-term readiness to persevere against the enemy and against hardships, and to work together under leadership to achieve the common goals."[2] In terms of components that might be evaluated by polling techniques, the Survey considered the following as indicative of morale:

1. The individual's personal willingness to go on with the war, or negatively, his war weariness; the attitude he would have toward national surrender.

[1] Adapted from The U.S. Strategic Survey (Morale Division). *The Effects of Strategic Bombing on Japanese Morale.* Washington, D.C., U.S. Government Printing Office, 1947, pp. vi + 262. Dr. Burton Fisher was the director of the study and was in charge of its planning, the field operation, the analysis of the results, and the preparation of the final report.

[2] *Ibid.*, p. 10.

2. His personal acceptance of the purposes of the war and his sense of identification with the common goals.

3. His confidence in the possibility of victory.

4. His confidence in the ability of his military leaders to achieve victory and to protect the people from attack; his belief in the will and ability of the civilian leaders to take care of the home front.

5. His feeling of group solidarity, as manifested in his conviction that all elements in the population are working together and making equal sacrifices.

6. His psychological and physical well-being.

In short, morale is defined for the purposes of the Survey as "confidence in victory, and social solidarity."[1]

Factors Influencing Japanese Morale.   In order to determine how morale, defined in this manner, was affected by aerial bombing, it was necessary for the Survey to assess the effects of other factors which might have influenced it, such as the military and naval defeats which brought the war steadily closer to the home islands; the war weariness and privations deriving from Japan's long-drawn-out military adventure beginning with the "China incident" in 1932; the maladministration of the war effort and of the home front; United States propaganda broadcasts and air-borne leaflets; the growth of communist and other sentiment politically opposed to the government; the entry of the Soviet Union into the war; and the efforts of Japanese authorities to suppress defeatism by fostering both hope of a last-minute "divine" intervention and a determination to resist invasion.   In addition to such changing or growing influences, it was necessary to consider the effect upon Japanese morale of the stable political, social, and religious structure of the Japanese society.

METHOD

In order to ascertain the effects of the air attacks on civilian Japanese morale, the U.S. Strategic Bombing Survey resorted primarily to the method of polling a random sample of the Japanese people.   To corroborate the results of that poll, several particularly well-informed Japanese were questioned at length, and intensive study was made of confidential reports prepared during the war by such Japanese agencies as the regular police, the special (or "thought" police), whose task it

[1] *Ibid.*, p. 11.

was to suppress defeatist and antigovernment sentiment, and the Japanese Cabinet Board of Information. The present chapter, however, is concerned only with the sampling technique.

The circumstances under which the polling was carried out imposed certain handicaps and limitations on the directors of the Survey. Since the study concerned the feelings and attitudes of the people during the air bombardment, the questioning had to be begun as soon as possible after the surrender of Japan and concluded with the least possible delay. The longer the time that elapsed after the beginning of the occupation, the less reliably would responses mirror the changes in morale before that date. Actually, the work of interviewing was completed by December 29, 1945, four months after American troops had landed on the islands, and about a year and a half after the heavy bombing attacks had begun.

The time limitation on the collection of data created a space limitation as well. It was necessary to minimize, as far as might be, the amount of traveling to be done by the interviewing teams and their military escorts, because of hazards in entering areas not yet occupied by United States authority. As a consequence, the Survey left unrepresented about 10 million (*i.e.*, about 14 per cent) of the Japanese population, namely, the people residing in the eastern parts of Kyushu and on islands other than the two main ones. However, since these people had been spared heavy bombing, the directors of the Survey consider that their omission does not seriously affect the results.

The necessity for coping with tendencies which might bias the findings was clearly recognized. The Japanese who were interviewed might be likely to try to curry favor with their conquerors or to oppose them defiantly. The interviewers, as representatives of the Strategic Bombing Survey, might tend either to maximize or to minimize the effects of bombing attacks. Between analysts and respondents lay the barrier of language and the incalculable possibilities of distortion produced by deep-rooted differences in culture patterns. The reader will recognize in various aspects of the procedures adopted by the Survey an effort to cope with these problems.

The polling method used by the Survey can be studied most readily by dividing it into four component elements: (1) the selection of the population sample, (2) the actual interviews, (3) the recording of the responses, and (4) the treatment of data obtained.

1. Selection of the Sample. *The first step was to make sure that the sample included a balanced representation of the major gross divisions of the Japanese people.* In addition, it had to be so chosen as to permit close study of those groups of people who were particularly affected by bombing, specifically, the residents of large, industrial cities, of atom-bombed Hiroshima and Nagasaki, and of rural regions to which there had been a large migration of evacuees.

To select its sample, the Strategic Bombing Survey resorted to the method of *stratification.* Instead of choosing names purely at random from a list of the entire Japanese population, *e.g.*, by methodically taking every thousandth name in the census list, the population was first divided into sections, or "strata," on the basis of a priori ideas as to the factors which might have had an effect upon morale, and samples were then selected from each stratum. The procedure is analogous to that of the assayer who decides to test samples of ore from the top, middle, and lowest sections of a vein, rather than from a random collection of specimens representing the vein as a whole.

The criteria governing the division of Japan into strata, for the purposes of the Survey, were (1) the population density of the area, (2) the extent and nature of its bombing experience, and (3) its location within the country.

The strata were of two basic types: incorporated cities (*shi*, in Japanese) and rural areas (*gun*).

Strata of *shi* were established according to the following principles:

1. There are four major industrial areas in Japan, each of which suffered heavy bombing: the metropolitan districts of Tokyo-Yokohama, Osaka-Kobe, Nagoya, and Yawata. Within the first three of these areas lie five of the six largest cities of Japan. Because of its size, each of these five cities was constituted a stratum in itself, thus assuring its representation in the sample. Those parts of the industrial areas lying outside these five cities were classified into six additional strata, some of which represented heavily bombed *shi*, others lightly bombed or unbombed *shi*. Thus, eleven strata in all were created out of the four industrial areas.

2. Kyoto, one of Japan's six largest cities, which lies outside the major industrial areas and was very lightly bombed, was made a stratum in itself.

3. Nagasaki and Hiroshima, together with the adjacent rural areas

in which evacuees from those atom-bombed cities took refuge, were constituted separate strata.

4. All cities of over 100,000 population, not already accounted for, were incorporated into one or another of six strata, according to their size, the extent to which they had been bombed, and their location in Japan.

5. *Shi* of less than 100,000 population were classified into 11 strata, according to the extent and character of the bombing they had undergone, their location in Japan, and their rate of population change during the period 1930–1940. Population change during this decade was chosen as a criterion for the establishment of strata on the supposition that it might be related to any special characteristics of recently developed industrial regions.

Whenever there was doubt as to which stratum a given *shi* should be assigned to, first consideration was given to the degree of its bombing experience, second to its size, and third to the region in which it was located.

Rural areas were divided into strata according to the following principles:

1. Three rural strata were made up of the *gun* areas surrounding the Tokyo-Yokohama, the Nagoya, and the Osaka-Kobe industrial regions. These were areas in which great numbers of the nearby urban residents had sought haven.

2. Nine additional rural strata were made up according to population density, the extent of bombing, and location within Japan. *Gun* of a population density below 140 persons per square mile were not classified into strata and are therefore not represented in the sample.

In all, 31 strata were created from the Japanese urban areas and 12 from the rural districts. The populations of the urban strata varied from 300,000 to 600,000, while those of the rural strata varied from 2,000,000 to 4,000,000. Hence, though the population of Japan is about one-third urban, the average number of persons included in each urban stratum was only one-eighth the average number in the rural strata. This discrepancy, which might seem to produce an overrepresentation of the urban population in the total sample, is justified by the directors of the Survey on the ground that the urban areas suffered almost all of the heavy bombing and therefore required the most intensive study. In calculating the frequency of opinions expressed by the Japanese generally, the lack of balance between the proportions of urban and rural residents interviewed was redressed by appropriate statistical weighting.

From each of the strata (except those which consisted of single cities), one city or rural district was chosen at random for inclusion in the sample. The total number of interviews to be made was first divided between the urban and the rural populations in a ratio which made it approximately eight times more likely for an urban resident to be interviewed than for a rural resident. The proportion corresponds to the population ratio between urban and rural strata described above.

TABLE I

Age, Sex, and Education of the Subjects of the Sample

Education, years	16–29 years, per cent		30–44 years, per cent		45–70 years, per cent	
	Men	Women	Men	Women	Men	Women
0–5	3	3	9	11	37	61
6	8	16	23	33	17	15
7–8	43	33	45	30	29	14
9–11	34	42	13	22	10	7
Over 12	12	6	10	4	7	3
Total	100	100	100	100	100	100

The total number of interviews designated for all urban and all rural strata, respectively, was then allocated among the individual strata in proportion to their populations.

The actual persons to be interviewed were chosen at random from census lists and other population records by sampling teams which visited each of the 43 points selected to represent the 43 strata.

Table I above shows the constitution of the entire sample in terms of age, sex, and education.

Interviews usually took place about two weeks after the sampling teams had done their work. The only persons on the lists who were exempted from the interviews were members of the armed forces (since the Survey was assigned the task of studying civilian morale only); those under sixteen or over seventy; the seriously ill, demented, or otherwise unfit; and the institutionalized. Interviewers were not always able to locate all the persons listed, since some had moved away or could not be found. However, the interviewers were expressly forbidden to substitute other persons, and they were required to make every effort to trace and interview missing ones. The purpose of this rule was to prevent any possible bias which might affect the random character of the sample. The interviewer, had he been allowed to substitute respondents of his own choice for those on the list whom he could not locate, might have emphasized in his selection people of stable residence, or those whose accents he readily understood, or men, or women, or some other category. The result would have been an overweighting of the sample in one direction or another.

A total of 4,075 persons was designated by the sampling teams, of whom 2,523 were in cities, 1,189 in rural areas, and 363 in areas hit by atomic bombs. In all, 3,135 of these were actually interviewed.

2. The Interview. The selected sample of Japanese civilians described above was questioned by members of ten teams, each consisting of nine interviewers on the average. Initial contact with the person to be questioned was made by a Japanese-speaking officer who was not of Japanese ancestry. This was done to avoid arousing suspicion that reports of the interview would fall into the hands of the Japanese "thought police," an attitude that might have developed had the respondent believed that the program was under the control of his countrymen. The actual questioning was carried on by American citizens of Japanese ancestry (Nisei), apparently because it was impossible to recruit a sufficient number of linguistically qualified people who were not of Japanese origin, to man the teams. Few of the questioners were "ideally qualified" for the task, according to the Survey report. To compensate in part for their lack of professional training for the job at hand, the interviewers attended a three-day course of lectures, and they held at least two practice interviews before going into the field. During this training period, recordings of the practice interviews they had made were played back to them, discussed, and criticized. Other means used to maintain interviewing standards included precise and detailed instructions to the interviewers and, while the survey was in progress, visits to the teams by a group of roving experts. The work of each team was under the direct supervision of a trained social scientist.

At the beginning of the interview, the following formula was used in order to "structure" the field, *i.e.*, to set the person interviewed in the proper frame of mind:

> I am Mr. (name of interviewer), representing the American government. We are much interested in the wartime experiences (or conditions) and present conditions of the Japanese people. In this connection we are interviewing people of various classes, ages, and occupations, both men and women. We would be grateful, therefore, if you would answer a few questions. Please be assured that what you say here will be used only by the American authorities and will be released to no Japanese person.[1]

When it appeared advisable, paraphrased versions of the formula, or of parts of it, were used to reinforce the "structuring" in the course of the interview. The interviewer was urged to encourage answers by respondents in terms of their personal experiences and attitudes, to seek for the reasons that lay behind the attitudes, and to make sure, as far as possible, that the answers were made with reference to that time in the past which most of the questions concerned. It was emphasized that the interview would not serve its purpose if it produced only "yes," "no," or simple factual answers.

The avoidance of "yes," "no," and simple factual answers clearly differentiates the method of the Morale Survey from the method employed by many commercially sponsored opinion polls. However, it creates serious difficulties in the analysis and statistical treatment of the responses. On the basis of such answers as the Survey demanded, it would be impossible, for example, to calculate what percentages of the total population declared that their morale was, or was not, affected by bombing. Defenders of the Morale Survey method claim, however, that the procedure employed avoids a spurious objectivity in estimating opinion, an "objectivity" that is arrived at only by forcing responses into a few rigid patterns predetermined by the polltaker.

The insistence of the directors of the Survey upon avoiding such rigid patterns is shown by the way in which the series of questions was arranged. The question series began with queries which required little thought to answer and which were designed to put the respondent at his ease. Questions eliciting the expression of attitudes concerning morale followed. However, use of the words "air raid" and "bomb-

[1] *Ibid.*, p. 167.

ing" appeared only in questions posed toward the close of the interview. The reason for this arrangement of questions was the desire
to avoid suggesting that the respondents answer questions in terms
specifically of the air attacks. Such suggestions might prejudice the
very findings which the Survey was assigned to discover.

Much care went into the wording of the questions. Prepared first
in English, the questions were translated into colloquial Japanese by
an analyst of Japanese ancestry who was familiar with contemporary
Japanese speech. They were then retranslated into English and
compared with the original version. A number of changes were made
following preliminary test interviews. The English version of the
questions which follows is a literal translation (and therefore unavoid-
ably awkward) of the series as it was given:

1. In general, how are things going with you now?
2. Do you feel you are better or w orse off now than you were during the war?
3. What things worried you most during the war? Any other worries?
4. What sort of work were you do ing, from the beginning of 1945 to the end of
the war?
5. How was your working capacity during this period as compared with other
years?
6. How were your working conditions during this period? [To be asked only
of those gainfully employed]
7. Now, we were talking a little while ago about what you were doing from
January 1945 to the end of the war. How many working days were you absent
from your work during this period? [To be asked only of those gainfully employed]
8. What prevented you from going to work on those days? [To be asked only
of those gainfully employed who missed work days in 1945]
9. During the war, what did you think was Japan's greatest strength in waging
the war?
10. During the war, what did you think Japan's greatest weakness was?
11. In regard to the way your leaders conducted the war, what did you think of
it during the war?
12. In regard to the way your leaders took care of the home front welfare,
what did you think of it during the war?
13. How did you feel about the changes in government during the war, at the
time the changes occurred?
14. Did the people's attitudes and conduct toward each other change during
the war?
15. Did you think that all kinds of people in Japan suffered alike in the war?
16. As the war wore on, did you ever begin to have doubts that Japan would
win?
17. When did you first feel certain that Japan could not attain sure victory?

18. Did you at any time during the war come to a point where you felt you could not go on with the war?

19. How did you feel when you heard that Japan had given up the war?

20. In regard to the policies taken by occupation-troop headquarters, how do you feel things are working out?

21. Now that the war is over, how do you think you and your family will fare in the next 2 or 3 years?

22. In your opinion, what changes should occur in Japan in the future?

22a. What about the Emperor?

23. During the war, what did you think would be in store for you and your family, if Japan lost the war?

24. Did you know about American propaganda leaflets which were dropped during the war?

a. What were the leaflets about?

b. What did you think of it (them)?

25. During the war, did you ever hear about any anti-Japanese radio broadcasts?

a. What did you hear?

b. What did you think about it?

26. During the war, did you think that your home town would be bombed? Or did you think it would be spared?

27. During the war, did you think that Japan would be bombed or did you think it would be spared? [To be asked only of those who did not believe their home town would be bombed, in reply to question 26]

28. When the American planes bombed Japan, on which side did you feel the responsibility lay?

29. How did you feel about the Americans, during the war?

30. During the war, what did you think about the way the newspapers and the radios described the air raids on Japan?

31. Did you ever hear about the Americans announcing they were going to bomb cities before they actually did? (What did you think about it?)

32. What do you recall about the first time American planes flew over Japan? (What did you think about it?)

33. In your opinion, how well was your home town protected against air raids?

34. What did you think about the atomic bomb?

35. What bombing experiences have you personally had?

[Questions 36 to 41 to be asked only if respondent lived in a bombed area during a bombing period]

36. Can you tell me more about your experiences? (Tell me what happened, what you did, how you felt.)

37. What kind of bombing do you think is worse—day or night?

38. What kind of bomb do you think is worse—incendiary or explosive?

39. Were you more and more afraid as the raids continued, or did you get used to them?

40. How good were the special measures and welfare services after the raids?

41. How much help did the people who were not bombed give to those who were?[1]

3. The Record. Each interviewer took full notes in the course of the interview. As soon as possible thereafter he wrote up his report. Sound recordings were made of about one in every seven of the interviews. Substantial excerpts from two of the interview reports follow:

SAMPLE INTERVIEW 1

Personal Data: Housewife, 65 years old. Four years of schooling. Religion, Sect Shinto. Interviewed in suburb of Nagasaki, November 16, 1945.

Responses:

Q. In general, how are things going with you now?

A. The problem that is uppermost in my mind is the food situation, but as my husband and I are old we don't need too much—the rationing is pretty slim but we are both around 70 years old so we haven't much more time to live. We have a niece living with us that adds to our comfort—I worry about my husband because he is partially invalid. I'm relieved the air raids are over; that was a strain on my nerves—especially trying to help my husband down to the shelters.

Q. Do you feel you are better or worse off now than you were during the war?

A. I feel pretty good now. (Why?) Well, the raids are over for one thing and my husband will become better, I hope. During the night when it rains it's bad for him to be in the shelter. We haven't really too much to worry about. We've lived a full life so it doesn't matter what happens to us now—I'm not as bad off as those with 2 or 3 children that have to worry about the food rationing.

Q. What things worried you most during the war?

A. My worry was for my husband. It was 3 years ago when he was attacked with paralysis and now one side of his body is lightly paralyzed. When there were air raids I had to carry him down to the shelters—sometimes when the raids were too often I used to cover him up with quilts and go to the shelter. Then I worried the most 'cause I was afraid he would be hurt from some debris or bomb.

Q. What sort of work were you doing, from the beginning of 1945 to the end of the war?

A. I was a housewife—I'm old now so I can't go out to work—my husband works in the post office and my niece works in a factory which helps us to get along.

Q. How was your working capacity during this period as compared with other years?

A. There was no change in my capacity. I did the same old housework—and my health was good so I tried to run the house as before—the only difference was the lack of food that cut down the meals.

Q. During the war, what did you think was Japan's greatest strength in waging the war?

[1] *Ibid.*, pp. 162–164.

A. I thought that our spirit, which was to fight to the end, was our strength. The soldier will also fight to the end and the people will back him to the limit. Also, I heard constantly on the radio that our Air Force and Navy was stronger than America's and I believed that—we also brought out all our idols to pray to them for strength to wage war against America.

. . . .

Q. In regard to the way your leaders took care of the home front welfare, what did you think of it during the war?

A. At times I hoped for more services and welfare; it wasn't too much but the leaders were handicapped because they didn't have the material to aid the people. The rationing was a little hectic and also I suppose the leaders with money bought food from the black market—but also others did too.

. . . .

Q. Did the people's attitudes and conduct toward each other change during the war?

A. Of course they would change—everyone became a little tense with nervousness. Each one was worrying about food and how to feed the family. I guess it was natural for them to worry about themselves, but we also tried to aid the war by obeying the rules.

Q. Did you think that all kinds of people in Japan suffered alike in the war?

A. I don't believe everyone suffered alike—the farmers and those above the common people had more to eat—the upper class could buy in the black market while those without money had to depend entirely upon rationing—people with children suffered the most.

Q. As the war wore on, did you ever begin to have doubts that Japan would win?

A. I had some doubts every time we were raided. I always thought if airplanes could fly over Japan we would have to fight hard—so when I heard about the Doolittle planes over Tokyo, I thought for a moment that we might lose if we didn't work and fight hard.

Q. When did you first feel certain that Japan could not attain sure victory?

A. I was only certain when the war ended—I was not sure until it ended. I listened to the radio and it seemed as if we were doing all right—of course if it wasn't for the atomic bomb the government would not have surrendered.

Q. Did you at any time during the war come to a point where you felt you could not go on with the war?

A. No. I felt downhearted and scared every time the planes came over, but I never thought I would quit fighting or praying for victory.

. . . .

Q. In your opinion, what changes should occur in Japan in the future?

A. That I can't say—I can't think that deeply. There should be changes I guess, but I don't know what.

Q. What about the Emperor?

A. He should be kept for the sake of the people—he was never wrong—he was the one who ended the war—I believe no one should touch our Emperor.

Q. During the war what did you think would be in store for you and your family, if Japan lost the war?

A. I always thought we would win but after the surrender rumors began to fly that the Americans would enslave the women and shame them and all the young girls left for some place also. But in a week they returned and I heard they felt foolish upon returning. . . .

Q. When the American planes bombed Japan, on which side did you feel the responsibility lay?

A. I believe the responsibility lies with the Americans—war is war and soldiers must fight soldiers but to kill innocent children and people is bad—why, over at my sister's place in Yamanishi machi, they bombed all the residential districts and completely neglected the military points which were on the other side of the tracks—that is inhuman. Also the use of the atomic bomb was inhuman—all those lovely girls being cremated by the use of such a bomb!

Q. How did you feel about the Americans, during the war?

A. I thought they were inhuman—when they were killed, I was happy; when any of our soldiers were killed, I cried. At Okinawa my husband's two brothers died. They told me that Americans were savages, just wanting to kill and kill.

Q. During the war, what did you think about the way the newspapers and the radios described the air raids on Japan?

A. They reported fairly well. Of course sometimes I felt that it was colored because they said no planes were lost but I knew that some must have been lost in the battle.

. . . .

Q. What did you think about the atomic bomb?

A. It was horrible. I saw a bright light and then windows smashed and everything began to fly around. It was around 11.00 AM. My husband was standing outside and I was bathing him when it happened. He was all naked and we were astounded because just the flash and then the flying debris. My husband was cut on the face and head by flying glass, but I was fortunate.

Q. What bombing experiences have you personally had?

A. Only the atomic bomb's concussion—no other experiences in actual bombing —the atomic bomb was terrible—the people were burned and the town was burning after the flash—people were running toward our place with terrible burns (tears in her eyes). That night they slept on the roads everywhere—some collapsed during the day due to the effect of burns. People would stop by and ask for water which was the most urgent need of these people. They were so upset that they couldn't think of food. It was a horrible night—crying and screaming. I can't describe the burns (wiping her eyes) that were on these people and the odor of burning flesh was in the air. It was so awful you have to see it before you can actually describe or even talk about it—it's hard to comprehend. Some father, with his entire family dead, would be yelling to die so that he would not have to live alone. [1]

. . . .

[1] *Ibid.*, pp. 217–220.

Personal Data: Man, 25 years old, single. Welder in aircraft parts plant. Interviewed in Osaka, November 20, 1945.

Responses:

Q. In general, how are things going with you now?

A. I'm living with my Dad in the basement of a building. Just the basement is left; the rest of the building was burnt down in the air raids of August. Dad is paying the rent monthly by giving the landlord 10 cigarettes out of his rationed amount (90 cigarettes per month). Mom took my three younger brothers to evacuate in the country (Hyogo prefecture) and I miss her very much. Not knowing how to economize on household expenses, Dad and I are having a pretty tough time to make ends meet. I wish mother was back here to see and take care of us. Water seeps into the basement after a rain and rises sometimes to about a foot and a half. It's very damp and filthy there and I know it's not good for our health, but we can't do anything about it cause we have no place to go, and in the first place we don't have the money to move.

Q. Do you feel you are better or worse off now than you were during the war?

A. I think it's worse off now. During the war, we had a somewhat easier time to make our living. Our rice ration amount was 2 go, 3 shaku instead of the present 2 go, 1 shaku and we were able to get more fresh vegetables too. I haven't tasted vegetables for about 4 months now. People whose houses were not bombed don't know the real feelings of us who lost everything in the air raids. They look upon us like we are beggars or bums and I don't know why. I feel very small.

Q. What things worried you most during the war?

A. What worried me most were the continuous air raids. After all, I like to live and it is natural that I didn't want to be killed by the bombings.

Q. What sort of work were you doing, from the beginning of 1945 to the end of the war?

A. I'm a welder at Hisaeda Bros. Aeronautical and Industrial Company, manufacturers of aeroplane parts and accessories. Products were delivered to Kawakami Aircraft Company. I worked from 7:30 AM to 6 PM making 1.50 yen.

Q. How was your working capacity during this period as compared with other years?

A. It was getting lower each day due to lack of food. We've tried to increase the efficiency by working every day but we couldn't keep it up. Our resistance couldn't keep it up. Our resistance couldn't stand the pace.

. . . .

Q. During the war, what did you think was Japan's greatest strength in waging the war?

A. I learned through the press, radio and the president of our company that we had the unique and incomparable Kamikaze Corps. They were harassing the enemy very much.

Q. During the war, what did you think Japan's greatest weakness was?

A. Black market racketeering. I should say that 7 out of 10 persons were unpatriotic and were dealing more or less behind our backs. It was disgusting.

. . . .

Q. Did the people's attitudes and conduct toward each other change during the war?

A. Stealing and robberies became numerous. Clerks in the bank became arrogant and unkind. I've noticed more among the women. I don't know why. Streetcar operators (women) would cuss up and down to old men or women and sometimes it made me so mad that I felt like punching her nose.

Q. Did you think that all kinds of people in Japan suffered alike in the war?

A. I've seen directors of companies and government officials so drunk that they could hardly walk and I knew that they were leading a life of luxury. A guy couldn't get drunk unless he had enough to eat, I think. Merchants usually have something in their hands to barter with, but not us. All we had to do is to say to ourselves that it couldn't be helped cause we weren't born rich or well-to-do.

. . . .

Q. When did you first feel certain that Japan could not attain sure victory?

A. When the B-29s would come over our city boldly, by the hundreds in day-time, and would not meet any opposition, I knew then that we were sunk.

Q. Did you at any time during the war come to a point where you felt you could not go on with the war?

A. People used to say "The hundred million would prefer defeat to dishonor," or "shoot the works," but I doubt if half of the people were thinking that way. In my opinion I can't die in honor unless my stomach is full.

Q. How did you feel when you heard that Japan had given up the war?

A. I learned the news by reading the paper that night of August 15th. I felt miserable and wretched because what I did and endured these long years of sacrificing burst like a bubble. I couldn't sleep that night. I was broken hearted, and still I couldn't cry.

. . . .

Q. In your opinion, what changes should occur in Japan in the future?

A. We should forget that we had a war once with America. Promote and encourage importing and exporting.

Q. What about the Emperor?

A. He should be left on the throne. He is a living god to me sometimes, and I like to think that he is a human as we are sometimes. It puzzles me so much that I can't make up my mind which to believe—god or human. Maybe we have thought him a god too much.

Q. During the war, what did you think would be in store for you and your family, if Japan lost the war?

A. We were told by the radio and press that males—from babies to 65 years old—would be murdered, and all the women and girls would be molested. I believed it.

. . . .

Q. What do you recall about the first time American planes flew over Japan?

A. When I learned through the press that the first American planes flew over Tokyo very low and machine-gunned several hundred public school children, it made me boiling mad. I was very glad to hear that one of the planes was knocked down.

Q. In your opinion, how well was your home town protected against air raids?

A. It is like a toy. I feel very foolish to think that I've spent considerable time in air-training (practice bucket-relaying). Most of our air-raid wardens weren't there when actual bombings occurred. Can't blame them, because it's too terrifying to be in the midst of it.

Q. What did you think about the atomic bomb?

A. Even a small explosive can do a lot of damage. When I learned that a single bomb has a destructive power equivalent to 2,000–50,000 bombs, it made me shudder with fear. On the other hand, I realized how far back we were behind in science to keep up with the rest of the world.

. . . .

Q. Can you tell about your [bombing] experiences? (Tell me what happened, what you did, how you felt.)

A. It sounded like a heavy shower pouring down. I ran into the shelter and stayed in there. I found out that my home was just a ball of fire when I came out. The sky was full of black smoke and it was like a dark night. I moved into a shack which was saved from burning and we had to borrow even chopsticks from the neighbors, as all our belongings were gone. I was awake all night, feeling miserable and lonesome.

. . . .

Q. How much help did the people who were not bombed give to those who were?

A. All they said was "We are sorry for your misfortunes" and we didn't receive any help from anyone, anywhere.[1]

Complete interview reports of this character were collected and forwarded to Swarthmore College for analysis by a technically trained staff. It was the task of this staff to prepare a system of classification adequate to accommodate the many shades of opinion which the respondents expressed under the stimulus of the questioning. On the basis of this classification system, cards were punched and machine tabulators were used to obtain statistical data.

4. Treatment of the Data. For the most part, the results of the investigation are given as they issued from the machine tabulators employed. One procedure used in putting the data into usable form merits special description because of its interest from the viewpoint of method.

The attempt was made to construct an index which would provide

[1] *Ibid.*, pp. 221–223.

a rough over-all quantitative measure of morale. The method used to accomplish this was as follows. Four members of the Morale Survey analysis staff independently listed the questions the answers to which they thought would be especially significant as indicators of morale. A majority of the judges agreed on 19 questions. Responses to these questions were then divided into high-morale and low-morale types. A random selection of 163 interviews was specifically scored for these 19 questions, and an analysis made of the 29 cases at the high end of the morale distribution and the 29 cases at the low end. The analysis showed that of the 19 questions on the trial list, 7 were conspicuous in their ability to discriminate between the extremes of the distribution. These were questions 11, 12, 15, 16, 17, 18, and 19, given above. (It should be noted that none of these questions involved the use of the terms "air raid," "bombing," or the like.) The Morale Index was constructed on the basis of answers to these 7 questions, one point (positive or negative, as appropriate) being allotted to each answer. The range of the Index for any individual, therefore, was from +7 for highest morale to −7 for lowest.

RESULTS

Since the primary interest of the present chapter is in method rather than in results, only a few of the salient findings of this sampling of Japanese opinion are reported here. In summary of those findings, as confirmed by other methods of ascertaining Japanese attitudes, the Survey makes the following statement as to the effects of bombing on Japanese morale:

At the time of Pearl Harbor the Japanese people were a little weary of the China war and were not spoiling for a fight with the United States. Their first reaction to the news of war was apprehension; but in the wake of the early Japanese victories their spirits rose markedly. Thereafter, and especially after the loss of Saipan, their morale began to disintegrate. The process was one in which an accumulation of prolonged war weariness, social unrest, increasing consumer shortages (especially of food) and a succession of military reverses weakened the will to resist. Then air attacks brought direct and immediate pressure on large segments of the population, and morale abruptly went into decline.

Analysis of an important component of morale—confidence in victory—indicates that once the decline set in, in the latter part of 1944, morale cracked at an ever increasing rate. . . . Military reverses and air raids were said by the Japanese to have been the most important factors in causing them to doubt victory or to become certain that Japan could not win. Consumer shortages were relatively much more important in making individuals feel unable to continue fighting than in causing them to feel uncertain of victory.

The importance of the air attacks in depressing morale is indicated by the fact that Japanese said they were:

The most important single factor in causing them to have doubts of victory.

The most important single factor in causing them to feel certain of defeat.

The most important single factor in making them unwilling to continue the war.

Their greatest worry during the war, and the thing which made most of them happy that the war was over.

Supporting morale were a number of factors from which the Japanese drew strength to continue, namely:

Fear of the consequences of defeat.

Faith in the "spiritual" strength and invincibility of the nation.

Obedience to and faith in the Emperor.

The black-out of information about the war.

Despite these, however, morale did fall and deterioration of the social fabric became general. People became critical of their leaders and lost confidence in one another. Even though the unity of the nation was falling apart, people were not able to organize for revolt; they simply became more and more obsessed with finding individual solutions to their own severe and urgent personal problems.[1]

To support the contention that bombing was followed by a precipitous break in Japanese morale, the charts reproduced below (Figs. 51 and 52) indicate that doubt as to the possibility of Japanese victory and a feeling of personal unwillingness to go on with the war underwent a sharp increase from the time of the first large-scale bombing of Japanese factories on June 15, 1944.

Figure 51 shows that although only 10 per cent of the population doubted the possibility of victory in June, 1944, the proportion of doubters increased to more than 80 per cent in less than 15 mos. Figure 52 shows that personal unwillingness to continue the war increased in similar fashion during that period. However, this unwillingness developed more slowly than did doubt as to Japanese victory, and it never characterized so large a proportion of the population. Evidently a great many people were willing to go on with the war, even though they were no longer confident that their country would win.

These charts show a time relationship between the beginning of heavy bombing and the accelerated growth of attitudes indicating

[1] *Ibid.*, p. 1.

deterioration of morale. But the existence of a time relationship does not necessarily mean that there was also a causal relationship. Coincidentally with the first major bombings, the island of Saipan fell to the forces of the United States, and the Tojo cabinet, under which the war had started, resigned. Conceivably it was events of this kind, rather than the bombing, or in addition to the bombing, which caused

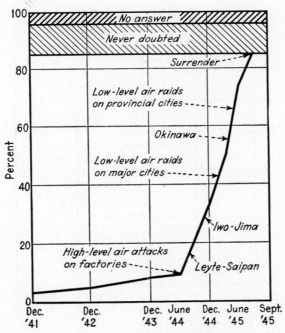

FIG. 51. Growth of Doubts of Victory.

This chart shows the percentages of Japanese who said that they began to doubt victory, at various stages of the war. The chart is based on answers to the following questions: "As the war wore on, did you ever begin to have doubts that Japan would win? When was that?" (This is No. 16 of the question list, followed by the request to specify the time to which the answer referred.)

the break in morale. These possibilities can be examined by referring to Table II, which shows what reasons were assigned by the Japanese respondents themselves for their doubts of the achievement of victory by the Japanese.

The table shows that although only about one-third of those who questioned the possibility of Japanese victory stated that the air attack was a reason for their doubt, this figure somewhat exceeds the percentage of persons giving "military losses and reverses" as a reason, and far exceeds the percentage naming any other cause. Furthermore, tabulation of the responses given by those who conceded that they had become personally averse to the continuation of the war yields similar results. Thirty-five per cent ascribed their unwillingness to the air

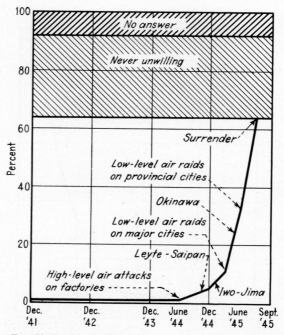

FIG. 52. Growth of Unwillingness to Continue the War.

This chart shows the percentages of Japanese who said they were unwilling to continue fighting, at various stages of the war. The chart is based on answers to the following questions: "Did you at any time during the war come to a point where you felt you could not go on with the war? When was that?" (This is No. 18 of the question list, followed by the request to specify the time to which the answer referred.)

attacks, including the atomic bombing, whereas all other reasons cited were given by far smaller proportions of the group.

Another method of ascertaining the effects of bombing was a comparison of the morale, as determined by the Morale Index scores, of respondents in areas which differed as to the extent of the bombing to which they had been subjected. This comparison is presented in Table III.

Although in general the findings by this method are in the expected direction, the differences among the respondents in the various areas are not very great and by themselves do not furnish strong support for

TABLE II

Percentages of Respondents Giving Various Reasons for Doubting Japanese Victory

Doubted victory:	Percentage
Because of the air attack	34
Because of military losses and reverses	28
Because of knowledge of shortages of war materials	7
Because of consumer shortages	5
Because of belief in greater strength of enemy, generally	5
Because they always had doubts of possibility of victory	3
Because of miscellaneous, or unspecified reasons	14
No doubts of victory:	
Never doubted Japan's victory	11
No doubts indicated, but later felt certain of Japanese defeat	2
No answer	4
	113[1]

the designation of air bombardment as the principal demoralizing factor. However, the Survey points out that by the time the interviews took place many persons had been evacuated from the major

TABLE III

Morale in Relation to Experience with Bombing

Bombing strata	Had relatively low morale, per cent	Had relatively high morale, per cent
Large cities, heavily bombed; high destruction	56	44
Tokyo	50	50
Smaller cities, heavily bombed; high destruction	51	49
Smaller cities, heavily bombed; light destruction	46	54
Lightly bombed and unbombed cities	47	53
Rural communities	51	49
Urban evacuees	61	39

bomb-target cities. Those who remained in the heavily bombed areas, therefore, probably represented a heavy concentration of people who, for a variety of reasons, would be likely to have had high morale.

[1] The percentages add to more than 100 because some respondents gave more than one answer.

This hypothesis is strengthened by the frequency of markedly low morale among evacuees from bombed cities (see Table III). However, the relatively small differences in level of morale, as inferred from the Morale Index, of people having different degrees of bombing experience should remind us again not to overlook the effects on morale of the general war situation, as well as of specific factors other than bombing, *e.g.*, shortages of essential commodities, military reverses, and political upheavals.

Concerning the effects of the atomic bombs, data from residents of the Hiroshima and Nagasaki areas show that although this weapon did impair the morale of many persons, it did not have the universally demoralizing effect that it often is supposed to possess. In fact, comparison of the findings in two critical measures of morale for the region subjected to atomic bombs and for the rest of Japan (Table IV) shows

TABLE IV

*Percentages of Respondents Asserting Absence of Doubts of Victory and of Personal Unwilling-
ness to Continue the War among Residents of (1) the Hiroshima and Nagasaki Areas,
and (2) the Rest of Japan*

	Hiroshima and Nagasaki areas	Rest of Japan
Never had doubts of victory....................	19	11
Never were personally unwilling to continue the war.	39	28

that morale was somewhat higher for the former. However, it may be that many of the residents of Hiroshima and Nagasaki, both of which cities had previously been spared heavy air attack, did not separate in their thinking the fall of the atomic bomb and the surrender of Japan which took place only a week later, so that their answers reflecting their morale referred to a time before the catastrophic explosions. It is clear from other data that the A-bomb did cause a sharp drop in morale among many respondents from these regions. For example, of people living in Hiroshima and Nagasaki who reported that they became unwilling to continue with the war, 45 per cent ascribed their discouragement to the atomic bomb, as contrasted with only 15 per cent of the respondents in the rest of Japan.

Morale among the Japanese varied according to the occupation, age, sex, and education of the individual. In terms of the Morale

Index, for example, the intelligentsia (professionals, semiprofessionals, managers, and officials) proved somewhat weaker than the population as a whole, 60 per cent of this group falling in the lower half of the total distribution of the Morale Index scores. Morale proved lower

TABLE V

Percentages of Respondents of Three Age Groups and of Both Sexes Who Stated that Group Unity Had Been Weakened, that Suffering Had Been Unequally Distributed, and that They Were Never Personally Unwilling to Go on with the War

Age group	Weakened group unity		Inequality of suffering		Never personally unwilling to go on with war	
	Men	Women	Men	Women	Men	Women
16–29	54	49	48	47	31	35
30–44	54	44	50	40	23	28
45–70	41	26	40	25	26	24

among the young and middle-aged than among those over forty-five, and lower among the men than among the women. Table V above indicates the percentages of men and women of various ages (1) who said that Japanese group unity had weakened during the war, (2) who

TABLE VI

Percentages of Respondents of Five Educational Levels Who Stated that Group Unity Had Been Weakened, that Suffering Had Been Unequally Distributed, and that They Were Never Personally Unwilling to Go on with the War

Education, years	Weakened group unity	Inequality of suffering	Never personally unwilling to go on with war
0–5	26	24	20
6	36	33	23
7–8	46	42	30
9–11	56	57	35
Over 12	68	62	42

stated that suffering had been unequally distributed, and (3) who asserted that they, personally, had never been unwilling to continue the fight against the enemy.

An ambiguous picture is presented when the data are analyzed in terms of the education of the respondents. As appears in Table VI above, the more schooling a Japanese had, the more ready he was to believe that the war had weakened those pseudofamilial ties which bound each Japanese to all others of his nation, and the more convinced he was that the national trials had been borne unequally. Nevertheless, the table also shows that the better educated Japanese was the more likely to want to fight on. The Survey suggests a reason for this apparent inconsistency. Although the better educated Japanese was more likely to have been informed of his country's military defeats and its withering chances of victory, he was usually wealthier than the majority of his countrymen, had suffered less from shortages, and had more to lose in case of defeat.

DISCUSSION

Obviously, without any intended cynicism, there is no sure way of testing the validity of the Morale Survey except by repeating the "experiment"—bombing followed by survey—a resort hardly to be recommended. However, the results, on the whole, appear to be valid, especially since they agree with statements made by individual Japanese possessing special sources of knowledge and with records of Japanese agencies concerned with Japanese opinion.

This problem of validation of results is one which besets almost all opinion polling, even when it is feasible to "try the experiment again." Those who conduct polls designed to discover which candidate a community will vote for can claim only that their findings show whom those members of the community who express opinions would have voted for had their expressed opinions been their real ones, and had they cast their ballots at the time the poll was taken. What can be concluded from the ascertained fact that most of a representative group of housewives declare a preference for a certain design of ironing board? It does not necessarily follow that the same percentage of housewives want to buy ironing boards, nor that those who do will actually purchase ironing boards of this design when they finally appear in the shops.

Despite limitations of this character, the scientific usefulness of opinion polling appears to be beyond question, and it would appear that the real task is to eliminate as many sources of error as possible. The Morale Survey is a contribution to this task. First in importance, perhaps, is its insistence upon free rather than controlled expression of opinion on the part of the respondents, that is, upon the "What do you think about . . . ?" rather than the "Do you think that . . . ?" kind of question. How many people who answer "yes" when asked whether they will vote for a particular candidate really mean "I'll vote for him unless he continues talking in the vein of his last three speeches"? How many people who say, "I don't know," really mean "I haven't decided whom I'll vote for, but unless X shows some gumption, I'll probably vote for Y, even though I generally don't like his views"? Such shades of opinion do not lend themselves to quick, easily and cheaply made summaries. It is clear that the restriction of answers to "yes," "no," and "I don't know" may afford only the roughest of guides to the real opinions of those questioned. Hence it is difficult to determine from such answers how people really feel or what their future behavior actually will be, for example, whom they will finally decide to vote for on Election Day.

However, the method of "stratification" adopted by the Survey is open to criticism on certain grounds. From one point of view, it implies a mistrust of the principle of random selection as the basic method of arriving at a representative sample. The polltaker who uses "stratification" seems to fear that elements in the population which he considers significant in terms of his problem may be overlooked or inadequately represented if he depends altogether on chance in his choice of those to be interviewed. He therefore permits random selection to operate only within the strata he has established. By this means he assures himself that the opinions expressed by people in each stratum exert an influence upon the total sum of opinions in proportion to the population of the stratum.

In a situation in which time and expense are of little importance, there would be no reason for such a departure from the method of chance selection of the sample to be polled. Any section of the population which constitutes a significant proportion of the whole would be correctly represented by an adequately large sample chosen purely at random. What then is the justification for the establishment of strata?

In the case of the Morale Survey, the best justification is the practical consideration that the method was an economical one, economical of time and perhaps of life.[1] A sample taken from the national popula-

---

[1] Two matters are to be recalled in this connection: first, that the occupation of the Japanese Islands by the forces of the United States was far from complete at the time the investigation was undertaken, and second, that the planners of the Survey were convinced

tion at large would necessarily have included individuals living at widely scattered points.   Interviewing them would have required a great deal of additional travel time for the Survey's teams. as well as the jeopardy of their personal safety.   Granted the limitation on size of staff, the result would have been a smaller total sample, or a longer interval between the end of the war and the questioning, or both.   It was decided, therefore, to limit the interviews to persons residing in a relatively small number of places in Japan.

It may be argued also that stratification constitutes a hedge against hidden errors which might distort seemingly random procedures.   For the selection of a sample by chance is by no means so simple a matter as may appear at first sight.   Even honestly manufactured dice are likely to be a trifle "loaded."   Polltakers have long recognized that making a choice of names from a telephone directory results in a sample not of the population at large, but only of that part of the population wealthy enough to subscribe to telephone service.   Other sources of error in sampling, however, are less easy to recognize.   For instance, within the telephone directory itself people whose names begin with "O" do not necessarily represent a valid sample of all the subscribers; there is likely to be an abnormally large proportion of folk of Irish origin among them.   The polltaker's decision as to which groups are significant in the analysis and should therefore be properly represented in the sample constitutes a safeguard against unforeseen distortion which any system of random sampling may produce.

---

that the validity of the results would be weakened if any considerable time elapsed between the surrender and the interviews.

INDEX

A

Accommodation, 203

Acidity and stomach activity, 103

Action currents (*see* Action potentials)

Action potentials, cerebral, 217–232
in alcoholic stupor, 224
at awakening, 222
apparatus for recording, 216–217
effect of auditory stimulation, 222
in epilepsy, 224–232
in hypnosis, 223
in infants, 224
during sleep, 222
(*See also* Alpha waves; Berger rhythm; Beta waves; Delta waves; Gamma waves; Random waves; Saw-tooth waves; Spikes; Spindles)
muscular, at awakening, 437
in deaf-mutes, 431–439
during dreams, 431, 434–436
during imagination, 427–430, 437
in investigations of motor theory of thinking, 426–439
from nerve trunks, 216, 217
during problem-solving, 437
during sleep, 434–437
during verbal reactions, 429–439

Activity and general condition in migration, 27–39

Acute anterior poliomyelitis, pathology of, 189–191
prognosis and treatment of, 193–194
symptoms of, 191–193

Adaptation, to darkness, 123
differences between rods and cones, 123
effect of vitamin A on dark adaptation, 135
to light, 123

Adjustment, significance to, of dark adaptation, 135
of emotional responses, 85, 105

Adrenin, 83, 95

Adrian, E. D., 217, 218

Adrian principle, 217, 218

Age, differences in, in relation to differences in morale in wartime, 480–481
and migration in salmon, 32–35
and reaction to interruption of tasks, 69

Aggressiveness, projection of, 445–454

Agnosia, visual, 186

Airsickness and perceptual conflict, 377

Albino, vision in, 124

Alcoholic stupor, cerebral-action potentials in, 224

Alcoholism, conditioning treatment of, 321–322

All-or-none principle of nerve conduction, 217

Allport, G. W., 242

Alpha waves, 218, 222, 224

Ambivalence, 457

Amentia, 185

Amplifier, vacuum tube, in study of action potentials, 216, 217

Amtman, L. E., 89

Anderson, O. D., 336, 351

Anger, bodily changes in, 85, 92
facial expression in, 108, 112
induced by hypnosis, 451–454
(*See also* Aggressiveness, projection of; Resentment)

Animal psychology and learning study, 170

Anxiety, through perceptual conflict, 376
in ulcer patients, 98, 100, 104, 105

Aphasia, and brain function, 186–187
and language areas in brain, 186*n.*
mass-action theory and, 186–187
principal types of, 186

Apparatus, air plethysmograph, 269
amplifier, vacuum tube, 216–217
balloon, for study of gastrointestinal tone, 92–93
for conditioning vasoconstriction, 269–270

C